Roadside History of

SOUTH DAKOTA

Linda Hasselstrom

Cover Painting *"The Prairie Is My Garden"* by Harvey Dunn
South Dakota Art Museum, Brookings, SD

Mountain Press Publishing Company
Missoula, Montana 1994

Second Printing, February 1998

For permission to quote from *South Dakota History*, we gratefully acknowledge the South Dakota Historical Society and the following:

Ruth Ann Alexander, "South Dakota Women Stake Claim: A Feminist Memoir: 1964-1989" (Winter 1989). Copyright © 1990 by the South Dakota State Historical Society. All Rights Reserved.

Lorna Herseth, ed., "A Pioneer's Letter" (Summer 1976). Copyright © 1976 by the South Dakota State Historical Society. All Rights Reserved.

Ruth Seymour Burmester, ed., "Jeffries Letters" (Summer 1976). Copyright © 1976 by the South Dakota State Historical Society. All Rights Reserved.

Special thanks to Westerners International, Oklahoma City, Oklahoma, for permission to quote Badger Clark's verse from *Sun and Saddle Leather*.

Maps by Trudi Peek

Library of Congress Cataloging-in-Publication Data

Hasselstrom, Linda M.
    Roadside history of South Dakota / Linda Hasselstrom.
      p. cm. — (Roadside history series)
    Includes bibliographical references and index.
    ISBN 0-87842-262-5 : $25.00. — ISBN 0-87842-236-6 (pbk.) : $18.00
    1. South Dakota—Tours. 2. South Dakota—History, Local.
3. Automobile travel—South Dakota—Guidebooks. 4. Historic sites—South Dakota—Guidebooks. I. Title. II. Series.
F649.3.H37 1994
917.8304'33—dc20
                                        94-26168
                                         CIP

Mountain Press Publishing Company
P. O. Box 2399
Missoula, MT 59806
406-728-1900/FAX 406-728-1635

For George,
who knew better

CONTENTS

ABOUT THE AUTHOR

Linda Hasselstrom, pictured here with her navigator and travel companion Frodo, helps run the family ranch near Hermosa, South Dakota. Her previous books of prose and poetry include: *Windbreak: A Woman Rancher on the Northern Plains* (Barn Owl Books, 1987), which testifies to the difficulties of surviving bitter cold and severe heat in this country; *Going over East: Reflections of a Woman Rancher* (Fulcrum, 1987), which considers Westerners' relations with the land; *Land Circle: Writings Collected from the Land* (Fulcrum, 1991), a book of poems and essays; *Dakota Bones* (Spoon River, 1993), a collection of poetry; and she edited a reprint edition of the fur trade classic *Journal of a Mountain Man: James Clyman* (Mountain Press, 1984). Her own press, Lame Johnny, published more than twenty books for other authors before she closed it to spend more time writing and working on the family ranch.

In 1989 Hasselstrom was named to the South Dakota Hall of Fame, received the Governor's Award for Distinction in Creative Achievement in the Arts, and won the Western Writing Award from the Center for Western Studies in Sioux Falls. In 1992 the *Rapid City Journal* included her among its Ten West River Notables.

PREFACE

This is, first, not a conventional history, because I am not a historian. South Dakota has had historians, in one guise or another, since long before the first white men crossed the Big Sioux River and said, "Look at that," no doubt in French. Very good historians have written about South Dakota; I've listed my favorites at appropriate spots, and a fat bibliography will point you to more of the tons of reading material about the state's history.

I am not a historian; I am a writer. I read a great deal and write fiction, poetry, and nonfiction. Considerable nonsense has been written lately about "creative nonfiction," a term that implies, to me, that the writer is adding a little imagination (or lies, if you favor the short Anglo-Saxon word, as Fred Manfred does) to the truth. When I'm writing nonfiction, I keep fiction out of it to the best of my ability.

But this book is a different matter. If a historian has related a story that fascinates me, tickles me, or captures the essence of something I believe is true about my home state, I've included it without worrying much about whether it really happened or not. If it *seems* true and *ought* to be true, that's what's important here.

South Dakota has always been somewhat handicapped because no one, not even its residents, can decide if it's quite Midwest or West. The reason for the confusion is that it's both. Farming governs the land east of the Missouri River, known as East River, and ranching governs West River. Never the twain shall meet. Into the vacuum moves myth, and West River, especially, has had its share. Indians, cowboys, gold, Mount Rushmore, and Crazy Horse all grew larger than life, and historians have produced volumes about who fired the first shot or whether evidence exists for this or that. All such subjects are legitimate, and a surprising number of historical events remain unwritten; someone else is welcome to them. What I'm after is the nugget that tells me what sort of place this state is, and that information must be influenced by my own partialities.

Ultimately, the state's nature comes from the people who live here, so you'll find plenty of people wandering along the roadsides in this history: old trappers, modern Indian artists, and lawmen who couldn't even hold a gun, let alone shoot one. All of them added a grain to the mountain that is South Dakota's yesterday.

Highway History

Recording history along highway lines may at first glance seem like a distortion. But modern highways, after all, were usually built upon older routes. South Dakota's highway 34 was an early Indian trail; part of SD 79 was the stagecoach trail from Cheyenne, Wyoming, to Rapid City, South Dakota; and US 85 follows the route of the Marquis de Mores's stage line. The pathways devised by humans who change the land and its culture, whether trails or highways, are the arteries through which the blood of history flows.

The western music you'll hear as you drive is a part of that history; if you don't like it, open the window and listen to the meadowlarks and redwing blackbirds singing on fence posts. These are sounds heard more clearly from the secondary roads than from the freeways. Interstate highways are built for speed and efficiency; they all look alike, and their identical facilities—fast-food joints, self-service gas stations, and the like—are filled chiefly with travelers. Only the details of the land through which they run and the people who live along them particularize such trails; you have to get off the interstate to really see and taste the country and the people who inhabit it. Smaller highways, the twisting veins that wander through each town and dip into the valleys, give you time to scent the season, to mosey along and get the flavor of whatever state you're in. During the Dirty Thirties, migrating farmers who had lost their land said they could tell where they were by the taste of the dust.

I have driven every highway covered in this book, so the history arranged along each one is filtered through my observations and interests, though I try to be objective. Most of us, when young, believe our home town and state are uninteresting and lifeless; we leave as soon as possible. Often, as maturity grows, we return for values we didn't appreciate in youth: clean air, pure but scarce water, open spaces, and spare prairie beauty. Those qualities are more important to me now, so they get more emphasis here than big buildings and expensive tourist traps constructed around historical tidbits.

The perspective in the pages ahead is that of a second-century South Dakotan who has worked most of her life at the business of ranching. As a custodian of the land, I am influenced by hindsight; one hundred years after statehood, I believe that many of our advantages and disadvantages, our triumphs and defeats, have sprung from the way successive populations have treated the land and natural resources, as well as one another. The prairie, for all its apparent toughness, is fragile and could be lost to us if we don't sensibly choose among varied choices of development. Those opinions affect everything I write and do; you're forewarned.

Early historians and record keepers were even more opinionated critters; they often ignored or mocked the subjects they wrote about. The oral history of the people who lived here before white settlement wasn't considered part of the real historical record until recent times. Neither were the tales of ranchers, cowboys, and artists, who were generally seen as being tributaries of the main interest of the state: development (defined as profit). In examining the state's business and industry, I've been influenced by friends passionate about subjects as diverse as mining, railroad trains, firearms, celebrated buildings, farming, rodeo, and small towns.

Particulars of This History

In this book, the state is divided into four geographic regions. East of the Missouri River is tallgrass country, lowlands made good for farming by rich soil, abundant glacial lakes, and other surface water. The Missouri River and its man-made great lakes created by dams are a second region, lying on both sides of the river. West of the river are the rolling shortgrass plains—once home to buffalo, now to herds of cattle and dryland wheat—decorated with limestone buttes. The state's fourth region is the southwest, including the Black Hills and Badlands. All four zones lie on the great Missouri Plateau, sloping from high in the northwest corner of the state to low in the southeast.

The introduction to each quarter of the state lists books that will provide more information on the region. Books that offer additional background on the state are listed in the bibliography.

Who's a Native?

Historians, journalists, and speakers have wrestled for years with what to call the tribes who inhabited North America before whites arrived. The term "Indian" preserves Columbus's error in thinking he'd arrived at the Indies, whereas the term "Native American" sometimes offends white folks born in America who consider themselves as native as anyone else. Tim Giago, a well-known Indian newspaper columnist from the Pine Ridge Reservation in South Dakota, says, "Any politically correct thinker who believes Native

American is the preferred identification tag for the Lakota or any other tribe is wrong." I've followed his lead in using "Indian" as a general term; for specifics, I use the tribal name. I use "Lakota" for those Indians who form the largest tribal group in the state, because this term seems to be preferred by the tribal members themselves.

Lakota was originally an exclusively oral language, not a written one. Spelling words that originate in such a language is always tricky. Paul WarCloud Grant's *Sioux Dictionary*, published in 1971, sorts English words in alphabetical order and gives the Lakota pronunciation only, not a spelling. It's of no use when one begins with a Lakota spelling from a map or another source and seeks the English meaning; in those cases, I have used the spelling offered by the source.

And Finally

Errors surely exist; if you've never made a mistake, feel free to point mine out. Otherwise, smile smugly, read on, and keep quiet.

The editor requires me to use nonsexist language; I am not sexist, so I have complied wherever possible. This manuscript written in the twentieth century will not offend twentieth-century ideas of right and wrong.

But the requirement strikes me as an ironic commentary on the differences between modern times and the times that are the subject of this history. The men and women who made history in Dakota in the seventeenth and eighteenth centuries were doing the best they could to survive in their own time; little did they know how they would be judged. The first explorers who slipped cautiously across the Plains and wandered, amazed, up a valley in the Black Hills were men; count on it. Their society dictated that white women stay home wearing crinolines over their pregnant stomachs.

Women who couldn't or wouldn't accept those limitations were probably right behind those first explorers, however. Wearing pants, they tried to speak in low voices except when swearing at an ox team; whenever they got a chance, they puzzled their colleagues by disappearing behind bushes. Only by pretending to be men could they have a man's freedom. Faced with that fact in their society, they didn't make up a new term, or find a therapist, or pass a law (mainly because they couldn't vote yet)—they acted. When they started coming to the West in large numbers, they modified society in record time. Even the women who were content to wear skirts demanded the vote: Female suffrage was ratified in western states first. Ranch women roped and branded their own cattle, used weapons when necessary, and swore if they felt like it; still do.

That's one of the keys to the differences between yesterday and today. Action. Of course, Dakota Territory had plenty of tough and nasty guys, men who shot Indians and raped women. They were operating within the limits of their beliefs, just like the rest of us, and some of them didn't survive long. Even the God-fearing, church-going, profit-promoting men whose pictures appear in dusty state histories and hang in government offices committed acts now thought unseemly, acts that aren't in the history books; we named streets and towns after them anyway. There's not much sense in blaming them now; they acted as they were taught.

If we're smarter and morally better than they were, perhaps we should stop deploring their errors and act to correct them. Humans can be persuaded; laws can be changed. The important point about the West, the thing that made it different from the East yesterday and today, is that it contains natural elements that are not moved by persuasion. A blizzard can still kill you, as can a bison or a fall from a cliff. The West is still home to wilderness, and wilderness can't be analyzed; it acts. If we need the qualities it can give to humans, as I believe we do, we have to take some action ourselves to see that we hang on to the wilderness we've got left—before the folks who will be called "entrepreneurs" in tomorrow's histories find ways to profit from it all and in the process destroy it.

ACKNOWLEDGMENTS

One of the most interesting old sources of information is *South Dakota: A Guide to the State*. Compiled in 1938 by the Federal Writers' Project Staff of the Works Progress Administration as part of the American Guide Series, it was arranged by tours along the state's existing roads. For convenience in this book, I refer to it simply as the WPA guide.

Other backbones of research include Herbert S. Schell's revised *History of South Dakota* and Jennewein and Boorman's territorial history, *Dakota Panorama*, first published in 1961 and recently republished. Various authors with uneven skills researched and wrote separate chapters, so it's not always reliable as a source, but it is always interesting. John R. Milton's bicentennial *South Dakota*, Robert F. Karolevitz's *Challenge: The South Dakota Story*, and *The Making of the Two Dakotas* by Helen Graham Rezatto were also extremely useful.

Last Grass Frontier, the South Dakota Stock Growers' history, edited by Bob Lee and Dick Williams, helped me considerably with information on early cattlemen. *Black Hills Hay Camp*, a book of photographs and historical notes compiled by Dave Strain, was invaluable. Bob Lee's *Gold, Gals, Guns, Guts*, the bicentennial history of Deadwood, Lead, and Spearfish, drove me crazy by neglecting to include documentation for stories from the region's newspapers, but some of the material was too good to resist.

Lakota history is a delicate and often-disputed matter. The Lakota didn't put much stock in footnotes, but they staked their personal reputations on truth—a concept difficult for modern society to grasp. For their version of historical events, I've sought advice from my Lakota friends and trusted authors who relied upon the oral tradition from the mouths of those who lived it, including Stanley Vestal's *Sitting Bull*, Mari Sandoz's *Crazy Horse*, and Dee Brown's *Bury My Heart at Wounded Knee*.

I have informally "studied" South Dakota history since I was five years old with certified teachers, listening to tales told by older family members at holiday gatherings and reading dusty library books ferreted out with the help of a generation of librarians. I've read "real" history, complete with footnotes, and experienced, or been told, bits of history that couldn't be footnoted for several reasons. I've heard from men and women who worked on highways, on ranches, and on government-funded dam-building projects. Ranchers have told me how they became good rifle shots killing rabbits for food when bullets were hard to get in the 1920s. Drinking coffee and practicing invisibility, I've listened in on conversations in truck stops and farmers' cafes, scribbling wildly in a notebook balanced on my knee. All of this is included in my definition of history. Many of those people had no idea I was writing it down (I didn't always know it, either); they have my thanks, and—if necessary—my apologies.

Other people have given me more specific and direct help. For nearly forty years, a succession of friendly, intelligent people at the Rapid City Public Library have guided me through reference books, taught me the intricacies of interlibrary loan, patiently answered my questions, and allowed me the privilege of sitting cross-legged in the stacks, looking for something I can't quite describe to them. In recent years, one or two of them helped me stand up when my knees wouldn't. They treat all their customers the same, but I especially thank librarians, including Rapid City's long-gone Story Lady, who read to me when I was five years old and helped me learn to love books and writing.

Special thanks:
- to my husband, George Randolph Snell, who fed me when I forgot to cook during the long summer in which I completed much of the research for this book and who died in autumn 1988, for patience with my workaholic ways;
- to eminent historian, explorer, wildlife expert, philosopher, collector of rare books on South Dakota history, and curmudgeon Lawrence Perry, for research assistance and advice;
- to historians James D. McLaird, Helen Rezatto, and Bob Lee, for special research help, and to Margaret Phelps of Hermosa, posthumously;
- to Sue Hey, for help with translations;
- to David Alt, for geological clarification; and
- to Jerry and other friends, you know who you are, for patiently listening to my complaints about the difficulty of this job. Aren't you glad it's over?

SOUTH DAKOTA CHRONOLOGY

2 million years ago   Glacial lakes form in eastern South Dakota

24,000 B.C.   Giant short-faced bears, mammoths, and peccaries die in sinkholes near Hot Springs

10,000 B.C.   Prehistoric people hunt buffalo and tan hides near Bear Butte; Paleo-Indians leave cliff drawings and artifacts in the Black Hills

5,000 B.C.   Paleolithic cultures decline with prehistoric animals on the Great Plains

A.D. 500   Mound builders appear east of the Missouri River

1000   Nomadic tribes occupy the Black Hills

1250-1400   Agricultural people migrate to Dakota from southern Minnesota

1300-1400   Woodland Indians build burial mounds in eastern South Dakota

1500-1800   Crow, Iowa, Cheyenne, Arapaho tribes hunt around Black Hills

1640s   French priests from Wisconsin encounter Lakotas

1654-1660   Pierre Radisson meets Lakotas while exploring the headwaters of the Mississippi River

1673   Jesuit Father Jacques Marquette and explorer Louis Jolliet become the first white men to travel on the Mississippi River, June 17

1679   Daniel Greysolon, Sieur de Luth (or Duluth), reports visiting Sisseton and Wahepton Lakotas

1701   De L'Isle map shows "trail of fur traders" to Sioux Falls area

1704   French report 100 Canadians along the Missouri River

1708   Robert Cavelier, Sieur de LaSalle, claims knowledge of silver on the Missouri River

1731-1744   Pierre de Varennes, Sieur de la Verendrye, explores Dakota, Montana, and Saskatchewan, building a chain of French forts

1738   De la Verendrye reaches the Missouri River on December 3

1743   Francois and Joseph de la Verendrye winter near Bear Butte and bury a lead plate near Pierre, which remains there until found by three teenagers in 1913

1750-1790	Lakotas drive Arikaras up the Missouri
1760	Arikaras and Mandans trade horses with Kiowas, Comanches, and Pawnee
1763	Hudson's Bay Company establishes a fur post on the Big Sioux River
1768	French build a fur post at Waubay Lake
1776	Oglala Lakota chief Standing Bull leads a war party west to the Black Hills
1785	Pierre Dorion is the first permanent white settler in the area that becomes South Dakota
1794	Jean Baptiste Trudeau (or Truteau) winters near Lake Andes
1795	Registre Loisel ascends Missouri River and establishes a trading post near Pierre
1800	Spain cedes Louisiana Territory to France
1803	France sells Louisiana Territory to the United States
1804-1806	Lewis and Clark chart a course to the Pacific Ocean; Robert Dickson establishes a fur post at Lake Traverse
1811	Manuel Lisa brings a tourist to the upper Missouri
1812	Lisa moves to Pierre and persuades Teton and Yankton Sioux to remain neutral in War of 1812; Sakakawea (Sacajawea) dies at Manuel Lisa's fort
1817	Joseph LaFramboise establishes a fur post on the west bank of Missouri River near mouth of Bad River
1819	H. P. Moers establishes a trading post at Big Stone Lake
1823	Gen. William Ashley's fur trappers fight Arikaras north of Pierre
1831	The Yellowstone is the first steamboat to reach Fort Tecumseh (Fort Pierre)
1833	Painter Carl Bodmer goes to Pierre with Maximilian
1837	Painter Alfred Jacob Miller ascends the Platte River via Fort Laramie
1838	John C. Frémont and Jean Nicollet visit Hole in the Mountain Pass east of Sioux Falls
1840	Father Pierre Jean De Smet begins missionary work with Indians on the Great Plains, possibly discovering gold and conducting the first baptism west of Missouri River in South Dakota
1843	John James Audubon visits Dakota Territory

1851	Treaty of Traverse des Sioux signed
1854	Lt. John L. Grattan and 29 men are killed by Lakotas, launching the Great Sioux War
1855	Gen. W. S. Harney leads an expedition against the Sioux; Paul Narcelle starts a ranch near Chamberlain; the U.S. Army buys Choteau's Fort Pierre
1855-1857	Lt. G. K. Warren leads a scientific expedition in Dakota
1856	Town site is surveyed at falls of the Big Sioux River; F. V. Hayden explores the fringes of the Black Hills and reports finding gold
1856-1857	Fort Ridgley and South Pass Wagon Road is surveyed through Woonsocket and Wessington Springs
1857	Grand Council of Teton Sioux brings seven bands together at Bear Butte; settlements begin at Sioux Falls, Flandreau, and Medary on the Big Sioux River; Norwegians arrive in southeastern South Dakota
1857-1858	Dakota settlers send representatives to Washington, D.C., asking territorial status
1859	First permanent white settlement at Yankton
1861	Dakota Territory created
1862	Sioux uprising in Iowa, Minnesota, sends Sioux hostiles to Fort Thompson
1864	Ft. Wadsworth (later Ft. Sisseton) established
1865	One of Dakota's first wagon roads marked west from Big Sioux River
1866	Ft. Sully established east of Pierre
1873	Railroad reaches Yankton
1874	Gen. George Custer leads exploratory expedition from Ft. Abraham Lincoln to Black Hills; Russell-Collins party searches for gold; grasshoppers strike eastern settlers
1874-1879	Black Hills gold rush, the Old West's last
1875	Col. Richard Dodge commands military escort for Jenney-Newton expedition to Black Hills; Ben Ash sights Hills from north
1876	Custer killed at Little Big Horn
1878	First telephone at Deadwood, two years after Bell's patent
1880-1881	Severe winters hurt ranchers; settlers moving in
1881	First artesian well drilled at Yankton
1882	Whites discover Wind Cave near Hot Springs

1887	Thoen Stone found near Lookout Mountain, Spearfish
1889	North Dakota and South Dakota admitted to Union
1890	Wounded Knee massacre; Sioux reservations opened to white settlement; Fremont, Elkhorn & Missouri Valley Railroad reaches Deadwood
1890-1915	Cattle companies spread on unfenced range; homesteaders, barbed wire take over
1892	July 5 hailstorm with 6-inch hail blinds 16 horses, destroys crops
1896	Populist movement; William Jennings Bryan wins in state by landslide
1899	Black Hills National Forest established, one of first with timber sales, multiple-use management plan
1903	Earliest recorded snow Sept. 15
1905	Orman Dam begun for Belle Fourche Reservoir
1909-1910	Cheyenne, Standing Rock reservations opened to white settlement
1917	State-operated rural credit system establish; SD one of first states to prohibit liquor sales; farm prices rally, then drop
1919	Custer State Park established
1920s	Farm protest groups like Non-Partisan and United Farmers leagues demand end to farm foreclosures; evictions, forced sales; state has highest per capita debt in nation
1922	Nine state banks fail
1923	Thirty-six state banks fail; 71 percent fail during 1920s, depositors lose $39 million; in 10 years, bankers initiate 34,419 farm foreclosures
1925	American Legion Junior Baseball begins
1927	Gutzon Borglum begins carving Mount Rushmore; Calvin Coolidge visits "summer White House" at Game Lodge, inadvertently begins tourist industry; Rapid City Air Lines begun
1929	Depression officially begins Oct. 28; railroad trip from Rapid City to Gillette, Wyoming, takes 27 hours
1930	Original "Deadwood Dick" dies; state per capita income falls from $358 in 1930 to $129 in 1933
1932	Farm Holiday movement calls strikes, pickets to prevent sale of livestock, grain, milk, to force prices up; Tom Berry elected first governor from west of Missouri River

1933	Civilian Conservation Corps organized at Ft. Meade; Agricultural Adjustment Act brings relief to some farmers
1934	First "black blizzard" of windblown dust; 95 percent of arable land in state damaged; prohibition ends; first balloon ascension from Strato Bowl; mining stock rises from $50 to $300 per share; many farmers become miners
1935	State sales tax passed; Explorer II balloon leaves Strato Bowl
1936	Three state records broken: hottest with 120 degrees, Gann Valley; driest with 2.89 inches of moisture, Ludlow; coldest with -58 at McIntosh; second Strato Bowl flight sets world altitude record
1937-1941	CCC repairs Orman Dam, builds Sheridan Lake Dam, and 10,000 other check dams in state, plants 22.7 million trees, employs 26,500 workers
1940	Census shows 642,961 people, almost 50,000 fewer than 1930
1940-1948	Federal soil conservation programs begin; farm prosperity improves
1941	Rapid City selected for army airfield, later Ellsworth Air Force Base; Provo chosen for Black Hills Ordnance Depot, later called Igloo; Gutzon Borglum dies, son Lincoln finishes Mount Rushmore
1944	Congress passes Flood Control Act authorizing dam-building projects in upper Missouri Valley; German prisoner-of-war camp established at Ft. Meade
1947	Korczak Ziolkowski begins carving Crazy Horse Monument
1948	Oahe Dam begun on Missouri River
1949	Four-day January blizzard kills hundreds of cattle; ranches, farms isolated for weeks
1952-1963	Four Missouri River dams completed in South Dakota
1953	Rapid City Air Force Base named after Brig. Gen. Ellsworth, killed in crash
1960	Last Chicago & Northwestern passenger train runs
1968	Indian Civil Rights Act protects Indians from unreasonable search, jailing without due process or trial, ensures freedom of speech, trial by jury
1969	Vine DeLoria publishes *Custer Died for Your Sins*
1970	Federal census lists 14 U.S. cities with populations greater than entire state of SD
1972	Rapid City flood kills 238 people, destroys $100 million worth of property

1973	Siege of Wounded Knee II lasts 71 days as AIM confronts FBI, federal forces; EROS satellite center established at Baltic
1979	Last eight-party telephone line eliminated in state
1980s	About 126,000 in state public schools; teachers' salaries 50th in nation
1980	Census shows 690,178 people in state; George McGovern loses senate seat to Jim Abdnor; voters reject tax reform measure; prostitution ends in Deadwood; Sioux tribes awarded over $100 million for Black Hills land, but Oglala reject offer, file suit
1981	Gov. William Janklow announces sale of 50,000 acre-feet of water to ETSI, Inc.; AIM activists camp in Black Hills
1982	Ziolkowski dies
1984	ETSI abandons $1 billion contract for water; EAFB gets B-1 bomber; strip-mining permits issued for northern Black Hills
1985-1986	Record snowfall, 200 inches in Deadwood area
1989	South Dakota Centennial; tourism now brings $576 million to state annually, serves 6 million visitors, creates 16,600 jobs

State Animal:	Coyote
State Bird:	Ringneck pheasant
State Fish:	Walleye
State Insect:	Honey bee
State Tree:	Black Hills spruce
State Mineral:	Rose quartz
State Gem:	Fairburn agate
State Flower:	Pasque flower

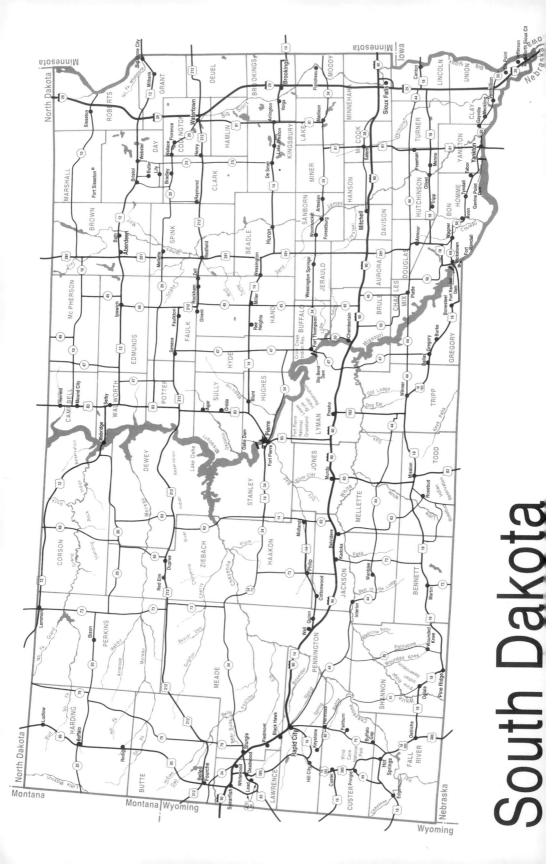

South Dakota

SOUTH DAKOTA:
LAND OF INFINITE VARIETY

Visitors who whisk through South Dakota on an interstate highway may think the state is only a flat stage setting for the Black Hills and Mount Rushmore. But South Dakota's nickname is "land of infinite variety"; that's a clue that there's more here than meets the eye.

The state is full of contrasts and contradictions; within a few minutes, you can find someone with an opinion opposite to yours on any topic, and in a few places you can still find a nickel cup of coffee to drink while you argue.

South Dakota's people create its character, and we are a blend of Old World bloodlines and values unique to the American West. Our ways are a mixture of nearly mythical old times and new; contrasting elements of the past, present, and future are all apparent. South Dakotans are fascinated by mammoth bones 26,000 years old and forget that a sophisticated satellite overhead is photographing every move. Our ranchers still wear broad-brimmed hats and black silk neckerchiefs, but some own computers and word processors. We love solitude and the smell of pure high country air mingled with the sharp odor of sagebrush; an old saying asserted that cow manure smells like money. Conversely, we also want wider highways (those who acknowledge the importance of tourism to the state economy might say the exhaust from tourists' cars smells like cash).

South Dakotans listen to more western music than rock and roll but pay to keep a public radio station broadcasting symphonies. We relish roast buffalo, Rocky Mountain oysters (the testicles of young cattle), fresh-caught trout, and Bohemian pastries made from recipes hundreds of years old, but crowded fast-food joints have appeared on the outskirts of every major town and a few minor ones.

A few state residents have car phones, yet some have no telephones at all. In some areas, mail is delivered only three times a week, unless it rains or snows, in which case it may not be delivered for weeks; in cities, though, people send messages instantaneously via fax machines.

Most rural Dakotans still leave their car keys in the ignition but also have a loaded rifle in the gun rack. An out-of-state visitor might see this as a mixed signal. It isn't: Don't try to steal the pickup.

We don't wear our guns strapped to our hips much anymore, but weapons are still readily available. Nonetheless, South Dakota consistently makes news as one of the least violent spots on the globe. The state ranked forty-eighth in overall crime in 1989; only North Dakota and Virginia had less. However, the *Rapid City Journal* reported in late 1990 that violent crime increased 19 percent over the previous year, compared to a national increase of only 5 percent. That total does not include crimes on Indian reservations, where, as elsewhere in the state, crime seems to be increasing as the population grows and becomes more diversified.

Even other Midwesterners—including Garrison Keillor's mythical Lake Wobegon residents—joke about South Dakota's provincial habits. But the state's list of firsts includes the first performance of "The Star Spangled Banner," forty-two years before it became the American national anthem. A car made news here fourteen years before Henry Ford turned his first crank, though newspaper writers predicted the noisy, dangerous contraptions would never catch on. Today many rural people in western South Dakota think nothing of driving a hundred miles for groceries or a concert yet find no contradiction in grumbling about how much of the scenery is disappearing under pavement; most of us have never seen a real traffic jam.

Before television invaded our homes, we didn't know how different we were from the general population; we thought everyone wore cowboy hats or seed caps and leather belts with names carved into the back. In recent years we have become conscious of our incongruities and flocked to shopping malls to buy sleazy, bright clothing that makes us blend in with people from the rest of the country. Our speech is losing its local spice as we adopt the slang blasted into our living rooms each night.

East and West River

Though ranchers and farmers are lumped together under the term "agriculture," their approaches have been utterly different. When cattle ranchers arrived, they did little to change the nature of the plains, but farmers broke up the sod with their plows and tried to turn both the fertile, flat eastern sector and the arid, hilly western sector into uniform, fenced, traditional farms. From this difference, often unacknowledged, springs many of today's differences of opinion on the use of land. Throughout the state's history, many folks have been in favor of drawing a dividing line at the 100th meridian, midway between the current eastern and western state boundaries, to resolve the conflicting interests of eastern farmers and western ranchers.

Unofficially, the boundary between the two halves of the state is the Missouri River; hence, the two regions are referred to as "East River" and "West River." Early explorers noted that the Missouri seemed to be a dividing line between two different climates and topographies. Stanley Vestal's 1945 book *The Missouri* described the river as "the great divide, where the West begins, a social barrier between two cultures, two climates, two ways of life," pointing out that the woodlands, lakes, and farms dominated the east bank while buffalo plains and ranches ruled the west.

More recently, historian James McLaird from Mitchell noted some widely recognized differences, including some that have never been fully explained: "In the western half of the state, rivers flow from west to east; in eastern South Dakota, they flow from north to south. Western South Dakota is in the Mountain Time Zone, whereas eastern South Dakota is in the Central Time Zone. Generally, pronghorn antelope and rattlesnakes are found west of the river. Popular field guides to bird life that print one volume for the eastern and another for the western United States divide the country along the one hundredth meridian, approximately in the middle of South Dakota."

McLaird later notes, "Vegetation also differs, the East River region being known as tall grass country, and West River as short grass

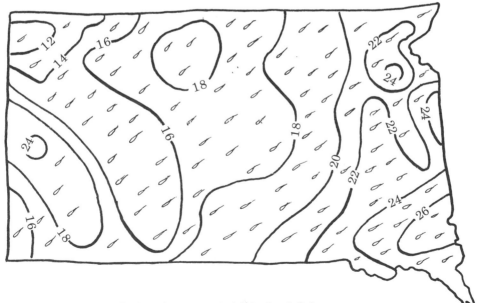

Inches of annual rainfall in South Dakota.

country." This difference is particularly significant, in that it is linked to economic discord. The dominant business east of the river—in what was tallgrass country before most of the prairie was plowed—is farming, and corn is one of the most important crops. The soil is fertile, well drained, and rich, and rainfall is greater than twenty inches. Trees were cleared from many farming areas east of the river, including cottonwood, oak, and elm, and their descendants grow vigorously where they are not plowed under, especially along streams and gullies that have intermittent flows from heavy rains. West of the river, the dominant grasses are grama and buffalo grass; crops include dryland wheat, sorghum, barley, rye, and flax. Elsewhere, cattle graze on unplowed rangeland. Plowing in the homesteading era of the late 1800s and early 1900s destroyed grass and topsoil that in some cases has not yet been restored.

East River has been called the Heartland, the Corn Belt, the Breadbasket, the Middle Border, and the Prairie Plains; terms applied to West River include the Great Plains, the Empty Quarter, and the High Plains. In 1931 Walter Prescott Webb named three characteristics to define the Great Plains: They are flat, treeless, and semiarid. Webb located the boundary at the twenty-inch-per-year rainfall line, between the 98th and 100th meridians along the Missouri River. Ian Frazier, in a more recent and idiosyncratic definition, settled for describing the plains in terms of what they do *not* have: woodlands, moisture, mountains, lakes, desert, and farmland.

No strict division is really possible: The river does not run in a straight line, and vegetation, soil, and rainfall change gradually rather than abruptly. Moreover, any definition that involves people must take their opinions of themselves into consideration.

Two States or Three?

Pat Halley, a Boston writer, looked at cultural rather than topographical features and observed three distinct "states" in South Dakota: East River, West River, and a third one, often ignored: "Indian" South Dakota.

The Scandinavian-American residents of East River, said Halley, feel they are more sophisticated than those in West River; they drink a lot of black coffee, "root for the Minnesota Twins and Vikings, and wear seed caps and call themselves farmers if they are involved in agriculture." They view the western end of the state as "a nice place to visit."

By contrast, West River residents see those in the other end as "snobby." By heritage western European, West River folks drink their

4

coffee with cream and sugar, "root for the Denver Broncos and wear cowboy hats and call themselves ranchers if they're involved in agriculture." They think of the eastern end of the state "as a place they'd rather not visit."

Halley's third state, Indian South Dakota, includes nine Indian reservations. In this "state," unemployment is often high, wages low (when businesses exist at all), and diseases such as alcoholism more prevalent than in the general population. Halley notes that Indian citizens were here first and now want more of their land back, a claim that particularly bothers West River South Dakotans. Indian South Dakotans are not as visibly committed to coffee, sports, or agriculture as South Dakotans from neighboring states, but theirs is the strongest culture. Residents of Indian South Dakota observe a less defined notion of time. They tend to believe that they got along just fine for a long time without either East River South Dakota or West River South Dakota at their borders and could easily do so again.

Halley's observation that Indians are not included in the state's culture is astute; other writers have charged the state with outright racism. However, there are signs of improvement. For example, cowboys and Indians whose grandfathers once shot at each other formed an environmental coalition calling itself the CIA (Cowboys and Indians Alliance). The group attracted international media attention when it used a combination of Indian spirituality and western Anglo independence and toughness to defeat a huge corporation's plan to test ammunition in a Black Hills wilderness valley.

Though Halley's definition contains humor, it also hints at more serious divisions with implications for the modern state and its people. The population of East River tends toward homogeneity: Many of its white, Anglo-Saxon inhabitants assume that everyone goes to a Protestant (probably Lutheran) church and lives in a conventional nuclear family. Folks who don't fit into those tidy categories—writers, artists, Indians—find more acceptance, or at least solitude, west of the river.

Most history is made by people who don't realize they are making it. Though a few South Dakotans who dreamed of greatness postured as if in front of a camera, most simply looked forward to their next paycheck, next meal, next enemy attack, or next child. Folks from dozens of nationalities, religions, and races have contributed something unique to the personality of the state, though—like the nation—it has traditionally been governed by white Anglo-Saxon males. The history of women and nonwhite pioneers has been hidden for years in their unpublished diaries and books; many of those documents are now being studied and published by scholars, and we can expect substantial changes in how we view our past as a result.

Turner and the Frontier's Closing

At an 1893 meeting of the American Historical Association, Frederick Jackson Turner read an essay that set a pattern for historians who followed. At that time, Americans, particularly Easterners, looked toward their European ancestors for models of government, society, and behavior. The United States was seen as a descendant of European culture.

Turner changed that view by asserting that the frontier had created the American character and that the traits we see as uniquely American—democracy, individualism, and nationalism—were a direct result of the pioneer experience. The existence of an area of unsettled land, said Turner, along with "its continuous recession, and the advance of American settlement westward, explain American development."

Turner's thesis added that the frontier period of American history was finished, that a hundred years after the Constitution was adopted, American civilization was ready for a new era of development in the conquered wilderness. He believed the first western frontier closed about 1890 with the destruction of Indians and wild animals that threatened settlers. Not coincidentally, 1890 was the year of the Wounded Knee massacre, when the last Lakota were driven, bleeding, to their reservations. From that time on, the Plains were no longer home to a nomadic civilization that left few permanent traces; whites seemed determined to change the land as much as possible to create "civilization."

Turner's declaration that the frontier was closed promoted nostalgia and created fantasies about the heroic antics of frontier folks. Seductive dime novels and movies distorted reality a bit more. Today, inhabitants of the Plains are annoyed and discouraged when we are perceived only as cardboard figures in an empty place with scenic backdrops. When we try to discuss serious land-use conflicts between ranchers and Indians, the rest of the country envisions us waving six-shooters, garbed in paint and feathers, thundering into the sunset. The land we regard as home is often thought of as a collection of stunning photographs, not the place we make a living. How can we expect fellow Americans to treat us like responsible citizens if they don't really see us?

Turner's thesis has incited considerable historical interpretation since his time; his views were attacked soon after his death in the

1930s, and today historians regularly dismiss his theories. Most agree that he legitimized the frontier as worthy of historical study, but few, if any, accept his view as valid.

Powell's Vision

At roughly the same time Turner was propounding his frontier thesis, a one-armed military man with a clearer vision than most of his contemporaries offered the Great Plains an extraordinary opportunity. If the leaders of the time had listened, many of the region's current problems might have been averted.

John Wesley Powell surveyed and mapped much of the West on hazardous treks, including one down the Colorado River into the Grand Canyon. He understood better than anyone else of his time the arid nature of the Great Plains. In 1878 he published a document later described as "quite possibly the most revolutionary document ever to tumble off the presses of the Government Printing Office."

Powell said the West should not be divided into tidy rectangular fields the way eastern farmlands had been, following a model drawn from Europe. Rather, land should be utilized according to the availability of water. He saw three possible categories of land—timber, irrigable, and pasture—and suggested that all holdings be tied to specific water sources and rights. He said: "The grasses of the pasturage lands are scant, and the lands are of value only in large quantities. The farm unit should not be less than 2,560 acres . . . the small streams of the general drainage system and the lone springs and streams should be reserved for such pasturage farms. . . . The pasturage lands will not usually be fenced, and hence herds must roam in common."

Powell might have been writing a blueprint for the way cattle ranchers had already organized western South Dakota. He even noted that in some districts, pastures would have to be much larger than his suggested acreage (which was sixteen times what the government allotted), explaining that ranchers already living in the region thought his limit too low. He suggested that the ranchers be allowed to divide the land themselves, acting cooperatively, as many had already done. Powell was not always right; he called the coal fields he had surveyed "inexhaustible." Little did he realize how prolific his countrymen would be!

In 1889 Powell addressed the North Dakota constitutional convention, and a supporter of his views spoke to a similar convention in South Dakota. Both pointed out the stark differences between the eastern and western halves of the two newly created states. Beyond the 100th meridian, Powell advised, settlement should be halted until clear policies to protect the scarce water and fragile land could be developed. "I tell you, gentlemen, you are piling up a heritage of conflict," Powell told one Congress, "for there is not sufficient water to supply the land!"

Prophetic words, but few listened. To read Powell's report today is to read a plan that could have stopped the disasters of the past hundred years. Our forefathers created havoc by blindly plowing, irrigating, and fertilizing the plains. They lacked experience and ignored Powell's prescient arguments. Irrigators outshouted him by promising "forty million forty-acre farms!" Shortsighted greed triumphed over a long view, as it has done depressingly often in our nation's history.

Into the Twentieth Century

As the nation entered its second century, a hunting and camping president, Theodore Roosevelt, led a national trend toward conservation of natural resources that previous generations had vigorously exploited. His South Dakota friend, Seth Bullock, helped; the nation's first national forest reserve was in the Black Hills. At the same time, the government began imposing regulations and fees on cattle raisers here who used public lands to graze their animals.

Though much of the Plains diversified its economy during the 1920s, the states last settled (including the Dakotas) gained less from national improvements. For example, whereas other parts of the West became cosmopolitan by absorbing new Hispanic, Oriental, and black residents, South Dakota remained largely white, Anglo-Saxon and Protestant, its Indian population little noticed. Homesteaders first avoided, then invaded the reservation lands of the Lakota as the government passed allotment acts dividing up the land. Land tenure on the Indian reservations in the state is still an uneasy mixture of white lessees and Indian owners, as the natives try to become self-supporting on the barren land left them by government treaty.

Other cultural upheavals that affected Plains dwellers included the fight for women's suffrage. In this case, for once, the western states led the nation; by 1918 all but four states west of the Mississippi River had extended the vote to women, finally granted to all American women with the passage of the Nineteenth Amendment to the Constitution in 1920. As women's roles changed, they began getting jobs in addition to their duties as housewives. But for years in South Dakota, rural women had few opportunities to take any outside jobs other than teaching school.

Politics: The Ultimate Puzzle

The conflicts between urban and rural interests, as well as between farmers and ranchers, may help explain why state officials are traditionally Republican but citizens often send Democrats to Congress. Woodrow Wilson once said, "I can't, for the life of me, in this place be certain that I can tell a Democrat from a Republican." He wasn't speaking of South Dakota, but he may as well have been.

The differences between South Dakota's state and national politics parallel the differences between its eastern and western halves on many issues concerning the environment and economic development. As I wrote in *Going over East*, a collection of essays about ranching in South Dakota:

> Many of the proposals for what is termed "bringing money and jobs into the state" center on the arid western half, while most people who might call themselves "environmentalists" live in the more metropolitan eastern half. Putting together coalitions of individuals dedicated to sensible but environmentally sane development has proven to be complex; ranchers won't talk to members of the Sierra Club, and intellectuals sometimes seem to believe that ranchers live only to slaughter prairie dogs and overgraze public land.

Like many of its neighbors, South Dakota is a little confused about its role and position in the modern world. Traditional agriculture, once the state's economic basis, is changing. Young men and women who stayed on to work the family ranch or farm in earlier generations now follow their fathers' advice and leave the state for higher education; they either don't return or return as urban professionals. Many large ranches have been sold to out-of-state investors because residents couldn't afford them. Small-town business districts are disappearing, partly because they can't compete with corporations doing business on a national scale and partly because large towns such as Rapid City and Sioux Falls serve ever larger areas.

Modern South Dakotans seem to mingle pride in their state with a vague embarrassment that it isn't more urban, more western, more populous, or more original in some undefined way. Some of the same misconceptions that influenced the state's early history (often for the worse) still seem to govern its modern leaders. A higher percentage of the population still relies on agriculture for income in North and South Dakota than in any other states in the Union. However, tourism has replaced agriculture as the most profitable industry, leading to conflicts between those two interests.

South Dakota, like other states in the region, frequently points to its low taxes, well-trained workers, cheap land, and wide open spaces to lure businesses into the state. A brochure recently distributed by the Governor's Office of Economic Development proudly notes that the state has no corporate income tax, no personal income tax, no personal property tax, and no business inventory tax. It adds that the state has the nation's ninth lowest rates for workers' compensation, second lowest energy costs, and third lowest unemployment insurance costs. South Dakota's workers are described as superior because they are used to working long hours for low pay. In short, the state's official "promotional" literature attracts businesses by advertising circumstances that workers in other states have condemned.

Weakening Environmental Laws

Elected officials have weakened environmental laws and offered incentives to industrial developers as a way of keeping young people home and employed, but they fail to see that too much development may ruin both of the state's top money-makers: tourism and agriculture. Deb Rogers Miller, executive director of the Technical Information Project, Inc., an environmental research organization, says reclamation laws are "almost nonexistent. The company must submit a plan—and the Board of Water & Minerals approve it—but no standards exist to which the plan must conform." The quality of the plan is up to the board's staff at the time.

Still, old values persist. Another gold rush has begun in the Black Hills, as sophisticated chemicals and techniques have made it possible to mine paying quantities from the low-grade ores discarded in piles of tailings by the earlier rush. The modern miners use bulldozers and cyanide, but citizens are reluctant to regulate the industry because of the jobs it has provided. In fiscal 1984, when the severance tax rate on gold mining was 6 percent of gross, the state made $7.35 million; legislators sympathetic to the mining industry dropped the tax to 2 percent of gross plus 8 percent of net, and gold revenues in fiscal 1985 dropped to $3.56 million. Because of the reduced tax, the state now enjoys five or six times as much gold mining but earns much less revenue.

At the same time, when state agencies impose laws to protect air, water, and land from misuse, other citizens, notably ranchers and farmers, protest that such laws interfere with personal liberty and the freedom to use their land as they choose. Indian citizens, adapting to white ways, have turned to media events and the courts to reassert their claims to the land they held when the whites appeared.

In the future, South Dakota and other western states may have more to lose than ever before. The money men from the East now want to do more than simply haul away the dwindling natural resources of the West; the trains that rush east with coal to fire the nation's engines return filled with garbage that Easterners don't want buried in their backyards. Garbage is now considered a smart investment in South Dakota. Despite challenges from environmental groups, lawsuits, bankruptcy, and other difficulties, businessmen from outside the state spent five years trying to save a plan to dump a million tons of the nation's garbage every year in a landfill near the town of Edgemont. An editorial in the *Rapid City Journal*, joking that the state's new motto might become, "We'll Take It," read: "Give us your heaped, huddled trash dumpsters, your straining Hefty garbage bags yearning to be free. . . . South Dakota—Trash Can for the Nation." Even tribal governments are negotiating with large waste-handling companies to provide hazardous or toxic garbage dump sites.

Choosing to become a garbage dump seems inconsistent with the standards demanded by both the state's primary industries, tourism and agriculture. A few years ago a slick operator talked Edgemont into importing 270,000 tons of sewage ash from Minnesota, convincing local citizens the gold and other precious metals extracted from the stuff would make them rich. The company defaulted, and the state ended up burying all the ash that hadn't already been blown around the landscape. One member of the state's Board of Minerals and Environment ought to get a medal for adhering to the pioneer motto of "making do with what you have": She developed a pottery glaze from sewage ash.

The Future of the Sunshine/Garbage State

When I came home from college with one bumper sticker that supported George McGovern for president and another about saving the whales, a man waited for me outside a truck stop in the middle of the night to tell me, "Your kind isn't wanted here." I wasn't sure if he meant Democrats or environmentalists; both groups enjoyed about the same popularity in South Dakota.

But in spite of his ire, I was simply reflecting the contradictions with which I grew up in this paradoxical state. To most residents of the nation, now living far from where they were born, being from somewhere else might seem unremarkable, but it still ranks as an insult here. Critics are often accused of being from somewhere else just before they are advised to return there; the slogan "love it or leave it" is alive and well.

However, with many people leaving overcrowded metropolitan areas for states like South Dakota, where land prices are lower and the quality of life higher, more residents are not native-born. The insult is losing its sting, and the attitudes of these new citizens are changing the state's image of itself.

We desperately want to be proud of our differences from the nation, but we're haunted by a sneaking suspicion that we are second-rate. When a few of our citizens made headlines for being willing to accept fried sewage ash because it might contain gold, we were delighted to be in the national spotlight for a change but embarrassed by the jokes about our gullibility. State officials can speak one minute of the benefits of burying every kind of garbage from radioactive sludge to used tires, then swing into a lyric about the state's natural beauties and tourism the next, apparently not realizing that the two businesses may be incompatible. We may have to choose between them; worse, the choice may be made before we understand it.

South Dakota and its neighbors are still reluctant to abandon the idea that mechanized agriculture can make the plains "bloom like a garden," but we are beginning to deal realistically with the arid climate—just in time, say the experts, to get ready for dust bowl conditions that will make the 1930s look like a picnic. Meanwhile, social scientists suggest that the entire center of the nation will continue to lose population, and some have suggested that a strip from Texas to North Dakota be converted to the greatest wildlife park in the world, given back to the bison and antelope. Disagreements over these topics should keep the nickel coffee sloshing and the hot air smoking for years to come.

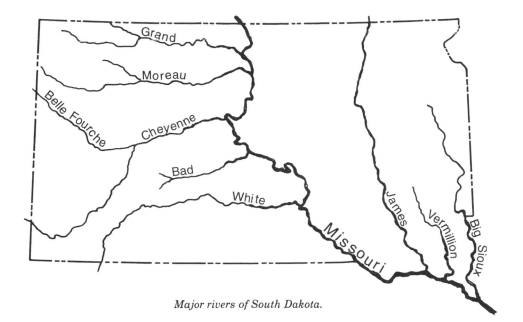

Major rivers of South Dakota.

1 - Eastern South Dakota

PART ONE

Eastern South Dakota

Glaciers and weather shaped the landscape of eastern South Dakota, which in turn influenced the state's history and politics. Two million years ago, masses of ice advanced into today's eastern South Dakota in two segments; one crawled southeast, leaving a six-hundred-foot cliff along the Minnesota River, and the other pushed southwest, carving a three-hundred-foot drop along the valley of the James River.

The two ice sheets joined during the Pleistocene epoch, roughly two million years ago, and buried the entire eastern portion of the state. Geologists think that near Aberdeen the glacier piled up sixteen hundred feet of ice, exerting forty-five tons of pressure on every square foot of ground it covered. Moving several inches a day, it bulldozed the landscape. Rocks embedded in the sole of the glacier cut long grooves in the bedrock, and silt and clay polished its surfaces.

When the Ice Age ended, melting glaciers left piles of sediments called moraines. Hills and ridges of the glacial lakes region, called *coteau des prairies* (hills of the prairie) by the French, are actually moraines. Huge chunks of ice were embedded in the moraines. The glacial lakes in eastern South Dakota were created about ten thousand years ago, when the last of a series of glaciers retreated across North America, leaving melted ice in glacial lakes and deep depressions called "prairie potholes."

Some of the lakes formed in this manner have no outlet, so the water can't escape except through evaporation. Some lakes have collected minerals over the ages; Medicine Lake, for example, contains half again as much salt as seawater and was once bottled and sold for its curative powers. The Works Progress Administration and other federal agencies helped build nearly seven hundred lakes prior to World War II to supplement the two hundred or so glacial lakes existing in the northeastern corner of the state; all together, these lakes cover more than twenty-three thousand acres. The Soil Conservation Service built more than a hundred small lakes, and the

U.S. Indian Department (before it became the Bureau of Indian Affairs) created more than two hundred. Look on the map; both sides of I-29 form a patchwork in blue.

Wildlife still abounds, especially in parks and refuges. The lake region contains species of plants more common to eastern forests: sugar maple, basswood, oak, elm, and ash. Wildflowers bloom everywhere: touch-me-nots, Dutchman's breeches, wood lilies, aster, gay feather, pasque flowers, and jack-in-the-pulpit. Plants and animals native to marshes, woodlands, grasslands, and croplands all exist in close proximity. For example, western grebes look like incredibly fast snakes racing each other on the surface of Sand Lake northeast of Aberdeen. Waubay Lake is the only refuge in the nation where all five members of the grebe family live, along with golden eye ducks, for whom this is the southernmost breeding spot known. White pelicans and thousands of geese gather in noisy flocks. Wildlife is everywhere, remnants of the native prairie recorded by writers such as Laura Ingalls Wilder and painters such as Harvey Dunn.

The Indians

After the glaciers retreated, about ten thousand years ago, this region became a wildlife paradise that attracted hunting bands of Indians. Prehistoric burial mounds and tunnels indicate that Woodland Indians lived in northeastern South Dakota, probably in temporary shelters of brush, between A.D. 300 and 1400. They buried their dead in earthen mounds, especially near rivers. Artifacts found in the mounds include pottery, stone knives and hammers, and shell beads from both marine and freshwater mollusks. A roadside park eight miles east of Sisseton and one and a half miles south of the highway contains several mounds; others are found in Hartford Beach State Park, northeast of Milbank; in Mitchell's Southside Park; near the mouth of Twelve-Mile Creek near Milltown; in Sioux Falls; west of Faulkton; and at Brandon.

Probably every tribal band developed stories around the discovery or origin of a particular spot. Most of these are lost, but some Lakota experts have recorded fragments. In one saga, the buffalo, revered for its usefulness, was the source of another valuable food— corn. Another told of a goose who had a vision of a sunny southern land and was driven out of the goose tribe for being different. The goose flew away to the south alone. When she reappeared strong and healthy the following spring, her family finally believed her. The upland plover's plaintive song was explained as the cry of a baby lost on the featureless prairie after its mother put it down while

A trapper holds the broad flat tail of a large beaver under his chin. Mountain men and trappers considered beaver tail a delicacy; its fat provided a necessary supplement to their lean-meat diet. —State Historical Society of North Dakota

digging roots; other tales told why birds should not be held captive and how the meadowlark acquired his yellow breast and black tie.

Indian legends supplied some of the names for the lakes of this region: Enemy Swim Lake, Red Iron Lake, Blue Dog Lake, Punished Woman's Lake. Lake Kampeska, originally called the Lake of the Shining Shells, contains a pile of rocks called Maiden Isle, where Indian warriors competed in throwing rocks into the water to win the favor of a local beauty. Angered by her refusal to choose a husband, they put her on the island and threatened her with starvation. A pelican fed her fish until her lover returned to rescue her. Other stories say the rock pile was the place where Wakan Tanka, the Great Spirit, stood when he spoke with the tribe.

Arrival of Whites

White explorers were drawn to the area by the ease of traveling on the chain of rivers and lakes, as well as good hunting and trapping opportunities. Fur traders followed, often living companionably with the Indians. Only when permanent settlers began moving into the rich region, plowing up the prairie and hunting the wildlife, did conflict between whites and Indians get serious. The settlers' vulnerability to Indian attacks drew military forces, and all this activity provided an incentive for the railroads, which attracted even more settlers, until the Indians were unable to survive by hunting.

Reports of early explorers, particularly those who traversed only the western part of the state, had said the region was a desert. As late as 1869, Ohio Congressman James Ashley argued that Dakota was "worthless for agriculture, arid, and grasshopper-ridden and that it must for a century at least be Indian land." Iowa newspapers called it that "barren, desolate, God-forsaken land," and Dakota promoters retaliated by accusing Iowans of trying to keep settlers in their own state with scare tactics.

Still, a few brave settlers followed routes marked by fur trappers and traders to discover rich, loamy, game-filled river valleys in the eastern part of the territory. Almost as soon as they unhitched their wagons, they were inspired to promotional fury in their desire for neighbors. In 1869 the Yankton *Union and Dakotaian* ran an ad typical of many: "WANTED IMMEDIATELY.—Twenty Thousand Farmers to know that Dakota has millions of acres of the finest Farm Lands in the country, which she proposes to give away to actual settlers."

Few promoters mentioned the weather, but immigrants flocked in. Deception followed deception. A couple of pseudoscientists combined a little knowledge with a lot of optimism and promoted the idea that rain follows the plow. A pioneer could be sure of adequate precipitation for crops by stirring up the sod anywhere, these men argued; the evaporation of soil moisture would bring humidity, rain, and prosperity. The "experts" believed, or pretended to believe, that the Plains had been a tropical paradise in the past and would be again if folks plowed wide and deep enough.

People tried homesteading all over the state, but those most likely to succeed settled in the eastern portion. Town site promoters, stagecoach services, and most other businesses encouraged homesteading simply because larger populations meant more profit. No one considered how many inhabitants the land might support; the concept of limits on abundance was inconceivable. Land locators overran every community; for a fee, they hauled home seekers out to open, unclaimed lands. Land offices posted photographs of potential homesites and crops reportedly grown in the area.

Locators also speculated in relinquishments—homesteads abandoned as worthless by their occupants and thus reopened for settle-

The Northern Pacific Railroad advertised low fares and a short route from coast to coast via northern Dakota Territory in this advertisement, published before statehood. —State Historical Society of North Dakota

ment. If a settler relinquished a homestead, the speculator simply brought in someone else to file on the relinquishment. Some land "sold" several times, much of it for as little as fifty cents an acre, dirt cheap! Other types of land fraud ran rampant throughout the entire country, and Dakota was no exception. Although the Homestead Act of 1862 mandated a limit of one quarter section (160 acres) per household, homesteaders with large families often managed to acquire several tracts by filing separate claims for every family member who was (or looked) over twenty-one. Lawyers and land speculators soon learned various other tricks.

The growth of homesteading brought railroads, which were needed to transport agricultural produce east to the cities. Though railroads eventually reached the entire state, they came to this region first and determined many elements of its development. The railroad's arrival in a particular locality caused a spurt of building; conversely, if the tracks missed a settlement, it often disappeared. Sioux Falls and Yankton were exceptions; though both were major towns, they never had mainline railroad connections.

During the 1850s, as settlers migrated through the northern Plains on their way to Oregon and California, railroad magnates mapped transcontinental railroads to help bring permanent white occupation to the valley of the Missouri River and its tributaries. By 1862 several railroad companies had been granted immense tracts of free land in return for their promise to lay rails from the East to the Pacific Ocean. Four corporations—the Union Pacific, Southern Pacific, Northern Pacific, and Santa Fe railroads—were granted more than 88 million acres from the total of a billion acres of public land between the Mississippi River and the Pacific slope.

This free land stretched for two hundred feet on each side of the track line and included additional land for stations and buildings. As if these advantages weren't enough, railroad companies were also granted every alternate quarter section, up to five per mile, on each side of the tracks. This unprecedented gift gave the railroads incentive to build, but it also handed them immense profits when they sold land they did not need (sometimes repeatedly and fraudulently) to homesteaders and speculators. Grants insured that many towns would be settled adjacent to tracks, guaranteeing the companies' continued profit from merchants shipping goods to and from the newly settled regions.

News accounts of the 1880s reported hundreds of land seekers riding trains to whatever fresh settlement lay at the end of the tracks, swarming off the cars at the last town. During a hasty meal in the nearest hotel, they'd ask directions of anyone who would talk to them, then rush toward the nearest unclaimed land in a buggy or wagon hired from a livery stable. Some farmers rented their teams and wagons for extra cash or hired themselves out as guides. The prairie within fifteen miles of every railroad siding was strewn with tents and makeshift shelters that homesteaders erected on their claims until they could build a permanent home.

Under such conditions, many of the towns in the eastern half of the state expanded rapidly, and speculators and businessmen went wild with predictions that each would become a major city. Skeptics said the "Great Dakota Boom" generated more paper railroads than real ones, as town site promoters assured lot buyers and homesteaders that a particular railroad was due to arrive any day. If the railway line didn't materialize, some of the towns vanished as quickly, their residents optimistically moving on to locate a real railway line.

Rail transportation became a key factor in the area's growth and modernization. Sioux Falls grew by more than a thousand people a year during the 1880s and topped ten thousand by 1890. During that same year, the final military confrontation with the Lakota took place in the remote western half of the state. Settlers there were still battling hostile Indians shoved west by white settlement, whereas progress in eastern South Dakota nearly kept up with that in more metropolitan regions. The two halves of the state have never been balanced; from that fact stems many of their differences.

Blizzards Wreak Havoc

Nature struck a blow against homesteading and other forms of development with an unusually severe twenty-four-hour blizzard in

October 1880. More than eleven feet of snow fell in a few hours in October, and snow continued to pile up through the fall and winter. Most of it was still on the ground when another storm struck the following February.

Hundreds of new settlers were caught unprepared for winter; railroads had not delivered winter coal, and food supplies and oil for lamps were short. Some families burned hay and corn, fences, even buildings and bridges to keep warm. Others moved in together, shared food, and ground wheat in coffee mills for flour. Thousands of stock animals died, and some of those that survived were trapped in barns and had to be fed and watered through holes chopped in roofs. Most railroad tracks were blocked by snow, but in December a train made it from Yankton to Elk Point using fifty bushels of corn for fuel.

In February, when most residents expected a winter thaw, another blizzard struck. When the thaw finally came in March, flooding did almost as much damage as the storms. Farmers already in danger of starvation lost buildings, livestock, stored grain—everything but their land and their lives. No one could escape on the blocked trails or raging rivers, and no relief supplies could be sent in. Settlers in Gayville, east of Yankton, were marooned on rooftops and haystacks and in barns, attics, and corncribs—wherever they were when the water caught them. About seventy-five people took refuge in the

The spring flood of 1881 caused a huge ice jam on the Missouri River, wrecking steamboats anchored for the winter and nearly ending riverboat traffic in Yankton, where this photo was taken. —Yankton County Historical Society

21

Meckling grain elevator, and more were trapped for several days on the upper floor of a granary, living on corn cracked in a hand grinder.

Huge blocks of ice broke loose and roared downstream; three bridges in Sioux Falls disappeared within fifteen minutes, and steamboats were wrecked on every major river in the territory. In Yankton, where an ice jam formed and then broke loose, the steamboats *Western*, *Butte*, *Helena*, *Black Hills*, *Peninah*, and *Nellie Peck* and the ferryboat *Livingston* were piled in shattered pieces on the bank.

Just eight years later, another terrible blizzard wreaked havoc in South Dakota. Temperatures dropped as much as seventy degrees in a few hours, reaching thirty below zero, and sixty-mile-per-hour winds accompanied heavy snow. The 1888 blizzard is remembered as the "schoolchildren's storm" because it caught so many of them on their long homeward walk. Many teachers became heroines by realizing how dangerous the storm was and refusing to let their students leave. Groups of children marooned in schoolhouses cooperated to keep stoves going, tied themselves together to get wood from an outbuilding or chop up a shed, shared the remnants of school lunches, and sang songs. A day or more later, most were rescued by groups of frightened parents who fought their way to the schools. Not all survived. A total of 112 South Dakotans died in the 1888 storm, along with 90 percent of the unprotected livestock and much of the wildlife.

As long as the memories of old residents lasted, these blizzards were spoken of with awe. Modern vehicles have made modern residents less fearful of the weather. However, every year, residents who ought to know better go out in bad conditions without adequate preparation or supplies, and some die. Though modern residents are better equipped for dealing with excessive snowfall, no Plains resident is entirely safe from the danger of blizzards, and several modern storms have caused severe disruption in the state.

Blizzards have affected not only humans but also wildlife. The 1880 storm virtually wiped out South Dakota's antelope population. Before settlement, antelope had been almost as plentiful as buffalo. Called "goats" by Lewis and Clark, who first saw them in 1804, antelope were not named, classified, and described by science until 1815. Because they could run sixty miles an hour, they could often escape hunters. The bitter storms of 1880 drove starving antelope down into the river valleys for food and shelter, where the deep snow made their speed useless. The hungry settlers butchered all they could find and even salted some down for summer meat. When spring came, an antelope was a rare sight in the region, and most of those remaining were wiped out in the 1888 blizzard.

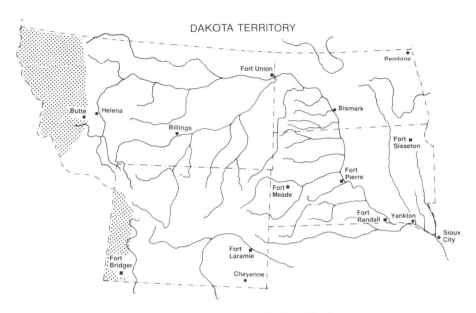

DAKOTA TERRITORY

Fort Union
Pembina
Butte   Helena
Billings
Bismark
Fort Sisseton
Fort Pierre
Fort Meade
Fort Randall   Yankton
Sioux City
Fort Laramie
Fort Bridger
Cheyenne

Shaded areas were not part of Dakota Territory.

A law passed in 1911 made killing antelope illegal, but by 1924 it was estimated that only 680 of the swift runners lived in the entire state. Careful management speeded their return, and by 1941 about 11,000 head existed; a hunting season was reinstated in 1942. Today the average number of pronghorn—the species' proper name—in the state fluctuates between 17,000 and 43,000.

Agriculture: Boom and Bust

When Dakota Territory became North and South Dakota, the thirty-ninth and fortieth states, in 1889, settlement east of the Missouri River was well advanced, and agriculture was the main business. But the boom of the 1880s collapsed, and droughts caused crop failures for several years. Most of the free land east of the Missouri River was taken up early, but many of the settlers were barely able to feed themselves, let alone make money. Governor A. C. Mellette begged eastern cities for money and food to help homesteaders survive the winter.

The farmers managed to hang on, and their fortunes took a turn for the better. Agriculture reached an all-time level of success with the boom that accompanied World War I; prices were artificially high, and farmers went into debt to plow up more land and buy more machinery. But when the war ended, farm prices fell by 40 percent; droughts, dust storms, and locust invasions worsened the effects of intensive cultivation. While the rest of the nation was making money, the farm states remained in a deep depression, and farmers began to move to town. The 1920 federal census showed that for the first time in its history, more of South Dakota's residents lived in urban rather than rural settings. The number of farms in the state has decreased steadily from the all-time high of more than 84,000 in 1931.

Rainmakers and Cash

Many of the region's inhabitants were victims of misinformation, believing they had come to a rich farming region with abundant rainfall. Before admitting the truth and succumbing to defeat, they tried everything. During the dry summer of 1893, the farming areas were invaded by rainmakers, usually shrewd con men, though a few actually believed they could help the desperate farmers by producing rain. Among the most common rainmaking methods were using artillery or dynamite to cause condensation or producing hydrogen gas in large quantities to stimulate existing clouds; sometimes the two were combined. Once the news spread, farmers unwilling or unable to pay for the services of a rainmaker pooled their funds, bought dynamite and ammunition, and blasted away at the sky in independent attempts.

A Kansas man named Morris worked this region, promising to produce a half inch of rain over a three-hundred-square-mile area for $500, payment after delivery. As farmers watched hopefully, Morris began mysterious operations, and dark clouds gathered. On the second day, a brisk wind blew the clouds east and Watertown received a downpour. Morris insisted that he'd fulfilled his part of the bargain and that the wind wasn't his fault, but he was persuaded to try again. On the last evening, a full half-inch of rain fell, and Morris received his payment.

Morris was immediately deluged with offers from farmers all over the state and moved his operations to Aberdeen. There he found a rival named Captain Hauser, who erected a contraption that emitted evil-smelling gas from the top story of a building. When Hauser's time was up, he had produced no rain. Within two days, Morris had produced another half-inch of rain, soaking the Fourth of July picnic; he again collected his money. Eventually, the rainmakers lost the public's confidence, and later farmers usually confined their rainmaking efforts to prayer.

For Further Reading:

Some surviving Indian legends appear in *Legends of the Mighty Sioux*, compiled by the Federal Writers' Project of South Dakota, illustrated by Oscar Howe, and first published in 1941. A 1987 reprint of the book includes an introduction by well-known Dakota writer Virginia Driving Hawk Sneve, who explains changes in public attitudes. *Dakota Texts*, first published in 1932 and reprinted in 1978, includes English translations of sixty-four legends collected by Ella C. Deloria, a Yankton scholar.

D. C. Poole, an Indian agent near Yankton for eighteen months immediately after the reservation was established, wrote about Sioux customs and the difficulties of his job in *Among the Sioux of Dakota*.

One of the best published accounts of homesteading was written by Edith Eudora Kohl; *Land of the Burnt Thigh* chronicles her experiences west of the Missouri River in the early twentieth century. Mary Worthy Breneman relied on her mother's memories to write *The Land They Possessed*, a story of German-Russian settlers set near Ipswich.

The Bones of Plenty by Lois Phillips Hudson vividly portrays the struggle of farm families in the 1930s. Hamlin Garland's books, *A Son of the Middle Border*, *A Daughter of the Middle Border*, and *Well-Traveled Roads*, all portray homesteaders. *Women's Diaries of the Westward Journey*, edited by Lillian Schlissel, quotes from some of the most intriguing, and least known, documents about what it was like to leave home and family for the prospect of a new life in the West.

Mari Sandoz's *Winter Thunder* was written about the experiences of a schoolteacher in the appalling 1949 blizzard. Laura Ingalls Wilder's books are widely reprinted, fascinating even to modern readers, young and old, and come from the author's real experiences. *The Golden Bowl* by Frederick Manfred is a fictional account of the Depression in South Dakota from his experiences.

Books by Indian writer Charles Eastman, some still in print, include: *Old Indian Days*; *Red Hunters and the Animal People*; *Wigwam Evenings: Sioux Folk Tales Retold*; *Indian Boyhood*; *Indian Scout Talks: A Guide for Boy Scouts and Camp Fire Girls*; *The Soul of the Indian*; *From the Deep Woods*; *The Indian Today*; and *Indian Heroes and Great Chieftains*.

North Dakota—Iowa
286 Miles

I-29 runs north-south through the eastern quarter of South Dakota. A traveler on interstate highways gains speed but loses contact with the details of the surrounding countryside. Still, from I-29 it is possible to see the height of what French traders called the *coteau des prairies*. On the north end, the *coteau* rises as much as five hundred feet above the surrounding lowlands of the Red River of the North; east are the valleys of the Minnesota River.

The extraordinarily flat prairie east of Sisseton was left by glacial Lake Agassiz, formed when glaciers blocked the Red River of the North. Water spilling out of the lake cut a channel fifty to ninety feet below the present bed of the Minnesota River. Sediment accumulating on the floor of the lake created the level prairies, one of the flattest landscapes in the world. The divide separating continental drainage north to Hudson Bay and south to the Gulf of Mexico lies between Lake Traverse and Big Stone Lake; the former is about nine feet higher.

Driving south into the lowlands along the Big Sioux River, especially from the bland fertility of the Red River valley, a tourist can hardly bear to pass without stopping to explore. The long slanting slopes are rich with trees and glittering streams, the windows of old farmhouses twinkling in the sun. Don't resist; the string of lakes and streams on both sides of the highway that once lured French trappers is dotted today with campgrounds and small towns and laced with roads back to the interstate.

SISSETON

Sisseton had a remarkably short settlement period, literally filling up in a matter of minutes. Once the Indians had been placed on reservations and allocated 160 acres each, the remaining land— 600,000 acres—was opened for sale to homesteaders at high noon on April 15, 1892. Hundreds of land seekers lined up at the edges of the new land ready to stake their claims. Cavalrymen carrying carbines kept them from getting a head start on each other. When the bugle sounded, the troops stepped aside, and settlers stampeded to choose their homesites.

Newspapers reported that about a thousand people came from Browns Valley, about five hundred from Travare, six hundred from

The original Fort Wadsworth, later named Fort Sisseton, included two log blockhouses like this one pictured in 1879 at Fort Berthold, on the upper Missouri River in northern Dakota Territory. —State Historical Society of North Dakota

Wheaton, and another six hundred from Waubay. A train on the Chicago, Milwaukee & St. Paul Railroad (the Milwaukee for short) carrying five hundred people was met at the end of the track by enterprising Indians, who sold mustangs to the settlers for the rest of the trip. By the end of the summer fifty buildings stood in town. The population of Sisseton in 1990 stood at 2,181.

Fort Sisseton

Fort Sisseton State Park is located on SD 10, twelve miles east and eight miles south of Britton on the Wadsworth Trail. This route, blazed by settlers in 1864, led from St. Cloud, Minnesota, to the fort.

Following the hostilities of the 1860s, settlers on the frontier remained nervous about possible Lakota attacks and wanted military protection. In 1864 the army established a guard outpost called Fort Wadsworth. Huge logs were set in a dirt embankment dug from a ditch in front of the walls. Two log blockhouses at the northwest and southeast corners made it possible to cover the walls with enfilading fire, and the three narrow entrances were easy to guard. Of

Modern volunteers in military uniforms reenact a cavalry parade at Fort Sisseton, named for the Lakota band settled nearby. In a battle, the extra men riding one horse of each pair pulling the cannon helped control the horses and served as replacements for gun crew members killed. The stone officers' quarters, stone barracks, powder magazine, and guardhouse were restored in the 1930s. —South Dakota Department of Tourism

this supposedly impregnable post, its first commander, Maj. John Clowney, boasted that he could "resist all the redskins in the northwest." This optimistic assessment went unchallenged, since most of the later conflicts with Indians occurred farther west.

There were occasional close calls, though. On April 19, 1866, word arrived that a war party was approaching. Samuel J. Brown, the post's chief of scouts, wrote a note to warn troops at Fort Abercrombie (near Wahpeton, North Dakota). The note was to be delivered the following morning. That evening, Brown (who was half Indian), rode forty-five miles to a scout camp on the James River at the mouth of the Elm River, near the present sites of Columbia and Ordway, northeast of Aberdeen. When he arrived there at midnight, he found that an error had been made: The Indians supposed to be hostile were actually runners sent out to tell local tribes that a treaty had been ratified.

A spring blizzard had begun (spring blizzards are often the most severe the Dakotas get in terms of snow depth and wind chill), but Brown felt responsible for stopping his incorrect message about the band's hostility. He headed back to Fort Wadsworth, lost his bearings and drifted southeast to a point he recognized on Waubay Lake.

By the time he found the fort, he was nearly frozen, and his legs were paralyzed; he never walked again.

Renamed Fort Sisseton in 1876, the fort was the military and social center of the area until its abandonment in 1889. By that time most of the original log structures had been replaced by stone and frame buildings. These were restored in the 1930s as a WPA project.

WATERTOWN

Watertown got its name from one of its early settlers, John E. Kemp, who hailed from Watertown, New York. But it could just as easily have been named for its location, in the center of the glacial lake region, between Pelican Lake and Lake Kampeska. Founded in 1879, the town is the seat of Codington County. In 1990 seventeen thousand people called Watertown home, just five thousand fewer than in all of Codington County. Promoters say it serves as a trade center for a hundred thousand people in northeast South Dakota and west-central Minnesota. Commerce here centers around agricultural products, including dairy products, wheat, flax, corn, oats, rye, barley, alfalfa, sorghum, hay and grass seed, and row crops such as potatoes. Cattle, hogs, and sheep are also sold here. The town has fifty manufacturing plants.

Provisions for early arrivals were sometimes crude. D. B. Lovejoy, in 1876, had little choice but to operate a hotel, as his was the only house in the region; the others had been burned in prairie fires. He shot buffalo fish and pickerel in the river for supper and kept a bundle of hay to spread on the floor for a spare bed; on one occasion seventeen people occupied it. In 1878 Mrs. Oliver H. Tarbell, the first white woman in Codington County, arrived and settled with her husband on the east shore of Lake Kampeska. By that time the area hosted a varied population typical of the time; many early fur traders and a few former military men had settled there after marrying Indian or part-Indian women.

The most vigorous homesteading activity was over by 1884, when the land offices in Watertown, as well as those in Yankton, Mitchell, and Sioux Falls, reported that only scattered bits of land remained open. Ambitious settlers were already pursuing statehood, and Watertown aspired to become the capital but withdrew in favor of Huron. A newspaper established as a weekly in 1887 survives today as the *Watertown Public Opinion*, and several buildings in the area are on the National Register of Historic Places, including a round barn and several elaborate private homes. The entire historic commercial district has been nominated for inclusion in the Register because of its neoclassical, colonial, and Georgian buildings.

A pioneer in modern moviemaking—one who never owned a camera—lived in Watertown and may have lost a historical treasure there. John Banvard was the inventor of "panoramic paintings," a popular form of entertainment during the 1850s. Panoramic paintings were extremely *long* murals. A narrator—usually the artist—told the painting's story while sweating assistants scrolled the long painting across a stage to simulate action.

Banvard developed the idea of panoramic painting as a child while boating down the Ohio River and watching the scenery moving past him. In 1841 he floated the Missouri and Mississippi rivers, sketching all the way, then he built a huge barn outside Louisville and began painting "The Great Three Mile Painting," perhaps the longest canvas in history. As empty canvas rolled off a giant scroll on one side of the artist, finished artwork rolled onto another. In 1846 he exhibited "a mile or so" of the work; the response was overwhelmingly positive, so he kept painting. The painting measured twelve feet high and showed various historical incidents along twelve hundred miles of the Mississippi and Ohio rivers. It took two hours to crank the scenes past enthusiastic eastern audiences. Banvard lectured about the painting and the history it depicted while his wife played waltzes on the piano.

In 1846 Banvard began a six-year tour of Boston, New York, London, and Paris. He charged fifty cents for admission, showed the work to two million people, and became a millionaire. Longfellow and Thoreau loved it; Banvard met Dickens and became the most famous artist of his time. Another of his panorama paintings showed the burning of Columbia, South Carolina, during the Civil War; drums, kerosene lamps, and colored tissue paper created battlefield effects. Other artists began experimenting, and Banvard's displays were soon upstaged by panoramas combined with live actors and horses on treadmills. By 1881 the broke artist moved to Watertown to be with his two sons, and he died there ten years later. His grandsons later remembered playing with "The Great Three Mile Painting," but today no one can find it. However, one of Banvard's smaller works is displayed at the Kampeska Heritage Museum.

BROOKINGS

Brookings County, created in 1862, was named for Wilmot W. Brookings, pioneer judge and legislator. It originally included parts of Moody, Lake, and Kingsbury counties before being chopped to its present size of 791 square miles. An individual of rare courage,

Homesteaders raise a windmill at a homestead near Brookings in 1898.
—South Dakota Agricultural Heritage Museum

Brookings spent much of his life not in the county and town named for him but in Sioux Falls. He was a graduate of Bowdoin College in Brunswick, Maine, and was admitted to the bar in 1857. In August of the same year, he arrived in Sioux Falls, then just a few cabins housing sixteen colonists surrounded by Indians. He may not have realized at first that he had fallen into fortune; he was immediately given charge of the legal affairs of the Western Town Lot Company, one of many early development companies. Ten of the colonists represented the Western Town Lot Company and six the Dakota Land Company. Competition for the money of settlers was fierce on the frontier, and the fledgling lawyer held a favored position.

Early the next February, while on a trip for his client, Brookings fell from his horse into the Split Rock River southeast of present-day Brookings. Darkness had already fallen, and the temperature was around thirty degrees below zero. When Brookings was unable to catch his horse, he knew he was in serious trouble. He'd freeze to death in minutes if he remained where he was, but settlement was sparse. The cold was extreme; the lawyer feared that even if he walked all night, he might become so chilled and drowsy that he would fall asleep and die. So he began to run. He ran all night and finally staggered into Sioux Falls the next morning, exhausted. Although the exact site of his mishap is unknown, he must have run at least twenty miles—a considerable feat for a man in good health, in good weather. When he arrived in Sioux Falls, his feet were frozen.

Dr. J. L. Phillips, fresh out of medical school, had joined the Sioux Falls colony. He treated Brookings for frostbite, but gangrene set in. In a desperate attempt to save Brookings's life, Phillips decided to amputate both legs below the knees. He had little equipment and no anesthetic, so he placed his patient on buffalo robes in Brookings's dirt-floored cabin. Frontier surgery without anesthetic usually required the presence of several burly assistants, who filled the patient with liquor, placed a soft rag in his mouth, and held his arms and legs. Phillips amputated Brookings's legs with a large butcher knife and a small saw.

The patient survived and took an active part in regional development. The first legislative assembly, an informal attempt to set up some rules for the new lands, met in 1859—before Dakota was even a territory—in Brookings's cabin in Sioux Falls. He was elected to the assembly, which promptly amended Minnesota laws to make them apply to Dakota, designated county boundaries, chartered several corporations, and petitioned Congress for territorial organization. None of these actions were legally binding, of course, as no government had recognized the territory, but they served notice on both local residents and the distant Congress that the settlers were serious, setting a pattern for the new region.

The men who held the meeting all became influential in the new settlements, and Brookings was one of them, even without his legs. He served in several offices both before and after the territory was officially established, bought from the government in present-day South Dakota in 1862, and later served as prosecuting attorney for Yankton County.

But Brookings wasn't through pioneering after his double amputation. In 1865-66 he supervised construction of the first road from the Minnesota boundary to the Crow Creek Indian Agency on the Missouri River south of Pierre. Though modern travelers may remark on the flatness of the state, this appearance is somewhat deceptive and partly a result of modern speed. The terrain rolls, which complicated early-day road building in much the same way that deep sea swells can complicate digestion. Brookings's job included finding a path that would be as level as possible so oxen didn't wear themselves out pulling loads up and downhill. In addition, he was required to remove rocks from the entire roadway, which was more than 150 miles long. Each time the road reached a creek, Brookings had to locate a ford that could be used by wagons and pave it with stone or gravel. In one place, workers built two feet of corduroy road— a bed of rock, covered with logs laid parallel to one another, covered with more rock and gravel. By the time the road-building party reached the Missouri River, only ten years before the Battle of the Little Bighorn, both men and money were exhausted.

Brookings served from 1869 to 1873 as an associate justice of the territorial supreme court and was a leading promoter of the Dakota Southern Railroad. In October 1872 a Dakota Southern locomotive, the *Judge Brookings*, crossed the Big Sioux River into Dakota Territory. By the following February, regular passenger trains began operating between Sioux City and Yankton.

The story of Brookings' life is symbolic of Dakota's early history. Its beginnings were crude, with brute strength and courage more valuable than education and polish. After the wilderness had been beaten back, men who had proven themselves adept at the crude skills of early frontier life often were the most successful leaders. No matter how informal or lawless their settlements may have been at first, the pioneers wasted no time in establishing schools, churches, and other symbols of what they considered proper society. For the village of Brookings, that point arrived in 1877; that's when the settlers nominated candidates for commissioner, register of deeds, sheriff, assessor, probate judge, treasurer, superintendent, district attorney, coroner, justices of the peace, and constables.

The arrival of tracks for the Chicago & Northwestern meant Brookings would prosper, and it outpolled Aurora and Volga to become the county seat. The railroad brought more settlers at once. In 1870, thirteen years after Wilmot Brookings became the sixteenth person living in Sioux Falls, the population of Brookings County stood at 163. By 1880 the county's population was nearly five thousand; ten years later, it had doubled, and the town of Brookings grew to fifteen hundred residents. As one of the best farming counties in the state, Brookings in the 1960s had nearly twice as many people in the county as in the city; and this changed only slightly by 1990, when the town's population stood at nearly fifteen thousand while the county registered twenty-five thousand. Brookings has long been known as "the city of trees," thanks to its residents who planted them over the years.

South Dakota State University

When the residents of Brookings voted to incorporate in 1881, the territorial legislature established South Dakota Agricultural College (now South Dakota State University) on eighty acres of donated land. The first building, Old Central, was used from 1884, when classes began with thirty-five students, until 1962, when it was razed. The first degree was granted in 1886. Enrollment was more than eight thousand students in 1991, an all-time high.

One of the university's priorities has been research on improving agriculture on the northern Great Plains. In 1990 $4 million in federal funds, matched by state money and augmented by cash reserves, was earmarked for construction of "biostress" laboratories to study how crops, livestock, and humans can better adapt to the region's environmental extremes. Researchers will work in advanced plant breeding, cellular and molecular biology, soil and water research, and livestock studies, including a focus on marketing meat products.

SDSU is home to a collection of paintings by one of Brookings' best-known residents, Harvey Dunn. A nationally known artist, Dunn made his living primarily as an illustrator, but he is most famous for his paintings of the pioneering landscape and people of his youth. Today his realistic depictions of the beauty and rigor of homesteaders' lives are popular even in his home state, where many people consider art frivolous.

Dunn was born in 1884 on a homestead claim in Kingsbury County. Historian Robert Karolevitz says young Harvey drew so many pictures on the blackboard at school that his teacher had to hide the chalk so she'd have enough to last through the term. In 1901 Dunn started attending classes at South Dakota's College of Agricultural and Mechanical Arts (as SDSU was then called), but his father, convinced that his son would remain a farmer, felt such education was unnecessary; he relented only after being persuaded by his wife. Dunn moved on to the Chicago Institute of Art in 1902 and never lived in his home state again.

At one point during his two years at the institute, some of his classmates told him he didn't have enough culture and sophistication to be an artist and urged the raw-boned farm boy to go back to his plow. Dunn ignored them and eventually became a successful commercial artist in New Jersey, receiving assignments from popular magazines such as *Scribner's*, *Harper's*, *Collier's Weekly*, *Century*, *Outing*, and *The Saturday Evening Post*. During the First World War he served with the American Expeditionary Force, sketching and painting while dodging bullets from vantage points so close to the front he made seasoned officers nervous. He rose to the rank of captain before leaving the military.

Late in life, he began vacationing in South Dakota to paint scenes of his boyhood, storing most because his regular eastern customers didn't find them appealing. In 1950 he hung forty-two framed canvases at the Masonic Temple in tiny De Smet, fifteen miles west of Brookings. The exhibit was such a success Dunn stayed in town all summer; more than five thousand visitors signed the guest book. The president of SDSU, Fred H. Leinbach, offered the College's Pugsley Union as a permanent home for the paintings, a brilliant idea that saved an important part of the state's heritage.

Even people who don't like art often display reproductions of Dunn's work in their homes. A frequent saying about Dunn is that "nobody liked his work but the people"—ordinary folks like those he painted. "A Driver of Oxen," for example, shows a sunburned man, eyes narrowed under the brim of his flat hat, his hand clutching a whip to control the ox team close behind him. "Buffalo Bones Plowed Under" shows a pioneer struggling to hold a walking plow in the tough sod, passing by the skull of an earlier prairie inhabitant, and "Pioneer Woman" gives us a close view of a woman standing before a crude dugout; her face, burned from the prairie sun, shows a strength deeper than cosmetic beauty. Other paintings depicted the hardships of winter and the spirit of the people who were able to endure in hope of spring.

Harvey Dunn posed for a photographer while painting in his studio.
—South Dakota Department of Tourism

Dunn's best-known painting, the one most often clipped from magazines and pinned on the walls of rural South Dakota kitchens, is a happy scene: "The Prairie Is My Garden." (It also found its way onto the cover of this book.) In it, an older woman with her growing daughter and little son are gathering flowers on the prairie. In the background, the homestead has grown from a dugout that sheltered the family in early days; now it includes a simple frame house. The woman wears an expression of quiet contentment, standing squarely on the earth, facing whatever may come. In her right hand is the sharp knife with which she has been cutting her bouquet. She's only picking flowers, but she might have to defend herself from danger with the same knife—and the same courage.

Oakwood Lakes State Park

Seven miles north of Brookings and ten miles west of I-29 on SD 30 is Oakwood Lakes State Park. This site saw a lot of action during territorial days. The Sioux called these lakes te-tonk-ha, "place of the great summer lodge"; they gathered around the lakes every summer to hunt, fish, visit, and feast. After the 1862 Sioux Uprising, soldiers deployed here to prevent the Sioux from drifting back into Minnesota dug breastworks that are still visible. Parapets originally about five feet high surrounded a log house with cannons mounted in two corners. In the 1860s the site also served as a camp for Indian scouts stationed at Fort Sisseton, ninety miles north.

The log cabin in the center of the park is built of hand-hewn logs, a historic remnant of pioneering days. In 1876 Hans Rolvig traded Eric Trygstad a milk cow for the logs to build the cabin. The home, originally located two miles south of Brookings, also served as the first Norwegian school in the area. Classes usually convened for a month at a time, but the school was permanently closed when authorities decreed that students should receive an American education.

Hole in the Mountain Pass

Maps from 1836 to 1879 located this pass at the point where Coteau Perce Creek drained to the southwest from Lake Benton into the Big Sioux River. Scientist J. N. Nicollet and explorer John C. Frémont, the "Pathfinder," visited Hole in the Mountain Pass on July 6, 1838. The July 8 journal entry describes the area: "Wood is not so rare here and it is found on every tongue of land which separates the lakes from one another and by which they communicate their waters with one another. The landscape is full of grandeur and beauty, the soil excellent, the trees of pretty growth, and several villages could be established on their shores. But there is no soul expanding its life here."

The pass was later used for the first "made" road into South Dakota—mostly rock piled to mark creek fords. Engineer Samuel A. Medary said the route was the only one possible for a railroad through or over the *coteau des prairies*. The railroad changed settlement patterns by encouraging the development of new towns, including Brookings, while several others, including Medary's namesake, disappeared because they were off the tracks.

FLANDREAU

Flandreau, a community of about two thousand, lies some twenty-five miles southeast of Brookings at the junction of SD 32 and SD 13. It serves a region historically active since the first fur traders entered. The Hudson's Bay Company built a trading post on the Big Sioux River in 1763; Joseph LaFramboise set up another post in 1822; and an American Fur Company post operated under Philander Prescott in 1831. Capt. James Allen's First Dragoons visited the Big Bend of the Big Sioux River in 1844, and by 1857 towns sprouted along the river, including Sioux Falls and Flandreau, both of which were laid out by the Dakota Land Company strictly for profit. A few woodcutters made a living on Big Sioux Point, at the river's mouth, supplying fuel for steamboats. Ferry and trading posts existed on the Iowa side of the river, at Vermillion, and at Yankton. In 1865 the Minnesota & Montana Wagon Road, one of Dakota's first, was surveyed and marked west.

Charles E. Flandreau, for whom the town is named, was an admirer of the early fur traders who explored and occasionally settled in the area. Like most trappers and hunters, he was French, a heritage reflected in town names all over the state. Flandreau arrived in the region in 1853 and fought the Minnesota Indian raiders in the 1862 Sioux Uprising. Later, when he was a judge, he said, "Had I been an Indian, I would have rebelled, too."

In the wake of the rebellion, sharp divisions developed between Christian and non-Christian members of the Sioux community. After the uprising, Christian Santee Sioux that lived around Flandreau and had peacefully coexisted with white settlers were punished along with the hostiles. Some of these Indians were reunited with a group from Iowa at Santee Agency at the mouth of the Niobrara River, west of Yankton. About a third of this group was Christian and in

A crude canvas awning sheltered white and Indian leaders at Fort Laramie, now in Wyoming, as they discussed the Laramie Treaty at the Peace Commission meeting in 1868. Gen. William Harney, at center with a white beard, helped draft the treaty. —South Dakota State Historical Society

constant conflict with non-Christian members of the tribe over how best to adapt to white civilization.

The Fort Laramie treaty of 1868 provided citizenship and allowed heads of families to choose 320-acre allotments of farmland. In 1869 twenty-five of the Christian Indians gave up their tribal rights, annuities—everything that marked them as Indian—and returned to Flandreau to homestead. Each family adopted an Anglo surname. Doing so, they reasoned, would help them be accepted as responsible citizens, a choice they believed would be best for their children. These courageous people settled at the site of the old Hudson's Bay trading post. W. A. Rogers conducted church services, and the families built log cabins along the river, where they lived without assistance from white authorities. Writer Ardyce Samp quotes a member of the group as saying there were "no wagon tracks" near the site— i.e., no roads.

After organizing as a congregation with forty-seven members, the group built a Presbyterian church with lumber hauled from Windom, Minnesota. By 1873 thirty-five more families had joined the community, including those of Old Flute, All Over Red, Iron Dog, and Big Eagle—signers of the 1868 treaty—and Iron Old Man, acting pastor, who later died in a blizzard. The new arrivals brought the community's population to 250, requiring a graveyard (still used) and a larger church. The second structure was built the same year as the town of Flandreau was platted and registered. The two Presbyterian churches were so near one another, though one had a white congregation and one Indian, that the same pastor often served both. Both congregations are members of the Dakota Presbytery.

The original church is now recognized as the state's oldest building and congregation in continuous existence, according to Samp. That first structure later became a school, then a ration house, and later a residence on the campus of the Riggs Institute. When it was scheduled for demolition, citizens organized to move the structure to the Flandreau museum complex on the east edge of town. Assisted by volunteers from Missouri, and using old photographs and newspaper accounts for reference, the congregation renovated the old church according to original designs. When the Rural Electrification Program came to the region in 1939, tribal members immediately requested new lights for the church and tribal council building, both of which had been lit by gas lanterns since 1873.

In 1892 the U.S. Indian Industrial School, later called Riggs Institute, opened on the other side of the river with ninety-eight students and twelve staff members. It was named for Stephen Return Riggs, a missionary who began working with the Indians in 1840. His translations of a hymnal and the Bible into the Sioux language are still used in reservation chapels and missions. Riggs's book, *Mary and I*, recounts his Indian experiences.

Famous Flandreauans

One of Flandreau's most remarkable inhabitants was Ohiyesa, who took the name Charles Alexander Eastman when he began his formal education. He attended mission day school in Flandreau, Santee Normal School in Nebraska, and college preparatory departments in Wisconsin, Illinois, and New Hampshire. He entered Dartmouth College on an Indian scholarship and earned a B.S., adding a medical degree from Boston University in 1890. He worked until 1893 as a government physician at the Pine Ridge Indian Reservation and later at Crow Creek and was an inspector at Carlisle Indian School in Pennsylvania.

Eastman is best known in South Dakota for his books on Indian life, through which he hoped to bring Indians and whites closer together. This remarkable man resigned his job in protest after the Wounded Knee massacre, where he found survivors at the site more than two days after the U.S. Army had left.

Flandreau's best-known white citizen is William "Bill" Janklow, elected governor of the state in 1978. Called "the prairie populist" by a national news magazine, Janklow became known for his flamboyance, a tendency to shoot from the hip and recover with remarkable agility, and his ability to think and talk on his feet— even, on one occasion, with his jaw wired shut after dental surgery.

As a lawyer on the Rosebud Indian Reservation, Janklow's style won him a reputation for aggressiveness. This image was strengthened when he prosecuted Indians who had rioted at the courthouse after the 1973 confrontation with federal troops at Wounded Knee. He was elected the state's attorney general, then won his campaign for governor by flaunting the "hip-shooter" label. When public safety is threatened, he argued, a strong executive takes quick, decisive action. He was credited with bringing Citibank and twenty-five hundred jobs into Sioux Falls, and he negotiated a complicated plan of sale and leaseback for state buildings that put more than $12 million into the state treasury. In 1985 he banned the import of foreign hogs treated with a drug banned in the United States and accompanied nearly the entire state legislature to Washington, D.C., to protest Reagan administration farm policies. He froze state hiring to reduce the work force by 10 percent and ordered a 5 percent cut in state spending. South Dakotans love state politicians who can make or save money, and Janklow was reelected in 1982 with over 70 percent of the vote despite being blamed for turning the state college campus at Springfield into a minimum security prison. Janklow hoped to move from the governor's mansion to the U.S. Senate in 1986 but was defeated in the Republican state primary by the popular Jim Abdnor.

EROS Data Center

Near Baltic, twenty miles northeast of Sioux Falls, is the Earth Resources Observation Systems (EROS) Data Center. A branch of the U.S. Geological Survey, EROS houses the government's central archives for nonmilitary satellite images and aerial photography. A low building contains more than six million negatives, beamed back daily from satellites orbiting as much as five hundred miles out in space, showing the land masses of the earth. The site also houses two million negatives of aerial photographs taken from government planes that fly at altitudes of sixty thousand feet. Opened in 1973, the center serves many purposes. African relief agencies have used the photos to find obscure road networks and reach remote areas in Ethiopia, and Ducks Unlimited orders photos to study the relationship between wetlands and duck migration routes in North America. EROS satellite photos proved that the fire in the damaged nuclear reactor at Chernobyl was still burning after Soviet officials said it was out. The facility is open to tourists, and any citizen can order photographs; four to six thousand reproductions are shipped a day.

SIOUX FALLS

The growth and development of the state's largest city—with more than a hundred thousand residents in 1990—demonstrates in microcosm the evolution of towns in South Dakota and across the Great Plains. Explorers drawn into the region by curiosity were followed immediately by profit seekers. Though early scouts remarked upon the beauty of a place or the abundance of wildlife, white settlers inevitably altered or destroyed these characteristics. As civilization grew more complex, natural beauty was invariably lost. After the vigorous labor of establishing towns and transportation routes, citizens found time for enjoyment; often their interest returned to the original enticements, and efforts were made to preserve whatever was left.

The Falls

The only records left by the earliest settlers in the Sioux Falls area, the Woodland Indians, were burial mounds; a few remain in Sherman Park. Later Indians called the river tchan-kasn-data, "thick-wooded river," and camped by it in peace, calling the water minne waukon, "sacred water." Explorers Nicollet and Frémont are often credited with visiting the area in 1839, though some authorities suggest that Nicollet may have gone only as far west as Minnesota's pipestone quarries before turning northeast. In 1844 an army expedition sent to ascend to the source of the Des Moines River camped about two miles northwest of the falls and visited them while searching for lost or stolen mules. Whites called the river the Big Sioux, and much of Sioux Falls' early industry centered around the water. As modern industry developed, the river became polluted; but the enduring falls emerged as the center of a park system.

Three viewing areas and walkways serve visitors to Falls Park, where an occasional careless person drowns. In McKennan Park stand the Pillars of the Nation, containing rocks from every state, as well as warheads and grinding stones left behind by Indians. White warfare is commemorated by the USS *South Dakota* Battleship Memorial, a monument to the most decorated battleship of the Second World War. The Shoto-teien Japanese Gardens, in Terrace Park near Covell Lake, lend an international touch with stone walkways, pagodas, and lanterns built by George Maddox before 1936 and restored for the state's centennial in 1989.

A full-scale cast of Michelangelo's statue of David stands in Fawick Park; public outcry over the sculpture nearly forced city fathers to add a kilt, but David remains nude, as Michelangelo made him. In deference to public sentiment, his back is turned modestly toward traffic, and he is deftly screened by trees. Michelangelo reappears on the nearby campus of Augustana College, where the only cast ever made of his masterpiece, Moses, stands—fully clothed. Both Michelangelo bronzes were gifts from Thomas O. Fawick, a philanthropist and industrialist from Cleveland, Ohio, who designed and built five of his Fawick Flyer automobiles in Sioux Falls between 1908 and 1910. President Theodore Roosevelt campaigned from the rear seat of one of the $3,000 cars, advertised as "America's first four-door automobile."

Along the east side of the river, bike trails following explorers' paths are part of a trail system begun in 1977 under the city's program to return the riverside to recreational, instead of industrial, uses.

Water at the falls flows over thick outcroppings of Sioux quartzite cemented with silica, showing ripple marks from wave action on the floor of an ancient continental sea. The pink rock was an important building and paving material for settlers.

As early as 1873, a Sioux Falls newspaper encouraged using the local stone for construction; the foundation of a schoolhouse laid that fall was of stone, as were the abutments for the first bridge over the river, built in 1875. At least one stone building went up in 1878, and by late 1879 at least one quarry was operating. The seven-story stone Queen Bee Mill began grinding grain that year; by 1881 it was turning out more than seven thousand barrels of flour a day. More than a hundred brick-fronted businesses lined thirty miles of improved streets.

The presence of the quarrying industry, with its complement of skilled stone workers, helped the territorial legislature decide to locate the penitentiary in Sioux Falls. Prisoners helped quarry the stone and erect the huge structure, now blackened by pollution, which still dominates the skyline. By 1885 three quarries were operating in Dell Rapids, one of which employed more than three hundred men. Quarrying was the principal industry in the county in 1887.

Hubbard and Riley supplied eight hundred thousand blocks to pave Phillips Avenue; soon afterward, speeding horse-drawn buggies disrupted city traffic. The stone is still useful to the city, though more modestly, as aggregate in concrete.

Early Sioux Falls

The settlers of Sioux Falls wanted to plow the rich farmland, not dig up rocks. After reading a description of Big Sioux Falls in 1856 or 1857, Dr. J. M. Staples of Dubuque, Iowa, organized a group of businessmen to form the Western Town Lot Company. (Modern authorities disagree on the precise date and the company's name.) Staples's cohorts included Dubuque's mayor, the editor of its newspaper, and a judge. The company hired Ezra Millard of Sioux City, Iowa, to find the falls and claim 320 acres for a town. Since the company had no legal authority to claim the land, it apparently hoped to succeed in simply squatting on it.

Millard arrived with a companion on a gray day. As he stood there admiring the falls and his cleverness in finding them, the two men suddenly found themselves surrounded by Indians. The warriors removed the bridles from the men's horses, turned them toward the south, and sent them fleeing in that direction. Millard's companion returned with a larger force in the spring of 1857 and laid out the town of Sioux Falls.

After being chased out by Indians a second time, the settlers again returned, this time with a sawmill, and they built a blockhouse. The only legitimate white residents of the land at that time were Indian-approved traders; all others were illegal squatters. But the squatters had time and a growing population on their side. About this same time, land speculators in St. Paul organized the Dakota Land Company to look for town sites in eastern Dakota. Their far-reaching plan included choosing multiple town sites, wrote John R. Milton in *South Dakota: A History*, hoping one of those sites would be "chosen eventually for the territorial capital, thus enabling the company to provide political offices and public contracts for its members and friends. One site so established immediately adjoined the acreage of the Western Town Company."

The squatters elected a legislature to help legitimize their land scheme; the election notices constituted the first printing in Dakota Territory. In both 1857 and 1858 the squatters sent representatives to Washington, D.C., as "elected" delegates to Congress. But Sioux Falls remained part of Minnesota's Big Sioux County, so Congress refused to recognize the squatter government.

When the Yankton Sioux sold the land to the government in 1858, some tribesmen burned settlements at Medary and Flandreau. Settlers scurried to Sioux Falls and built a shelter known as "Fort Sod," a one-hundred-foot-square stockade of logs and earth with walls three feet thick and eight feet high around a stone house they believed impregnable. Most of the fort's defenders soon fled to Yankton with a cavalry escort; a portion of the trail they used is preserved on the campus of Sioux Falls College. Author Wayne Fanebust, in *Where the Sioux River Bends*, says thirty-five men and one woman, all good rifle shots, voted to stay inside the fort until the danger passed; the woman made a flag from old flannel shirts. After a six-week siege, they were weak, having eaten nothing but fish and musty flour. Two men managed to slip a buggy load of food into the fort, avoiding the Indians via a roundabout route.

The Indians burned much of the town after the settlers fled and threw the local printing press into the river. When settlers cautiously returned to the town site two years later, they found the platen and spindle. In 1871 the remains of the press were raised from the river. Someone made the type bed into a door stop and sent the salvaged type lead to Vermillion, where it was used to print the *Vermillion Republican*. Despite journalism's rough start in the city, at least seven other papers and six magazines eventually took root in Sioux Falls, including the present daily, the *Sioux Falls Argus-Leader*, formed in 1887.

In the summer of 1858, Indians who may later have joined Inkpaduta's hostiles in the Sioux Uprising stole three horses from the new settlement. Joseph B. Amidon, who had arrived in town only the day before the theft, owned two of the horses. He and Samuel J. Albright, editor of the *Dakota Democrat*, offered a $100 reward for the scalps of the thieves or the return of the horses. A Boston newspaper promptly harangued the two men, calling it an act of savagery to offer a reward for murder; frontiersmen and city dwellers have often differed on the details of what constitutes civilization.

Despite Indian scares, by 1859 Sioux Falls City was the largest settlement in the region—though fewer than forty people lived there. The town had a grist mill, a newspaper, and mail service. Several historians say almost two thousand votes were cast in an election that fall; it was not unusual for the number of votes to exceed the number of settlers in frontier towns. Although it's hard to believe the citizens accepted such an election, no source explains the discrepancy and the elected territorial delegate went to Washington. While there, he lobbied Congress to grant territorial status to Dakota and claimed he had the support of eight thousand to ten thousand people. But Congress ignored the delegate's appeals, in part because it would then have to extend military protection to the new citizens, and the army had other priorities at the time.

Late in 1862, Amidon, by then a judge, and his hunchbacked son William were killed by Indians while gathering hay. Fanebust wrote that William had a dozen arrows in his hump but lived long enough to pull some of them out. A marker now stands on the site of their burial at the intersection of US 77 and Cliff Avenue.

Such incidents made settlers afraid to move to the new town, so promoters persuaded the federal government to establish a military post for protection. Petitions to Congress did no good until the end of the Civil War, when the nation was left with large numbers of unemployed soldiers. A company of the Sixth Iowa Cavalry arrived that spring to establish Fort Dakota just above the main falls; the company also marked off a military reservation seven by ten miles around the fort. Town promoters were immediately stymied again, as no civilians were allowed to settle on military land. Thus, the boosters worked just as hard to get rid of the army as they'd worked to get it there. Because government policy required that military land be auctioned in Washington, D.C., to the highest bidder, the promoters feared that wealthy Easterners could outbid them.

However, Richard F. Pettigrew, a college student traveling that summer with a government surveying party, saved the day and made himself wealthy in the process. His connections in Congress helped get a law passed allowing the land to be disposed of under federal preemption and homesteading laws. The grateful town promoters didn't forget young Pettigrew when they filed their claims; when he returned in the spring of 1870, he quickly became a leading citizen, climbing the steps to political success in traditional fashion. Dr. J. L. Phillips, the sawbones who had saved Wilmot Brookings's life by amputating his legs, claimed a quarter section that included the fort and present-day downtown Sioux Falls. Other promoters moved into the fort's old barracks and officers' quarters, transforming them into the center of a growing town.

Several authorities suggest that the nimble Pettigrew, involved in so many aspects of Sioux Falls' development, also was responsible for some deft maneuvering when Dell Rapids threatened to become the seat of newly formed Moody County. He had been elected to the territorial legislature but through a technicality was not seated yet. Still, his influence was considerable, and when county lines were drawn, Dell Rapids was suddenly on the edge of the county, not in the center as a leading city should be. The new boundaries also put a homestead belonging to Pettigrew's brother in the middle of the new county, right where the county seat, Flandreau, was eventually located. In another stroke of promotional genius, Pettigrew convinced the Populist Party to hold its 1900 national convention in Sioux Falls, where William Jennings Bryan was nominated as a presidential candidate.

By 1890, when he was a successful businessman, Pettigrew's thoughts turned to philanthropy, and he opened a zoo featuring buffalo, elk, and other animals native to the Plains. Though the original zoo didn't last long, the present Great Plains Zoo, opened in 1963, continues Pettigrew's plan. Nearly three hundred native Plains critters and animals from around the world live in an environment that allows them freedom and makes them visible to the public. The North American Plains exhibit features mule deer and native waterfowl in a six-acre natural paddock along the banks of the river. African aoudads live on a natural stone mountain built of Sioux quartzite, and children can have close encounters in the children's zoo, opened in 1970.

Adjoining the zoo is the Delbridge Museum of Natural History, open year round, with displays of five different climatic ecozones of the world: grasslands, tundra, temperate forest, tropical forest, and desert.

Pettigrew was similarly generous in expanding educational opportunities. The Norwegian Evangelical Lutheran Synod founded an academy at nearby Canton; in Sioux Falls, the synod sponsored a normal school with the help of Pettigrew and other enthusiastic citizens, who raised over $5,000 and donated four acres of land. By 1985 the college had more than eighteen hundred students. Augustana is also the home of the Center for Western Studies, dedicated to preserving and interpreting the history of the native and immigrant people of the prairie region.

Railroads Aided City's Development

The first train came to Sioux Falls in 1878, and within three years the population jumped from six hundred to more than two thousand. City leaders shrewdly encouraged development; by 1888 five railroad companies with connections to the East had been given land for a depot and rights-of-way. Eventually, seven railroads served the town, bringing agricultural products and settlers in and hauling goods to smaller towns around it.

The exchange stimulated the rapid growth of wholesale business, which in turn encouraged the city to become a regional manufacturing center. The national depression of 1893 stalled the city's growth, but by 1902, the *Argus-Leader* reported that twenty-three whole-

sale jobbing houses in the city had revenues of more than $4 million. During World War I, when fuel for other forms of transportation was rationed, trains were invaluable; livestock, for example, usually went by rail to St. Paul, Chicago, or Sioux City.

In 1909 John Morrell and Company opened a packing plant in Sioux Falls to provide pork for British Isles customers. In its first year, the company processed 89,000 hogs. The expansion of the livestock industry created a need for the Sioux Falls stockyards, the nation's largest by 1982, with more than forty acres of pens, a bank, cafe, clothing store, and commodity offices.

World War I provided yet another spurt of growth, though not all Sioux Falls businesses boomed during the war—quarries, for example, couldn't find enough railcars to haul stone and never recovered from the loss. Farmers and wholesalers unable to ship by rail bought trucks to haul their goods and produce, and that proved a harbinger of success in the postwar era. Such commercial and agricultural users could obtain gas during the war more readily than private citizens. Auto manufacturers and commercial trucking firms expanded to fill the growing need. During the first year the state required auto registration, in 1911, it counted only 480 vehicles; by the end of the decade, more than 100,000 cars and trucks traveled the state's roads. Developers naturally turned their attention to building better highways and away from older forms of transportation like railroads and waterways. As automobiles took over modern transportation, Sioux Falls profited from being on the crossroads of major highways; the town's continued growth was practically guaranteed in 1962 by its proximity and connection to the new interstate highway system. The junction of I-29 and I-90 lie just northwest of town.

World War II provided another impetus for development. An Army Air Corps training school for radio operators was established, graduating nearly fifty thousand servicemen in slightly more than three years. The war helped the economy of Sioux Falls by cutting unemployment, and high wages drew workers from surrounding small towns and agricultural centers. Thus, Sioux Falls' good fortune sapped the countryside of workers and raised wage expectations to levels that farmers could not afford to pay.

Meanwhile, housing boomed, as did the downtown area, where soldiers spent free time. When the training school closed late in 1945, its land and facilities were returned to the city. Some buildings were sold or dismantled for materials; area colleges and churches took others; and some barracks became private homes. The main part of the base was converted into the municipal airport facilities, named Joe Foss Field in 1955 in honor of a local flying ace who equaled Eddie Rickenbacker's World War I record of twenty-six enemy planes shot down. Foss was also shot down and rescued three times, receiving the Congressional Medal of Honor. After the war he commanded the state's Air National Guard, stationed in Sioux Falls, and in 1954 was elected governor for the first of two terms. In 1960 Foss became commissioner of the fledgling American Football League, later retiring to Arizona.

In 1955 city leaders convinced Congress to fund a big flood-control project; a series of dams north of town now regulate water. A federal Housing and Urban Development project benefited Sioux Falls enormously; parking lots replaced aging warehouses, and the city built a new public library, followed by new motels, banks, and office buildings. In its zeal, the city removed many old industrial structures, but what remains of the warehouse district is now on the National Register of Historic Places.

Scandal and Divorce

Like most cities, Sioux Falls would like to forget some aspects of its history. During the 1880s, the town became well known in the East for easy divorces. A ninety-day residency law, an abundance of unscrupulous lawyers, and judges who accepted fraudulent testimony made the town a mecca for people seeking a quick escape from marriage. Connie DeVelder Schaffer, writing for *South Dakota History* magazine, reported that between 1887 and 1906, Minnehaha County granted 1,124 divorces—one for every 2.26 marriages, while the national average was one divorce for every seven marriages.

The divorce law applied to the entire state. Although Yankton tried to promote itself as a divorce center, Sioux Falls was embarrassed by the notoriety. Still, local business leaders catered to the divorce trade by building three elegant hotels with ballrooms and luxury suites; department stores, florists, jewelers, dress shops, and gambling houses also flourished. Sioux Falls prohibited liquor sales, but drugstores were allowed to prescribe whiskey and brandy as remedies, so their business boomed. Law firms multiplied, and rich clients from all over the world sometimes paid extra for discretion or for ingenuity in applying the "extreme cruelty" provision of the law. One divorce resulted when a woman put her cold feet on her husband's back. Despite appeals from church leaders, the legislature was in no hurry to end the profitable business, but in 1909 a one-year residency requirement took effect, and the divorce industry in the city was virtually ended.

Most citizens also prefer to forget that the Ku Klux Klan was active in Sioux Falls in the 1920s; the *Argus-Leader* reported a march by nearly five hundred Klansmen through town in 1927. Few residents were black, so the northern Klan had to be content with attacking Catholics. Other forms of discrimination were practiced during World War I, when German-Americans drew unwelcome attention in Sioux Falls and throughout the nation. Clubs celebrating German heritage were disbanded, and teaching or speaking foreign languages in public schools became illegal. The German-language newspaper was closed, and several men—including the paper's editor and the distinguished Pettigrew, who publicly opposed the war—were arrested on suspicion of espionage.

Two events of the turbulent 1930s deserve mention. The so-called Dillinger holdup occurred on March 6, 1934, when six men robbed a city bank. A pursuing motorcycle patrolman was shot by one bandit, and the others forced their hostages to stand on the running boards of their escape car until they'd gotten out of town. After releasing their male prisoners, the thieves spread roofing nails on the road, took several female hostages inside the car, and drove on. Later they stole another car, released the women, and disappeared; they were never apprehended. Sioux Falls historians prefer to believe the holdup was committed by famous Chicago racketeers, but no proof exists.

Two years later, on December 31, 1936, the Larson Hardware Powderhouse exploded with a blast heard fifty miles away, destroying $20,000 worth of windows in Sioux Falls and splintering glass as far away as Dell Rapids. Authorities later announced that four tons of blasting powder and more than a ton of dynamite had been used in what was apparently an attempt to conceal a double murder. The blast left a crater fifty feet across and twenty-five feet deep; while cautiously examining it, law officers found a woman wounded by gunshots. Her story, never entirely disproved, indicated she and her boyfriend were part of a gang of Sioux City bank robbers. When she nagged him to quit the gang, both were shot, and the powderhouse was blown up just to hide the murders. Wounded, the woman had crawled far enough away to survive the blast. Three murderers were eventually caught and convicted.

ELK POINT

Lewis and Clark chose a point extending into the Missouri River for an expedition campsite late in 1804; their journals mention "elk sign"—explorer talk for elk manure. That night the scouts called a meeting to replace Sgt. Charles Floyd, who had died a few days earlier. To fill his post, the leaders nominated two privates from Pennsylvania, Patrick Gass and George Gibson, and blacksmith William Grattan. Gass won, garnering nineteen of a possible twenty-seven votes in what was probably the first election in South Dakota—and possibly the last honest and peaceful one. When the region's first general election was held in 1862, settlers in Brule Creek allowed minors and nonresidents to vote, and they stuffed the ballot box in an attempt to snatch county seat status away from Elk Point. At the same time in Charles Mix County, "even half-breeds" were allowed to vote, and campaign workers in the Red River valley threw in an extra hundred votes for their candidate for governor.

Elk commonly roamed this area as it became permanently settled. When Eli B. Wixon built a log cabin for travelers and a trade store

A team of horses used to harvest wheat in 1898. Each bundle was tied and shocked—arranged with others in a tipilike formation to repel rain or snow. Late in fall, the bundles were threshed in the field, or hauled to a barn for threshing or winter feed. —South Dakota Agricultural Heritage Museum

for Indians in 1859, three years after the military road from Sioux City to Fort Randall went through, he chose a site that remained above water during floods—an old elk walkway. At least one fur trading post had already occupied the same spot. History does not record where the elk walked after Wixon put his cabin in their path; perhaps the herds had been hunted to extinction or driven off by the traffic, as was much of the wildlife that drew the first explorers and trappers into the region.

Many early trappers settled in this area. The first child born in Elk Point, in 1861, was a grandson of Joseph LaBarge, a fur trader who traveled upriver on a steamboat in 1832 and was influential in Missouri Valley business for the next half-century. When Santee war parties began moving up and down the Missouri, Vermillion, and James rivers after the 1862 Sioux Uprising, a two-story hotel in Elk Point became the rendezvous point for citizen militia during the

Indian scare. When settlers began fleeing Sioux Falls after Judge Amidon and his hunchbacked son were killed there, Eli Wixon and a few others remained in Elk Point and built blockhouses for protection. Northeast of town, near a settlement hopefully called Richland, other settlers built Fort Brullé, which was abandoned in 1868 and dismantled in 1873. The fort's name was probably a variation on the Lakota band, usually spelled "Brulé."

Civil War veterans who fought for the North named Union County, which chose Elk Point as county seat by popular vote in 1865. The veterans had taken unusually speedy advantage of their benefits under the Homestead Act. A few minutes after the Homestead Act went into effect on December 31, 1862, Mahlon Gore filed the first claim in Dakota Territory, for land located about ten miles northwest of Elk Point. However, his claim was later jumped by Henry H. Fisher, and Gore never proved up. Frank Verzani, the seventh U.S. citizen to file a homestead claim, was actually the first man in the nation to prove title; his homestead adjoined the Missouri River in Clay County.

Once settlers began to move in, the area around Elk Point quickly adopted the necessities of civilization. Cabins and a store went up first, followed by a church in 1861 and a school. By 1867 the region had enough teachers to justify a week-long teachers' institute. The first flour mill began supplying white flour in 1873. Liquor undoubtedly came in with the first white traveler, and a local Women's Christian Temperance Union was organized in 1878.

JEFFERSON

While white settlers edged the Indians away from prime settlement land in North America, peasants in Ireland struggled to survive the potato famine. In 1859, ten years after the famine began, many Irish found their way to a settlement at Jefferson, about five miles south of Elk Point. Along with a group of French-Canadians, these colonists created a strongly Catholic community; Father Pierre Boucher, the first resident priest in the region, arrived in 1867.

Pioneers around Jefferson suffered the usual Plains hardships: smallpox, diphtheria, and drought. They also faced an unusual one: During the late 1870s, plagues of grasshoppers wreaked devastation severe even in a state that has grown used to agricultural adversity. Pioneers who told their stories in later years remembered a July 1874 day when someone recognized a dark cloud in the north as a swarm of grasshoppers; others spoke of the air being filled with white, glistening flakes at first mistaken for snow. The insects covered every surface; cattle and horses stampeded when their bodies were covered by them. The insects thudded against roofs and windows, sounding like hail. Within an hour, fields and gardens were chewed bare, and onions and turnips were eaten below the ground.

One farmer chased his cattle, fleeing from the swarm. Disgusted by the grasshoppers crawling up his pants legs, his daughter later reminisced, "he tied ropes around the bottom of his pants and around his sleeves at the wrists. When he came back about an hour later his clothes were in shreds, almost eaten away. He could not find the animals." Other homesteaders reported that the bugs ate cotton mosquito netting used for window screens, wooden window sashes, and the handles of pitchforks, rakes, and hoes. The grasshoppers crowded toward any source of food, stacks of them piling up around windows and doors, trying to get inside. People who tried to walk on the bare ground slipped, but those who walked through tall grass were nearly choked by the insects. When the grasshoppers had eaten everything else, they ate each other.

In frantic efforts to save their crops and end the plague, some farmers built bonfires and scooped grasshoppers into the flames; others set their fields on fire, hoping to destroy both the insects and the eggs they laid. A few farmers discovered that hogs ate the insects with relish but a year afterward claimed that their pork tasted like grasshoppers. Chickens and turkeys ate until they couldn't walk. One enterprising Jefferson poultry raiser turned his turkeys into his corn fields, then sold the fattened birds in a Sioux City market. For months afterward, when he heard complaints about the "strange taste" of the meat, he pretended to be puzzled.

The grasshopper hordes remained about three days, then rose into the wind and were gone. Many settlers could not face the loss of their illusions or the real loss of a bountiful life; some of the French-Canadian families, fearing starvation, returned to Canada the next winter. Later, historians reported that during the first infestation, grasshoppers covered an area from North Dakota to Texas and from the Rockies almost to the Mississippi River.

Two years later, Father Boucher, whose parishioners were still fighting the shock of the catastrophe, created a ceremony that had an uplifting effect. The priest announced a pilgrimage to three crosses erected at the edges of his large parish. With the priest at its head, a mile-long procession of church members, along with most of the other citizens of Jefferson, marched to all three crosses. The first cross was on a farm two miles west of Jefferson, the second three miles north of that, and the third on the church grounds, making the march eleven miles long. Prayers were recited at the crosses, and the expedition lasted most of the day. But residents of the neighborhood insist that no major grasshopper infestation has struck inside the area protected by the crosses since. The original crosses have been replaced with replicas and historical markers, and the pilgrimage is now an annual event.

Fourteen Mile House, built of logs by Francis Reandeau about 1861, originally served travelers on the military road. Before hotels and motels lined every traveler's route, roadhouses often served as stopping points where stage and ox drivers could rest and feed their teams or obtain replacement animals. Meanwhile, passengers could buy a meal and sometimes wash or rest. A wall of the original house is visible inside a renovated private home; the name Lyzimon Reandeau, son of the Frenchman who ran the establishment until 1872, is carved on a log in the wall. Several sources remark that the house and the businesses that grew up around it were originally named Willow, became Adelscat in 1869, and finally became part of Jefferson about 1873.

NORTH SIOUX CITY

Modern residents of areas along rivers often believe their fortunes would change if they could only have a bridge in a particular spot; citizens of Vermillion have been arguing that very point in recent years. In the past, before permanent bridges were common, overland travelers had to find other ways across waterways. Sites suitable for a ford or ferry were much prized and often the cause of feuding. Such was the case at the site of Pacquette's Ferry, widely considered the first in Dakota Territory. The historical spot is marked on SD 12, west of the Big Sioux River and north of North Sioux City.

In 1855 Capt. P. T. Turnley licensed Paul Pacquette to run a ferry across the Big Sioux River as the starting point for a military road to Fort Randall. But fifteen days before Pacquette's license was issued, a county judge named Moorhead had granted a ferry license to Henry Ayotte down the river at Sioux Point. Ayotte sold his license to Charles Ganon, who soon died, leaving Theophile Bruguier, a powerful man in the community, as his administrator. The Pacquette and Bruguier licenses were disputed in court for years, but the argument didn't keep both parties from making money in the busy community. Ferry rates were fifty cents for a team, twenty-five cents for a horse and rider, ten cents a head for loose stock and people on foot, and five cents each for sheep and hogs—big money in those days. In 1863, when troops assembled for the campaign against Inkpaduta after the Sioux Uprising, Camp Cook was established at the west end of Pacquette's Ferry, and the community attracted refugees from Indian attacks, eventually drawing more settlement than the Sioux Point region. The road and ferry served both military and civilian travelers until the Dakota Southern was built to Yankton in 1872.

I-90
Aurora County—Minnesota
129 Miles

Aurora, Davison, Sanborn, and Jerauld counties were the destination of many Norwegian settlers, among the first to migrate into the territory. Unlike some of the other immigrants, the Norwegians did not settle in compact, closed groups; they are scattered throughout nearly every township in the eastern part of the state. Most Danish immigrants stayed in Clay and Turner counties, in the southeast corner of the state; Swedes were compressed into the northeast corner; and Germans, one of the largest immigrant groups, collected along the James and Missouri rivers.

THE MILWAUKEE RAILROAD

The Chicago, Milwaukee & St. Paul Railroad extended east-west across South Dakota during the late nineteenth century. Known simply as the Milwaukee Road, it had a considerable impact on the pattern of settlement in South Dakota, establishing a number of towns along its tracks and rescuing others from oblivion. Several communities still bear the names of railroad company officials.

Firesteel was well settled before the railroad came in sight. According to legend, a railroad engineer charged with choosing town sites noticed a piece of driftwood on the ground and said, "This will never do for a town. Where water has been it may come again." Some of the residents of Firesteel laughed, but most moved to Mitchell. Two years later, in 1882, Firesteel was wiped out by a flood.

Plankinton, settled in 1880, was named for John H. Plankinton, a Milwaukee meat packer and director of the Milwaukee railroad. Shortly after Plankinton was established, Charles B. Clark took a soldier's homestead, indicated today by a marker four miles south of I-90 and US 281 and one mile west on a county road. Clark proved up in 1884 and lived there until moving to Mitchell, where he was a minister. His son, Charles Badger Clark, later became the first poet laureate of South Dakota and one of its most famous citizens. Ironically, the poem for which he is most famous, "A Cowboy's Prayer," is usually attributed to that prolific writer with no known address: "Anonymous." Though Clark lived for a time in Plankinton and attended Dakota Wesleyan University in Mitchell, he is most associated with the Black Hills, because he spent his teen years in Deadwood. He lived alone much of his life in a cabin called the "Badger Hole" near Legion Lake. (See the section on US 385—Custer.)

White Lake, first called Siding Thirty-six for its distance west of Mitchell, was named for a phenomenon seen on the lake, four miles north. From a distance, sunshine on the water caused it to appear white. However, the lake has never been full since pioneer days, so the illusion can't be confirmed.

MITCHELL

Mitchell, named in 1879 for Milwaukee Road president Alexander Mitchell, is located in the center of a farming region at a railroad division point, which explains its prosperity. Over the years, this part of the state has become increasingly sophisticated and increasingly metropolitan. By the 1960s, Mitchell's ten thousand people had made it one of the most significant towns east of the Missouri River. Hog raising remains a vigorous regional industry, and Mitchell, like Huron, Pierre, Scotland, Watertown, Woonsocket, Yankton, and Sioux Falls, was home to a meat-packing operation briefly during the 1980s. Dairies and flour mills have flourished at various times, as have livestock operations, grain shipping, and the sale of frozen eggs. Today Mitchell's population exceeds thirteen thousand.

This area lacks the rough, mythic qualities that characterize the state west of the river. The only nearby military fort was Old Fort James, also known as Fort Des Roches, located near a bend in the James River south of I-90. It is one of the least famous frontier forts; during its only major battle—the one in which the cannon was actually fired—one Indian and one horse were killed.

In another noteworthy incident, Mitchell once refused a gas-powered vehicle permission to enter the city. The machine, designed in the late 1890s by Louis Greenough and Harry Adams of Pierre, attached a two-cylinder gas engine to a wagon that could haul up to eight passengers. The inventors hoped to turn a profit by hauling passengers at fairs, but they didn't calculate on the fears of fellow citizens: Officials in Mitchell refused to let them bring the machine

Six men pose with a steam-powered tractor pulling a threshing machine. With a thresher in the field, men brought shocks of wheat to be separated from the chaff. The straw was collected for bedding while the wheat stores were reserved for human and animal consumption. The man at center is holding a bicycle. This photo was taken near Oldham, South Dakota. —South Dakota State Historical Society

inside the city limits. An editorial in the *Yankton Press & Dakotan* agreed with the decision, saying: "It is a dead moral certainty that the infernal machine will frighten horses and endanger the lives of men, women and children." Another writer, in a magazine published at Mission Hill, said, "The automobile is a plaything for idle minds and hands. It is also a very successful contrivance for killing people."

Prophetic words. But Dakota, perhaps because of its open spaces, seems to have attracted people who enjoyed trying to improve transportation. In 1880 E. S. Callihan moved to Woonsocket, northwest of Mitchell, in a covered wagon; three years later, he introduced the three-wheeled, steam-driven "autocycle"—a dozen years before Henry Ford displayed his first experimental auto, the "quadricycle," in Detroit.

In 1883 Dakota University was established in Mitchell by the Methodist church. The original structure was rebuilt of Sioux Falls granite in 1889 after a fire. Now called Dakota Wesleyan University, the campus is home to the Museum of Pioneer Life, founded by Hamlin Garland, John Dewey, and historian James Truslow Adams, among others. It contains manuscripts from Dakota writers, including O. E. Rolvaag, John G. Neihardt, Rose Wilder Lane, L. Frank

Baum, Frederick Manfred, and Garland. The Case Art Gallery displays sculptures, paintings, and prints by Gutzon Borglum, Harvey Dunn, James Earle Fraser, Oscar Howe, and Childe Hassam. The 1886 home of Louis Beckwith, a cofounder of the Corn Palace (see below), has been restored, as have a one-room schoolhouse, a depot, and a country church. Horse-drawn vehicles, early farm implements, and antique autos represent pioneer life in Dakota Territory and illustrate the changes caused by the settler's main weapon: the plow that broke prairie sod and prepared the ground for crops. The Indian Gallery and Native American exhibits show what pioneer culture replaced.

A prehistoric Indian village north of town on Lake Mitchell and a nearby hill are both called Medicine Butte. The village is a National Historic Landmark. The name comes from a rock cairn reportedly built by prehistoric Indians. Boehnen Memorial Museum contains exhibits of the artifacts and environment of these prehistoric farmers and hunters. The original village may have housed a thousand people living in about seventy lodges. Each lodge was about twenty feet by forty feet and strongly built of poles and grasses; it might accommodate as many as twenty villagers. A full-scale reproduction of a lodge is open to visitors at Prairie Village, along with a garden of native plants and a gift shop with crafts and books.

The Corn Palace

Mitchell is best known for the Corn Palace its citizens built in honor of the region's main business, agriculture. In 1892 local residents conceived the idea of a magnificent structure that would advertise the community's principal products during an annual harvest festival. Sioux City, Iowa, had held such a festival beginning in 1887, but the event went broke in 1891. Citizens of Mitchell decided they could succeed where others had failed. The Corn Palace was planned as a center for agricultural exhibitions, meetings, and entertainment. The first "Corn Belt Exposition" attracted crowds to the palace in 1892-93. Economic problems caused by drought and crop failures caused the celebration's suspension until 1900, when presidential candidate William Jennings Bryan was persuaded to speak. The fourth show was held in 1902, and it has been held annually since.

Several versions of the edifice have been built, each replaced by a larger structure. The current building, which holds five thousand people, was completed in 1921 at a cost of $300,000. The Corn Palace plays host to state wrestling and basketball tournaments, dances,

58

Mitchell's Corn Palace is illuminated at night to show the scenes worked in grain. Since the first palace was built in 1892, each series of panels has been different. —South Dakota Department of Tourism

circuses, and other forms of entertainment, attracting more than a half million tourists a year. It's the sort of place that must be seen to be believed; its effect is too enormous to imagine. "Pigeons cavorting on the outsides of the building" impair views of the Palace during the winter months, says a display inside, so it's best to see it in summer or fall. Local folks, exhibiting that dry South Dakota humor, call it "the world's largest bird feeder."

From the beginning, designers intended the Palace to be a display of native corn, grains, grasses, and other agricultural products. The first structure was one hundred by sixty-six feet and featured round towers topped with conical roofs; every outside surface was covered with sheaves of grain or ornamental designs made of colored corn.

Today, local farmers contract yearly to grow specific colors of corn, as well as specified amounts of oats, sorghum, Sudan grass, flax, millet, cane, and barley, for the yearly change of decoration on the Palace. Each year's design requires two to three thousand bushels of corn and forty tons of other bundled grains. Ten different shades of corn, many of them developed near Mitchell for use in the Corn Palace, are used to give lifelike hues to the scenes. When a severe drought ruined crops over much of the state in 1936, organizers cut evergreen boughs in the Black Hills as a substitute.

Each year an artist develops miniature scene panels made of corn. One year panels might show an Indian warrior and a settler, mounted Indians attacking a wagon train, or settlers plowing fields. The 1907 design featured geometric shapes, including an old Indian good luck sign resembling a swastika (causing considerable confusion when tourists saw the photographs after World War II). Designs have been contributed by various local artists, bound by little but the requirements of the materials, and the result is always spectacular.

In a burst of fantasy, minarets, turrets, and kiosks of a vaguely Moorish fashion were added to the final building in 1937; they are repainted frequently rather than covered with grain. One of the most fascinating permanent displays inside the building is the photographic history of the Corn Palace. The photographs themselves are marvelous, showing the vast assortment of designs that have enhanced the Palace. But it's also fun to eavesdrop on older visitors as they stroll the long halls, stopping before each picture to comment on the merits of the design and squinting to read the year as they recall the entertainment, who they came with, and how old their children were.

On permanent display inside are the six interior panels designed by Yankton artist Oscar Howe, a graduate of Dakota Wesleyan and the state's artist laureate, who designed the Palace's exterior panels between 1948 and 1971 (for more on Howe, see the section on SD 50—Vermillion). Mitchell is home to the Oscar Howe Art Center, where many of his linear abstract paintings hang.

During Corn Palace Week, traditionally held in mid-September, the street outside the Palace becomes the site of a carnival; inside, two or three shows are held daily by well-known entertainers. Headliners have included Tommy Dorsey, Lawrence Welk, Andy Williams, Bob Hope, the Mills Brothers, Jim Nabors, and Roy Clark. At first, some performers didn't quite know what to make of the unusual new venue. John Philip Sousa, the famous American bandmaster and composer, was invited to play the Palace in 1904. Perhaps naturally cautious, he wired back, "What is Corn Palace?" When town officials finally persuaded him to appear, he rode a train to the rough frontier town but refused to get off without receiving his $7,000 payment in advance. Two bankers waded through mud and rain to hand him the cash. Sousa was so impressed he played extra performances, and returned to town several times in later years. Other prominent visitors to the unique building have included Theodore Roosevelt, William H. Taft, and Franklin D. Roosevelt.

Among the Palace's most delightful souvenirs are color postcards showing various years' adornments; the entire one-hundred-year history is not yet available, but enough exist to form a fascinating record of the Palace's changes. Just around the corner is the Made in South Dakota Shop, which stocks nothing but handmade products of the state's writers, artists, and craftspeople, including Indian music, painting, jewelry, and hand-carved wooden toys.

Fraser and McGovern:
Mitchell Celebrities

Ironically, though nearly all Americans are familiar with the work of James Earle Fraser, he remains relatively unknown here in his home state. Fraser left South Dakota as a teenager, but the Dakota plains inspired two images that are among the best known in history. Fraser was born in Winona, Minnesota, in 1876 and moved to Mitchell at age four. His father, a mechanical engineer for the Milwaukee railroad, took his family with him on construction trips. Often they lived on the prairie in boxcars. Young Fraser stored in his mind images of buffalo, Indians, and other pioneer figures he later used in sculptures and coin design.

By the age of eight, he was carving in soft stone; at age fifteen he was studying at the Chicago Art Institute; and at nineteen he studied in Paris with sculptor Augustus St. Gaudens. One of Fraser's most famous pieces, "End of the Trail," a defeated Indian slumped on his tired horse, won first prize in the 1898 American Art Association competition. He completed a full-scale model in 1910 and in 1915 exhibited a piece more than twice as large at the Panama-Pacific International Exposition, where it won a gold medal over fifteen other works of art. Dozens of small replicas appeared everywhere, most of them illegal copies for which he received no royalties. The huge plaster original is now in the National Cowboy Hall of Fame and Western Heritage Center in Oklahoma City. Fraser later said the piece was inspired by the words of an old Dakota trapper he'd met as a child, who said, "The Indians will someday be pushed into the Pacific Ocean."

Even more widely known is Fraser's design for the "buffalo" nickel, with a bison head on one side and, on the other, an Indian's profile. The latter image was fashioned in 1911-12 from a composite of three Plains Indians: Iron Tail, a Sioux; Big Tree, a Kiowa; and Two Moons, a Cheyenne. A small model of "End of the Trail" and two eight-foot plaster casts of Lewis and Clark are at the museum in Mitchell.

George McGovern may be Mitchell's most famous former resident. In 1956 he became the first Democrat in twenty years to win a major office in South Dakota, becoming a U.S. Representative. Born in Avon, he considered following his father into the ministry. In World War II he won the Distinguished Flying Cross by flying a B-24 Liberator named the *Dakota Queen* on thirty-five bombing missions over Europe. On his return he studied history and joined the faculty of Dakota Wesleyan University in Mitchell at $4,500 a year. A man who wasn't afraid of risk, he left his teaching job to become executive secretary of the state's Democratic Party. In 1956 he defeated Harold Lovre in the First Congressional District, then beat popular Republican Joe Foss (another World War II ace fighter pilot and winner of the Congressional Medal of Honor) for the First District congressional seat in 1958. Two years later, McGovern was beaten by veteran politician Karl Mundt; loss turned into fame when John F. Kennedy appointed him head of the Food for Peace program.

In 1962 McGovern ran for a Senate seat vacated by the death of long-time Senator Francis Case. The campaign was bitter and close; McGovern beat Lieutenant Governor Joe Bottum, a lawyer from Rapid City, by something like five hundred votes out of a quarter million cast. His stand against the Vietnam War caused problems in conservative South Dakota, particularly west of the Missouri River and in Rapid City, where Ellsworth Air Force Base contributed heavily to the economy and where many young men enlisted in the military forces. In 1972 McGovern, the Democratic Party nominee for president, challenged President Richard Nixon's reelection bid. He didn't even carry South Dakota, where voters were bitter about his widely publicized opinions on racism and the Vietnam War, but he proved that prairie politics weren't entirely Republican and conservative anymore. In 1974 McGovern beat yet another winner of the Congressional Medal of Honor, Leo Thorsness, to regain his seat in the Senate, but in 1980 he lost to Rep. James Abdnor, riding Ronald Reagan's conservative coattails. Voters felt McGovern had lost touch with his home state and was too comfortable in Washington; he has remained there much of the time since.

US 212
Faulk County—Minnesota
143 Miles

The eastern part of US 212 zigzags along county and township lines, generally heading east-west through the rich lake and farming region between Faulk County and the Minnesota border near Watertown. Large pheasant populations find good shelter and feeding grounds in an area settled by vigorous, thrifty German farmers, with a few Swedes and Norwegians thrown in for flavoring.

FAULK AND SPINK COUNTIES

The towns in Faulk and Spink counties are small, widely separated, and their histories difficult to trace. Seneca is now only a post office. Orient, founded in 1887, was originally named for J. C. Campbell, from whom the Chicago, Milwaukee & St. Paul Railroad bought the town site. Campbell refused to approve his own name for the town, arguing that it would give him too much publicity. Rockham began in 1886; apparently it was named for Rockhampton, Australia, but no one seems to have a clue why. Zell, named for German immigrants, was platted in 1886, at the height of the homestead boom. Henry, according to the WPA guide, was one of several towns named for railroad officials' wives, daughters, or sweethearts; others in the area include Florence, Wallace, Lily, Bradley, Raymond, and Butler. One can only assume that the ladies' surnames were used in some cases.

The promotional rhetoric accompanying white settlement inspired many of these small towns to label themselves as "capitals" of some sport or resource. Redfield, for example, is called the "Pheasant Capital of the World" because H. A. Hagman released twenty-five Chinese ring-necked pheasants on his farm in 1908; today the pheasant is the state's bird and a major hunting industry. Nearby Clark, founded in 1882 and named for territorial legislator Newton Clark, bills itself as "South Dakota's Potato Capital" and offers tours of the french-fry processing plant.

Frankfort, founded in 1882 by the Western Town Lot Company, may have been named for Frankfort I. Fisher, an early settler who explored the area in 1878 and distinguished himself by shooting the last buffalo in Spink County. (Perhaps pheasant hunting helped compensate for the loss of the buffalo; pheasants don't eat as much, and hardly ever injure hunters.) Frankfort aspired to be the territorial capital when the two Dakotas were one, bidding $100,000 and 160 acres of land. Other contenders included Aberdeen, Canton, Huron, Mitchell, and Ordway in present South Dakota, and Steele, Bismarck, and Devil's Lake in North Dakota. With some sophisticated wheeling and dealing, Bismarck won.

Northwest of Redfield is the tiny town of Athol, named for Athol, Massachusetts, named in turn by some nostalgic Scot immigrants for the holdings of Scotland's Duke of Atholl in Perthshire, where the original gleaming white castle is still open to visitors. The duke

is the only individual in Great Britain allowed to maintain a private army (twenty-four men); his own bagpiper plays daily.

FAULKTON

Faulkton was platted in 1886 by the Western Town Lot Company. Both the town and the county of which it is the seat were named for Andrew Jackson Faulk, Dakota Territory's third governor. Faulk was a printer, lawyer, and coal company superintendent from Kittaning, Pennsylvania. Unfortunately, one of his distinctions was being the father-in-law of the worst in a long line of crooked Indian agents. In

1860 Faulk was designated a trader to the Yanktons. His son-in-law, Walter A. Burleigh, was agent of the Yankton tribe. Both men were interested in town development and bought a plot on which the town of Bon Homme was later laid out. In 1866 Republicans chose Faulk as their candidate for territorial governor, an appointed position hinging on the removal of Governor Newton Edmunds; this was effected with the help of Burleigh, and Faulk was duly appointed.

Faulk was popular with Dakotans, partly because he seemed to have a nose for trends. He was one of the first men to insist on advertising Dakota Territory, especially the Black Hills. He tried to prevent the latter region from becoming part of an Indian reservation because of the mineral and timber potential. Like many people during that time, he didn't care much for Indians and favored opening all lands suitable for farming to white settlement. However, he later worked to secure relief for them after a devastating grasshopper infestation.

Burleigh, Faulk's son-in-law, was involved in many money-making schemes in the new territory, including the sale of twenty-five hundred acres of land near Springfield to a Hutterian colony, and was unusually adept at fleecing the Indians and the Indian bureau while he served as agent. Burleigh's daughter was listed as a teacher to Indian children, though no school existed on the reservation; his thirteen-year-old son drew $80 a month as a clerk; and his father-in-law was on the payroll as a worker. Burleigh's attitude was not unusual for the time; the official War Department position was that settlement of Dakota should be delayed until all Indians were pacified or dead. Indian cattle were kept at Burleigh's farm near Bon Homme, about thirty miles from the agency, where he instructed herdsmen, "We get a calf or two apiece from them." His hired hands butchered an Indian beef at least once a week and sold what wasn't used on the farm back to the Indians. Despite these activities, Burleigh was later exonerated of any wrongdoing, chosen as a delegate to Congress for two terms, and served two terms in the territorial legislature. He maintained, "I was the only honest Indian agent. I gave the Indians half and took half myself."

Faulkton was also the site of an infamous county-seat war. Its competitor was nearby LaFoon, now a ghost town, five miles east. LaFoon won the first county-seat election, setting off a controversy that involved allegations of election fraud and malfeasance against Territorial Governor N. G. Ordway. In 1886 Faulkton became the crossroads of two railroad lines, gaining considerable economic advantage. Many residents of LaFoon simply jacked up their buildings and hauled them to the rival town; county offices followed.

Ironically, though LaFoon is only a memory, Faulkton today has no rail service.

An unusual Faulkton resident was Dr. Abbie Ann Hall Jarvis, who became the first licensed woman physician and the first licensed woman pharmacist in the state. A middle-aged parent with no previous college education, she came with her husband and children to Redfield in 1880, just in time for the famous blizzard, which struck October 17. As provisions became scarce, neighbors shared what they had; most of the winter they survived without vegetables, sugar, salt, pepper, coffee, or tea. Five families shared a coffee mill for grinding wheat, which they used as a coffee substitute and made into a rough flour. The only available meat came from starving antelope that wandered close to houses. No one had any matches, either, so fires were shared. Jarvis later told her daughter, Annette, that when she found an old match in the pocket of one of her husband's old jackets, she was so astonished she lit it—and then was appalled at the waste.

According to Annette, who wrote her mother's story for *Daughters of Dakota*, Jarvis decided to become a doctor because her father had been one. Accompanied by her daughters, she entered the Woman's Medical College in Chicago, graduated fourth out of twenty-four in 1898, and returned to Faulkton to practice. She became a familiar sight to county residents in her white apron; local children believed she carried babies in her black satchel. For years she drove her own buggy, often alone, to care for the residents of the county; when automobiles became available, her daughter often drove her to house calls at night. Jarvis died in 1931.

REDFIELD

Redfield is the seat of Spink County, one of the flattest counties in the state—or anywhere else. One fellow, "thinking he was going down hill, started out at an altitude of 1,304 feet and after six miles bottomed out at 1,302 feet," says David Holden in *Dakota Visions*. The elevation of the county varies less than fifteen feet except where streams have cut small valleys. Most of the county was once covered by glacial Lake Dakota, which left behind the rich soil that has made it one of the great wheat-producing regions in the world. Potatoes, oats, and barley are also grown locally.

The first post office in the region was at Stennet Junction, established in 1879; when the railroad arrived, this site laid out by the Western Town Lot Company in 1880 was renamed Redfield, after a railroad official. Early citizens argued over whether Redfield or Ashton, a few miles north, should be the county seat (and thus the business center) of the developing region. The arguments escalated in 1884 into the "Spink County War."

In the 1880 election, according to the WPA guide, Redfield was chosen as the county seat, but the county records remained in Ashton. In the 1884 election, the number of votes cast exceeded the number of eligible citizens in the county; the names of dead men appeared on some ballots, as well as those of railroad workers, and Redfield won again. Eager for the benefits of county-seat status, a group of

Redfield residents stole the government records from Ashton one night and hauled them home. Before morning, about three hundred armed men, many of them Civil War veterans, gathered in Ashton. Nervous county officials in Redfield began to consider the unpleasant possibility of actual combat. Soon about fifteen hundred men from the northern part of the county, armed and calling themselves the "Army of the North," established a camp outside of Redfield. They sent the Redfield mayor a message, allowing him two hours to evacuate the women and children before they intended to invade the town and recover the county records. They might even burn the town.

A special Chicago & Northwestern engine was chartered to Watertown, and from there a group of officials raced to Milbank, where they obtained an injunction against removal of the records from Redfield, based on the 1880 election results. Marksmen were posted to protect the negotiators, and when the injunction was brought back to Redfield, the impromptu Army of the North dispersed with only a little grumbling. A judge in Ashton issued warrants for sixteen leading Redfield citizens for stealing the records from his town; he eventually dismissed the charges with the comment: "Not proven; but don't do it again."

Though this was one of the more nerve-racking county-seat fights in the state, it wasn't the only one, and some in other midwestern states were bloodier and more lawless. The settlers weren't moved by sheer patriotism; their biggest inspiration was money. Once a governor declared a county organized, he named temporary officers and a temporary center of county government until a special election could be held. Then the politics got interesting. Territorial Governor N. G. Ordway, for example, was famous for stalling the organization of a county until he'd been thoroughly bribed, both with cash and with lots in the chosen town.

Not all governors were quite so obvious about it. But even if the governor was honest, the developers still had plenty of opportunities for skullduggery. Promoters often staked out towns near the center of the county and bought the land for $1.25 an acre; if they won the county seat, they could subdivide and sell each acre for hundreds of dollars. Some promoters invested in several towns, knowing that if any should be chosen as a county seat, they'd make a profit. After a county seat had been chosen, residents of nearby towns would sometimes put their flimsy wooden dwellings on horse-drawn wagons and haul them to the new government center. If somebody stole the county records—and there weren't many to steal at that early period of settlement—and made the settlers move again, they could be testy.

Redfield's Most Renowned:
Peter Norbeck

South Dakota's first native-born governor, Peter Norbeck, embodied the possibilities of the frontier. The son of a Lutheran minister, he was born to Norwegian immigrant parents in 1870 in the cellar of a crude frontier home near Vermillion. He was largely self-educated, though he attended public schools and the pre-freshman course at the University of South Dakota in Vermillion. When he was sixteen, Norbeck's family homesteaded in Charles Mix County along the Missouri River northwest of Vermillion. In 1892 he perfected a drilling apparatus for deep artesian wells and soon became head of a company that operated dozens of gasoline-powered drilling rigs and employed more than a hundred men. In 1901 Norbeck moved to Redfield and by 1908 became one of South Dakota's wealthiest businessmen.

Norbeck's political career began in 1892 when he was elected constable of his township in Charles Mix County. After leading the local Republican Party in 1906, he accepted nomination for a seat in the state senate. Cannily, he transported his drilling crews to polling places and won the race easily. In 1914 he was elected lieutenant governor. By now a leader in the state's Progressive movement, he advocated state-financed rural credits that would allow farmers to borrow money for short periods at low interest to finance seasonal operations. He also supported a bank deposit guarantee law and regulation of securities sales. Farmers increasingly troubled by bank foreclosures saw him as their ally. In 1916 he ran for governor and carried the election by more than twenty thousand votes.

As governor, besides asking for rural credit, Norbeck asked for money to construct arterial roads and to establish a wildlife refuge system. He also requested money to supply free textbooks for schoolchildren. He called for a state office to help farmers market crops and instituted studies on workers' compensation, state hail insurance, state-owned flour mills and terminal elevators, development of water power resources, and a state-owned coal mine. He was also supporter of Prohibition and advocated the adoption of a unicameral state legislature. Though he made little headway with the latter idea, he pushed the rest of his initiatives through the legislature.

Norbeck is best remembered for his work on behalf of a state park in the Black Hills, an idea he first proposed in 1905. More than sixty thousand acres in Custer County were set aside as a state game preserve in 1913, and Norbeck helped by adding thirty thousand acres of federal lands to form Custer State Park in 1920. He also helped design a scenic highway, which was completed in 1922 under

The log and plank ceiling used in this prairie homestead kept the interior cleaner than sod over logs, used for many roofs. The furniture is ornate, whereas many settlers used shipping boxes. Typically, the stovepipe ran along the ceiling to leave as much heat as possible inside. —South Dakota Agricultural Heritage Museum

Governor Henry McMaster, who succeeded him. Norbeck's work on behalf of the environment shifted into high gear when he was elected to the U.S. Senate in 1920; he promoted federal highway bills, backed the idea of a sculpture on Mount Rushmore, and helped attract President Calvin Coolidge to vacation in the Hills, giving force to the idea that tourism could become a major industry in the state.

Norbeck's legacy to his home state has not survived as he might have wished. His program to encourage state ownership of key industries eventually failed, except for a state-owned cement plant at Rapid City. His idea to build a hydroelectric plant along the Missouri River failed because of inadequate financial support; however, the sites had already been investigated, and the main stem dams were authorized under the Flood Control Act of 1944. Again, Norbeck began with a concept that was farsighted for his time; that the dams now threaten to create more problems than they solved should not be blamed on him.

DEUEL COUNTY

One of the most important officials in any county is the assessor; that's who counts the families and estimates the value of their holdings for tax purposes. Assessors are seldom popular with their neighbors. Byron James Cochrane, Deuel County's first permanent white settler, performed this tough job for forty years and earned the respect of his neighbors by demonstrating some of the qualities found in many Dakota pioneers.

His granddaughter, Evadna Cochrane Burba, recalling his life for the *South Dakota High Liner*, wrote that early each April the assessor packed his record books "in a metal suitcase wrapped in oil cloth." Wearing a "shaggy bearskin coat and robe, heavy union suit, two pairs of overalls, two heavy shirts, one over the other, and a warm cap with ear flaps," and four-buckle overshoes, he toured the county in his buggy. Housewives apparently loved Mr. Cochrane, especially because he was known to be a discriminating eater. If he stopped at mealtime or stayed the night, the home had been honored. "The Norwegian ladies," writes Burba, "had on hand a variety of special baking. *Sandbakkels, fattigmand*, or crisp, and man-sized cookies were served with coffee. Fried meat stored in lard from fall butchering, pickles tangy and cool from the cellar, and fruit canned the previous summer enhanced the meal."

Cochrane also shared his neighbors' suffering and pleasures. While he was assessor, his house burned, and grasshoppers and tornadoes destroyed his crops, but he persevered. "If coffee is served in heaven,"

Farmers pose with an early steam-powered tractor near Oldham, South Dakota; at right is a 1914 Model T. —South Dakota State Historical Society

his granddaughter concluded, "certainly the pot must have been shoved to the front of the stove at his approach." The pioneer is the subject of a biography published by the South Dakota State Historical Society, and a marker stands on the site of his cabin, south of Lake Cochrane on a county road.

US 18
Douglas County—Minnesota
96 Miles

The eastern portion of US 18 runs east-west between the Charles Mix County line, west of Tripp, to near Canton, on the Minnesota state line east of I-29.

HUTCHINSON COUNTY

Several evangelical Protestant settlements were established in the county during the late nineteenth century by German-Russians unable to find land in eastern states. Their cohesion brought other immigrants from neighboring regions around the Black Sea, and many current citizens trace their ancestry to the "German-Rooshians," as they are called locally.

Tripp was the site of one Americanization school started as part of a nationwide campaign to teach the English language and American values to immigrants. The community stands on a hill between farming ground on the east and, on the west, a sparsely settled zone of clay soil, with fewer farms and groves of trees. Tripp was founded early, in 1866; like Tripp County (which lies west of the Missouri), it was named after Bartlett Tripp, chief justice of the territorial supreme court. Born in Maine in 1842, he became a schoolteacher, lawyer, surveyor, educator, chairman of the first state constitutional convention, and U.S. Minister to Austria-Hungary. He was also an incorporator of the University of South Dakota at Vermillion and a trustee of Yankton College.

Olivet was not on a railroad line, but it became the Hutchinson County seat in 1871 and has tenaciously held that position. In 1878 the Free Methodists built a sod church, which doubled as a courthouse until the official one was constructed three years later. Here the highway rises over a divide separating the drainages of the Missouri and James rivers.

Menno actually bears the name intended for Freeman, ten miles northeast; when railroad officials were nailing up the town signs, they accidentally switched the two. Freeman was supposed to be called Menno because it was an early Mennonite colony; conversely, Menno, founded in 1879, was supposed to be called Freeman after an early settler of the community. Menno eventually became a center of German-Russian immigrant culture. In Freeman, Mennonites and Hutterians gather every October for a two-day Schmeckfest, with beer and German food served by women dressed in traditional costumes. People of Norwegian, Swedish, and Irish ancestry come from miles around to join the fun.

Hutterians and Mennonites

The Hutterian Brethren colonies of Rosedale and Rockport lie along the James in the southern part of Hutchinson County. The Hutterians may be the oldest communal group in the Western world. The correct and preferred term is "Hutterian," though most of their neighbors call them "Hutterites." The name originated with founder Jacob Hutter, a Moravian preacher burned at the stake in 1536. Several Hutterian groups originated within the Mennonite theological tradition, but they prefer not to be called Mennonites. However, Mennonites include Hutterians among their members, and the main difference between the two is the latter's communal organization. Both groups suffered persecution in both Europe and America and were often forced to move and forfeit their property.

Both groups sent delegations abroad to the United States in 1872-73 to investigate the settling opportunities. They visited Minnesota and the Dakotas and asked President Ulysses Grant for certain concessions, such as exemption from military service. Grant could not agree to all their requests, but several groups came anyway, migrating to Kansas, the Dakotas, Nebraska, and Minnesota. Some Russian Mennonites came to Yankton in 1873, settling in Turner County. The following year about sixty Hutterian families arrived in Yankton and took land south of Bon Homme, beginning steady migration. One estimate indicates that by 1957 about eighteen hundred Hutterians lived in South Dakota in seventeen colonies. At that time, they controlled approximately seventy-nine thousand acres of farmland.

These religious settlers inadvertently made one of the worst ecological blunders of all time, introducing one of the widespread scourges of the West—tumbleweeds. As Ray Ring explained in *High Country News*, the immigrants planted crops in the spring of 1873 using seeds brought from the steppes of the Russian Ukraine. Lurking somewhere in their sacks of flax seed from back home were seeds of another, far less desirable plant: *salsoka kali*, also known as *salsola pestifera, salsola iberica,* or just plain old tumbleweed. The new arrival lost no time taking root. Literally from that moment on, the accidentally introduced tumbleweed spread through the West like— well, like white men.

The weed thrives on disturbed land, and drought just seems to encourage it; both conditions were present in Bon Homme County. The plants can grow up to six feet in diameter, then break loose and roll happily across the terrain, dropping seeds everywhere. The Russian tumbleweed has become the most successful weed in the world, spreading rapidly, and the story isn't over yet; as land conditions worsen, tumbleweeds seem to thrive. In 1980 Mobridge, South Dakota, north on the Missouri River, made world headlines when the streets were filled with windblown tumbleweeds, blocking access to the hospital and burying thirty homes up to their roofs. Burning them was out of the question, and even heavy equipment had a hard time shoving the packed mass out of the way.

Characteristically, Westerners have made a variety of attempts to extract something good out of this chronic problem. Tumbleweeds have been hung with tinsel and shiny ornaments and used as Christmas trees, or spray-painted and propped up in art galleries to provide ambience. They've been ground and compressed into logs for fireplaces and fuel pellets for power plants (not bad ideas—the weeds contain roughly the same amount of thermal energy as wood). Now researchers are experimenting with making the tumbleweed into cattle feed; it is hardy and adaptable to drought and can be harvested two or three times in a growing season, yielding a total of six tons an acre. Some folks are even trying to convince humans to eat it; *The Tumbleweed Gourmet*, published by the University of Arizona Press in 1987, features recipes for Jellied Tumbleweed Salad and Cream of Tumbleweed Soup.

Once the origin of the weed was known, suspicious people spread rumors that it had been introduced as revenge by Russian Mennonites in return for earlier religious persecution against them. When Hutterians refused to register for the draft during World War I, eligible men were arrested by county sheriffs and sent to army camps. There, some were forced to remain outside during the rain or to run at the point of a bayonet; others were put in dungeons without blankets, fed on bread and water, or manacled to walls so they had to stand on tiptoe. In one colony a hired non-Brethren worker mixed ground glass into the flour in an attempt to increase anti-German sentiment by making it appear as though the colonists supported the Germans. Gangs of youths stole and sold Hutterian sheep and cattle. The Hutterians offered $10,000 to a relief committee in lieu of buying Liberty Bonds, paid their regular taxes, and contributed to the Red Cross, but the persecution persisted. Many colonists were forced to move to Canada but returned after the war when they were allowed to perform services in forestry in lieu of military service.

CANTON

Canton's first settler appeared in 1861 but was quickly frightened away by the fear of Indian attack. Others returned, however, and by 1866 the settlement appeared on maps as Commerce City. In 1867 several men claimed land in the vicinity but spent the winter together in shacks on the proposed town site for safety. The next year, several men built a combined blockhouse and general store. When it became the county seat, residents voted to change the name to Canton—an oddity in this vast inland sea of Scandinavian, Bohemian, and Indian names—because they believed it to be exactly opposite to Canton, China, on the globe. The first newspaper was printed in 1872, and the Milwaukee Road reached town in 1879.

By 1882 at least six churches were operating, along with several secret orders and a chapter of the Women's Christian Temperance Union. The town included three banks, several lumber companies, hotels, real estate and loan offices, grain dealers, thirty or forty mercantile houses, millinery shops, blacksmiths, wagon makers, and saddle makers, as well as a fair sprinkling of doctors, lawyers, and ministers.

O. E. Rolvaag, the Norwegian-born author of *Giants in the Earth*, one of the best fictional accounts of early pioneering life, lived in Canton, where his novel takes place. Rolvaag's book emphasized the difficulty of isolation for the settlers, especially the women, who moved from the eastern forested lands to the broad prairies. Rolvaag continued the story of these settlers' lives in two sequels, *Peder Victorius* and *Their Father's God*.

Another famous Canton native was Ernest Orlando Lawrence, inventor of the cyclotron, a key device in the development of the atomic bomb. A graduate of Yale University, he received a 1939 Nobel Prize in physics, and the 103rd known chemical element, Lawrencium, was named for him. He died in 1958. Merle Tuve, developer of the "radio proximity fuse" used in World War II, was also born in Canton.

Today, Canton's nearly three thousand residents host the Sioux River Folk Festival annually in August and lure hikers to trails through the nearby Newton Hills.

Turkey Ridge

Nearby Turkey Ridge is a community but not officially a town—at least, not by the definition that insists towns must have post offices. Nevertheless, its businesses supply a farming area with many necessities. The ridge for which the area is named runs northeast and southwest near the town of Wessington Springs. Many wild turkeys were once found in the woods that cover it, but farming and settlement have damaged their habitat; few are seen today.

US 12
Edmunds County—Minnesota
169 Miles

US 12 runs east-west across the eastern third of the state from the west side of Edmunds County through the northern farming region to the Minnesota state line near Big Stone City.

IPSWICH

When US 12 was first completed, it was called the "Yellowstone Trail" and extended from Plymouth Rock, Massachusetts, across the entire nation to Seattle's Puget Sound. Ipswich, home of the Yellowstone Trail Association, celebrated the road's completion by building a memorial arch over the highway. After several moves, the arch is now in the city park. The small towns along the highway, like Ipswich, once were the social and economic centers of the rural communities surrounding them; today, most of those towns are dwindling, as people trade in larger centers.

When the area was opened to settlement, it was fertile and rich with game. Both Bowdle, laid out in 1886, and Roscoe, named for Roscoe Conkling, a U.S. senator from New York, were railroad-inspired boomtowns. Bowdle, named for a local banker who represented railroad interests, was an important sheep- and wool-shipping point in the early 1880s. German farmers migrating into the area brought diversified farming practices, decreasing the region's reliance on grazing. Both Bowdle and Roscoe, a day's buggy ride apart, filled up fast enough to challenge Ipswich for the position of county seat, but the contention was short. Both towns were hard hit by the great blizzard of 1880-81, and their populations have been declining ever since.

Dakota winters brought fierce blizzards and snow deeper than many homesteaders had ever seen. The man on top of the drift is probably aiming his rifle as part of a pose, since the women and children seem specially dressed for the photographer. —State Historical Society of North Dakota

Ipswich was settled all at once in 1885 when a large group of German Catholics moved in; the town was officially founded a year later. Charles H. Prior, superintendent of the Chicago, Milwaukee & St. Paul line, named the town for his birthplace in England. Ipswich's development was meteoric, even in a territory where towns could appear and disappear quickly; within two weeks it had three newspapers and two banks and was the Edmunds County seat. But as Ipswich grew, other small towns in the county inevitably died; the list includes Edmunds, Freeport, Georgetown, Beebe, Craven, Gretna, Loyalton, Powell, and Vermont City. All were established with lofty hopes, but all were doomed to extinction when settlers gravitated toward the largest town in the neighborhood.

Ipswich was once the nation's greatest shipping point for bison bones, which were sent eastward to be ground up for fertilizer. For a time, it shared distinction with Eureka as the largest primary wheat-shipping center in the nation. It was also briefly an important sheep- and wool-shipping point, and its candle factory supplied local churches for years.

ABERDEEN

By 1884, when the boom slowed in the eastern half of the state because much of the good land was filled, Aberdeen's land office reported that unimproved lands still constituted 80 percent of the area. Unimproved land was valued at $5 an acre, improved land at $15. Some settlers left as quickly as they had come; some went home, while others moved on to new land, and some pieces of land were sold and resold.

Fur traders came early to the rich Aberdeen area. A trading post was operating by 1822 at the mouth of the James River, probably run by Joseph LaFramboise, who ran another post at Flandreau. Colin Campbell of the Columbia Fur Company probably manned a post near Groton between 1822 and 1827, and Zephyr Recontre established several posts on the lower James River. William Dickson, the half-Yankton son of Robert Dickson, wintered at the Oakwood settlement in the early 1830s.

Dickson's presence is particularly interesting, since he represented the second generation of fur trade families in the state. Donald Parker wrote in *Dakota Panorama* that by 1805 the elder Dickson, an agent of the Hudson's Bay Company, had a post on the east side of Lake Traverse, "opposite the favorite camp site of Chief Red Thunder, his Yanktonais brother-in-law." Dickson, a Scot, actively worked for the British during the War of 1812, enlisting Sisseton warriors to aid the cause. After the war, when his business had been destroyed, historian Doane Robinson says Dickson moved back to the South Dakota side of Lake Traverse and continued trading. With Lord Thomas D. Selkirk, another Scot, he tried to form a British colony in the Red River Valley. When British and American officials reached agreement on the Canadian boundary, both Scots were arrested and tried in St. Louis. But by 1822, Robert Dickson, along with Joseph Renville and others, had formed the Columbia Fur Company and established trading posts at the mouths of the Vermillion, James, and Niobrara rivers, with the chief post on Lake Traverse. Apparently his son was extending the family business to the west.

Another Scot, Alexander Mitchell, was president of the Milwaukee Road. When the tracks reached the site of a new town in 1881, it was named, not coincidentally, Aberdeen for Mitchell's birthplace. The Milwaukee was taking a calculated risk in extending its lines into barely settled land. At the same time, it bought the Southern Minnesota Railway and built a parallel line through Flandreau to Madison, South Dakota, southeast of Aberdeen. Three other railroads extended their tracks to Aberdeen, making the city a major center for the shipment of agricultural products. Consequently, for

78

a time Aberdeen was the second largest city in the state. Today its population is nearly twenty-five thousand.

When Brown County was organized in 1880, Columbia, northeast of Aberdeen, was the county seat. Aberdeen citizens began battling for the honor and wrested it away in 1887, and Columbians apparently haven't forgiven them yet. A historical marker at Columbia says the county seat was lost to the larger town by "legislative gerrymandering, frequent elections, [and] several court actions."

An early passenger on the northern line was Hamlin Garland, who went on to become one of the state's best-known writers. In *A Son of the Middle Border*, he recalled his arrival in Aberdeen and emphasized how closely civilization followed wilderness on these Plains: "Aberdeen was the end of the [railroad] line, and when we came into it that night it seemed a near neighbor to Sitting Bull and the bison. And so, indeed, it was, for a buffalo bull had been hunted across its site less than a year before."

In *Main-Travelled Roads*, his first collection of short stories, Garland vividly described the twelve-mile walk from Aberdeen to his father's homestead at Ordway, near present-day US 281.

> The whistle of gophers, the faint, wailing, fluttering cry of the falling plover, the whir of the swift-winged prairie pigeon, or the quack of the lonely duck came through the shimmering air. The lark's infrequent whistle, piercingly sweet, broke from the longer grass in the swales nearby. No other climate, sky, plain, could produce the same . . . weird charm. No tree to wave, no grass to rustle; scarcely a sound of domestic life; only the faint melancholy soughing of the wind in the short grass, and the voices of the wild things of the prairie.

Aberdeen is notable for the number of trees along its streets, planted by early citizens who missed the forested areas they had left behind. It is now an oasis on what was originally a treeless prairie. The town site, located in ancient Lake Dakota, is so flat that careful engineering was required to ensure drainage in city streets. Early residents included Americans from states farther east, as well as German-Russians and a broad range of Scandinavians. A substantial population from Alsace-Lorraine came to Aberdeen by way of the Odessa region of Russia. In the early 1930s their native culture was still in evidence; their brightly painted houses were fronted by vegetable gardens instead of lawns, and older women wore bright silk head shawls.

In 1883 the ethnic makeup of the region changed with the arrival in Aberdeen of three hundred members of a Welsh colony. Most of the group, primarily bachelors, lived in a single large house (known as the "Big Shanty" or "Shanty Mawr") about ten miles south of

Ipswich until they moved to their own houses and homesteads. Many had to travel east or return to Wales to find brides, until an enterprising group of single Welsh women took homesteads in the county. The community—naturally—grew. Later, the Big Shanty was moved to Powell, twelve miles south of Ipswich, and turned into a post office; it was destroyed in a 1911 tornado. Other Welsh communities were established in Aurora, Miner, Lake, Marshall, Brown, and Moody counties.

About the time of the First World War, the Industrial Workers of the World (IWW) established its national headquarters in Aberdeen. Within a few weeks, the group was accused of five murders and several fires; a local group called the Home Guards raided IWW headquarters and ordered its members to stay outside the city limits. In retaliation, IWW farm workers boycotted the state in an effort to hamper the harvest, but local clerks and businessmen helped farmers pick the crops in defiance of the union.

Four-year Northern Normal and Industrial School, now Northern State University, was founded in 1902; the original buildings now form a quadrangle. Presentation College was originally founded as a junior college but has four-year enrollment and three campuses: one at Aberdeen, one at Eagle Butte, and one at McKennan Hospital in Sioux Falls.

L. Frank Baum

L. Frank Baum, the creator of the world of Oz, lived in Aberdeen as a youth and apparently drew some of his inspiration from the prairies surrounding it. Arthur R. Huseboe, in *An Illustrated History of the Arts in South Dakota*, says Baum came to Aberdeen in July 1888, having been unsuccessful as a theatrical producer and as a salesman for the family oil company. With the help of relatives, he opened a general store, expecting to profit from the Dakota boom. But the gold rush in the Black Hills was over, and the store went out of business. Baum bought the weekly *Dakota Pioneer* and operated it for over a year as the *Aberdeen Saturday Pioneer*.

Baum lived through the blizzard of 1888 and the drought and difficult times that succeeded it in South Dakota. During this period he spent only a few days in Kansas, so it is legitimate to assume that his inspiration for the whirlwinds and drought that Dorothy experienced in *The Wizard of Oz* was really South Dakota weather. Unfortunately, one may also infer that when he described the poor shack where Dorothy lived with her downtrodden Uncle Henry and Aunt Em and wrote of "the great grey prairie" around it, he was also thinking of South Dakota. Other authorities have suggested that the Wizard's preparations to leave Oz by balloon reflect Baum's experiences at the 1890 state fair in Aberdeen, and some trace the use of green spectacles by Dorothy and her friends at the Emerald City to a newspaper column Baum wrote about a federal farm agent visiting a drought-damaged farm. A 1968 essay by Henry Littlefield calls *The Wizard of Oz* a parable on the Populist agricultural reform movement Baum observed in South Dakota. Baum's political intentions aside, his book has sold more than seven million copies, been translated into twenty-seven languages, and, with Judy Garland's help, become one of the most popular movies in history, making him clearly South Dakota's most influential writer.

BATH AND BRISTOL

Like Ipswich, Bath and Bristol were named by Chicago, Milwaukee & St. Paul official Charles H. Prior for towns in his native England. At that time, railroad sidings were constructed at ten-mile intervals, so those two towns, along with Webster, Andover, and Groton, grew quickly.

Pioneer women welcomed an excuse to get together. Here they are engaged in a quilting bee held in a well-built log-and-frame home in northern Dakota Territory in 1883. —State Historical Society of North Dakota

An early settler in Bath was Walborg Strom Holth. At eighteen, she had married a widower with children almost as old as she and was a widow herself before her second son, Severin, was born. She inherited a prosperous business that kept her comfortable the rest of her life and enabled her to travel in style, unusual for women of the time.

In 1891-92 Mrs. Holth visited her eldest son, Christian, at his homestead near Sand Lake. Apparently he enjoyed a little higher standard of living than the average homesteader, but his mother was still disappointed. "Oh well! if one isn't too spoiled it perhaps can pass," she remarked in a letter to a stepdaughter in Norway. Inside, "we have first a kitchen, which is also Christian's bedroom, our dining room and usually our sitting room. . . . Christian's bed serves as a sofa and otherwise we use just anything to sit on out here in the far west." The day Mrs. Holth arrived, a heavy rain had fallen, and "a deluge of small frogs were hopping about between our feet." Still, the pioneers ate well from "a food cellar which is well filled with potatoes, roots and milk. . . . We live on geese and ducks and prairie hens for dinner while for breakfast and supper we have sandwiches."

DAY COUNTY AND WEBSTER

Webster, founded in 1881, was named for homesteader J. P. Webster. The WPA guide says Webster was surrounded by a farming community populated by Norwegian, Scotch, English, and German settlers. The town included a livery, real estate office, jewelry store, grain elevator, bank, general store, newspaper, and saloon. As a railroad supply point for Fort Sisseton, about twenty miles north, it was considered a gateway to the lake region that originally drew the Sisseton and Wahpeton Sioux.

A mixture of prairie, woods, and ponds, this was prime summer Indian hunting land; it was once called "The Buffalo Republic" because of the vast herds that migrated through it. After these animals disappeared, bird hunters came to the area. In the early 1900s, the skies were literally darkened by flights of migrating wildfowl, and market hunters from Minneapolis and Chicago arrived to profit from mass slaughter. They traveled by horse and buggy to the lake region with cases of shells, hunted all day, and shipped their take of ducks and geese to city markets, receiving one dollar for each bird. The Migratory Bird Law of 1913 ended the unregulated hunting. The area now supports diversified farming, dairying, and livestock growing, and Day County's population is nearly seven thousand.

Light buggies such as this one speeded travel, especially if hitched behind fast two- or four-horse teams. In light two-passenger buggies, market hunters could make a quick trip to the lakes in eastern South Dakota and hunt profitably all day.
—Rose Mary Goodson

Many of the small settlements in this area became railroad sidings when the tracks were laid. Day County's first settlement probably originated as a fur post set up by French trader Francis Rondell in 1868 at the west end of Waubay Lake. Known officially as Station Fifty when the railroad reached it in 1880, the name was later changed to Blue Lake, then to Waubay in 1885 to match the lake to the north. The word is an approximate translation of a Sioux word for "where wildfowl build their nests." Summit, just east of I-29, stands at the height of the *coteau* and, at two thousand feet of elevation, may be the highest town between the Mississippi and Missouri rivers. Marvin was called Grant Siding when it was founded in 1882, but when the post office was established, citizens felt the name should be more dignified. One man noticed a Marvin safe in the office where the group met and suggested it as a good "safe" name.

Seven miles north of Webster on SD 23 occurred what may have been the first—but not the last—death by prairie fire in Dakota. Widow Betsy Dalager, her five children, and her mother Guri Schobakken had come to Day County by ox-drawn wagon in May 1884. By 1886 the family had a house, a barn, a well, and several cows, and they had carefully plowed the necessary fireguards. On April 17, John Dodd, who lived three miles south, set a fire to burn out his slough. A strong wind took the fire out of control and burned haystacks near Mrs. Dalager's barn. She and her mother, seeking to save the livestock, were trapped by the fire in the flaming barn. Betsy ran out, her clothes burning, and jumped into the well. Her mother burned to death. The children found safety in the plowed firebreak and, after the hot earth had cooled, helped their mother out of the well. Mrs. Dalager was badly burned and was later crippled by rheumatism, but for thirty-six years she ran her farm from a wheelchair, a symbol of the courage of pioneer homesteaders.

Another courageous deed took place near Webster some twenty years before the widow Dalager's misfortune. A Sioux named Solomon Two Stars, employed as a U.S. Army scout at Fort Wadsworth (later Fort Sisseton), spotted a band of half-breed outlaws wanted for a murder in Minnesota. Three were killed, one escaped, and one was captured—a renegade nephew of Two Stars. The nephew confessed to participating in the murder. The scouts were under strict orders to take no prisoners, so Two Stars faced a choice. He could have contrived to let his nephew escape or he could have asked one of the other scouts to shoot him. But Two Stars, following the code of the frontier, carried out his duty. Fifty years later he said, "I shot him before my tears should blind me."

MILBANK

Milbank grew partly because it was close to Lake Traverse and Big Stone Lake, which lay on the fur traders' water route into Canada. It is intriguing to compare early observations of the area with the way it looks today. In 1808 Thomas Anderson wrote of a buffalo hunt near Big Stone Lake with a party of Indians. Traveling up the lake by canoe, the group hadn't sighted buffalo yet when they heard "a

Most homesteading families in territorial days traveled in rigs like this old lumber wagon.
—Rose Mary Goodson

84

rumbling noise, like rolling thunder, at a distance, causing the whole country to quiver and shake." Before them was a bay crowded with buffalo swimming in all directions, and "as far as the eye could see, the prairie was black with these animals." Typical of hunting parties at the time, Anderson's party took only the choicest pieces of the buffalo they shot—tongue, hump, a few steaks or ribs—and left the rest to rot.

When the Milwaukee reached the settlement in 1880, a railroad division headquarters attracted many Irish and Dutch families to work on the line and open shops. Big Stone City won the first election for county seat that year, but the railroad's arrival soon made Milbank's population greater, so the controversy was reopened. In a twist on the usual scenario, the official records were not stolen from Big Stone City; Milbank simply called itself the county seat and started a new set of records. Confused citizens filed important papers in both towns, just to be safe. When a court finally recognized Milbank's claim in 1883, Big Stone City demanded reimbursement for the money it had spent on campaigning.

Jeremiah Milbank was one of the directors of the Milwaukee when the town was founded. *The Dakota Huronite* of May 31, 1883, said, "Ground has been broken at Milbank for the $15,000 church to be built and presented to the town by J. Milbank of New York."

Hamlin Garland described Milbank as a boomtown filling rapidly with land agents and settlers: "[T]he flock of shining yellow pine shanties strewn upon the sod gave me an illogical delight, but then I was twenty-one—and it was sunset in the Land of the Dakotas!" When he saw the valley of the James River for the first time, he said it was "as illimitable as the ocean and level as a floor." By 1990 the town's residents numbered nearly four thousand.

According to David Holden in *Dakota Visions*, at first glance the Milbank area appears to boast "only the usual corn, beans, and Norwegians." But there's more than meets the eye. When Dutch settlers moved there in 1878, they were one of more than twenty-five ethnic groups in the region, with unique industries such as a wooden shoe factory. Milbank flour mills operated on wind power in pioneer days, providing a necessary service for this vast wheat-growing region. Ironically, the railroads that brought the settlers soon made it more cost-efficient to ship the wheat elsewhere than to grind it locally; only one wind-powered flour mill is left in the area (it is open to visitors).

East of town are the granite quarries, supplying rich red granite for tombstones found in practically every cemetery in the nation. Part of a massive formation that reaches from Big Stone City to

Montevideo, Minnesota, the granite is among the oldest rock on earth, dated at 4.2 billion years. Only on the moon have older rocks been found. When I visited the Scottish stonemason from Maryland who made the bronze plaque for my husband's stone, he said little until he realized I was from South Dakota. "Milbank!" he said enthusiastically, "Best granite in the world!" While he explained why Milbank stone is superior, his wife whispered that she and her husband visit granite quarries on vacation—but have not yet come to South Dakota.

Six large companies produce the Milbank tombstones, leaving pyramids of waste material piled on the surrounding plains. Local folks insist fossil shark teeth and the vertebrae of some unidentified creature have been found in one quarry. Some of the first granite gravestones erected in the state are still standing in an abandoned Indian cemetery in the hills northwest of Milbank. Since the quarries opened, more than twelve hundred acres of granite have been produced, enough to cover an area of fourteen square miles.

Another distinctive local feature is Blue Cloud Abbey, a monastery whose monks work with Sisseton Indians. The abbey was named for a Christian Yankton Lakota man who was born in 1833, abandoned by his parents, and raised as a warrior by his grandfather. Blue Cloud grew up under the influence of two fur-trading uncles and was a scout and guide for U.S. Army mapping expeditions on the Powder River and in Utah. He traveled to Mandan country and attended the 1851 treaty conference at Fort Laramie, Wyoming, with Father Pierre De Smet. During the Minnesota uprising, Struck-by-the-Ree sent him to warn white settlers. In 1877 he was appointed head chief of the Yanktons when the hereditary leader left the tribe. He died in 1918. Work by Indian writers from around the nation was for many years published by a small but important publishing house sponsored by the abbey and directed by Brother Benet.

More local color: Milbank was the site of a sports milestone that has influenced the lives of thousands of youthful baseball stars. In 1925 the South Dakota Department of the American Legion founded the nationwide organization of Legion Junior Baseball there.

BIG STONE CITY

In 1819 Hazen P. Moers, an American, set up a trading post on the south shore of Big Stone Lake; some authorities claim it was the first post in what became South Dakota. Maj. Stephen H. Long's expedition camped there on July 22, 1823, while surveying the Red River region. J. C. Beltrami, a member of the party, wrote in his journal, "In the evening we stopped at the middle of the lake, just

where it takes a northerly direction, where a magnificent wood and a little traders' settlement were crossed by the River of the White Herons or Ho-ka-San-be-Wa-Kpa which falls into the lake on the southern side."

James Hayes, in charge of the trading post in 1845, listed the furs he had on hand, including nearly eight hundred buffalo robes, more than ten thousand muskrat skins, over a hundred mink, seventy-seven raccoon, twelve otter, two bear, two beaver, and twenty-one fisher. In 1852 Levi Bird, another proprietor, listed eleven packs of muskrats, a hundred foxes, sixty wolves, a hundred mink, six fishers, nine elk, twelve beaver, and thirty badgers. A sighting of any of those species (especially elk or wolf) today would make news all over the state.

On nearby Big Stone Lake, Moses Moreau and Solomon Robar established a fur post in 1865, then turned to farming in 1873 when the Indians who supplied their furs were put on reservations. In the fall of 1878, John Marten settled on the north fork of Whetstone Creek northeast of Milbank. Because the main road west crossed his homestead, he thriftily established a ferry, which operated only at high water.

"Big Stone" refers to the region's generous granite endowment. The town was first known as Inkpa City, apparently in honor of the renegade Inkpaduta, who may have camped nearby after the Sioux Uprising. The town has been more popular as a summer resort than a year-round residence. Chautauqua assemblies during and after the 1890s attracted large crowds to the lake shore for programs of drama, readings, music, and public lectures. Boating facilities, hotels, skating rinks, and bathhouses were built where Moreau and

Robar's trading post once stood. Swimming and fishing were popular, but boating was often hazardous because of the high waves created by winds on the huge lake.

Today a cheese factory is open to visitors. A brick factory functioned for a while, as did a corn cannery established in 1904 on the state line, but in modern times these small businesses have been unable to compete with larger metropolitan concerns. Big Stone City now has about six hundred residents.

US 14
Hand County—Minnesota
160 Miles

In this part of the state, US 14 runs east-west between the western border of Hand County near Ree Heights and the Minnesota state line, east of Brookings. Like the other east-west highways in eastern South Dakota, it begins near the eastern edge of the high, rolling tableland along the Missouri River and plunges down through some of the richest farming country in the state.

In 1912 the highway became part of the Black and Yellow Trail, another label for the route from eastern cities to the Black Hills and the Yellowstone; this one was established by a group of Chicago investors. In 1991 officials from several South Dakota towns formed an association with the goal of promoting the trail to tour bus companies and families from adjoining states as a long weekend trip. South Dakota's part of the trail winds through about thirty towns, including Brookings, Huron, Pierre, Harrold, Highmore, Miller, Wessington, Iroquois, De Smet, Lake Preston, and Volga, before merging with I-90 at Wall and heading for Wyoming. The association hopes to raise money through grants, membership fees, and individual donations, using the funds to get tourists to leave I-90 and explore the adjoining rural areas and small towns.

The western end of the area is more hilly and more tree-covered than the eastern section. The Lakota Indians found good hunting in the drainages that led to the breaks of the Missouri River. West of Miller, prehistoric Indians drove a buffalo herd over a clay cliff around six hundred years ago, before the hunters had horses. On top of the hill above the jump site are two to three hundred tipi rings, rock symbols, ceremonial sites, and other signs of the activity that accompanied a successful hunt.

The rolling character of the land that made it ideal for nomads made it less attractive to homesteaders who planned to farm, and many gave up during dry years. When homesteaders moved out, cattlemen rapidly replaced them. A highway marker mentions the ranchers' motto—"good grass makes good beef"—and even in dry years, unplowed land like this produced rich, nourishing grass. Early brands registered by ranchers in this area included the Monkey Wrench, the 77, the RL Rail, the JO, the Triple 1 Quarter Circle, and the Quarter Circle 2. The historical marker three miles west of Miller on the north side of the highway is one of several in the state that give instructions in proper reading of brands.

REE HEIGHTS

"Ree" was the nickname used by early explorers and trappers for the Arikara Indians, who inhabited the region until being driven out by the Sioux. The Ree Hills, a rolling, well-watered grassland three miles south of town, suggested the name of Ree Heights. The knolls were well known to travelers when white settlement was sparse; wooded ravines offered hidden campsites, wood, and water,

Most travel in territorial days relied on oxen or horses, but this enterprising settler was ahead of his time, using wind power. —South Dakota State Historical Society

and the heights furnished lookout spots, making the area attractive to anyone who had reason to be cautious. When this was Indian country, of course, wariness was important to all white travelers; later the hills became a hideout for horse and cattle thieves, according to tradition. Later, bullwhackers used the hills as a convenient place to graze teams while scouting the trail ahead.

The life of settlers on this frontier is detailed in the letters of Wilburn Wallace Jeffries, a homesteader who lived near Ree Heights. (The letters—written to his wife, Nellie, and brother-in-law, Solomon Huntington—were edited by Jeffries's granddaughter, Ruth Seymour Burmester, for *South Dakota History*.) Jeffries got "no fernature with the Stove," like most homesteaders, but he praised the warmth of his shanty and wished his family were as comfortable as he. Imagine spending a few nights sleeping at forty degrees below zero as he did: "my floor is double thickness the sides are double also with a thickness of tar paper between the boards. The roof is one thickness of lumber, sheets of tar paper and one thickness of Sod on over the paper so that you may see that I do not suffer with the cold while indoores."

Jeffries was proud of the stove. Like many homesteaders, he burned hay, and he boasted that the stove would take seven twists of hay at one time. When the hay supply ran low, however, his choices seemed clear: "I had to doe something either freeze or let the horses starve I studied the thing over and finally shouldered the Crowbar and started out and it took me just one minit to knock it [the stable?] into wood."

To his brother-in-law, Jeffries wrote frankly that anyone intending to homestead should have another source of income. "Hardly think you can get a School here at Ree heights No schoolhouses built in this Co yet except at the RR stations; and thare is more Red Headed old maids here than you can shake a stick at in a week, came here to get married and failed taken up land gone to teaching [w]hile planting Beans on the Sod Now you see what your chances are yourself Wages are for teachers $35-$40." Jeffries predicted that bad weather would drive away the women homesteaders: "Wait untill we have a Siclone, thare will be a better demand for men teachers Sol, the only way you can make it pay to come here is to take a claim and watch your chances for a School." He also suggested an alternative job: "Dr Crown at Miller this season will sow 1,200 acres to wheat, 800 to flax. Thare is your chance for Work He will learn you how to raise grain Go West, boy while youre young."

Jeffries, like some other male homesteaders, had little respect for independent females who homesteaded while teaching school, but many of the women proved up on their claims. In her letters about homesteading in Wyoming, Elinore Pruitt Stewart noted that homesteading provided an option for women who wanted to get away from cleaning houses and getting married just to support themselves.

MILLER AND WESSINGTON

Miller was founded in 1880 and named for its first settler, Henry Miller. St. Lawrence, just three miles east, was established as a railroad siding first, but in 1881 settlers persuaded railroad officials to add a siding at Miller, so the smaller town lost population. Other small towns along US 14, such as Vayland, Wessington, and Wolsey, are slowly disappearing, leaving only fragments of their history. (One fragment that should not be lost: A man named Tommy Fastwalker achieved local fame by crossing the sixty-mile width of Hand County in one day.) Miller's position as the seat of Hand County keeps its population fairly stable.

Wessington, which should not be confused with the larger town of Wessington Springs to the south, was originally a railroad stop named Aqua, probably because trains took on water there. It was renamed Wessington for the nearby Wessington Hills in 1882.

How the hills, an abrupt range of the *coteau des prairies*, were named is a matter of dispute. One story says they bear the name of a teamster who worked for Col. W. H. Nobles; in 1857 Nobles laid out a road from the Minnesota River to the Missouri and discovered a medicinal spring in the hills. Another story says they were named for a Captain Wessington, who was reportedly captured and tortured to death there by Indians in 1863. Local residents, who prefer this version, like to show a charred tree in the hills as "proof," though there's no way of telling when the tree was burned and no other evidence to support the claim. Still another story says that the hills were named for a missionary who held open-air meetings there.

HURON

On the state fairgrounds in Huron, a historical marker proclaims the James River as the dividing line between North America's humid and semiarid territory—the literal beginning of the West. Dozens of other places have so proclaimed themselves, but Huron, though it is well within the area usually designated as "eastern" South Dakota, has more justification than most. Drought and crop failures sometimes forcefully persuaded farmers that they weren't in the East anymore; the dust storms of 1933-34 were so severe that much of the topsoil was moved to the roadside ditches. Conservation programs encouraged the planting of tree belts to discourage blowing dust.

Huron was staked out in 1879 when a man named John Cain and others claimed land on the east bank of the James River. Not long afterward, surveyors for the Chicago & Northwestern Railroad camped nearby and selected the west bank as railroad division headquarters at the instruction of Marvin Hughitt, president of the railroad. The Chicago & Northwestern—through its subsidiary, the Western Town Lot Company—bought title to 880 acres and built depots, a roundhouse, shops, and offices. Town organizers were so busy they didn't get around to celebrating the Fourth of July until the *fifth*, but they did it in fine style: with a baseball game. Unfortunately, before nine innings had been completed, the last bat in Huron was broken, and the game was left unfinished.

Hughitt or another railroad official named the site for the Huron Indians, a confederation of four tribes that lived in the region east of Lake Huron. The name is said to be a corruption of a French word meaning "wild boar," because early pioneers in the East thought the Indians had a wild and unkempt appearance. It's doubtful whether any Hurons ever visited Dakota; perhaps Hughitt was operating on the assumption, still evident in some areas, that all Indians were alike.

Naturally, the railroad's arrival started a land rush. The Huron district land office covered seven counties and during 1882-84 recorded 38,501 claims. By 1884 some land was still available in Hughes, Potter, Hyde, Hand, and Sully counties. Canny railroad officials established "homeseeker specials," trains that offered lower rates for settlers examining land; thousands took advantage of the offer. By 1913, for example, early Hutterian colonies at Yankton and Bon Homme had been followed by daughter colonies, one of which was established at Old Huron. The War Department installed a signal station nearby in 1881, followed by a weather bureau for the state.

Huron was incorporated by the Dakota territorial legislature in 1883, the same year a bill naming the city as the capital failed. In 1885 the Republican Party called its first "state" convention at Huron and nominated candidates for office under the new, unratified constitution. The Democratic Party ignored the whole thing and fielded no candidates, so only Republicans were elected. After the constitution was approved and statehood was achieved, Huron and Pierre battled it out for the honor of becoming the capital; the debt Pierre incurred in winning the campaign took thirty years to pay off, so Huron may be glad of losing.

Still, because it is situated on the west bank of the James River in the center of a level prairie, Huron has remained a hub for the rural communities and small towns around it. The economy was originally based on agriculture, including grain and dairy production, poultry raising, and livestock raising. Industries to process this abundant farm output also flourished, including a meat-packing company and a brewery. Labor unions came to town early and grew strong, starting with the Brotherhood of Locomotive Firemen, whose charter was issued in 1883 and signed by Eugene V. Debs, candidate for U.S. president on the Socialist ticket; twenty-two other unions flourished at various times.

Huron now sports two railroad lines, several bus lines, numerous hotels, an airport, a country club, two golf courses, a tennis court, thirteen city parks, jogging tracks, and several recreation areas. The city encourages a convention business and emphasizes its ethnic mix by hosting the South Dakota State Fair, an annual Indian celebration, and public Scandinavian ludefisk suppers. Today, with a population of around thirteen thousand people, Huron occupies nine square miles.

Hubert H. Humphrey, who became vice president of the United States in 1964, spent part of his youth in Huron and Doland; a local establishment has been renamed the Hubert H. Humphrey Drug Store to take advantage of his fame. Another local celebrity is Charles Partlow (Chic) Sale, who gained national recognition as a humorist. Sale was born in Huron in 1885 and spent the first eleven years of his life here. His book *The Specialist* was called the "mirth of a nation" and sold more than a million copies.

Frontier Feminists: Mamie and Gladys Pyle

Mamie Pyle was an astute politician and hard worker for women's suffrage. The state constitution of 1889 permitted women to vote only in school elections. As president of the State Equal Suffrage Association, Pyle engineered a clever and unusual lobbying effort in the state legislature in 1913. She and her supporters decided they would no longer stop legislators in the hallways to beg them to extend the vote to women. Instead, says Dorinda Reed in *The Woman Suffrage Movement in South Dakota*, the committee obtained a room and a conference table and summoned legislators by note, using a privately paid page. The tactic was successful:

> Believing that he was being summoned by some important state official, each legislator would come, be interviewed, and then would consider it such a good joke that he would say nothing and wait for his neighbor to get caught. The ladies had interviewed nearly the

entire membership before the men began comparing notes. Later, the members of the legislature always referred to this procedure as "the Campaign of Committee Room 2."

These efforts helped ensure passage of a bill to amend the state constitution and extend the franchise to women. However, the amendment failed to win a majority of the popular vote, as required. Not until 1918 was a suffrage amendment added to the state constitution. The following year, South Dakota ratified the suffrage amendment to the federal Constitution.

When South Dakota's women voted for the first time in 1920, Pyle became the state's first presidential elector, and Dr. Helen Peabody, head of All Saints Girls' School in Sioux Falls, was elected its first woman delegate to the Republican Party's national convention. Pyle also served as president of the South Dakota League of Women Voters and president of the Presbyterian Women's Association of the Huron Church and was a member of the Women's Christian Temperance Union, the Young Women's Christian Association, and the Twentieth Century Study Club. At eighty-one, she was selected as the state's Mother of the Year. All three of her daughters graduated from Huron College and became schoolteachers; her son, John, earned a degree from University of Michigan Law School. Three of the children left South Dakota, but Gladys, the youngest, remained.

Ironically, when Gladys Pyle was once asked about the greatest influence in her life, she didn't mention her mother, widowed at thirty-six, who not only raised her children but was active in politics. Instead, she named her father, once South Dakota's attorney general, who died when she was eleven years old. After teaching for a year at Miller High School, Gladys became superintendent of schools at Wessington. When the schools closed during the influenza epidemic of 1918-19, she volunteered as a nurse and later took care of her brother John's sick wife and child. She taught for a total of eight years and later said teaching was the most significant part of her life. During 1921-22, she lectured all over the Midwest, training women to become active in political parties.

In 1922 Gladys Pyle became the first woman to run for the state legislature—and the first to be elected to it. In 1923 she fought for ratification of a child labor amendment to the state constitution, which failed, and worked for a bill to permit women to serve on state juries, which later passed. Gladys was appointed assistant secretary of state, the first woman assistant in a state constitutional office, and served until resigning to run for a second legislative term. At the end of her second legislative term, she was again appointed assistant secretary of state; she was elected secretary of state in

1926, serving for two terms. In 1930 she became one of five candidates for governor; she lost her bid but was appointed state secretary of the Securities Commission by Governor Warren Green, serving from 1931 to 1933.

Pyle served briefly in the U.S. Senate in 1938, which made her the first elected female Republican in either house of Congress. In 1940 she ran for mayor of Huron but finished second. Retiring from public life, she became an insurance agent and served on the Board of Charities and Corrections. Toward the end of her life she received awards recognizing her work for the state, including an honorary doctorate of letters from Huron College. On her ninetieth birthday, October 4, 1980, she was honored by Gladys Pyle Day in Huron; she died March 14, 1989, in a nursing home there. Her home is open to the public.

Gladys Pyle's example is still an inspiration for women who have had a struggle in South Dakota. Historian and feminist Ruth Ann Alexander noted in *South Dakota History* that in 1964, when women were searching for advancement opportunities in the United States, South Dakota ranked no worse than other states; its congressional delegation, state legislature, and local governments remained

> bastions of male domination. Private clubs, Jaycees, Rotary, and Kiwanis excluded women. Few female students enrolled in engineering, science, agriculture, medicine, or law at the universities, and the business school discouraged female applicants. A woman in the clergy was a rarity. Women were paid less than men—the average figure was about fifty-nine cents for the male dollar—in banks, businesses, schools, colleges, and even as lifeguards at local swimming pools.

During the 1980s some of that discouraging picture began to change. Gladys Pyle would be pleased at the number of women elected to the legislature, to county and city commissions, and as mayors. A woman is president of the University of South Dakota. In 1975, according to Alexander, "only 43.9 percent of the total student population in public and private colleges [were] women; in 1988, women comprised 55.8 percent of the population. In 1975, women made up 16.7 percent of the medical school enrollment and 19 percent of law school; in 1988, the number of women in medical school had jumped to 29.5 percent; in law school, to 41.8 percent."

Still, women have always had to struggle for equality in this pioneering state, which seems odd since they homesteaded it right beside the men. Even the most fundamental rights have been slow in coming; for example, not until 1988 did women legislators finally get their own toilet in the state capitol building. Prior to that time, the men's toilet had simply been partitioned for use by women!

DE SMET

De Smet was founded in 1880 and named for Father Pierre Jean De Smet, a Jesuit missionary who ascended the Missouri River to South Dakota in 1839 to Christianize the Indians. He is believed to have learned about the existence of gold in the Black Hills from his Indian friends. He advised them never to tell the whites about it, adding that gold made the white men crazy and they would do anything to get it. Rumor has it that De Smet found a valuable vein of gold and resisted the ultimate temptation by covering it up.

Father De Smet traveled throughout the Northwest, from St. Louis to Oregon and into Canada, with fur traders and trappers. He carried neither weapons nor money; the Indians accepted him peacefully and called him and similarly garbed priests "the black robes." He was a passenger on an American Fur Company steamboat in 1850, when cholera broke out among the crew. Though Father De Smet contracted malaria (called ague on the frontier), he left the steamer whenever possible to help the sick and dying Indians, who were particularly vulnerable to and suffered greatly from smallpox. Unwittingly, he probably spread the contagion. In 1851 De Smet walked from the Yellowstone River to the Black Hills and then on to Fort Laramie, where he attended the great council between U.S. commissioners and Indian representatives, preaching to the captive audience of ten thousand Indians. He died at age seventy-two in 1873, three years before Deadwood's gold rush began.

Because it lay at the heart of a dairy region, De Smet was once called the "Cream City." Today its thirteen hundred residents are developing other industries. Raven Industries, which manufactures outdoor sportswear, established a plant here in 1977 and made clothes worn in 1989 by climbers ascending Mount Everest.

The *Real* Little House on the Prairie

Four of Laura Ingalls Wilder's popular novels, nostalgic stories of homestead life, were set in the De Smet area, where Charles and Caroline Ingalls and their daughters Mary, Laura, Carrie, and Grace lived. The Ingalls homestead site is located south of town near De Smet Forest, a small roadside park. The Laura Ingalls Wilder Pageant is presented each summer with a cast of twenty-five community volunteers at a site overlooking the Ingalls homestead and the "Big Slough" and adjacent to the five cottonwoods planted by Charles Ingalls for his daughters. More than seven thousand people attended the presentation in 1989, and twenty-one thousand visited the Ingalls home and museum. Children can ride free in horse-drawn wagons before the performance.

Wilder wrote of the fall and winter the family spent at a railway construction camp in *By the Shores of Silver Lake*; the site of the camp was a mile east of town, and the lake is actually Lake Henry. The family then moved to De Smet, site of *Little Town on the Prairie*, living in the Ingalls store briefly, before moving to a homestead across the Big Slough. After the October blizzard of 1880, the family returned to town for *The Long Winter*. Later, in *These Happy Golden Years*, Laura wrote of her romance and marriage with Almanzo Wilder and their life in a claim shanty two miles north of De Smet, where their daughter, Rose Wilder Lane (later a journalist and author), was born.

A year after the Panic of 1893, Laura and Almanzo left Dakota, traveling with thousands of families who had lost homes and land;

Ma and Pa Ingalls's home in De Smet has become a tourist attraction, thanks to the literary works of their daughter Laura. Visitors can see other sites mentioned in Laura Ingalls Wilder's books, including the three-room surveyor's shanty the family occupied and the Big Slough. —South Dakota Department of Tourism

with a team, wagon, and a hidden $100 bill, they were better prepared than most. "That's your last sight of Dakota," Laura told her seven-year-old daughter; she took notes on the trip for a letter published later in the *De Smet News*. William T. Anderson, writing in *American West*, notes that in the letter, her first published work, Laura expressed sentiments unusual in a white woman, especially coming only four years after the Wounded Knee massacre: "If I had been the Indians, I would have scalped more white folks."

The *Little House* series is a valuable record of pioneer life as well as some fine reading; many Dakota families have passed complete sets of the books from one child to another down the years, and they are read aloud in many grade schools. The stories are exciting, and their author always insisted that they were all true, written from her memories. She was seventy-six when her final book appeared in 1943. After Almanzo died in 1949, Laura stubbornly remained alone on her farm; she died there in 1957. With Rose's help, the home

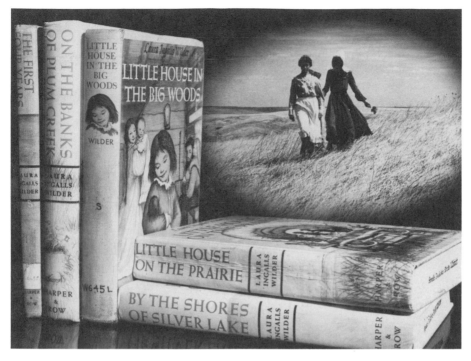

Laura Ingalls Wilder's books have enthralled readers for years, letting them experience some of the realities of homesteading through the author's words. —South Dakota Department of Tourism

became a shrine with a nearby museum; other cabins the Wilders inhabited on their trip west have been saved and are now visited by thousands of tourists yearly.

Another famous local landmark is the birthplace of Harvey Dunn (see entry for I-29—Brookings), one of South Dakota's best-known painters. He was born March 8, 1884, in a homestead shanty three miles south and a half mile east of Manchester; fifty years later, only low mounds of earth marked the Dunn homestead. So far the site has escaped becoming a tourist attraction.

LAKE PRESTON AND ARLINGTON

Explorer John C. Frémont named this natural lake, covering 480 acres, in 1839 for William Campbell Preston, senator from South Carolina. The town was known simply as "Preston" when the first post office was established in 1879 but took the name of the nearby lake in 1881 at the direction of the federal postal delivery system to avoid confusion with Preston, Minnesota.

Postal service officials were frequently concerned with such mix-ups. A settler in Dakota might consider it unlikely that anyone could confuse his town with one in, for example, Arkansas, but the postal service thought differently and often refused to acknowledge a name. In some cases, naming a town proved to be quite a struggle. Arlington, founded in 1880, was called Nordland by the Dakota Central Railroad Company because of the many Norwegian settlers in the vicinity. The postal service accepted Nordland, but officials of the Western Town Lot Company objected, saying the name would mislead other settlers into believing the town only accepted Norwegians. In 1884 county commissioners renamed the town Denver, but the postal service refused to accept this change and instead dubbed the town in honor of Arlington, Virginia—apparently giving up one sort of confusion for another. For a short period, the post office referred to the community as Nordland, the railroad station bore the name Denver, and the town's signs read Arlington. Settlers must have wondered where they were.

VOLGA

Celebrating Volga's golden jubilee on August 29, 1929, the *Volga Tribune* said the town was so named by Chicago & Northwestern Railroad officials either because it wanted to attract Russian settlers or because the Missouri River was the railroad company's goal (Volga means "great river" in Russian). Another explanation advanced by the newspaper is that a railroad official called it after the town and river of that name in eastern Iowa, which makes a little more sense. The town was laid out in 1879 when three early residents each donated forty acres for a town site, hoping to attract a railway company. By that fall, J. Harris's hotel, grandly named the Pioneer House, was in business, but accommodations were a little crude; army blankets were used as room dividers.

Several early histories remark upon the fact that this region, though settled in pioneering times, attracted such solid citizens that it had almost none of the wild and woolly reputation of the gold rush and cattle towns farther west. Occasionally, local residents apparently became jealous of the western reputation and stirred up a little trouble. According to one story reported in the WPA guide, a salesman from Chicago came to Volga in 1880 and drove to the site of a trading post at nearby Oakwood. The nervous visitor believed the country was dangerous, and some local men decided not to disappoint him. That night they lured him into a drugstore for some high-stakes gambling and drinking. As soon as the salesman had a sizeable chunk of change on the gaming table, the locals staged a violent quarrel. The drugstore's owner rushed behind the counter and emerged waving a huge cheese knife while another man charged out of the back room clutching a shotgun. Three players rushed the man with the gun, who fired a shot safely but unnervingly through the ceiling. By the time things settled down, the salesman had bolted, leaving his money as it lay on the table.

US 281

North Dakota—US 18 at Douglas County

194 Miles

US 281 is an old two-lane highway that runs almost straight north-south from the northern border of the state near Frederick to the southern border with Nebraska. By the system of divisions used in this book, the part of 281 that lies in eastern South Dakota ends at the Douglas County line; the remainder is discussed in Part Two.

The highway can be hazardous for drivers who insist on high speeds, because neighborhood farmers drive cumbersome farm machinery on it, but the trip is pleasant if you drive slowly enough to look at the countryside. Most of the communities on the route flourished in the early 1800s but are declining today as people move from rural areas into metropolitan centers. Many of these little towns began as investments for railroad companies and have declined along with the companies themselves. Originally, railroads profited both by selling land to the settlers and from hauling whatever crops they raised to market. But as rail shipping prices rose and highways were established, farmers began using trucks for transportation. Some towns still have businessmen who supply a few necessities: groceries, gasoline, perhaps propane. However, modern citizens find it faster and more efficient to shop in central towns such as Aberdeen, so small towns like Frederick, Barnard, and Westport are losing the elements that held their communities together: newspapers, churches, stores, and people.

Though the region's population has plummeted steadily for a century, however, some inhabitants have done their best to increase it: The Schense quadruplets and the Fischer quintuplets both were born in this locality.

GHOST TOWNS AND LEGENDS

The highway intersects a region that was prime homesteading country during the 1880s, an era known as the Dakota Boom. As farming has changed in the 1900s, the region has followed a familiar pattern: Farmers have steadily acquired more land, more machinery, and bigger mortgages. Deserted farmsteads outnumber inhabited ones, and the countryside is dotted by ghost towns with names considerably longer than their main streets, sturdy names taken from cherished villages left behind: Columbia, Winship, Detroit, Amherst, Claremont, Putney, New Dehli, Rudolph. To modern travelers, speeding past, these hamlets much resemble one another; yet their largely unrecorded histories are as vivid as any in the archives.

Ashton, for example, was probably named by settlers for the groves of ash trees in its original location on the James River, five miles south. When settlers moved to the spot where the railroad crossed the river at Redfield, the original town gave up and died.

Another unlikely legend is sometimes offered for the naming of Tulare. The story says two brothers were riding the train when it stopped on an uphill grade near the town. During the long delay, the pair entertained passengers with so many tall tales that they were nicknamed the "two liars," and the expression, contracted to "Tulare," became the town's name. The word may also have been used to suggest a marshy region with abundant tules, or rushes. The naming of Bonilla is equally baffling. One authority says it was named in 1884 for Gen. Manuel Bonilla, a president of Honduras, though it's difficult to imagine why such a person would have a town named after him here. Alternatively, the name might be a corruption of the French words for "good village," *bonne ville.*

There is more certainty about the origin of other names. Corsica was named for immigrant workers who provided cheap labor for the railroad in the 1900s, and Stickney, platted in 1905, honors J. B. Stickney, veteran depot agent for the Milwaukee railroad. Douglas County recalls the fame of "the little giant," Stephen A. Douglas of Illinois, a lawyer, judge, and Abraham Lincoln's opponent in the famous presidential debates of 1860. Beadle County was named to honor Brig. Gen. William Henry Harrison Beadle, a pioneer scholar, educator, lawyer, legislator, and soldier. Aurora County was named for the Roman goddess of the dawn by six women, wives of the first

Abraham Lincoln was busy with political affairs, such as his debate with Stephen A. Douglas, but he found time to appoint his personal physician to an important post in Dakota Territory.

settlers in the county, during a meeting in a sod shanty to organize a literary club. When the subject of county names arose, one woman suggested Aurora because the name symbolized their hope that the free homestead land would bring the dawn of a new era for settlers.

Brown County recognizes Alfred "Consolidation" Brown. He came to Dakota Territory in 1874 and became a legislator from Hutchinson County. While in office he advocated that several small counties be combined into larger ones. When his work was finished, a single nameless county remained, split by the James River, and associates persuaded him to name it after himself. Thus, Brown County is named for a man who, as far as anyone knows, never visited it.

Spink County is named for a skeptical pioneer, S. L. Spink, a New Yorker who came to Dakota as territorial secretary in 1865. He didn't believe the stories he'd heard about the severity of Dakota blizzards.

During one January storm he set out to test a blinding blizzard for himself by walking to a store one and a half blocks away. By feeling his way along a strip of fence between three houses, he arrived safely. As he rested from the minor ordeal, the storekeeper warned him that he'd been lucky. Undaunted, Spink set out for the return trip. Within only a few steps he became confused, lost his way, and wandered helplessly for two hours. Although a man of unusual size and strength, Spink was completely exhausted by the time he stumbled into the home of a neighbor.

Benjamin Harrison, twenty-third president, signed documents admitting both Dakotas to the Union on November 2, 1889. Tactfully, he shuffled the documents so no one could tell which was signed first, saying, "They were born together—they are one and I will make them twins." The relationship is sometimes fraught with sibling rivalry. —State Historical Society of North Dakota

Hamlin Garland: Dakota Writer

Writer Hamlin Garland homesteaded with his father near Ordway in 1881, and many of his books deal with the pleasures and drudgery of homestead life in the area. Garland rode the train from Minnesota to Aberdeen, then walked twelve miles to his father's claim near Ordway. He described the flat expanse as depressing, the town as ugly, and the little park along the muddy James River as pathetic, "with its tiny unkempt grove of water elms and box elders filled with flimsy cabins and huts."

His first impressions of the prairie through which he walked to find his claim were more encouraging; he found "delicate" beauty and "a weird charm" in the plain, despite its flatness. Its "lonely unplowed sweep" gave him the sense of being "among the men who held the outposts—sentinels for the marching millions" of homesteaders approaching from the east. He walked for two hours, "seeing Aberdeen fade to a series of wavering, grotesque notches on the southern horizon line." To the north, he said, another wavering, shadowy line "gradually took on weight and color" until it became Ordway, the village where his father was busy "founding his new home."

Garland worked for $2 a day on his father's claim but left after two weeks to look for a teaching job. Then he worked as a clerk, a carpenter, and a teacher in various locales. In the spring of 1883, he returned to Dakota Territory determined to get a claim of his own and settled thirty-six miles west of Ordway. He helped his father establish a store, which also served as the post office and the town's social center. Later, after he had left Dakota for a writing life, he wrote about winter as the settlers experienced it: "Winter! No man knows what winter means until he has lived through one in a pine-board shanty on a Dakota plain with only buffalo bones for fuel."

Admitting that he had settled on land he hoped to prove up and sell, Garland sympathized with those who planned to build a home. They'd worked all spring in hope of a crop, but with winter beginning they had little money and no coal. Many of them would have frozen to death without burning the buffalo bones. Homesteaders who were taking over an abandoned claim were required to visit it every thirty days. After being trapped in his shanty in three successive blizzards, with seventy-mile-an-hour winds and temperatures of forty below zero, Garland sold his claim for $200 and moved to Boston, where he spent the rest of his life writing about the hardships of life in Dakota.

David Holden remarks grumpily in *Dakota Visions* that Garland "blew [the blizzard] through almost every book he wrote" and that his images have been affecting the nation's picture of South Dakota

ever since. The author's descriptions of snowstorms, poverty, and homesteaders whose health broke with hard labor under difficult conditions, says Holden, "leaves one with a feeling of having just made a rest stop on the way to hell."

Though Garland's portrait of farming wasn't pretty or encouraging, it was undeniably true for many farmers; modern writers and historians, particularly as they examine the diaries of homesteading women, have demonstrated that the pastoral life was not a stroll through the daisies and wheat fields. Any county history is likely to include instances of suicide, individuals packed off to asylums, grasshopper plagues, and railroad tracks covered so deeply with drifting dust that snowplows were required to clear them. Many old-timers in the northeastern corner of the state remembered finding pioneers when snow melted in the spring, sitting where they froze during a blizzard, and one or two histories insist men froze to death walking and were found, dead in mid-stride, in the spring.

MELLETTE

Mellette, settled in 1878, was named for the last governor of Dakota Territory and first governor of South Dakota, Arthur Calvin Mellette. He appears to have been a man with the best attributes we associate with the pioneering era. Born in 1843 in Indiana, Mellette had little formal education but taught himself German and Latin while plowing on the family farm; he was admitted to the University of Indiana at the age of eighteen. The Civil War was beginning, and he volunteered early; a high bounty was paid to volunteers, but when his invalid brother was drafted, Mellette chose to enlist as a substitute, forfeiting the bounty. He later completed Indiana University's law course and was invited to join in practice with Col. Thomas Brady, a former Civil War commander who had been much impressed by his sacrifice. Mellette also helped Brady manage a newspaper and was elected superintendent of schools, district attorney, and an Indiana state legislator.

Seeking relief for his wife's poor health, Mellette moved his family to Colorado and then to Springfield, Dakota, making him the only territorial governor who moved to Dakota voluntarily rather than as a result of government appointment. He was registrar of the land office, then moved to Watertown, where he was active politically. He visited Washington, D.C., to work for statehood, spending more than $16,000 of his own money. An 1885 convention named a slate of territorial officers, but the group realized the national Democratic administration would be unlikely to admit an overwhelmingly Republican state and adjourned. Mellette reconvened the impromptu legislature in 1886 and suggested the assembly demand the right to form a state, but the effort failed.

When Mellette was appointed territorial governor in 1889, he was a close friend of President Benjamin Harrison, and nine months later he was elected governor of the new state. His term was marked by a long drought, which damaged the state's reputation for prosperity, and by the tragedy at Wounded Knee. Mellette was unique in that he flatly refused to levy taxes beyond the strict requirements of the constitution. He raised money to aid drought-stricken farmers from private sources, even traveling to Chicago and other eastern cities for help. These missions angered businessmen, who accused him of presenting a negative image of South Dakota—charges still made today against environmentalists, farmers, and ranchers who dare to admit that the state is sometimes hot, dry, and conservative. Mellette distributed the private money he collected to needy farmers, contributing more than $3,000 of his own for administrative costs. He was criticized for this benevolence and blamed for the tough economic times.

After his term as governor, Mellette practiced law in Watertown. But his health was poor, and a few months later William Walter Taylor, state treasurer and Mellette's friend, broke him financially and created a scandal that dogged the state's Republicans for years. In 1895 Taylor absconded with more than $300,000 of the state's money and fled to Latin America. Mellette, who had acted as one of Taylor's bondsmen, was forced to surrender $15,000 to the state and turned over all his real estate to pay off part of the bond. Penniless, Mellette moved his family to Kansas, where he practiced law until his death the next year. He is buried in Watertown.

Honest Arthur C. Mellette lost everything he had, but the story wasn't finished. Two banks in Deadwood loaned the state money, and two railroad corporations—the largest property taxpayers in the state—paid their taxes early. The legislature also authorized the sale of bonds to pay off the debt, and eventually about three-quarters of the stolen money was restored. Taylor inexplicably came back to the state, was jailed for two years, and moved to Chicago upon his release, where he promptly abandoned the wife who had been faithful to him during his jail term and married another woman. His antics inspired a song:

> *Oh have you seen our Wandering Willie*
>
> *In his journey through your state?*
>
> *He wears a gripsack on his shoulders*
>
> *And he walks with a waddling gait.*
>
> *Yes walks with a waddling gait.*
>
> *Oh walks with a waddling gait.*
>
> *His grip's well filled with solid cash,*
>
> *So he walks with a waddling gait.*

According to musicians, the song's many verses, outlining Willie's guilt, escape, and the light penalties he paid, was sung to the tune of an emancipation song, "Kingdom Coming," also known as "The Year of the Jubiloo."

ARMOUR

Philip D. Armour was both a railroad director and a well-known meat packer—and thus a potential employer—when this town was founded and named for him in 1886. In recognition of the honor, he purchased a bell for the town's first church. The hundredth anniversary edition of *The Armour Chronicle*, published in 1986, says prices for lots in the original town ranged from $225 to $375. Electricity came to town in 1907, followed closely by the first car, a fourteen-horsepower machine built by International Harvester. At its peak the town boasted five livery stables, nine grain elevators, four banks, five or six hotels, several restaurants, five saloons, a cigar maker, and a racetrack.

Armour's first major fire burned eighteen businesses on Main Street in January 1891. Fires were a common hazard in prairie towns, often hastily built of flimsy materials, but Armour seems to have been especially flammable; it suffered major blazes in 1916, 1926, 1931, 1932, 1934, 1952, and 1959. The volunteer fire department, formed in 1892, still operates, holding an annual Firemen's Ball in December.

SD 34
Jerauld County—Minnesota
126 Miles

SD 34 runs east-west between Wessington Springs and the Minnesota state line. The highway closely follows the route of an Indian trail that connected the pipestone quarries in Minnesota to the Three Rivers of the Sioux, a sanctuary near what became Fort Thompson on the Missouri. Many modern highways, especially in the West, follow old trails of this type; by the time motorized travel was accepted, such trails were so well marked and so hedged by settlement that using an old route was more convenient than carving out a new one.

WESSINGTON SPRINGS

This town was settled in 1876 under the name Wessington but found itself renamed Elmer at the postal service's insistence. Repeated petitions from citizens finally convinced the department to change the name to Wessington Springs after the natural springs in the nearby Wessington Hills. The WPA guide says the town was founded in 1880 by a group of settlers under the Reverend A. B. Smart, who wanted a community begun "on a strong, pure basis of temperance, education, and Christianity." In keeping with this idea, the Free Methodists in 1887 founded an academy. Twice fire destroyed the school's administration building, and twice it was rebuilt. In 1964 the institution became a private four-year high school.

One of the most unusual events in the town's history was a balloon ascension in the summer of 1893. The balloonist—no one seems to know what he was doing in Wessington Springs—sat on a trapeze below the gas bag, according to the WPA guide. He tried to improve the entertainment value of his act by tying a hard slipknot to release the parachute by which he intended to return to earth; most performers simply cut the rope. With a band playing, the balloonist did tricks on the trapeze, hanging by his knees, by one hand, and finally by his toes. However, when he was ready to return to earth, he could not release the parachute's knot. Crowds watched helplessly as he rose into the sky and disappeared. When the gases in the balloon eventually cooled, he descended again and landed only a few hundred yards from his starting point.

A historical marker in Prospect Hill Cemetery in Wessington Springs tells the heroic story of Cleveland T. Hall, credited with carrying the message that saved Washington, D.C., during the Civil War. Gen. Jubal Early of the Confederacy defeated Union forces in the Shenandoah Valley, then crossed the Potomac and routed Gen. Lew Wallace's divisions at the Battle of Monocacy, leaving the road to Washington open. Communications between the Union field commanders and the city had been destroyed.

Hall, serving with General Wallace, suffered seven bullet wounds and two saber cuts in the battle. Nonetheless, he rode through Confederate lines to warn the capital. Rebels shot several horses from under him, but each time he grabbed another mount and continued. He reached Washington in time for the army to deploy a thousand artillerymen under the command of a Captain Dupont, repelling General Early's forces at the city's limits. Hall, like many other Civil War veterans, moved to Wessington Springs in 1882; he married Nettie C. Weems, a pioneering woman doctor. In spite of this intelligent choice of a wife, he died at forty-seven from the wounds suffered at Monocacy twenty-two years earlier.

WOONSOCKET

The not-so-subtle mind of Chicago, Milwaukee & St. Paul Railroad agent Charles H. Prior appears in the name of Woonsocket, named for a town in Rhode Island; one source claims the name is Indian for "city of mists," which seems unlikely. The Fort Ridgely and South Pass Wagon Road, which passed through the present town site, was surveyed in 1856-57, but the town was actually formed at the junction of the two Milwaukee Road rail lines in 1883. Within nine months the population had swollen to 1,800, inspiring railroad workers to nickname the place "Boom-strucket." As often happened in pioneering villages, the first child born after incorporation was named for the town—Ralph Woonsocket Elliot, a tough handle to carry.

Typically, the first building in town was a saloon, but a minister appeared on the first Sabbath after settlers began drifting in, according to a local history written by S. S. Judy and Will Robinson. Arriving in total darkness, the Reverend J. B. Currens stepped off the train from Mitchell into water and mud that nearly filled his shoes. He stumbled toward the only light he could see, tripping over piles of lumber that would become houses and stores, bumping into haphazardly parked wagons, and falling into mud holes. He even ran into a cow that was stabled in the middle of the street.

When he knocked at the door of the hotel, he was informed that he was too late for supper. The hotel was unfinished: Walls weren't plastered, wood shavings covered the floor; and no beds had been built. The minister and five other men propped themselves up in chairs around the wood stove and tried to sleep. About midnight, the proprietor and his wife came in with two new straw ticks they had made after their guests arrived, and the six men arranged themselves on the floor to sleep the rest of the night, sharing one blanket. Sleep still didn't come easily; men yelled and fired pistols around several busy saloons. The next day, apparently undaunted, the Reverend Currens held services in a carpenter's shop.

Old-timers sometimes wistfully relate a story, which also appears in the WPA guide, of what Woonsocket could have become. Early in the town's history, it seems, a man named Post asked town fathers to donate land on which he would build a cereal factory. But officials were skeptical of the stranger's intentions, despite his assurances that Woonsocket, in the heart of the grain belt, would benefit from establishment of his business. Woonsocket refused Post's request, so he took his proposal to the more agreeable officials at another grain-growing town—Battle Creek, Michigan. The problem with this story, of course, is that Battle Creek is the home of Kellogg's cereals, not Post's.

John Brown's Mound

In the middle of Sanborn County is a single huge dune called Big Mound or, for no apparent reason, John Brown's Mound. According to legends related by Judy and Robinson, a dugout in the mound was the haunt of horse thieves. Behind the dugout, stories say, was a large cave, where stolen horses could remain hidden. One settler camped near the mound allegedly lost his oxen and never found them. After repeated thefts in the neighborhood, officers hid and watched the dugout all day without seeing anything suspicious. During the night, they asked at the dugout for food and shelter; while they ate, one heard a horse whinny behind a curtain. The officers investigated and found enough evidence to take the thieves to trial at Elk Point, where they were convicted.

Robinson comments delicately that "what is fact and what is legend, perhaps, has become confused over the years as regards this mound." Nevertheless, he proceeds to tell of one Belcher, a cattleman who came to live with his wife in the dugout. One summer, another rancher grazed his cattle nearby and became friends with the couple. When it came time to sell this man's cattle at Fort Thompson, the Belchers helped load them on the ferry. When the final load of cattle embarked, Mr. Belcher didn't get on the ferry; instead, he rode his horse into the river. Suddenly, "a rifle bullet knocked him from his horse and into the stream. The cattleman and the new widow proceeded west" with the valuable herd; apparently she was a lot friendlier with the neighbor than her husband suspected.

FORESTBURG

After glacial Lake Dakota drained away down the James River, sand blowing off the old lake bed turned the entire region into a wilderness of dunes. The sandy soil makes the county a prime center for pumpkins, squash, muskmelons, morel mushrooms, and watermelons; Forestburg is known as the "Watermelon Capital of Dakota."

The area's first real road, the Fort Ridgely and South Pass Wagon Road, crossed the James River seven miles north of the present town in 1857, where a rock ford constructed by Col. W. H. Nobles still exists, along with a monument to his achievements. O. E. Rolvaag's *Giants in the Earth* mentions that the original settlement was located on the homestead of Sanborn County's first white settler and first postmaster, William T. Santee. Santee noticed that fires, often deliberately set by farmers as a way of clearing land, had destroyed much of the region's timber. He changed the name of the community to Forestburg to encourage protection of the remaining grove of trees so settlers would realize that trees were an asset. When the Milwaukee railroad reached the area in 1883, the town was moved two miles north of the site of Santee's homestead to its present location.

In 1903 H. A. Rodee, who owned the original grove in a horseshoe bend of the James River, noted that neighborhood residents used the area for picnics. He cut down many of the 150-year-old trees (though one elm remained that three men with joined hands couldn't reach around) and built an amphitheater, dance pavilion, hotel, and cottages for summer use, calling the area Ruskin Park. Chautauquas, plays, programs, meetings, and picnics soon made the bare area he'd created from a forest the cultural center of the county, where residents erected tents for summer camping. Dancing, roller skating, golf, tennis, baseball, boating, horse racing, and automobile racing were included in the entertainments, and the mile-long racetrack was, said the editors of the WPA guide, "known to racing drivers from Indianapolis to Denver as being one of the fastest dirt tracks in the world." A railroad station accommodated special trains of vacationers.

ARTESIAN

Originally called Diana, the town took on its current name when residents realized it lay in the center of a basin of water under such pressure that it would shoot from the ground. The first U.S. discovery of artesian water was in Yankton, says Robert Karolevitz in *Challenge*, where a contractor agreed to drill a well to 1,500 feet for $4 a foot. On August 29, 1881, at 460 feet, the first artesian gusher came in; the water shot into the air and spilled down hillsides. The well at Woonsocket was reckoned the world's most powerful, with a stream of water that rocketed 96 feet into the air. News spread fast; soon everyone in the region was drilling wells that gushed fountains of water. Promoters, wildly exaggerating as usual, predicted that the water was without limits and that Dakota would have fountains on every quarter section; most folks allowed the water to run without restrictions. As pressure dropped, wells dribbled instead of gushing, excitement dwindled, and everyone went back to farming and praying for rain.

PRAIRIE VILLAGE

Prairie Village, an outdoor museum, is west of Madison; it preserves some of the flavor of pioneer days with a sod house and almost sixty other restored historic buildings from the area, plus an

1893 steam carousel with hand-carved wooden horses. In 1961 local citizens created the Prairie Historical Society, dedicated to preserving antique machinery in a living museum.

Each August for nearly thirty years, the village has been the site of an annual Steam Threshing Jamboree, attracting more than twenty-five thousand people. Both gas- and steam-powered harvesters demonstrate grain threshing, wagon trains wind toward town from all over the country, more than three hundred antique cars and machines parade, and workhorse teams compete in plowing and pulling contests. Displays include the Chapel Car Emmanuel, a railroad car specifically designed and constructed as a moving church to reach pioneers who hadn't gotten around to erecting one yet. Old-style melodramas are presented to visitors, and fiddlers keep the tunes lively.

One of the buildings at Prairie Village is the Opera House, where Lawrence Welk first played. The building was originally constructed in Oldham in 1912 by Socialist Party members, who had been refused permission to meet in the Main Street Opera House. Party backers financed the new structure, which featured a balcony, stage, fly system, and modern seating. After Theodore Roosevelt destroyed the Socialist Party movement, membership declined, and the hall was eventually sold to Tom McAllister of Madison. "With typical prairie frugality," wrote Ardyce Habeger Samp in *South Dakota High Liner*, McAllister chiseled the last three letters from "Socialist," turning the building into the "Social Hall."

By 1916 the community had organized a chautauqua, which presented programs of speeches, music, and entertainment, leaning heavily on ethnic humor, the style of the day. In 1924, when Lawrence Welk was traveling through the state with other musicians looking for work, they discovered the Potato Festival in Oldham. Welk played his accordion in the lobby of a small hotel for tips and was asked to bring his band to the Opera House to play for a dance.

That dance started Welk on the road to success—sort of. After his debut in Oldham, Welk formed his own band in 1927. The group was heading to New Orleans when they were stranded by a blizzard in Yankton. The next morning Welk wandered into the studios of radio station WNAX and was offered an audition by Chan Gurney, owner. When he returned with band members, they discovered Gurney intended to put them on the air live. By the time they'd played the first selection, phone lines were jammed with calls from listeners wanting more. After the band played again in the afternoon, Gurney offered them a week-long contract, then a second, and before long Welk and his group had been in Yankton for nine years. After he grew so famous that ten secretaries handled over two hundred thousand letters a week, Welk still answered all South Dakota mail personally.

MADISON

Lake County, twenty-four miles square—and it is almost precisely square—was organized in 1873 and named for its most obvious feature. The county's primary town, Madison, lies in the center and was named for Madison, Wisconsin. It was originally settled in 1875; by 1880 more than twenty-six hundred people lived in the town. The first train arrived in 1881, and settlement boomed, with smaller towns such as Junius, Ramona, Nunda, and Rutland scattered around it. The same year settlers established a state normal school, but it didn't begin offering classes until 1883; the first building burned in 1885, but the school persisted and was later dubbed General Beadle State College, in honor of its first president, Brig. Gen. William Henry Harrison Beadle. Later named Dakota State College, it eventually became Dakota State University.

Beadle was colorful and controversial, the way Westerners prefer their characters, and the kind of man necessary to the complicated process of civilization. Beadle has been called the patron saint of Dakota schools, but he was also accused of rebelling against the Union. Appointed surveyor general of Dakota Territory in 1869 by President U. S. Grant, Beadle became active in school affairs in Yankton. He battled for legislative matters and statehood constitutional provisions he considered essential, particularly regarding school land. In the legislature, he successfully promoted the township system for administration of rural schools, including a basis for electing school board members and for allowing several townships to establish a single, consolidated high school, farsighted provisions for his day.

In 1879 Beadle was appointed territorial superintendent of public education by Governor William Howard, a job for which he received only $500 a year; he worked at other jobs to bring in an additional $1,000 a year, enough to support his family. Then as now, two sections of each township (numbers 16 and 36) were reserved by federal law for state use in supporting schools. The reserved land constituted one-eighteenth of the land in the territory, or more than five million acres—an area larger than the state of Massachusetts. Beadle noted that because surveying funds were inadequate, squatters were appropriating choice lands that should be reserved for schools. He'd heard a rumor that speculators planned to persuade Congress to sell school lands cheaply but felt that Dakota's citizens should make decisions about the lands—which would require statehood.

Many of Beadle's school land provisions were included in the state constitution. A floor was set on the price of school lands to prevent speculators from acquiring it cheaply; lands containing minerals could not be sold for less than their appraised value; and all money from the sale of school lands was invested as a permanent school fund, with only the interest spent.

Many of these ideas influenced other western states, and a historical marker on the Dakota State University campus credits Beadle with saving twelve million acres of school lands in North and South Dakota, Montana, Idaho, Wyoming, and Washington. Beadle served as president of Dakota State University from 1889 until 1905 and as professor of history from 1905 until 1912. He died in 1915.

Grouped around Madison are remnants of other pioneer villages, most founded by various development companies in the late 1800s. Fedora is one such town; local legend says the original name was Miner or Miner Center, but because that name was too common, residents petitioned for a new name that reflected the popularity of fedora hats in Christopher Winters's store. Vilas was established by the Western Town Lot Company and named for Col. W. F. Vilas, an attorney who later became U.S. postmaster general. Howard was named on July 4, 1881, for a recently deceased son of Judge J. D. Farmer, who owned the town site. Winfred was named for someone's daughter; Junius for the son of a Milwaukee railroad agent.

Just west of Madison stands Lake Herman, once a resting place on the Indian trail from the pipestone quarries in Minnesota to Fort Thompson. White settlement began in 1870 when William Lee, John Walker, and Herman N. Luce arrived and built the Lee log cabin. Luce's cabin, built next, is preserved in a state park on the eastern shore of the lake. In four graves near the cabin lie the bodies of Luce's daughter Mary; a Mr. Abbott, a trapper and brother of Mrs. Luce killed in a blizzard in 1878; Mrs. Abbott, the mother of Mrs. Luce; and Mrs. Luce herself, who burned to death in 1881. The lake was named not for Herman Luce but for Herman, Wisconsin, where he grew up.

When Herman Luce settled on the lake, he found twenty to thirty feet of clear water filled with northern pike. The surrounding land was covered with eighteen to twenty inches of rich, organic soil. But as settlers plowed up the native grasses to plant crops and applied fertilizers and, later, pesticides, the soil began to disappear at the rate of one inch every hundred years. Much of it washed into the lake and other reservoirs, slowly filling them. Lake Herman now

This statue of Brig. Gen. William Henry Harrison Beadle used to stand in a special niche under the state capitol building rotunda. During the centennial year, Beadle's likeness was moved to make room for a new sculpture by a contemporary artist. Controversy accompanied the change, including protests from schoolchildren and teachers. —South Dakota State Historical Society

contains ten to twelve feet of silt and is filling at the rate of one inch every ten years. The first two feet, according to biologists, accumulated over eight thousand years, while the last eight feet built up in the last hundred years. Under present conditions—that is, if traditional farming practices continue—this lake and others in the region will last only another twenty to thirty years.

US 81 runs north-south the entire width of the state between the North Dakota and Nebraska state lines. Because of the geographical division of this volume, this segment ends at US 18 between Turkey Ridge and Menno; the last few miles are discussed in Part Two. From the North Dakota line to Exit 180, a couple of miles north of Watertown, US 81 is also I-29, covered separately.

SALEM

Salem was probably named by O. S. Pender, its first storekeeper and postmaster, for his hometown in Massachusetts. Soon after being settled in 1880, the town started spelling its name backwards ("Melas") to avoid confusion with a town named Salena; but Salena didn't last, so Salem resumed its forward spelling. Many state historical guides insist that Salem takes its name from a Hebrew word meaning "peace." This is absurd; the Hebrew word is "shalom." And most of the settlers were Scandinavians, though a cluster of Irish immigrants lived nearby. Three miles south of Salem, US 81 crosses I-90.

The seat of McCook County, Salem thrived for a while in the 1800s because it was the most important railroad point between Sioux Falls and Mitchell; however, with the rise of modern transportation, its location has hastened its downfall, as residents drive to one of the larger cities to shop. A series of crop failures speeded Salem's decline.

Salem celebrated its centennial in 1980, but David Holden gripes in *Dakota Visions* that townsfolk concentrated only on the area's brief white history, ignoring several million years of prehistory, eight thousand years of Indian settlement, "and the natural heritage responsible for the fertile soil upon which man's livelihood depends." It's unfair to single out Salem, but the point is valid: Most citizens of the twentieth century pay little attention to cultures that precede ours—yet without them, our culture would not exist.

In the town's hundredth year, 6,444 people were spread across Hanson County's 573 square miles. The population had dwindled more than 2,000 since 1945 and nearly 4,000 since 1925. The steady decline is typical of small towns in farming country. The 1990 census reported another severe decrease; Hanson County had only about 3,000 people, and Salem had about 1,200.

McCOOK COUNTY

Organized in 1873, McCook County drew its name from Edwin S. McCook, a Civil War general appointed secretary of Dakota Territory in 1872. He came from a family known as the "Fighting McCooks" of Ohio, and he shared his rank in the war with five other McCooks. The new secretary probably expected a long and illustrious career in the West. Unfortunately, he collided with a little man who had a pistol, promptly ending McCook's career and his life in 1873.

Robert Karolevitz explains in *Challenge* that the conflict was really a political argument that got out of hand. At a public meeting in Yankton called to discuss the problem of how to pay off bonds backed by the county for construction of the Dakota Southern Railway, McCook tangled with Peter P. Wintermute. Though many citizens favored the railroad, the political maneuvering connected with it caused confusion and hostility.

General McCook, a big man weighing 200 pounds and standing six feet tall, supported Governor John A. Burbank, one of the railroad's directors. But the general had enemies; an editor at the *Dakota Herald*, for example, called him an "ignorant, vainglorious, drunken lout, who is an eyesore to our people and a depression upon the good morals of this community." Wintermute, a banker, weighed only 135 pounds. Both men visited a Yankton saloon and billiard parlor in the basement of the St. Charles Hotel next door to the courthouse where the meeting on the Dakota Southern was being held. Reports on the incident vary, but Wintermute apparently ran out of cigars and asked McCook for a smoke or for money to buy one. McCook refused, insultingly, and Wintermute attacked him. The big general easily threw the little banker to the floor; some observers say he rubbed Wintermute's face in the contents of a spittoon. Then the general went back upstairs and headed to the courthouse, and the banker went home to clean up.

By that time, more than a hundred men had gathered in the courthouse to hear arguments on the Dakota Southern. Suddenly shots were heard, and McCook, blood pouring from his chest, charged through the door toward Peter Wintermute, standing inside the room with a smoking pistol in his hand. Though the general was mortally wounded, he threw the banker to the floor, and more shots were fired. Finally someone stepped on Wintermute's arm and took the pistol away. McCook tried to throw the banker through a window before the justice of the peace arrived to arrest Wintermute, and friends helped McCook back to his hotel room. The attending physician was Dr. Walter A. Burleigh, later a notorious Indian agent. McCook remained conscious for a while but, after following Burleigh's advice to send for his family, died early the next morning.

Wintermute was first convicted of manslaughter, but at a retrial in Vermillion almost two years later he was declared not guilty. Seventeen months later, money and health gone, he died in New York from consumption he may have gotten in his Dakota Territory jail cell, and two careers that might have concluded in the history books came to early ends.

FREEMAN

Freeman suffered from considerable confusion on the part of railroad officials. When workers were nailing signs bearing the names of new towns to the depots along the line, the name-boards of the neighboring towns of Freeman and Menno were accidentally interchanged. Thus, Freeman is named for an early settler of Menno, and Menno is named for the settlement of Mennonites at Freeman. The WPA guide of 1938 noted one problem of the close-knit Hutterian settlement: "It has been said that around Freeman and Bridgewater the woods are full of Tschetters and Hofers, with several Glanzers and Kleinsassers among them. More than forty families of Tschetters are recorded, so many in fact, that they are distinguished from each other by numbers."

A noteworthy event in Freeman's history was the Battle of the Cows, which made the little town a focus of international tensions and drew the attention of a New York newspaper in 1921. According to Reuben Goertz, an expert on Hutterian history, dairy herds in Germany were depleted after World War I, and milk and meat became so scarce that children suffered. The American Friends Service Committee (Quakers) began buying cows to feed children. One such shipment originated in Hutchinson County, with farmers from a wide region donating cows. Not everyone was in favor of the program, however, and some American Legion members tried to stop shipments; the Ku Klux Klan may have been involved. By March 1921 more than three hundred cows were held in pens near Scotland, and two hundred more at Tripp. That night about twenty-five carloads of men, and about thirty more on horses, swept down on the herds—guarded by four unarmed boys—and opened fire. Cars were driven over frightened, bawling, stampeding cattle; many were killed or injured. Others calved in the bedlam.

The next day, volunteers rounded up the remaining cows and drove them to a pasture west of Kaylor, southwest of Freeman. A fenced corral was turned into a stockade, and two to three hundred deputized farmers stood guard with rifles and shotguns; some hid behind tombstones in a nearby cemetery. American Legion wives provided hot food. Late that night, about thirty cars roared up to the stockade. As they paused, perhaps to reconsider, the sheriff assured them the first man to cross a fence would be fired on by two hundred men. The attackers retreated. Later, fourteen men were arrested, charged with carrying concealed weapons, and fined for their part in the stampede.

Controversy ensued; some say Governor Henry McMaster refused to intervene, but a U.S. marshal came to Tripp. About seven hundred cows were loaded on twenty-six train cars, which carried guards and passed at double speed through towns where threats had been made. The guards had plenty of work; the cattle had to be milked and fed daily as the train headed east. Once they were loaded on a ship, the milking continued for the eighteen-day passage to Germany, where people lined both sides of the locks in the Wesser River to greet the shipment. The men handed out free milk all the way upriver.

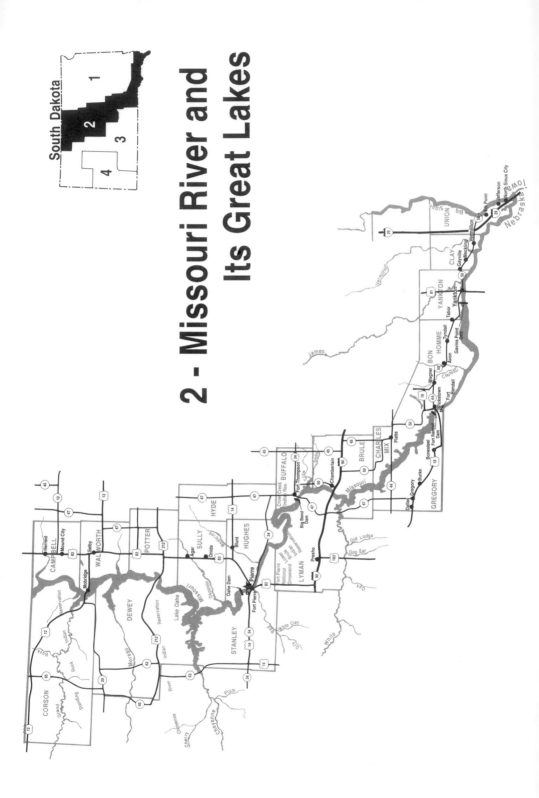

2 - Missouri River and Its Great Lakes

PART TWO

The Missouri River and Its Great Lakes

The Missouri River is like a great vein running through the heart of the Dakotas. The ease of traveling on or along the water lured Indian tribes and explorers into the region. Later, furs and other wealth flowed, as does the water, to the east and south. Because the fur trade centered in St. Louis, most of the money made from this harvest of animals from the rich bottomlands and prairies remained there. Modern Dakotans sometimes reflect that as the state began, so it continues: Many modern resources are produced in a way that sends the profits out of state, while problems and shortages remain in South Dakota. When the river was dammed, it was made to serve the state by providing electric power, irrigation, and tourist dollars. But the dams flooded land given to Indians driven out of eastern Dakota by settlement, exacerbating racial conflict. The dams also deprived downstream states of flows they could use for irrigation and tourism.

The Missouri straddles the most important invisible historical feature in South Dakota—the hundredth meridian. East of the line the land is generally considered tallgrass prairie, fertile and well watered. West of the line are the great short-grass prairies, land of the cowboy hat and the horse trailer, where men wave at passersby with one finger raised over the steering wheel. Near the river, the grass in some years resembles its pre-settlement quality, but only because much of this land is part of the Fort Pierre National Grasslands. Parts of these grasslands are divided into community pastures leased to ranchers for grazing, and others provide government game refuges and recreation sites where hunters may find game that reminds them of pioneer days. Plowing is not allowed.

The state often leads the nation in the production of oats, rye, and flaxseed and is among the top three in honey, sunflowers, and

Carl Bodmer's painting of the "Missouri River Snags" shows the dangers to boats on the tricky Missouri. When high water hid snags and sandbars, piloting became dangerous; recently, divers have located wreckage from steamboats sunk on the muddy Missouri bottom in the early 1800s. —State Historical Society of North Dakota

alfalfa hay and seed, crops produced in the strip of land on both sides of the river. Yet this region has few major highways and only five middle-sized towns—Mobridge, Pierre, Chamberlain, Yankton, and Vermillion.

Indians in Competition

Historians believe that a severe drought in Nebraska and Kansas started the Arikara people moving northward along the Missouri River valley. In the sixteenth century, the central Dakota tribes reached the peak of their development, with fortified villages set on high plateaus along the Missouri to take advantage of the protection, game, and water furnished by the river. Outside each cluster of earth houses stood picket stockades behind deep ditches; villagers gardened, stored food, and worked inside the protective fence. In the early seventeenth century, their most prosperous period, at least thirty-two solid, permanent villages lay along the river, with four thousand warriors to defend them.

Carl Bodmer's painting of the "Mandan Village and Bullboats" from Travels in the Interior of North America *shows the earth lodges of the Hidatsa and Arikaras that existed until white men's diseases wiped them out in the nineteenth century. The round bullboats were made of untanned buffalo hide stretched over a frame of willow sapplings.* —State Historical Society of North Dakota

The Arikara were not nomadic; they settled permanently along the river, governing themselves through a loose confederacy with chiefs in each village. They hunted game, grew gardens, made pottery and baskets, and were busy traders, swapping extra corn, vegetables, and a native tobacco for meat, skins, and buffalo robes. They probably first acquired horses in trade with the Kiowa, Comanche, and Pawnee, who stole or bought them from southwestern Spaniards; by 1760, horses were a regular trade item and served to keep their relationship with the Lakota mutually beneficial.

After 1700 the Lakota and other tribes were pushed west, competing with the Arikara for game and forcing them to concentrate in fewer and more heavily fortified villages. By the end of the eighteenth century, warfare and smallpox had cut the Arikara population to two villages. They first encountered white fur traders at the mouth of the Grand River in northern South Dakota. Initially, the Arikara welcomed the meeting, believing they would have new customers for trade and perhaps protection from the stronger tribes. In 1832 an Arikara remnant moved into North Dakota with a frag-

A marble monument marks the spot where the Verendrye brothers buried a lead plate claiming a vast region for France; it was found in 1913 by schoolchildren and is on display in the State Historical Museum in Pierre.
—South Dakota State Historical Society

HERE ON
MARCH 30,1743,
THE VERENDRYES
BURIED A LEAD
TABLET TO CLAIM
THIS REGION FOR
FRANCE. THIS
TABLET FOUND
ON FEB. 16,1913, IS
THE FIRST WRITTEN
RECORD OF THE
VISIT OF WHITE
MEN TO
SOUTH DAKOTA.
ERECTED BY
STATE HISTORICAL
SOCIETY
AND FT. PIERRE
COMMERCIAL CLUB
1933

ment of the Mandans, another once-numerous tribe of peaceful farmers who could not withstand the invasion of the warlike tribes and the whites, with their dubious gift of alcohol and their diseases—smallpox, tuberculosis, scarlet fever, venereal disease, and the common cold—against which the Indians had no defense.

At the same time, other Indians were moving into and around the central Plains. According to French priests who visited the area in the 1640s, the Lakota lived west of Lake Superior on the headwaters of the Mississippi and were armed only with bows and arrows. Before long, several tribes in the region were drawn into conflict when the French and British, both eager for territory in the New World and needing help from armed Indian allies, supplied the Cree with guns. The Cree began to push the Lakota south, and the Chippewa, also given guns by traders, pushed another Lakota band southwest. At roughly the same time, with game in the eastern woods more difficult to find, the Lakota discovered the usefulness of bison and started pursuing the herds west, into the James River valley in

Dakota and eventually to the Missouri. Their activity encouraged the Omahas and Poncas to drift south into Nebraska.

The Fur Trade Opens

Fur trappers and traders visited the heart of the Plains beginning in the 1600s, using rivers to transport furs and supplies. The French had particularly strong claims in the central Plains because they'd ventured here so long before most other explorers. About 1743 the Verendrye brothers entered the state from the west or northwest, trekked east to the Missouri, and then headed north to Canada, passing by Bear Butte on their route. While near Fort Pierre, they met a white man who said that a Frenchman had lived for years three days' journey away, but they didn't investigate.

The Verendryes left a metal plate claiming the region for France. Written in Latin and French, it was found in 1913 near the mouth of the Bad River by three teenagers—Leslie Stoup, Harriet Foster, and George O'Rielly—from Fort Pierre. The enterprising O'Rielly suggested that they sell the plate for type metal and headed toward the local print shop, carrying the precious artifact. Fortunately for history, the group met two state legislators who convinced the teenagers to take it to Doane Robinson, state historian. Happy historians gave the discoverers a reward of more than $700, and the plate became the property of the South Dakota State Historical Society, where it's displayed. A Verendrye monument stands in Fort Pierre, where the tablet was found; cross the railroad tracks and take the first street to the right about half a mile to a hill.

The late 1700s were busy on the Missouri. In 1783 English traders began to visit the Mandans in North Dakota, arriving through eastern Canada and sometimes descending along the Missouri into southern Dakota. Jacques d'Eglise, representing Spain, was on the Upper Missouri between 1791 and 1795. But most of these excursions were visits only, intended to find a route to the western ocean or to anything that might be valuable; most of these pioneers did not intend to trade or settle.

That changed in 1794, when a group of St. Louis merchants with vision and an acute eye for profit formed the Commercial Company for the Discovery of Nations of the Upper Missouri, usually referred to as "the Missouri Company," and sent Jean Baptiste Truteau (Trudeau in some sources) up the Missouri. The company's lengthy instructions to Truteau make it clear that speedy profit wasn't their only motive. Truteau was ordered to build a trading post at the Mandan villages, gather news of any waterways that might furnish

Thirteen states, including the two Dakotas, were eventually carved from the Louisiana Purchase acquired by President Thomas Jefferson for nearly three cents an acre. —State Historical Society of North Dakota

a continuous water passage between the Atlantic and the Pacific, note the location of Indian villages and how they were led, and make observations of plant and animal life. Like Lewis and Clark, Truteau was an agent of ambitious plans to build a new empire.

Truteau, caught by the Teton and Yankton Lakota and forced to "trade at a loss," as Donald D. Parker politely says in *South Dakota History*, spent the winter in a cabin somewhere near the present Fort Randall Dam. The Omahas followed him, settled down nearby, and "compelled Truteau to give them goods on credit."

Enter the United States

France sold its territory west of the Mississippi River to the United States as the Louisiana Purchase in 1803, partly because Napoleon was determined to keep the riches of the region away from the British. With satisfaction and foresight, Napoleon said of the sale, "I have just given to England a maritime rival, that will sooner or later humble her pride."

The Louisiana Purchase of 1803 changed the Plains by changing their white owners. Thomas Jefferson referred to the unknown land he'd bought as "The Great Interior Valley" and believed the land would forever support the nation of farmers he envisioned. Workers, he thought, need never be locked in factories to earn a living; the Louisiana Purchase would allow everyone to farm happily for generations.

Before the era of Plains agriculture, however, there came the era of the fur trade. This industry reached its peak between 1830 and 1840 and kept the Missouri River currents busy. The most important fur post was at the mouth of the Teton River, or Bad River, at what became known as Fort Pierre. An estimate from 1830 said shipments to St. Louis from the country above the Big Sioux River included about 26,000 buffalo robes, 25,000 pounds of beaver fur, more than 37,000 muskrat furs, 4,000 otter furs, and 150,000 deer skins.

Hundreds of Indians and trappers hunted the rivers and lakes of the West, harvesting furs and decimating the wildlife population until around 1840, when the market for dressed fur declined in Eu-

Thomas Jefferson had a deep scientific interest in the huge chunk of continent he bought from Napoleon for $15 million. He persuaded Congress to provide $2,500 to outfit a scientific expedition led by Meriwether Lewis and William Clark and dubbed it the "Corps of Discovery."
—State Historical Society of North Dakota

rope. Toward the end of the fur trade period, a few ex-traders settled along valleys and began raising cattle or cutting wood to supply steamboats. They hunted buffalo for food, but they were not farmers or ranchers, and most retired to St. Louis or points east. Many of them left behind children by Indian wives; these mixed-blood descendants still live in South Dakota, a reminder of the early exploration.

Traders bargained for furs with the Lakota as the tribe began its move westward to the Plains, forced out by white settlement in areas to the east. Right behind the traders and Indians were more settlers, eager to farm the rich soil along the river valleys. Groups of settlers clustered along the north-south line now made by the highway; as railroads and other enterprises moved in, some communities died or were moved to a train stop, whereas the population of others exploded with merchants serving the farm and military economy that dominated Dakota Territory.

Flood Control and More

The Missouri River appears docile to travelers on the highway, but it has violent seasons. It goes on periodic rampages that change its channel, creating new land and wiping out old. In March 1862 an unusual ice gorge formed near the mouth of the James River, flooding the entire valley. Another damaging flood struck in the spring of 1881, after an unusually severe winter. The WPA guide says a village called Green Island was destroyed; within two hours after the first mass of ice struck, every building was drifting with the current. "Settlers 30 miles downstream told of seeing a building float by and of hearing bells tolling uncannily as the structure bobbed up and down in the surging river."

Dakotans dreamed for years of controlling the wild Missouri, which an Interior Department study in 1945 referred to as "water in the wrong place at the wrong time." In 1943 and 1944 alone, devastating Missouri floods caused more than $100 million in damages. In 1944 Congress passed the Flood Control Act, combining a plan by Col. Lewis A. Pick for flood control and navigation with a plan by Bureau of Reclamation engineer William Sloan for irrigation and power generation. The Pick-Sloan Plan provided for construction of a hundred dams and reservoirs along the length of the Missouri and its tributaries.

Four of the five biggest dams were built in South Dakota. Oahe Dam, constructed between 1948 and 1964 near Pierre, is the largest rolled-earth dam in the world; standing 242 feet high, it holds back water for some 250 miles upstream. Next along the river's southward course is Big Bend Dam, north of Chamberlain, which was built between 1960 and 1966. Just north of where the river begins forming the border between South Dakota and Nebraska is the Fort Randall Dam; begun near Lake Andes in 1946, it was completed ten years later. Farthest south is the Gavin's Point Dam near Yankton, which was built between 1952 and 1956.

The resulting lakes are not conveniently called by the names of the dams; that would be too simple. Instead, Lewis and Clark Lake is behind Gavin's Point, Lake Francis Case is behind Fort Randall Dam, and Lake Sharpe is behind Big Bend; more logically, Lake Oahe lies behind Oahe Dam. The statistics on Lewis and Clark Lake illustrate the size and power of the dams: Though only forty-five feet at its deepest, it holds water drained from 280,000 square miles and has 90 miles of shoreline.

The plan was supposed to stop flooding, provide clean, cheap hydroelectric power, provide a stable channel for downstream navigation, and promote irrigation. Within limits, it has done all but the latter.

Despite below-average rainfall during many years since the dams were built, enough water has remained to promote tourist facilities centered on the dams. The river and lakes buzz with powerboats; the air hums with fishing lines and electricity. The dams generate

Carl Bodmer painted a panoramic view of Fort Pierre, including an Indian lookout and tipis surrounding the fort, about 1833. —South Dakota State Historical Society

cash as well as power; money comes from sport and commercial fishing as well as recreation. As much as twelve million pounds of commercial fish are shipped to markets in Iowa, Illinois, and New York. Dozens of new recreation-oriented businesses have sprung up. The purity of the waters of the great lakes of South Dakota, compared to that of the natural Great Lakes, makes fishing attractive to trophy seekers as well as ordinary fishing enthusiasts—in South Dakota, you can actually eat the fish you catch.

The dam plan, however, has not been an unmitigated success. There have been, and will be, negative effects of the flood control project. As the river bluffs erode with the rise and fall of water, silt is building up, filling the lakes. Roger Holtzmann says, "downstream navigation may not be possible at all after the year 2000 unless drastic (expensive) measures are taken." In short, a project undertaken in part to improve navigation may stop it instead. In recent years, more potential trouble has surfaced. South Dakota has argued for reduced flows to downstream states so its lakes can remain high enough to support the increasingly lucrative recreational industry. Several states dependent on the river for irrigation, navigation, and their own recreational activities have threatened lawsuits to determine whose water rights take precedence.

Roy Houck, whose Triple U Ranch now lies beneath Lake Oahe, thinks the dams' effects will get worse in the future. Besides flooding many ranches and farms, the dam obliterated four town sites, although Cannonball and Forest City were small and might have disappeared anyway. Cheyenne Agency, the Cheyenne River Indian Reservation's largest settlement, was moved fifty miles west to Eagle Butte. Pollock, on the Missouri's east bank three miles from the North Dakota border, survived after its five hundred residents elected to stick together. Once the new town site was selected, a mile south of the previous position, residents chose their new homes by lot. Old homes and business properties were assessed, and owners were paid full value. Then the Army Corps of Engineers allowed them to repurchase their homes at salvage value, as low as twelve cents on the dollar.

Though promoters of the reservoirs promised they would cover little valuable land, more than six hundred thousand acres of river bottomlands are underwater today. Nearly fifty-six thousand acres on the Standing Rock Reservation and over a hundred thousand acres on the Cheyenne River Reservation were flooded, and reservation life was seriously disrupted. More than a third of the state's Indian families had to be relocated, which has led to years of related problems. The flooded land was the only timbered area on the reserva-

132

Indians parade with a large drum on the side of a horse endorsing "Pierre for Capital" in this undated photo. —Courtesy of James Aplan

tions, as well as a refuge for much of the wildlife, and plants for medicine, dyes, and other uses grew there. Some experts estimate that the dams reduced wild game and plants on the reservations by 75 percent, reducing the Indians' ability to carry on their normal lifestyle in a state where they are already among the poorest inhabitants.

Another issue involves the loss of historical information about the Indians and early white settlers as archaeological sites along the river are destroyed by erosion. Some sites are accessible to vandals and boaters, including looters who profit from the illegal sale of artifacts. Other sites, higher on the bluffs, are endangered as banks are undercut by wave action. In this region, settlements and trade posts were drowned by the waters of Lake Oahe. The names of forts that once sheltered traders and drew trappers read like a list of explorers: Manuel Lisa, LaFramboise, Galpin, Pierre, Bennett, Sully, Tecumseh, George, Teton, Hale, Randall. Many answers to our questions about seventeenth-century relationships between traders and the tribes might be lost at such sites—buried, covered by water, eroding with the dam's rising and falling action, probably lost to history forever.

James Haug, the state archaeologist, testified in 1991 that the Army Corps of Engineers is pursuing a "deliberate policy of neglect" by gutting its regional archaeological staff and manipulating its budget to guarantee that no money is spent protecting the sites. Haug made his charges in testimony before the House Subcommittee on Water Resources in Washington, which is looking into the feud between upstream and downstream states over how the Corps manages water releases from the river's six reservoirs. One of the three archaeologists in the Omaha, Nebraska, office responsible for Corps projects in a district that extends from Colorado to Iowa said the charges were untrue. It should be noted, however, that the shoreline of the Upper Missouri River alone is as long as the Atlantic Coast of the United States.

The story of the consequences of damming the mighty Missouri will probably continue as long as water flows in the river.

For Further Reading:

Stanley Vestal's *The Missouri* tells much of the history of the region drained by the river. Joseph Mills Hanson's *Conquest of the Missouri* tells the story of Capt. Grant Marsh, famous steamboat pilot who brought wounded back from the Battle of the Little Bighorn. Herbert Hart's *Tour Guide to Old Forts of Montana, Wyoming, North and South Dakota* is a quick guide to the fur trade and forts, but it is frustrating in its brevity. Mari Sandoz's *The Beaver Men* is an entertaining source of information on the era of the fur trade.

Faye Cashett Lewis's story, *Nothing to Make A Shadow*, tells of her experiences homesteading with her family near Dallas, west of the Missouri River, in 1909. Elizabeth Cook-Lynn's books, *The Power of Horses and Other Stories*, and a novel, *From the River's Edge*, show both the strength the Indians derived from their connection with the land, and their bitterness over its loss, as well as showing how Indians were treated by whites on and around the reservations. Cook-Lynn grew up at Fort Thompson on the Crow Creek Indian Reservation.

This segment of I-90 runs east-west between the western borders of Lyman County near Vivian and Aurora County east of Kimball. Much of this stretch of highway crosses the high plateaus flanking the river, with dramatic views from the bluffs on either side. As the highway swoops down the ragged bluffs to a bridge near Oacoma, one can look upstream to older crossings and downstream to Lake Francis Case, which makes the river appear wider and more impressive than it would naturally be. Trees clothe the gullies slashing downward; waterfowl feed on the river and use it for a flyway. In spring and fall, watch for flocks of geese, cranes, and other migratory species. On the east side of the river is a rest area with excellent views and good walking trails.

A good deal of history was transacted in this region by the Indian tribes and white explorers; the Missouri River provided a natural highway for anyone with a canoe. On September 16-17, 1804, Lewis and Clark camped a mile and a half above Corvus Creek, later called American Crow Creek, north of the present site of Oacoma. They called their camp "Plumb" or "Pleasant Camp" and stayed two days "dressing skins, drying, washing and mending their clothes." Two years later, on August 28, 1806, they used the same campsite as they were returning home.

Few whites settled in this area until after the Indians were moved to reservations. When Samuel H. Morrow surveyed the area in November 1868, he found a ranch on American Creek but did not name the rancher. An early homesteader, Iva King, told of an experience that exemplifies the kind of misunderstandings that arose between white and Indian. She was washing her baby's clothes in the kitchen when some instinct prompted her to check on the child in the next room. She found four Indians warming themselves at the stove. One bent over the cradle, then picked up the child. Terrified and presuming that her child was being kidnapped, Iva threw herself against the outside door. The Indians spoke, but she understood nothing. Thinking she had to barter for the child, she snatched up a plug of her husband's chewing tobacco, pressed it into the Indian's hand, and jerked the child away from him. Her husband returned in the evening, laughing. He'd met Flying Eagle and three of his friends on the ferry, and heard how Iva had given the man tobacco as a present for admiring her child. Unfortunately, many Indian-white misunderstandings resulted in far more tragic consequences.

PRESHO

The state marker on Presho's main street is notable for retaining the phony dialect only used by Westerners in movies. Here's a sample, in case you don't get to Main Street:

HOW COME THEY CALLED IT PRESHO: Wal partner, in 1862 when the Civil War was being fit and Dakota Territory took in everything South of Canada to the Rocky Mountains, the legislature gave a ferry license across the Old Muddy down at Yankton to J. S. Presho. Come 1872 they were casting round for a name to call a great big new county they were carving out of the Great Sioux Reservation. Someone said Presho and that was it. It was 1889 til the Guvment started to small down that big reservation and let white folks in. The whites came on filtering in and hankering for mail.

There's much more, if you "hanker" to read it. You'll find friendly folks in Presho. But if you hear anyone talking the way this sign reads, they'll be tourists.

Presho's busiest era probably was the early 1900s, when land was taken from the Lakota reservations in the area and awarded to homesteaders by lottery. Registrars filling out forms for the hopeful lined both sides of the street, using dry-goods boxes and nail kegs for tables. Between the officials were hot dog and coffee salesmen screaming advertisements; popcorn and peanut vendors pushed through the crowds. Even notaries used megaphones to announce their services; the post office stayed open all night, as did hotels, saloons, motion picture theaters, and gambling houses. According to the WPA guide for South Dakota, "eight minutes after the first town lot was offered for sale in 1905, a bank, composed of two barrels and a plank, opened for business. At first the bank operated day and night in serving the frantic rush of homesteaders, and the cashier was compelled to carry a six-shooter and all the currency with him when he went to lunch."

For a time, Presho's population stood at nearly three thousand people (almost five times its current number of residents) and the town was one of the busiest points for baling and shipping hay in the United States. Between 1890 and 1915, farmers plowed up nearly half of Lyman County, but they had crossed the river into arid country, and the boom didn't last. Today, the Fort Pierre National Grasslands lies in northwest Lyman and adjacent counties where homesteaders visualized farms.

LOWER BRULÉ INDIAN RESERVATION

A few miles northeast of Presho is the Lower Brulé Indian Reservation. Brulé leaders Iron Nation, White Buffalo Cow, and Little

Pheasant signed a treaty in 1865 agreeing to live on a reservation twenty miles long and ten miles back from the Missouri River between White River and Fort Lookout. The eighteen-hundred-member Lower Brulé tribe was to get $6,000 a year, with a $5 bonus going to farming families. The next year the Indians planted grain and were pleased when their harvest yielded two thousand bushels. That same year, agent Joseph Hanson estimated eight hundred "hostiles" and seven hundred "friendlies" living on the reservation, and he noted that they acknowledged no chief. Since the Lakota followed chiefs only for specific purposes and none of their people had any prior experience in farming, it wasn't unusual that they had no real leadership for their new life. The reservation was later enlarged and moved to north of Fort Lookout, where the band held 472,550 acres.

"Brulé" means "burnt thighs" or "burned backs." According to one version of the Lakota legend, the name resulted from a disastrous raiding expedition against the Pawnees in Nebraska. The Pawnees, on learning of the hostile party's approach, set fire to the prairie and caught the raiders in the flaming trap. Some died, but the majority escaped and returned home severely blistered. Other tribesmen derisively called them *sicangu*, meaning "burned thighs," later translated by French traders as *brulé*, "burned." Some modern members of the tribe now prefer to call themselves *sicangu*.

CHAMBERLAIN

Brule City, fifteen miles below American Island at the narrowest part of the river, was settled in 1879 and became the first county seat when settlers assumed the railroad would cross there. But the tracks were laid along American Creek to a site named for Selah Chamberlain, a Chicago, Milwaukee & St. Paul Railroad official. The town became county seat in the 1881 election, with twenty-five families in residence. The Indian name of the area, Makah Teepee, meant "mud house," in honor of a recluse who lived there in a dugout. The Sioux no doubt found such behavior odd and preferred the airy height of their tipis.

The winter of 1880-81 brought deep snow followed by the inevitable spring floods that shoved thick river ice up onto holdings adjoining the river. Much of the construction of the previous year was destroyed, so the railroad didn't actually reach Chamberlain until 1882; the first train crossed the river in 1905 during a Fourth of July celebration.

Materials for Chamberlain's first buildings were brought in on the steamboat *C. K. Peck*; during the 1880s and 1890s, service by boat and rail brought dozens of passengers a day. By 1890 two

Steamboats like the F. Y. Batchelor *hauled building materials upriver to Chamberlain and brought furs downriver. In this undated photo, the steamboat carries troops from Fort Yates, headquarters of the Standing Rock Reservation on the Missouri River.* —State Historical Society of North Dakota

hundred businesses were established in town. For about twenty-five years, Chamberlain was a busy cattle-shipping city that served as the railhead for the cattle-raising White River valley to the west and the Crow Creek and Lower Brulé reservations upriver.

During Chamberlain's busy early years the notorious Nelson Road House stood at the junction of American Creek with the Missouri, just north of town. Some roadhouses were tidy hotels, and the notorious ones furnished extra amenities: beds equipped with tiny livestock, liquor that might be brewed in the back room, and the companionship of females who specialized in relieving the traveler of his money. This one was constructed with timbers two feet apart, and the spaces were filled with mud bricks; the outside walls were boarded over and the inner walls covered with plaster. The roof was thatched with long grass, later shingled over. Custer and his troops used the house as a headquarters on their way to the Black Hills in 1875.

Chamberlain has always been a stopping place for people on their way somewhere else, a fact that largely explains the community's development. Land seekers stayed in town long enough to arrange for homesteads, then packed their belongings on wagons or train cars and moved on to settle between the Cheyenne and White rivers. During this century, there have been periodic booms. During the thirties, a Civilian Conservation Corps camp drew hundreds of men from farms and ranches to find work with the Work Projects Administration, including building a Boy Scout camp on American Island. In the 1940s, large deposits of low-grade manganese were found along the river near town, but the deposits cannot be mined economically. The building of Fort Randall Dam brought another boom in the 1960s.

Chamberlain's location on the east slope of the river valley, its many parks, and the fact that much of the development catering to tourists is built on the outskirts of town, close to I-90, has kept the community quiet and beautiful, though civic leaders might have preferred growth. In recent years, with the town's population at around two thousand, developers have begun to work to exploit the town's history as a means of keeping some of the traffic over the bridge in town long enough for tourists to leave some cash. A major marina is planned, and the Brulé tribe plans to build a casino. Various state and county roads lead north and south to beautiful, and generally free, sites for fishing and camping up and down the river.

St. Joseph's Indian School was established in 1897 as St. Viator's College. One of the school's unique modern features is the Akta Lakota Museum, opened in 1991. A $2 million renovation project turned a former school building into a round museum facility, with displays of more than a thousand artifacts of prairie Indian life arranged inside to tell the story of Lakota culture. The collection was begun more than sixty years ago, some of it by the family of Lydia Bluebird from 1880 until 1900.

American Island

Once a site of several fur posts, American Island was nearly a mile south of Chamberlain. A monument stands at the western end of the bridge approach of US 16, the old highway, but the island is only a memory: The waters of Fort Randall Dam covered the island in 1953.

When Lewis and Clark passed the island on September 17, 1804, they said, "this island is about a mile long and has a great perpotion of Red cedar on it." In 1811 Astor's Pacific Fur Company party called it Little Cedar; in 1843 Audubon called it Great Cedar Island. In 1855 western topographer Lt. G. K. Warren called it Second Cedar Island, and it appeared that way in Colton's 1857 atlas. The island was a regular stopping place for explorers, fur traders, steamboat

men—who replenished wood supplies—and people interested in recreation. Fort Aux Cedres and Pilcher's Factory, or Fort Recovery, used it as a woodlot and pasture in the 1820s.

In 1889 Congress gave the island to the city of Chamberlain as a park, but by 1911 the Milwaukee railroad had filled the channel on the west side. In gold rush days, travelers crossed the river on a ferry. In 1893 an enterprising businessman built a pontoon bridge to connect the island to the east bank of the river; he charged a two-cent toll to walk across, twenty-five cents to drive a team. The floating structure was built on the deck of flatboats tied side by side; when river steamers approached, one end of the bridge was let loose and allowed to float free so the steamboats could pass through. Unsafe in high water and freezing weather, the pontoon was still a link between the markets at Chamberlain and the open range to the west,

Meriwether Lewis.
—State Historical Society
of North Dakota

and cattle could be induced, with a lot of shouting and swearing, to tiptoe across it.

In 1905 the Milwaukee finally built a bridge across the river, but teams and cars continued to cross the river on the ice. In 1920 Charles Bolling and his wife were drowned, orphaning their nine children; the deaths inspired a drive to raise funds for a highway bridge. In 1923 the state legislature passed a bill authorizing five bridges over the Missouri, including one at Chamberlain. In 1925 a state highway bridge was built—the piers are visible upstream as you cross the river on the more modern bridge.

US 212 runs east-west between the Dewey County line and the western boundary of Faulk County. Between La Plant and Gettysburg, the highway crosses Lake Oahe, northernmost of the state's four reservoirs along the Missouri River. On the west side of the Missouri, much of the highway runs through the Cheyenne River Indian Reservation.

CHEYENNE RIVER INDIAN RESERVATION

This arid, sparsely settled region was probably busier and more populous during the fur trade days than at any time since. During the era of the big ranches, many of these outposts of civilization bustled with trade; cowboys rode on horseback to town on Saturday nights to drink and stock up on tobacco, and Indian families drove their buggies many miles to buy supplies. Today the region is sprinkled with dying towns with unusual names and histories, but many of the latter will be forgotten as old-timers die. Indian leaders on the Cheyenne River and Standing Rock reservations have studied various ways of bringing economic development to the region, including legalized gambling. Much of the reservation land has traditionally been leased to white ranchers, and conflicts over these arrangements have also made local politics interesting.

A smattering of tiny towns are strung along the highway west of the Missouri. Parade was originally named after George Paradis, a French fur trader who lived with the Indians; its most famous native is Norm Van Brocklin, a star quarterback and coach in the National Football League. Nearby Ridgeview was named for its position on the divide between the Cheyenne and Moreau rivers, and La Plant was named for George and Fred La Plant, pioneer ranchers. The latter town was officially founded by the Chicago, Milwaukee & St. Paul in 1910, but it had long been a prairie trading post for Indians as well as cowboys from the surrounding ranches. Like many of these isolated villages that sprung up in the era between the ranching and homesteading eras, it was strung haphazardly along a hillside, as though people simply stopped their wagons temporarily beside the trail.

The ghost town of Mossman, primarily a shipping point for cattle, was named after Burton C. "Cap" Mossman, who founded the Diamond A Ranch in 1903 on the open range. Amadee Rousseau guided Mossman over the reservation, helped him find a location, and became his first foreman. The ranch carried about fifty thousand head of cattle at its busiest, but by 1909 Mossman had been forced by incoming homesteaders to buy or lease a great deal of the land he had previously used for free.

Mossman got his nickname as the leader of the Arizona Rangers, a group of lawmen he helped found in 1901. Bob Lee reports in *Last Grass Frontier* that "he was a nervy fellow and personally ran down the notorious Mexican rustler-bandit, Augustin Chacon, who was hanged for his depredations in the Southwest." Later, he was range manager of the Hansford Land and Cattle Company, a Scottish firm that ran the famous Turkey Track outfit on the Pecos River in New Mexico. In 1907 he bought out the Sword and Dagger and later purchased the Turkey Track holdings in New Mexico and ran cattle there as well as in South Dakota. He sold out in 1944 and retired to Roswell, New Mexico. One of the original founders of the National Livestock Association, Mossman is honored in the Cattlemen's Hall of Fame of the Saddle and Sirloin Club of Chicago.

East of the river, Gettysburg was settled about 1884 by Civil War veterans of the Union army, one of several towns whose names reflect the war: Others include Lebanon, Union, and Appomattox. The year after its founding, Gettysburg was involved in a county-seat flap

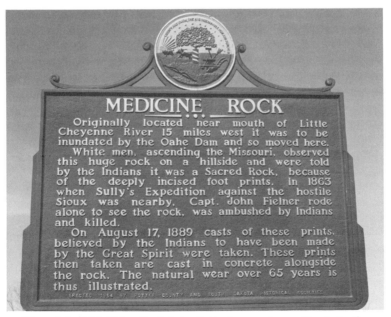

The original Medicine Rock is in Gettysburg and a replica is in the Cultural Heritage Center in Pierre; this sign along US 212 explains the rock's importance. —South Dakota Department of Tourism

with Forest City. Residents of the latter declined to turn over the legal records of Potter County; a delegation of battle-scarred veterans cleaned their rifles, went to Forest City, and got the records. Forest City has disappeared from the map.

An intriguing Indian landmark, Medicine Rock, was originally located about fifteen miles west of town; the site is now under the waters of Lake Oahe. The rock, which has since been moved to Gettysburg, is covered with impressions of huge handprints and footprints. The rock may have been first observed by white men during the Atkinson-O'Fallon Peace Treaty expedition of 1825, but subsequent river travelers mentioned it. Capt. John Fielner, a member of Gen. Alfred Sully's 1863 expedition against the Santee Sioux, rode alone to see the rock and was ambushed and killed by Indians. Sully pursued and captured the attackers, then beheaded them and placed their heads on tall poles as a warning to other Indians. On August 17, 1889, concrete casts of the prints were made, and the replica is displayed at the Cultural Heritage Center in Pierre.

US 18
Gregory County—Douglas County
82 Miles

US 18 runs east-west across the southern third of the state between Dallas, on the Gregory County line west of the Missouri River, and the Douglas County line near Tripp, on the east side of the river.

Because many tourists stay on I-90, towns in this region have mounted an advertising campaign to lure travelers to "the scenic route." Attractions include the Fort Randall Dam at Pickstown; six state recreation areas for camping, fishing, boating, and hunting; and the benefits of small-town hospitality. Hunters can find deer, grouse, pheasant, and prairie dogs; boaters will find numerous beautiful campgrounds with boat ramps: Randall Creek, Joe Day Bay, North Point, White Swan, South Scalp Creek, North and South Wheeler, Pease Creek, Whetstone Bay. Many of these sites are also accessible from land and are rarely crowded. People who simply like to enjoy scenery will find some of the most unspoiled stretches of river below Pickstown.

The scenery has not changed drastically since George Catlin came upriver with Pierre Chouteau, Jr., on the *Yellowstone* in 1832. The steamer ran aground on a sandbar above William Laidlaw's fort at the mouth of the Teton River, near present-day Pierre, so Chouteau took twenty of his men and set out cross-country toward the fort on foot, two hundred miles distant. They must have had a severe case of cabin fever because grounded vessels usually floated free or could be pushed free within a few hours. Catlin was already used to hardship and probably thought anything was better than being stranded on a stationary steamboat, so he joined the group with his painting equipment, "canvass, paints, and brushes, with my sketch-book slung on my back and my rifle in my hand."

The trip provided scenes of buffalo and landscapes that fascinated Catlin. He wrote of the "simple beauty and serenity of these scenes of solitude" and how feeble and small he felt, walking and carrying his gear across the plains "without a hill or tree to mark his progress, and convince him that he is not standing still." A modern traveler could easily recapture a sense of this isolation by walking some distance from the highway in this area. Much of the landscape Catlin saw still exists today; the human traffic through the region has not left many marks here.

Below Pickstown, over a thousand acres of prairie have been preserved in their natural state as the Karl Mundt National Wildlife Refuge, created and paid for by the 7-11 convenience store chain. The largest wintering population of eagles in the continental United States spends the winter here in the huge cottonwoods along the river, though their numbers have declined since the large dams were built, putting many cottonwoods underwater; other trees have replaced them in a few areas. In recent years, eagles have frequently been killed by pesticides that wash into the river via rainfall. In addition, the pesticides damage eagle reproduction.

GREGORY COUNTY

Gregory was founded as the county seat in 1904 and named for John Shaw Gregory, a member of the first territorial legislature in 1862 and later an Indian agent for the Poncas. Like Mitchell, Gregory once built a "corn palace" to celebrate agriculture, but the idea lacked enthusiasm, possibly because settlers soon discovered the land is better suited to grazing than farming.

Numerous smaller towns cluster around Gregory. To the east is Herrick, founded in 1904 and named for Samuel Herrick, who helped release the Rosebud Reservation to white settlement (114,769 people registered for 4,000 homesteads of 160 acres each). Six miles east of Herrick is St. Charles. It was originally named Hampton by Charles A. Johnson, a banker from nearby Fairfax who furnished land for the town site, but the post office rejected the name. West of Gregory is Dallas, founded in 1907 and named for the well-known city in Texas by the Jackson brothers, early settlers. When they guessed that the railroad would miss the town, they moved it in time to be ready for a land opening the same year; within a few days Dallas grew from two hundred to two thousand people. The town expanded to include seven churches, a library, a water system, electric lights, and a three-block-long business district; the WPA guide says, "Farm machinery was sold by the carloads, and soon rippling grain fields replaced endless stretches of dun prairie." Not for long.

Another nearby town, Burke, was founded in 1904 and named for Charles Burke of Pierre. Burke served in the state legislatures of 1895 and 1897 and in the U.S. Congress from 1899 through 1907 and 1909 through 1915; he became commissioner of Indian Affairs in 1921.

In 1905 Laura Belle Hegarty Schulze came from Iowa to homestead near Burke with her husband, John, and small son. Reflecting on her pioneer experiences in *Daughters of Dakota*, she found much to enjoy, though she regretted having no telephone. To ease the loneliness, neighbors tried to meet each Saturday to visit, play, and sing, and she found "an intense spirit of friendly cooperation, when hard times came along, when a baby was born, and through sickness and death." Among her friends were the Indian families of Red Leaf, who became a minister, and Fool Hawk. Mr. Red Leaf entertained Mrs. Schulze by singing "Nearer My God to Thee," but she didn't care for the Indians' habit of entering her home without knocking. Another Indian friend, Mrs. Emory, taught her how to make bead necklaces of the abundant wild roses.

The origins of Bonesteel, twenty miles east of Burke, can be traced to H. E. Bonesteel, an early settler who joined the J. L. Turner Mercantile firm at Springfield in 1872. The firm of Bonesteel and Turner became widely known for freighting before he moved to the town that bears his name in 1902, the same year the railroad arrived. The town boomed and busted with the land lotteries, but getting a homestead in the dry land was easier than keeping one. By 1905 the town had only about seven hundred people. Today it has only about three hundred residents.

During the 1904 lottery, Bonesteel attracted an underworld element of gamblers, confidence men, and liquor salesmen, alongside the settlers, businessmen, and promoters who hoped to profit from homesteading. Jim Nelson, the local police chief, chose that moment to retire, perhaps more quickly than he'd originally planned. With no police force, the town was wide open to criminals. Citizens organized to drive the unlawful elements out of town, and several people on both sides opened fire. Patsy Magner, one of the town's leading businessmen, later said there were two hundred of the bad men and that their slogan was, "stand for no pinch." Under the headline, "BONESTEEL HAS HOT EVENING," the local newspaper reported, "The bad men simply mobbed the officers, took their clubs and guns, pounded them up and took their stars." One tough was killed, and two were wounded on each side of the fracas. The sheriff asked for troops, but things quieted down before his request was granted. Still, the "Battle of Bonesteel" made national headlines.

Fort Randall

Fort Randall was established by Brig. Gen. W. S. Harney in 1856 and named for Col. Daniel Randall, deputy paymaster of the U.S.

Gen. John Blair Smith Todd held the post of sutler at Fort Randall; he was also a land speculator and traded with the Indians. One of the few Democrats in a Republican territory, General Todd later settled in Yankton. He wrote a memorial to Congress asking that Dakota Territory be established; when it was, he became its first delegate to Congress.
—South Dakota State Historical Society

Army. The fort's first permanent commander was Col. E. Lee, Second U.S. Infantry.

In 1875 some of the post's military personnel, members of the International Order of Odd Fellows Lodge, decided to build a lodge room, a church, and a library for the fort. George Bush, post carpenter and a discharged soldier, designed the structure, which the men built in their free time from chalk stone hand-sawed from nearby quarries. When the fort was abandoned in 1892, the ruins of the church were left standing, a beautiful building resembling a medieval monastery. Two windstorms and a direct lightning strike ruined the roof, but the remaining structure was stabilized by the Corps of Engineers in 1953 and can be seen by visitors.

PICKSTOWN

On the east side of the Missouri River is Pickstown, a community created in 1946 for construction workers on the Fort Randall Dam project. Lake Andes, founded in 1904, was named for the nearby lake, which was named either for Edward Andes, a surveyor for the American Fur Company, or for an early fur trapper named Handy who had settled nearby. According to the second story, the lake was first known as Handy's Lake, then Andy's Lake, and finally Andes Lake, or Lake Andes.

One of the earliest white settlers of South Dakota lived near here. In 1794 St. Louis merchants formed the Missouri Company and sent a St. Louis schoolmaster, Jean Baptiste Truteau, up the river with eight voyageurs. His mission was to negotiate trade with the Sioux, Arikara, Mandan, and any other tribes he could find. By fall, Truteau knew he would have to winter on the Missouri, preferably hidden from the Sioux and Poncas, as neither tribe was universally friendly.

On a spot where his group could have concealment, firewood, and water from a large spring, he built a cabin called (perhaps ironically) Ponca House. This was probably the first structure built by white men on South Dakota's stretch of the Missouri River, but historians aren't sure exactly where it was, though locals sometimes speak of picking up artifacts there. Lewis and Clark noted its remains in 1804 but called it "Pawnee House" because of confusion over the word "Ponca" on the map they carried.

Lewis and Clark also spent three days unsuccessfully hunting for an ancient volcano they had been told existed in the Bijou Hills. In 1812 fur trader Louis Bissonette of St. Louis, whose nickname was "Mr. Bijou," built a fur post at the foot of the hills on the river.

By 1877 a community named for him had developed, with a postmaster, newspaper, and bank.

US 83
North Dakota–Nebraska
241 Miles

US 83 runs north-south between the North Dakota and Nebraska state lines. Its northern half lies east of the Missouri River, often within sight of it; after crossing to the west side of the river at Pierre, the highway lies higher on the tablelands. Massive power lines march across the horizon, carrying power generated by the dams. Be alert for slow-moving farm machinery in these short rolling hills; a standard wide load of hay fills the entire road, leaving only the narrow shoulder or the ditch for other drivers.

Clues to the region's economy appear in beehives lining fences, tall blue silos and fat steel Butler buildings storing cattle feed, and white stucco grain elevators overshadowing small-town main streets. Billboards advertise brands of grain and herbicides. Shelterbelts, some planted as homesteaders' tree claims, protect fields; some careful farmers leave unmown grass in the watercourses to prevent erosion. Those small triangular sheds you see in farmyards shelter female pigs and their litters in spring.

Pack a lunch; many small towns on US 83 have gas stations, but few have coffee shops or restaurants. A church may encourage community togetherness and farmers may gather to gossip around a coffee pot in a corner of the gas station, but modern times find local residents driving to larger cities to visit shopping malls. Without enough business, the cafes that used to be town social centers have closed their doors and boarded over their windows.

CAMPBELL COUNTY

Herreid, located west of the hundredth meridian, wasn't founded until 1901 with the arrival of the Minneapolis, St. Paul & Sault Saint Marie Railroad. The town was named for Charles N. Herreid, who became governor of South Dakota about the same time.

During the 1920s Herreid was among the dozen or so South Dakota towns chosen to initiate a new "Americanization" program for immigrants. A law passed in the legislature that year required all persons aged sixteen to twenty-one who could not speak, read, and write English at the fifth-grade level to attend night school. Immigrants, whose sincerity in wanting to become citizens had sometimes been questioned, signed up for the program and wore buttons stamped "Americanization School, South Dakota." Many immigrants, either to show their patriotic zeal for their new country or as a result of the Americanization efforts, refused to teach their children their native tongue. In 1940 various languages were still often heard in business places and homes, but as first-generation immigrants die, Dakotans are becoming exclusively English-speaking.

Eight miles south of Herreid is Mound City, the seat of Campbell County and home to only about a hundred people. Even so, it is not the smallest county seat in the state; that distinction is held by Olivet. The county has lost about 60 percent of its population in the last fifty years, an average of forty-two people per year; the 1990 census found fewer than two thousand residents. With the labor pool shrinking, farmers have had to hire mechanical help, often on credit, in the form of those huge tractors you're dodging on the highway. Folks chatting in the remaining coffee hangouts are worried.

Mound City was named for nearby Indian burial sites, but you have to ask local residents to point them out; they aren't advertised (this region still hasn't discovered tourism). Children who grew up here often found arrowheads made of flint from the Knife River in North Dakota; the Arikara Indians collected or traded for the material and brought it home to shape. Farmers occasionally find insignia of soldiers and Indian relics, indicating that some unrecorded conflict between white soldiers and Indians might have occurred here. However, no documentation has been offered.

In the Footsteps of Lewis and Clark

West of Mound City, a scenic state road—numbered 1804 because it follows Lewis and Clark's upriver route—runs along the eastern side of the Missouri River past Waneta Bottoms and Bramble, giving a view of the waters backed up by Oahe Dam. The Pocasse National Wildlife Refuge, northwest of Mound City on Spring Creek, is a hideout for sandhill cranes on their migration routes; several lakes, including Sand, Salt, McClarin, and Campbell, serve as landing places for cranes, ducks, and other wild waterfowl. Lake Hiddenwood State Park offers campsites, and boat ramps have been placed along the river for water access at West Pollock, Point of View, Shaw Creek, Indian Creek, Walth Bay, Swan Creek, Dodge Draw, and other points on the east side of the river. Deer and other wildlife are abundant along the water and in the marshes surrounding it. A campsite of the Lewis and Clark party lies just north of Pierre on Spring Creek, which the explorers called Stone Idol Creek for the rock they found (the origin of the name "Standing Rock Indian Reservation").

WALWORTH COUNTY

The hundredth meridian lies two miles east of US 83. State historical markers near Selby and Blunt are downright grouchy—not to mention grammatically inconsistent and badly punctuated—but they do have a point:

> For two generations the Insurance Companies and other world-wide lending agencies would not, as a matter of agreed policy, lend a shiny dime west of this line. Their reason was that some geographer had labeled it the EAST EDGE of the Great American Desert. Neither the geographer nor the insurance Companies had been west of 100 degrees. Today, more than a quarter of America's new animal wealth alone, is produced from that misnamed desert. This unrealistic, geographically limited loan policy, forced South Dakota into the farm loan business. Our Rural Credit Business cost us plenty and was a splendid illustration of why a State should not be in the loaning business. But South Dakota has paid all its debts in full. The 100th Meridian is just another bad memory. Historically however the 100th Meridian was a most important one in Western economy.

Selby, seat of Walworth County, was named—naturally—for a railroad official; after the Milwaukee Road arrived in 1899, the residents moved buildings from the old county seat, Bangor, to the railroad terminal. Presto! They had a new town. A historical marker stands on the site of the old one.

The Lakota called the lovely valley in which Selby lies Blue Blanket Valley, possibly referring to haze from the river or to a blanket of wildflowers that no longer exist. Some researchers suggest the name might have been that of an Indian leader or a reference to a variation on the traditional Lakota burial custom of wrapping the body in a blanket before placing it on the scaffold. No one is sure, but the name is still used in coffee conversation in the local truck stop.

SULLY COUNTY

Agar and Onida are symbolic of the past, both in expectation and reality. Agar, founded in 1910, was named for Charles H. Agar, one of the first county commissioners, and was once a major shipping

Remnants of the great buffalo herds that once covered the Great Plains now graze on the Sutton Ranch near Agar. —South Dakota Department of Game, Fish, and Parks

point for cattle raised on the surrounding plateaus. West of Agar is the Sutton Ranch, whose private herd of buffalo was started with three head from the Scotty Philip herd. The Suttons have experimented with breeding "cattalos," a cross between buffalo and native cattle that includes the characteristic neck hump.

Onida is a misspelling of Oneida, the New York hometown of the first settlers who arrived here in 1883. During the region's period of booming settlement, townspeople battled with nearby Clifton for possession of the Sully County seat. Today, Clifton has disappeared, and Onida is one of the few county seats in the state with fewer than 2,000 people. Its population is still dropping: In 1980 it had about 900 people; in 1990 it had only 761.

The original Fort Sully, established in 1866 on low land close to the river and abandoned in 1894, was important in the battles to take control of the Upper Missouri from the Indians. (A stone marker stands on the site, four miles east of Pierre on SD 34.) When that post was finally abandoned, because commanders felt the location contributed to illness among the personnel, the second was built south of the Little Bend, near Agar. The new fort boasted a band, a baseball team, roller-skating and hunting clubs, and a library. Nearly a thousand soldiers and staff occupied the fort's sixty-plus buildings joined by palisades. The forts and the county were named for Gen. Alfred Sully, who camped nearby in 1863 during his expedition against the Santee Sioux.

The land on which the fort stood was inundated by Lake Oahe, but with careful local directions and a four-wheel drive vehicle you can reach an overlook along the bluffs. Recent dry years lowered the waters of Lake Oahe sufficiently that several local people visited the site to photograph the remains of foundations. The former post hospital is now a granary on a nearby farm.

Arikara Villages

Thousands of Arikara probably lived along the river in this territory in prehistoric times, in sturdy homes built of mud, surrounded by fields of corn, tobacco, and three kinds of squash. On the south side of Fort Sully Creek, archaeologists have found evidence of a huge village estimated to have contained between two and three hundred lodges, with a total population of perhaps five thousand people. A similar village called the Arzberger (or Mush Creek) Fortress is located eight miles east of Pierre on SD 34. Almost fifty acres in extent, it was defended by a palisade and a moat, with numerous bastions. Archaeologists say that when it was occupied, probably in the 1600s and 1700s, it was the equal in engineering and planning of any similar structure that existed in Europe.

Several Indian ceremonial sites lie in the surrounding countryside, and the garbled explanations of their origins and meaning furnished by white scholars are often more intriguing for what they tell of whites than for their information on the Lakota. On Medicine Knoll, near Blunt, is a gigantic serpent outlined in rocks. According to some authorities, the knoll was so named because the Sioux performed rituals and gathered medicinal plants here. Actually, however, the Lakota gathered medicinal plants wherever they found them. The WPA guide says the serpent commemorates a young Sioux who was attacked by an Arikara enemy while he was on a vision quest; he sang loudly to attract the attention of his tribesmen who killed the Arikara. The serpent also resembles stone figures left by the Hopi, who say they journeyed to the four directions on the North American continent before settling at Oraibi, Arizona. Relax at the picnic table placed on the site and consider these questions in state-sanctioned comfort.

Carl Bodmer's "Interior of a Mandan Earth Lodge" shows the homes visited by such upriver travelers as Catlin, Lewis and Clark, and the Verendryes. The largest lodges were thirty to ninety feet in diameter, with ample room for stabling favorite horses and storing war shields and weapons. The occupants slept around the outside of the lodge in private niches and worked, ate, and visited near the fire in the center. —State Historical Society of North Dakota

On Snake Butte, a line of boulders ends with the outline of a turtle. Legend says this is a monument to an Arikara brave who was shot and wounded by the Sioux but ran to warn his people. A rock was laid where every drop of his blood fell on his desperate run, and the turtle was outlined where he finally fell.

Negro Settlement

Dakota has never had many black residents. A company of black miners remained in the Black Hills long enough to dig a little gold and give their name to a site that appears on some modern maps as "Negro Hill." But in the late 1890s four hundred black settlers claimed land along the Missouri River fifteen miles west of SD 83. The leader of the group was Norval Blair, a forward-thinking man who expected to profit with the coming of the railroad. Blair filed land claims for each of his six children. At one time their combined holdings totaled nearly $75,000, but real estate values dropped when the railroad failed to arrive, and drought and taxes further cut the value. Blair also owned an excellent string of racing horses, including Johnny Bee, the fastest horse in the state from 1907 until 1909. By 1938 only about a hundred black residents remained in the region. The nearest settlement, Fairbank, became a ghost town, then a mud hole, and is now covered by the waters of Lake Oahe, leaving only Blair Cemetery on a small knoll.

LOISEL'S POST

Registre Loisel's post on Cedar Island between Pierre and Fort Thompson was operated by the St. Louis Fur Company until fire destroyed it in 1810. The remains probably helped induce later travelers to stop at the same spot, where they were assured of firewood and a good spot to moor boats.

Because the river provided easy traveling, explorers who thought they were in untouched country often unexpectedly met folks who had been here awhile and could offer good advice. Lewis and Clark spoke of meeting Pierre Dorion, whom they said had lived with the Yanktons in southeastern South Dakota "more than twenty years and was high in their confidence." Joseph Garreau, who came to the Upper Missouri in 1787 and settled among the Arikaras soon after, was another valuable contact made on the river. On September 22, 1804, Lewis and Clark arrived at Loisel's post, describing it this way: "Log palisade 13 ½ feet high with sentry boxes at the corners, 65 x 75 in size. Four room house within, one room for storage, one for trade, a common hall and a family house."

Later on the same day, the adventurers passed the Medicine Knoll River, calling it the Reuben River for Reuben Fields, one of the party's hunters. J. N. Nicollet and John Frémont renamed it in 1839 after holding a Fourth of July fireworks display on Medicine Knoll twelve miles up the creek. In 1855 Lt. G. K. Warren camped in the same spot; an ex-fur trader named Paul Narcelle later started a cattle ranch on Medicine Creek. A careful look at the map will show two creeks by the same name—one just south of Pierre on the east side of the river, and the one Narcelle and others used as a campsite, on the south side of the river near the Great Bend, where Fort Defiance also stood.

FORT PIERRE

Ramsey Crooks and Robert McClellan traded on the upper Missouri between 1807 and 1810. In 1813 Manuel Lisa, whose upriver post had been burned by the Yanktons, moved to this area and set

Pierre Chouteau, Jr., agent for the American Fur Company, was on the steamboat Yellowstone *as it navigated the Missouri River for the first time. Fort Pierre was eventually named for him.* —State Historical Society of North Dakota

up a refuge for old and infirm Sioux. When he resigned as subagent for the Upper Missouri in 1817, Lisa reported that he had "from one to two hundred men in my employment, large quantities of horses and horned cattle, of hogs, of domestic fowls," creatures that must have been a source of great interest to the nomadic Lakota.

According to Donald D. Parker in *Dakota Panorama*, the second and permanent settlement was begun on the Missouri in 1817 at Fort Pierre when "Joseph LaFramboise, two half-breed Frenchmen, and a party of Sioux came overland from Prairie du Chien on the Mississippi." Their post, called Fort Tecumseh, was on the west bank of the Missouri just south of the mouth of the Bad River, named by the Teton Sioux after a flood drowned a village on its banks. Along the Bad River (now the Teton River), within the present city limits of Pierre, Father Christian Hoecken baptized twenty-five children of thirteen traders and trappers in 1840, the first baptism west of the Missouri River in South Dakota. Some historians consider Hoecken's action particularly important—to them, baptism signified Christianity, and Christianity was, of course, equivalent to civilization.

Fort Teton was established in 1827, nearly on the site of Fort Tecumseh, by Pierre D. Papin and Pascual Cerres and sold to the American Fur Company in 1830. A clerk there reported on May 24, 1830: "I forgot to mention that our old bull died yesterday morning." The death of the bull may seem of small historical importance—but if Fort Tecumseh had a bull, it must have had cows, too, indicating an established settlement. The post was rebuilt in 1832 and named Fort Pierre Chouteau, Jr., by Chouteau himself, though residents later dropped the surname. A tablet on a ranch one mile north of US 14 and half a mile east of the road to Oahe Dam marks the site of Fort Pierre Chouteau Trading Post. Furs are still bought and sold in Fort Pierre, so the fur trade is almost certainly the oldest continuously operating business in the state.

Chouteau may have had a compelling personal reason to write his name strongly on the history of the new region: He had doubts about his paternity. Different historians give varying versions of his background. Herbert T. Hoover, in *South Dakota Leaders*, says Pierre Chouteau, Sr., had abandoned his family in New Orleans after siring one son, Auguste, by his wife Marie, and returned to France for about fifteen years. Legally, Marie remained married, because neither civil law in New Orleans nor Roman Catholic law permitted divorce; however, she lived with Pierre Laclede after 1755, and had four children by him, including Jean Pierre, whose birth date Hoover gives as 1789. Some flaw exists in this reasoning, however, because by that time Mrs. Chouteau would have been fifty-six years old. If she didn't live with Laclede until 1755, perhaps Pierre Chouteau, Sr., was actually the father of the boy who bore his name.

Janet Lecompte, in *Mountain Men and Fur Traders of the Far West*, agrees with Hoover that Pierre, Jr., was born in 1789, but says that his mother, Pelagie Kiersereau, was Pierre Sr.'s first wife; that Pierre was a full brother to Auguste; and that a second wife bore five more sons, for a total of eight, most of whom became fur traders. The abundance of Chouteaus, their tendency to intermarry, and their habit of using the same names over and over may explain why historians have such a hard time keeping them straight. For example, Auguste's middle name was Pierre, and another brother's name Charles; Pierre, Jr., named his own son Pierre Charles, and after his death another son was named Charles Pierre.

Lecompte says Pierre, Jr., nicknamed "Cadet," entered the fur trade when he was fifteen as a clerk in his uncle Auguste's office and was issued a license to trade in his own name in 1807, when he was only eighteen. Because that is probably true, this is a good place to begin understanding Chouteau's history.

Pierre Chouteau, Jr., Hoover says, worked in lead mines on the Upper Mississippi before beginning an independent trading business, eventually joining Bernard Pratte in what became Pratte, Chouteau & Company. In 1827 he joined John Jacob Astor, managing the Upper Missouri outfit for the American Fur Company. Lecompte criticizes Chouteau and the other traders for their business methods; whenever a rival company dissolved, Chouteau hired its posts, employees, territories, and trade routes. In this way, he kept equipment and experienced traders from joining competing companies. Firms that attempted to oppose him were treated to "vicious price wars." If he couldn't crush the competition, he joined it; William Ashley's atypical venture of taking trade goods to mountain rendezvous so the trappers didn't have to come to him was so successful Chouteau bought into it. (However, he lost money on the deal annually and finally abandoned this part of his trade in 1839.) He used any method he could find to win a trade territory, says Lecompte, from political influence to liquor, and called it the price of a successful fur trade.

In the early days of the fur trade, relations between traders, trappers, and Indians were friendlier, more casual, and probably more honest than in later years. Once competition developed between companies, as investors realized how much potential profit existed in the fur trade, respect for the Indians' rights seems to have declined. Later, when some traders realized how vulnerable the Indians were to alcohol, honorable dealings with the natives became rare. To his credit, Chouteau tried hard to eliminate liquor in the fur trade about 1845, with the cooperation of the Sioux, but his efforts were hampered by the fact that he had used it in his own trade. Moreover, the competition from traders plying Indians with illegal whiskey was simply too great.

By 1838 Pierre Chouteau, Jr., controlled most of the trade in the entire region drained by the Upper Mississippi and the entire Missouri River. He held a virtual monopoly and was the principal supplier of goods, managers, and transportation, which made him, as Hoover says, "the foremost business magnate in pre-territorial Dakota history" and probably one of the most successful businessmen in the whole history of the state. Adds Hoover, "Nearly all legendary merchants of the upper Mississippi and Missouri Rivers were at some time in his employ: Alexis Bailly, Henry Hastings Sibley, Honore Picotte, P. D. Papin, and Theophile Bruguier, to name a few." Those names crop up again and again in Dakota's development history.

The fur trade was a lucrative business. In return for muskrat, deer, grizzly and black bear, beaver, otter, mink, fisher, martin, raccoon, wildcat, wolf, fox, skunk, badger, and lynx pelts and packages of buffalo tongue, Chouteau supplied traders and hunters with food and supplies that included pork, corn, tea, spices, clothing, iron, plows, riding equipment, building tools, and anything else needed on the frontier. Merchandise for the Indian trade included bright blankets, linen, calico, and flannel, along with decorative sewing items such as lace and ribbon, decorative metal such as hawk bells and medallions, beads of all kinds, household goods—and liquor.

To haul all this stock, Chouteau established the first regular steamboat service on the Upper Missouri; Lecompte says the suggestion came from Kenneth MacKenzie, but the boat was bought with Chouteau's money. The *Yellowstone* first went upriver in 1831, though it only reached the abandoned Fort Tecumseh; the next year, when Chouteau christened the new post in his own honor, the steamboat came back. On that trip, the *Yellowstone* continued on to Fort Union at the mouth of the Yellowstone River and returned to St. Louis

Tons of freight arrived on steamboats and barges like these tied up to the docks at Fort Pierre. Goods brought upriver from St. Louis stand waiting to be loaded onto wagons for the fifteen-day trip to the Black Hills. —South Dakota State Historical Society

Carl Bodmer drew "Keelboat Near Piegan Camp" when he traveled upriver with Maximilian, Prince of Wied. —State Historical Society of North Dakota

having averaged a hundred miles a day, an incredible feat of travel. Painter George Catlin noted that the steamer ran aground near Fort Pierre; too impatient to wait for it to float free, Chouteau chose to walk to the fort (see US 18, Gregory County). Such hazards were normal, and the delay doesn't necessarily affect the mileage average. The success of the *Yellowstone* led Chouteau and others to purchase more steamboats, including the *Diana*, the *Antelope*, the *St. Peters*, the *Burlington*, and the *Trader*.

Chouteau became completely blind in 1859 and died in 1865 at the age of seventy-six. Without his organization and enterprise, the entire history of the Upper Missouri might have been much different. Though he was at times ruthless in his dealings, he was no worse than other traders and businessmen (even modern ones) and better than most. But only his first name is recalled in the name of the state's capital city—and consistently mispronounced by people who have forgotten its significance.

Artistic Impressions of Fort Pierre

A modern traveler can visualize how the Fort Pierre region looked before it was settled by viewing the work of artists who visited in the earliest years of white development. George Catlin, Carl Bodmer,

Alfred Jacob Miller, Friederich Kurz, and John James Audubon all found their way up the water highway to the center of the continent during the nineteenth century. Catlin was first, coming upriver on Ashley's second keelboat trip in 1832 with Pierre Chouteau, Jr., Lucien Fontenelle, and other traders and trappers. He sketched from the deck of the keelboat, sketched in a canoe, and sketched in Indian camps; his scenes are important both as art and as a historical record, as are his extensive notes.

In his "Letter No. 26," Catlin noted that in Fort Pierre, thirteen hundred miles above St. Louis, he stayed with Laidlaw, a Scotsman who handled the American Fur Company's transactions from the Upper Missouri to the Rocky Mountains. His fort, said Catlin, was "two or three hundred feet square, enclosing eight or ten of their factories, houses and stores." Around it lay "the Missouri's most beautiful plains, and hemmed in by a series of gracefully undulating, grass-covered hills, on all sides; rising like a series of terraces, to the summit level of the prairies, some three or four hundred feet in elevation, which then stretches off in an apparently boundless ocean of gracefully swelling waves and fields of green." Because the modern town has still not climbed the surrounding hills, visitors to Pierre can see the same scene.

One of the poignant stories of the era concerns the portraits Catlin painted of a chief named Black Rock and his daughter, who Catlin said was both beautiful and modest. He rendered her name as Red Thing That Touches in Marching. The portraits so captivated trader Kenneth MacKenzie that he asked Catlin for copies to hang in Laidlaw's post. Several years later, the girl's father came to the room containing the portrait of his daughter and told Laidlaw that she was dead. "My heart is glad again," said the chief, "when I see her here alive." He offered Laidlaw ten horses and a tipi for the painting so he could see and talk to his daughter again. Laidlaw gave him the portrait but returned the gifts out of appreciation for what Catlin calls "the true grief that he expressed for the loss of his child." Both then and later, many whites believed the Indians incapable of such love.

Carl Bodmer came to Pierre the next year, with Maximilian, Prince of Wied, who was gathering material for his book, *Travels in the Interior of North America*, which Bodmer illustrated. Both spent considerable time with the Mandans, and Bodmer's paintings include "Horse Racing at Fort Pierre." Alfred Jacob Miller came to Fort Pierre by way of Fort Laramie in 1837; his paintings, too, have great historical importance, though his horses more nearly resemble delicately bred European chargers than the robust mustangs of the American West. John James Audubon was almost sixty when, in

1843, he came on the steamship *Omega* to Dakota Territory. He traveled with a party of fur traders and trappers and spent the summer sketching birds. His health failed before he returned to New York, and he died soon after.

The work of many of these artists, and others who lived their entire lives in the state, is displayed in the State Capitol in Pierre. One of the largest murals is a panel by Charles Holloway in the House chamber titled "The First Prayer." The painting depicts Ashley's keelboat coming up the Missouri in 1823, carrying fur traders and trappers. Jedediah Smith, more handsome and cleaner than any real trapper ever was, kneels in the center of the painting, wounded after a fight with Indians, praying for the dead.

PIERRE

Pierre was officially founded in 1878 as Mato, which means "bear" in Lakota. In 1880 J. D. and Anson Hilger of Bismarck, North Dakota, consigned a shipment of household goods to "Pierre on the east side of the river, opposite Fort Pierre," and the name persisted.

After Pierre was named South Dakota's capital, jubilant citizens built this wooden building with volunteer labor and materials in time for the January 1890 legislative session; the structure served until 1910. —South Dakota State Historical Society

162

South Dakota's capitol building at Pierre was modeled after the nation's capitol in Washington, D.C. The state sold eighty-five thousand acres of federal land in the central and western part of the state to finance the million-dollar building. —South Dakota State Historical Society

Once the railroad arrived in 1880, land agents and other promoters moved in, and the town's white population grew. But the region seemed destined to be a cow town rather than a homestead center; the grasslands to the west encouraged large ranches, though many suffered heavy losses in the blizzards of 1887 and 1888. In 1890, after a tough and costly battle with Huron, Pierre won out as state capital, and its future was assured, though it has never had the population of either Sioux Falls in the east or Rapid City in the west. The capitol building, modeled after its federal counterpart, was dedicated in 1910. South Dakota had been granted eighty-five thousand acres of federal land to help finance construction, but because the land was in the central and western part of the state, its sale didn't help much against the millions of dollars the structure cost.

One of the state's worst historical markers—and that's saying a good deal—stands in downtown Pierre on US 14 and reinforces stereotypes about the city. "PIERRE WAS A COWTOWN" it declares:

Yes sir, Mister, Pierre was a cowtown. Why they built the sidewalks two feet off the ground to keep the cows from spattering 'em up. The stockyards ran longside [sic] the river for half a mile and three ferries were busy night and day in the shippin' season fetching cows over from the holding grounds, where cattle from as far away as Montana were funneled into the railhead at Pierre.

Yes sir, Pierre had 14 saloons in which cowpokes could wet a whistle and it was cows that kept Pierre and kept Pierre awake with their endless bawlin' enroute east. Why one year more cows clumb [sic] aboard the cars here than ever happened elsewhere anywhere. Yep sonny, put it down, Pierre was a cowtown. West river ranchers wintered here and the brand books of 1902 and prior listed 75 brand owners with over 200 brands.

The rest of the marker lists early area ranchers and their brands. On the reverse is a short course in how to read a brand, in case you plan to pick up a few cows on your way through South Dakota.

Several locations in Pierre, as well as other towns, house artifacts from the state's history, though administration is subject to change as the state slashes budgets to meet changing economic conditions. The State Agricultural Heritage Museum is in Brookings, and the Smith-Zimmerman State Museum is in Madison. The Soldier's and Sailor's World War Memorial, directly across from the state capitol, once housed archival collections but is now home to Military and Veterans' Affairs. The sandstone memorial, built in 1932 to honor those who died in World War I, was placed on the National Register of Historic Places in 1983.

The South Dakota Historical Resource Center—modern language for "museum"—is in the Cultural Heritage Center. Dedicated at the state's centennial celebration in 1989, this is a unique earth-covered building north of the Capitol. Landscaping features native flora grown in sod taken from a plot of land in northeastern Jones County, so the outside of the building furnishes a living nature exhibit. Among predominant species in the sod are buffalo grass, blue grama, western wheat grass, green needle grass, and sideoats grama, with a scattering of native flowers, herbs, and small bushes. Nearby Hilger's Gulch is also being returned to native landscaping. An underground irrigation system will supplement rainfall, and the natural landscaping will require less maintenance than conventional lawn techniques. South Dakota granite covers the building's entrance.

Among notable exhibits inside is the amazing Sioux wood carving of a running horse, used as the center's logo. Lean as a whippet, the horse stretches in a full-out run. The carving, one of only two known complete horse sculptures done by Plains Indians, is believed to have been made in 1875 by a Sioux warrior as a tribute to a horse lost in battle and was donated in 1920 by the Reverend Mary Collins, a missionary on the Standing Rock Reservation.

Archival collections containing historical, genealogical, and immigration records, photographs, and newspapers are all stored in climate-controlled rooms in the 63,000-square-foot building. Exhibits at the center are divided into four main periods: prehistory to

1860, the settlement years of 1860-90, development from 1890 to 1940, and the modern era. Items shown include the Verendrye plate, Native American quilts, beadwork and quillwork, a tipi, horse-drawn carriages, western clothing and equipment, and the silver service from the battleship USS *South Dakota.*

Also in Pierre is the Discovery Center and Aquarium, housed in the renovated Pierre Municipal Power Plant on the west side of the Missouri River bridge. The center is a "science playground," with more than forty hands-on exhibits and an aquatic wing for native fish of the Missouri River. Visitors can climb inside a huge soap bubble or a drag racing car, paint with the "sand pendulum," build a miniature St. Louis Arch from wooden blocks, and make a tornado. Exhibits on conservation, water management, and natural history will also be featured.

One of Pierre's most famous modern citizens was Casey Tibbs, who became an international rodeo champion after spending his youth breaking broncs and herding cattle around the Plains. The youngest of ten children, he was born March 5, 1929, on land his father had homesteaded near the Cheyenne River. At ten, he broke his first colt; at fifteen, he ran away from home to become a professional cowboy. In 1951 Tibbs earned $80,000 and his first title as

Casey Tibbs of Fort Pierre, a world champion cowboy, rides a bucking bronc before admiring spectators at a rodeo. —South Dakota Department of Tourism

World Champion All Around Cowboy (his second came in 1955). He retired from the rodeo circuit in 1959 but returned in 1967 and went on to win twenty-two of the twenty-seven contests he entered that year. He did a little acting and stunt work in movies and made two documentaries—*Born to Buck* in 1967 and *Sioux Nation* in 1969; he also produced, directed, and played a role in *The Young Rounders* in 1973. Tibbs promoted rodeo as a healthy, clean sport, as much a part of America as baseball. A restaurant in Pierre once displayed dozens of silver-mounted saddles and trophies Tibbs won through his bone-breaking riding; the establishment later put those items in storage and installed an aquarium.

Oahe Dam

North of Pierre is Oahe Dam, named from the Sioux word *titankoahe*, which probably means "place of the big house" (though other authorities suggest "a place to stand upon" as a translation). The name derives from the establishment of a missionary school by the Reverend Thomas L. Riggs, son of Stephen Return Riggs. The elder Riggs visited Fort Pierre in 1840 and held services for about five hundred Yanktons and Tetons but had no time or money to establish a mission; that was finally done by his son, who founded the first Protestant mission in 1874. The church was moved from its original location when Oahe Dam flooded it; it now perches some-what incongruously atop the dam at the eastern end. The graves of Riggs and his family were not moved and are now under two hundred feet of water.

When completed, Oahe Dam was the largest rolled-earth dam in the world, 242 feet high. Begun in 1948, it cost something over $380 million by the time it was finally finished in 1964 and turned the Missouri River at this point into a lake longer than Ontario and deeper than Erie. It boasts the largest hydroelectric power plant of any Corps of Engineers project.

Fort Pierre National Grasslands

South of Pierre is Fort Pierre National Grasslands, one of several government-owned grasslands in the western part of the state. The area straddles US 83, its rolling hills home to antelope, deer, eagles, hawks, and various other species. Many ranchers graze their cattle here, marking the roads to their ranches with a variety of devices: a rifle silhouette, an old plow. At the junction of US 83 and I-90 stands Vivian, the only town in a wide stretch of grass between the interstate and river. It is named after the wife of Harry Hunter, a prominent lawyer, land agent, and representative of the Chicago, Milwaukee & St. Paul Railroad when the town was founded. At Vivian, US 83 joins I-90 for a short distance west to Murdo, where it turns south.

WHITE RIVER

The White River was named for its milky waters, which carry sediments eroded from the Badlands. In early accounts, the river was often referred to by explorers as the White Earth River. The Sioux name for the river translates as "Smoky Earth River," reportedly because when large numbers of people camped along it the smoke would hang in the air and blanket the entire valley. James Clyman, an experienced trapper who accompanied Ashley's second brigade through the area, incorrectly called the river White Clay Creek and said it was a small stream running thick with a white sediment, resembling cream in appearance, and having a sweet, pungent taste. "Our guide," he continued, "warned us from using this water too freely as [it] caused excessive costiveness [constipation] which we soon found out." In modern times, similar clays are the main ingredient of Kaopectate.

The river rises in Sioux County, Nebraska, enters South Dakota through Shannon County, and heads east to join the Missouri River just below Chamberlain. From the I-90 bridge, or the rest stop on the east side of the river, you can spot the creamy white water running beside the greener water of the Missouri for a short distance.

The site for the community of White River, the Mellette County seat, was opened for settlement in 1911, with land selling for $2 to $6 an acre. The area filled and emptied fast; the county's population in 1990 was about two thousand. Left behind are ghost towns and post offices with names both hopeful and derivative of the Indian and white cultural mix: Apex, Berkeley, Brave, Red Wing, Ringthunder, Bad Nation, Chilton, Cody, Farley, Runningville, Schamber, Gate Way, Neville, Jorgensen. Texsam was named for settler Samuel Texter, known as "Sam."

US 12
Corson County–Edmunds County
108 Miles

US 12 runs generally east-west. At Walker the highway begins to incline southeast, toward the river, which it crosses at Mobridge;

from there it flows straight east-west across Walworth County, with one jog south, to the western border of Edmunds County near Bowdle.

Driving over this rolling countryside has reminded many travelers of floating over an ocean of grass; the region's buttes stand like lighthouses. Occasionally the highway drops abruptly into a valley with a stream, green grass, and scampering wildlife. The city driver's eye may stop focusing in the emptiness and wide spaces, so it takes a little practice to look for details of abundant prairie life: a hawk riding thermals, or a coyote slipping out of a draw, muzzle dripping with water. Towns and homes seem puny and unimportant in this place of sky touching earth. Out of the corner of your eye, you may sense movement; you may imagine seeing the figure of a mounted warrior, silhouetted against the sky, a woman on a horse pulling a travois slipping down a grassy draw. Perhaps you do . . .

STANDING ROCK INDIAN RESERVATION

Towns in the area seem to have washed up on the shores of the Standing Rock Reservation or the Missouri River. Established for the Hunkpapa Lakota, the reservation covers Corson County and extends into North Dakota. To the south, the neighboring Cheyenne River Indian Reservation encompasses eastern Perkins County and all of Dewey and Ziebach counties, making a huge chunk of the surrounding grasslands primarily Indian land, with islands of white ownership.

When land on the Standing Rock Reservation was opened to white settlement in 1909, several groups of German evangelical Protestants from the Black Sea moved into the region; they were called— but only by fluent German speakers—*schwarzmeerdeutschen*. Today, whites and Indians have learned to live together, as shown by the mixture of names in the single thin telephone directory that covers small communities in the western third of the state: Schuchhardt, Schuelke, Schwalm, Swift Bird, Two Lance, Two Bulls, Wiedland, Witte, Wortman, Wunderlich, Woodenknife, White Woman, White Thunder, White Plume, White Horse, White Hawk.

Much of the area west of the reservation is in the Grand River National Grasslands. This place of great beauty is one of the few, even in South Dakota, where a hiker can escape the roar of traffic. Watch where you're going if you do; it's easy to become lost in the rolling grasslands. Experienced explorers look over their shoulders frequently, so they'll know what the view will be when they start back.

Indian and white leaders gather for the ceremony of moving the Standing Rock figure to agency headquarters at Fort Yates. Agent James McLaughlin stands at right of the stone, and Sitting Bull, in profile, at left. The two men clashed many times before the Indian leader was killed. —State Historical Society of North Dakota

The Sitting Woman

Fittingly, a pair of explorers named Lewis and Clark are responsible for naming the present-day Standing Rock Reservation. On their trip upriver in 1804 they saw an unusual rock formation and named a creek Stone Idol in its honor. In 1873 the U.S. government changed the name of the natural monument to Standing Rock, which became the reservation's name when it was permanently established in 1878.

To the Lakota, this rock formation was known as Sitting Woman. The tale associated with it, as told in *Legends of the Mighty Sioux* in 1941, is about a young woman who was scolded for having told her parents a lie. The girl's father told her she would have to stay in the tipi until she learned to tell the truth. Instead, she went out into the night, north toward a high butte, crying. Her father believed she wished to talk with the spirits alone, and the family went to bed. The next morning, the girl had not returned, but a strange object now stood on the high butte, something new. Several young men climbed it and "discovered a pillar of rock resembling a sitting woman. She faced the rising sun. The daughter of the chief had not returned; so it was believed that the girl had been transformed into a pillar of stone in punishment for her disobedient act." The stone was thereafter considered to be holy; it now stands on a pedestal in front of the Standing Rock Agency headquarters in Fort Yates, North Dakota.

Legends such as this were recorded by Melvin Gilmore, a professional ethnobotanist who spent 1912 among the Oglalas on the Pine Ridge Reservation and the next year with the Pawnee, Teton Lakota, Ponca, Santee Lakota, Omaha, Winnebago, and Arikara on the Fort Berthold Reservation in North Dakota. The Arikara version of the Sitting Woman story differs from the Lakota version. The Arikara girl of legend was beautiful, kind, thoughtful, earnest, and never idle. She was in the habit of walking alone to commune with all living creatures.

When she reached marriageable age, she told all her suitors she would not marry. "I am at home with the bird people, the four-footed people of the woods and prairies, the people of the flower nations and the trees," she said in explanation. She loved to work in the garden. Her grandmother reasoned with her and insisted that her duty was to marry and bear children for the tribe. The young woman protested but did as she was told. Three days after her marriage, she was back in her mother's house, saying that although her husband treated her well, she was not intended for marriage. She explained her feelings on a walk with her grandmother, and the old woman left her there, sitting by a clump of chokecherries with her sewing kit in her hand and her dog by her side.

When the young wife did not return home that night, men were sent to search for her and found her sitting on a prairie hill, turned to stone from her feet to her waist. By the time the youths returned with all the people of the village, the young woman had become stone as far up as her breasts. The medicine man opened the sacred bundle, withdrew the sacred pipe, and asked her to smoke with them so that they might communicate clearly. She refused, not because she was disloyal or unwilling to join her people but because, she said, "I am different by nature." To show her good will toward her people, she promised that whoever put a symbol of nature—wildflower in summer, a twig of a tree in winter—by the stone would be rewarded by being able to commune with nature. As she spoke, she turned completely into stone, as did her little dog, sitting at her feet and leaning close against her. In Gilmore's time the stone was still on the prairie being "revered by the people."

Another professional researcher traveled to the Standing Rock and Sisseton reservations during the same period, in 1911, to learn about Lakota music and make recordings of the best voices. Frances Densmore was the daughter of a pioneer Minnesota family and a talented musician; she recorded about three hundred songs and ceremonials during her stay on the reservation, commissioned by the Smithsonian Institute.

Robert Higheagle, a Lakota from Hampton University, helped Densmore record the voices of Sikaya, Brave Buffalo, and Holy Face Bear singing medicine and dream songs, and he assisted in translating the words. As traditional Lakotas confronted and mingled with whites, they debated whether it was legitimate to preserve traditional learning with the aid of tools such as tape recorders or if any white scholar, especially a woman, should be allowed to hear material that was once a tribal secret. If Frances Densmore hadn't gathered the material when she did, much of it might have been permanently lost.

Some Indians are turning to archives and elders to recapture elements of traditional society they believe will help them preserve their identity while adapting to modern times. One of these, Professor Beatrice Medicine, grew up on the Standing Rock. She studied at the state university at Brookings, received her master's degree in sociology and anthropology from Michigan State University, and earned her Ph.D. in anthropology from the University of Wisconsin. She taught across the nation before retiring to the reservation in 1988. She has lectured and written extensively and encourages Indian women to continue their education.

Sitting Bull

Stanley Vestal, who wrote the premiere biography of the only man ever chosen as chief over all the Lakota, Sitting Bull, acknowledges the difficulty of writing about a man who, until he surrendered at the age of fifty, had spoken with few white men. For the first forty-five years of Sitting Bull's life, the historian's only sources were the memories of old Indians "of high reputation." Vestal insists, in Sitting Bull: Champion of the Sioux, that such data is at least as reliable as the white man's method of footnoting references and checking facts in multiple sources: "Very few of those old-timers could be induced to repeat hearsay." In the case of any event that took place during battle, he explains, "old warriors generally insist on having two witnesses present to attest their statements." Few historians of any time could swear they relied on such rigidly honest reports.

Still, such information was not easy to come by. In the early years after Sitting Bull's death, many Indians who had known him well were afraid to talk, especially of the Custer fight, because they feared the soldiers would come and hang them or—later—that they would be punished by Indian agents. Even when they spoke the hard, plain truth to government agents, an interpreter often in-

Sitting Bull was respected for his spiritual qualities as well as his fighting skills. He never signed a treaty. He was shot to death while resisting arrest in 1890. Seventy-five years later, North and South Dakota fought over his bones. —State Historical Society of North Dakota

accurately translated their statements, either deliberately for his own purposes or by accident.

Though modern whites might scoff at such notions, the fact is that many Indian warriors, including Sitting Bull, suffered later for their part in an honest fight against whites who had attacked them, sometimes in a peaceful village with their women and children. Vestal felt fortunate to have spoken with these men before they died; he noted in his introduction to the revised edition of *Sitting Bull* that because of their deaths, a better biography is now unlikely. He added a heartfelt belief that the wall between whites and Indians was down, permanently—"we have buried the hatchet"—and predicted that as Sitting Bull became better known, South Dakota would erect "a fitting memorial to her great son; he is by all odds the most famous man ever born within her borders."

After being chosen for the position in 1868, Sitting Bull was the only leader who spoke for all Lakota. At first, he never attacked white settlements and insisted he wanted only to be left alone. He demanded that the federal government fulfill its promises made in previous treaties: that roads through reservation lands promised to the Lakota be closed; that forts in those lands be closed; that steamboat traffic through reservation lands be stopped; and that all whites except traders be expelled.

From today's historical distance, these seem to be reasonable requests; indeed, they seemed reasonable to many observers at the time. But the military and the Bureau of Indian Affairs, the two branches of government most involved with the Indians, worked against each other, confusing and angering both Indians and whites. Vestal concludes that "so long as the bureau kept on making friendlies out of hostiles, and the army persisted in making hostiles out of friendlies, neither department could possibly lack employment. Sitting Bull summed up the matter in a nutshell: 'The white men have too many chiefs.'"

On December 22, 1875, a message reached Standing Rock ordering all agency Indians back to reservations by January 31. After that date, they would be considered hostile and attacked. In *South Dakota Leaders*, historian Raymond L. Clow writes, "When it became obvious that few would comply, the matter was turned over to the United States Army." But the journey was impossible; cold and deep snow stopped troops who tried to march after tardy bands. Sitting Bull was more than two hundred miles away, at the mouth of Powder River, where he had offered shelter to agency Indians who had left the reservation because they were starving.

On March 17, Col. J. J. Reynolds Crook, thinking he was attacking Crazy Horse, attacked peaceful Cheyenne, burning lodges and food supplies. He was unable to capture the Indian ponies, on which the Cheyennes escaped to join Sitting Bull; the survivors were suddenly hostile. Finally out of patience, Sitting Bull declared war; Lakota and Cheyenne braves joined him by the hundreds, forming the largest band of Plains Indians ever brought together for battle. Vestal says the final total was two hundred lodges of Cheyenne and about twelve hundred lodges of Lakota.

On June 14, 1876, in a Sun Dance ceremony, Sitting Bull had a vision of soldiers "falling into camp" and being killed. Explaining his vision, he warned his warriors not to take guns or horses from dead soldiers. "If you set your hearts upon the goods of the white man, it will prove a curse to this nation," he said.

On June 25, when Lt. Col. George Armstrong Custer attacked the war camp, Sitting Bull's prophecy came true. The warriors separated after the victory. Crazy Horse went to the Bighorns and Sitting Bull headed toward Grand River. Spotted Tail persuaded Crazy Horse to surrender at Camp Robinson, Nebraska, the next spring; his three hundred men, one of the best-armed bands of Lakota, turned in barely more than a hundred guns.

Sitting Bull remained at large in Canada until July 19, 1881, when he brought his band back to Fort Buford, North Dakota. As a part of the surrender, Sitting Bull was promised a full pardon, and his people were promised rations, houses to live in, farming equipment, and a reservation in the Little Missouri region. But the promises were broken: His band was sent to Standing Rock Agency at Fort Yates, North Dakota, and Sitting Bull remained a prisoner at Fort Randall for two years. With the help of the Reverend Thomas L. Riggs of the Oahe mission, he was finally sent to Standing Rock on May 10, 1883, after other Indians explained that he had not killed Custer. He lived on the banks of the Grand River, near his birthplace in the heart of the reservation.

The agent for Standing Rock, Maj. James "White Hat" McLaughlin, worked constantly to break Sitting Bull's influence, organizing Indian police and creating rival chiefs among men who had surrendered early and been obedient and peaceful. Part of McLaughlin's plot was to send Sitting Bull away from the reservation to appear at meetings, patriotic gatherings, and performances of Buffalo Bill's Wild West show. While Sitting Bull was away, McLaughlin worked to undermine his influence on the reservation. Buffalo Bill respected the old chief and gave him a horse that could sit down and raise one hoof on command; as Sitting Bull was being murdered a few years later, the old horse went through his paces, creating a weird counterpoint to the action.

First, though, Sitting Bull had one more triumph. In 1888 another commission came to Standing Rock to arrange the cession of eleven million acres of Lakota lands at fifty cents an acre, pure thievery. Sitting Bull organized other leaders against the treaty, went to Washington to negotiate with the secretary of the interior, and finally agreed to $1.25 an acre. When J. J. Reynolds Crook, now a general, came back as a government representative in 1889 to get more Lakota land at the same price, Sitting Bull blocked the sale. When someone asked him what the Indians thought of it, according to Vestal, he said, "Indians! There are no Indians left but me!"

Lakota leader John Grass met with McLaughlin and signed the land cession agreement in secret. Shortly, McLaughlin ordered the

Indians to stop performing the Sun Dance and plotted to have Sitting Bull killed; his Indian police resigned, so he had to hire others who were not loyal to the chief. Though he was not authorized to do so, McLaughlin promised pensions to the arresting police and their widows and orphans, clear evidence that he expected a fight; Congress did not grant the pensions until nearly forty years later.

Sitting Bull was arrested in the middle of the night and dragged out of his house. Aroused by the commotion, his friends completely surrounded the police, but Sitting Bull agreed to go peacefully. Suddenly Catch-the-Bear, commander of Sitting Bull's bodyguard, appeared on the scene with a rifle, and Sitting Bull abruptly shouted, "I am not going. Do with me what you like. I am not going. Come on!

Come on! Take action! Let's go!" Immediately, Catch-the-Bear shot an Indian policeman; falling, the officer shot Sitting Bull, just as another officer shot the chief in the back. Either wound would have been fatal. While the police battled the friends of Sitting Bull, the old circus horse danced. Eventually, a hundred troopers of the Eighth Cavalry arrived to rescue the Indian police. Afterward, twelve Lakota lay dead, including four Indian policemen.

The only chief ever to lead all the Lakota was buried at Fort Yates on December 17, 1890, about two weeks before the Wounded Knee massacre. Muriatic acid and five gallons of chloride of lime were poured into the coffin. Newspaper reporters, perhaps the same ones who had printed rumors that Sitting Bull had personally killed Custer, published reports that the Indian department and military had plotted Sitting Bull's death; the *Chicago Tribune* called it an assassination, and others called it "cold-blooded, premeditated murder." Sitting Bull's relatives were taken to Standing Rock under guard, and while they were gone, most of their possessions were stolen, as was most of Sitting Bull's property, including cattle.

After the military post was abandoned and the bodies of soldiers removed from the cemetery and reburied at another post, Sitting Bull's grave was left, covered with weeds. Even in death, though, Sitting Bull was not allowed to rest easily. Newspapers of the day treated the story cautiously, but it appears that some citizens of Mobridge, thinking of profit, convinced Sitting Bull's three grand-daughters that he should be removed from his neglected grave and reburied near where he was born and died. The Indian bureau didn't object, as long as the relatives agreed and the body was not taken off the Standing Rock Reservation, but the state of North Dakota did. According to Bob Lee, writing in *Dakota Panorama*, "one night in the spring of 1954, a group of Indians and Mobridge citizens opened Sitting Bull's grave and spirited his decayed bones across the border into South Dakota before the North Dakota officials could prevent it. Sitting Bull's bones were reburied in a new grave on the west bank of the Missouri in the southeast corner of the Standing Rock Reservation."

If Vestal is correct about the muriatic acid and chloride of lime, it's hard to believe the midnight diggers found many bones. The site chosen for the new grave overlooked the Missouri River and was conveniently located near a highway. This time, the bones were encased in concrete to discourage midnight removal. Mobridge citizens, perhaps planning to expand the tourist trade in their neighborhood, financed a three-ton granite bust of the chief for the tomb. Carved by Korczak Ziolkowski, sculptor of Crazy Horse Monument,

176

the monument depicted the chief standing guard over his lands, as he had done for so long. A sign was posted to direct tourists.

But when the Oahe Dam was built on the Missouri, the impounded water that flooded so much reservation land also forced relocation of the bridge on the highway leading to the grave site and memorial. The site is no longer easily accessible; instead, it stands in isolation, overlooking the river and the northern prairies. "So," concludes Lee, "Sitting Bull—who wanted nothing from the white man except to be left alone in his own lands with his own people—finally found in death what he could not achieve during his stormy lifetime."

Probably few state residents share Vestal's opinion that Sitting Bull, besides being the most famous South Dakotan, is also the most interesting. "No one," said Vestal, "can ignore so many-sided a man . . . soldier, diplomat, organizer of the most unstable elements; his later roles of patriot, statesman, and prophet; the crushing defeats inflicted by his warriors upon hostile Indian nations and the armies of the United States." These achievements, said Vestal, should fascinate anyone who loves heroes. He also admired Sitting Bull's resolve "in the face of conquest, exile, starvation, treason, and death," qualities appealing to those who care for "lost causes and forsaken beliefs and impossible loyalties."

That description ought to appeal to South Dakotans, who have traditionally been champions of causes the rest of the nation gave up long ago (which afford considerable scope for humor to national news services) and loyalties that are scorned on a regular basis. However, South Dakotans are also stubborn, and as a result have steadfastly ignored the achievements of Sitting Bull and other Indians; no permanent monument to his greatness has appeared. He deserves the honors accorded other war heroes, however. Sitting Bull's job was to lead his people in battles against invaders of their lands, and he did it well. Sadly, many South Dakotans, a hundred years after statehood and Wounded Knee, are not quite ready yet to "bury the hatchet" or acknowledge the values of the original inhabitants in shaping the state's development, past, present, or future.

Indian Names

Names affixed by white explorers and settlers have replaced the more picturesque and metaphorical Indian names in many areas of the state, but in this territory, perhaps because so few white people ever lived here, many Lakota labels have remained: Little Eagle; Wakpala (meaning "creek"); Tatanka ("buffalo"); Bullhead; Red Horse Hawk; Broken Horn Bull.

Bruce Nelson, in *Land of the Dacotahs*, pays wry attention to the matter of Indian names and incidentally comments that, "save for their superior social and economic institutions," Indians were "discouragingly like white men." Now that Indians are trying to become a part of white society, he complains, one can hardly tell the difference "except for their names." Howard Fast, in his memorable novel *The Last Frontier*, has suggested that of all names, Indian names are the silliest. However, it may be argued that

> an Indian named Slow is not much sillier than a white man named Fast; that Corn Stalk, Red Top, and Strike-the-Ree are not per se more humorous than Roosevelt (Rose Field), Schwartzkopf (Black Head), and Eisenhower (Iron-Striker); and that Shake Tomahawk is no more ridiculous than that mighty name that has come ringing down the English centuries—the magic name of Shake Spear.

Nelson points out that the Indian naming system was simple and practical, depending on events that occurred when the individual was born or during childhood. Moreover, some of the humor whites found in the names resulted from sloppy translation or poor interpretation: One warrior called by the ignominious name Afraid-of-Soldier was a victim of mistranslation, his name really meaning "Their Soldiers Fear Him." In revenge, perhaps, the agent at Pine Ridge at the time of the Wounded Knee massacre, Dr. R. F. Royer, was called "Young-Man-Afraid-of-the-Indians" by the Lakota.

CORSON COUNTY

Most of the small towns along US 12 lie barely south of the dividing line between North and South Dakota. White Butte, founded in 1909, was named for the butte six miles south of town, composed of white chalk or limestone, which glitters in the sun. Early white pioneers called it "TX Butte" after the brand of Ben Garland, a rancher nearby. When a man named Orlando Giles was murdered nearby, it was briefly known as Giles Butte.

Thunder Hawk was named for nearby Thunder Hawk Butte, which in turn was named for a chief. Keldron, founded in 1909, may derive its name from a misspelling of the word "cauldron"; a ring of hills protects it and suggests the general shape of a huge kettle. Morristown sprang up in 1917 when thirty thousand cattle arrived from the Morris Packing Company of Chicago at the C-7 Ranch on the tracks of the new Chicago, Milwaukee & St. Paul Railroad. The shipping point was named for Nels P. Morris, head of the packing company and part owner of the ranch.

Watauga, according to W. J. Bordeaux, an interpreter in the early days of white habitation, was named for a Lakota word meaning "foam," or "foaming at the mouth." The name may be derived from a traditional story concerning hydrophobia, a much-feared affliction before introduction of the rabies vaccine. In it, a sleeping trapper is bitten by a maddened wolf during the wild chaos of rendezvous. In one version, the man dies; in another, the man is so loaded up with whiskey that the *wolf* dies. The tale appears several times in various fur trade histories and is always repeated as authentic, but it is never possible to document its actual occurrence.

The tiny settlement of McIntosh was named for two brothers who subcontracted to build the Milwaukee railroad grades across the Standing Rock Reservation in 1909. Although McIntosh has only about four hundred people, it is the seat of Corson County, which covers five thousand square miles and has a total population of about four thousand people. Nearby Walker was named for the owner of the W. I. Walker ranch, a major cattle-raising operation that shipped from this point.

The town of McLaughlin is named for James McLaughlin, the agent on the Standing Rock Reservation who battled Sitting Bull and author of a book titled, ironically, *My Friend, the Indian.* In recent years the community has gained notoriety because citizens believe a Dakota bigfoot wanders the area; folks have found large, humanlike tracks, and some claim to have seen the hairy creature. The road leading south out of town goes to Little Eagle, original campsite of Running Antelope and his band; the site is named after an Indian policeman killed in the struggle with Sitting Bull. Pow-wows held here each summer draw visitors, and a trading post operates at the center of town.

Wakpala lies a short distance southeast of McLaughlin. The name is Indian for "small brook," probably a reference to Oak Creek, which runs through the town. The small white church and buildings around it used to be St. Elizabeth's Episcopal Mission School and Home for Indian Children.

The Strip: Cowpokes and Cattle

Where the Standing Rock and Cheyenne River reservations met, a corridor of land six miles wide and more than eighty miles long—known as The Strip—was leased by the Milwaukee railroad and fenced after 1900 to make it easier for ranchers such as Murdo McKenzie, Cap Mossman, and Ed Lemmon to drive cattle to shipping points on the river. The Indians split a fee of twenty-five cents

Nat Love, thought by some historians to be the original "Deadwood Dick," was one of many black cowboys who came west seeking freedom by riding the open range. He posed for this picture in Deadwood with the tools of his trade—a gun belt and a well-used rope. His neckerchief could protect him from sun and dust and was also decorative; both his hair and his hat are more plentiful than those of the typical cowboy. —South Dakota Historical Society

a head for all cattle and horses using the corridor, but sheep traveled free, possibly as a plain statement that they didn't count in cow country. The railroad company provided water holes where natural water was unavailable. Among the ranching companies using The Strip were the Matador, the Flying V of the Sheidley Company, A. D. Marriott's H.A.T. outfit—which had three brands, shaped like square, pointed, and round headgear—and Mossman's Diamond A Ranch. The Indians who kept cattle also used this unique, and convenient, passageway.

The eastern end of The Strip was on the Missouri River south of Mobridge at LeBeau and Evarts. There cattle crossed the river on a pontoon bridge and were loaded into Milwaukee railroad cars for the long trip to eastern markets. A railroad depot, known as Glencross, drew settlers from North Dakota when the railroads were active. Trail City was known as Cheyenne Junction until 1912, then named for its location on The Strip. When rail lines established terminals west of Mobridge, Pierre, and Chamberlain, The Strip was no longer needed; the fences fell down and the shipping towns disappeared.

One important cattle-shipping center, Evarts, began in 1900 when the railroad reached it and was a lively town while the herds were coming through. Cowboy Jim O'Connell recalled hearing a Texan recite a toast in an Evarts bar:

We came into this world all naked and bare,
We've lived in this world through trouble and care;
When we go out of this world, we'll go God knows where,
But if we're good here, then we'll be good there.

Glenham, founded nine years after Evarts, was named because it was located in a glen. When the railroad began building track toward Mobridge, where a better place had been found for a bridge across the river, buildings from several surrounding communities were moved to Glenham.

Many of the small communities in this area are gaining some transient life from the recreation offered by Oahe Dam. Tourists and sports enthusiasts are attracted by hunting and fishing opportunities. New Evarts, a resort twelve miles southeast of Mobridge on SD 1804, offers camping, fishing supplies, and a restaurant and bar for people taking advantage of Oahe's recreation spots.

However, other towns were killed with the coming of the dam. The cow town of LeBeau, now largely submerged by the waters of Lake Oahe, was settled in 1883 and had attracted more than two hundred people before the pontoon bridge was built at Evarts; the town quickly faded. It was given new life when Evarts was in turn abandoned and the Milwaukee tracks extended closer to LeBeau. Again the settlement boomed—within three years it had almost five hundred residents.

Cowboys who worked on the reservation leases of the big ranches met at DuFran's saloon in LeBeau until Murdo McKenzie's son David was shot dead by an old Matador cowhand who was tending bar in December 1909. The story might have come straight from a Wild West novel but is reported as fact by Bob Lee in *Last Grass Frontier*. Lee says young "Dode" McKenzie was managing the Matador's reservation herds at the time. A personable man, he was well liked by the other cowboys and had inherited his father's tough frame if not his Scottish reticence. He was known to like his liquor and to get rowdy under its influence. "But those who were on the scene at the time insisted that he had not been drinking when Bud Stephens gunned him down in DuFran's saloon," says Lee. Later, a dozen rumors circulated: that Stephens and McKenzie had disagreed in Texas; that McKenzie had threatened Stephens; that some cowboys had convinced Stephens that McKenzie was out to get him. The final rumor has the ring of truth, but if so, the prank produced tragic results: "Stephens pumped three quick shots from his .45 into McKenzie's body as he came into the saloon. . . . Stephens' first shot slammed into McKenzie's chest and the bartender fired two more shots into his back as the wounded cowman staggered out of the saloon to die in the street. McKenzie was armed, but he never even attempted to draw his gun during the fracas."

Locals believed it was a clear case of murder and expected Stephens to be convicted; they said it was a second crime when Stephens was acquitted, in spite of the "six high-priced lawyers" hired by Murdo McKenzie to convict the old cowboy.

Stephens left town suddenly at the request of irate citizens, but the incident "marked the beginning of the end of LeBeau," says Lee. "The Matador cowboys boycotted the town and a few months after Stephens' trial in 1910 a fire of unexplained origin wiped out almost all of the Main street business houses." Volunteer firefighters noticed right away that the fire hose had been cut, as had the telephone and telegraph lines. "The street where McKenzie died was brightly illuminated by the flaming buildings which flanked it," but DuFran's saloon, ironically, did not burn.

MOBRIDGE

Founded in 1906, Mobridge got its name from a telegrapher's combination of the abbreviation for Missouri (River) and "bridge." The town lies at the east end of the Milwaukee railroad bridge over the river. By 1909 it boasted three general stores, two coal yards, two livery stables and an auto garage, an elevator, a blacksmith shop, and one each of the usual frontier amenities: jewelry store, millinery, drugstore, cigar store, furniture, bakery, shoe shop, hand laundry, and pool hall. However, it had five land dealers and four land locators eager to sell more lots. It became a cattle- and crop-shipping center, with a livestock sale barn and grain exchange.

Though they insisted on the purity of water drawn directly from the river, Mobridge citizens couldn't drink it until it had settled—

it was too muddy. For the same reason, laundry was actually shipped to Redfield, South Dakota, and Minneapolis, Minnesota. By 1911, however, a couple of steam laundries had opened in town, and the wash could be done locally. Folks also cut ice from the river in winter for use in preserving food; in 1913 one enterprising businessman cut six thousand tons of ice and sold it throughout the year from a warehouse. By January 1915 nearly a hundred teams of horses and two hundred men worked to salvage an average of seventeen thousand tons of ice a year.

Nearly four thousand people live here today, and the region is being promoted for its access to Oahe Dam recreational facilities, and its open, uncrowded atmosphere. Each July the town hosts a rodeo called, incongruously, the "Sitting Bull Stampede."

About thirty old Arikara sites exist within a ten-mile radius of Mobridge, and many of the artifacts are on display in the town's museum. Built on a horseshoe bend of the "old river," Mobridge is surrounded on three sides by shoreline. The southern part of the horseshoe, called Lower Bottom, is in Walworth County, and the Upper Bottom is in Campbell County. Both areas are alluvial, with heavy stands of cottonwood, willow, elm, and similar trees offering good cover for hunters near the river. State regulations allow a fishing enthusiast to catch more than 445 fish a day in the area in nineteen different varieties; limits include four walleye; five largemouth bass; fifty rock bass, white bass, crappie, bluegill, and perch; a hundred bullheads; five gallons of smelt; and one muskellunge. Some go after salmon; bait shop owners are usually happy to reveal where they're biting. The annual Bridge City Walleye tournament in June draws more than a hundred teams.

Manuel Lisa's Fort

Fur trade baron Manuel Lisa built a fort north of Mobridge in 1812. One of the most influential and intriguing characters in Dakota history, Lisa was one of the organizers of the Missouri Fur Company. In 1811 he left St. Louis to collect winter furs from the site of a post on Cedar Island, midway between Pierre and Big Bend, that had burned in the spring of 1810. He was also looking for his associate, Maj. Andrew Henry, who hadn't returned when expected. Lisa started upriver hard on the heels of John Jacob Astor's Pacific Fur Company expedition, led by Wilson Price Hunt. The members of the Astor party, generally called Astorians, were traveling up the Missouri on their way to the Pacific coast, where they would establish a trading post. This group left St. Joseph, Missouri, on April 21, 1811.

Manuel Lisa, a founder of the Missouri Fur Company and an important trader on the Upper Missouri.
—State Historical Society of North Dakota

Lisa's party of twenty keelboaters hoped to overtake the Astorians—nineteen days and about 240 miles ahead—so that both parties might more safely pass the hostile bands of Lakota. The race that followed stretched over two months and about eleven hundred miles. Lisa sent a messenger to catch the Astorians, and Hunt promised to wait—but immediately worked even harder to stay ahead. Ramsey Crooks and Robert McClellan, two traders in Hunt's party, believed Lisa was responsible for the hostility of the Indians Hunt met. They may have been right; Lisa later stirred up trouble between the Yankton and Missouri bands of Lakota. He reasoned that if the Indians didn't trust each other, they would guard their camps closely and not wander far. He encouraged them to plant crops, hunt, and trade with the Americans instead of joining the British in the War of 1812.

By June 5, Hunt's and Lisa's parties camped only a short distance apart near Pierre. Hunt and Lisa quarreled and nearly fought a duel, but two English scientists with Hunt's party separated them, and the parties traveled on opposite banks of the river for two days without communication. Near the mouth of the Cheyenne River they were delayed by a huge herd of buffalo swimming the Missouri and arrived together at the main Arikara village on June 12. Hunt traded goods for horses. In return, the Arikaras wanted primarily guns and ammunition for their war against the Lakota. After six weeks, Hunt's party continued west with eighty-two horses; their route was generally west from the Mobridge area along the Grand River. After some harrowing experiences they reached the Pacific and established Astoria at the mouth of the Columbia River. Lisa went on north to the Mandan villages near Bismarck.

Lisa divided the winter of 1811-12 between the Arikara and Mandan villages with eighty-seven men, trade goods, and barge loads of cows, hogs, cats, and chickens—probably the first domestic animals in the Dakotas. He built a fort just south of the present South Dakota boundary, and it served as his headquarters until it was destroyed in 1813. A town named Kenel later rose on the site where Lisa's fort had been built; the Lakota called it *Ho-ta*, "big city," for the large Catholic farm school and mission there. However, Lake Oahe's waters covered the site, so the town was moved to its present location northwest of Mobridge on SD 1806.

What might be called the state's first Thanksgiving feast occurred November 19, 1812, when the post was formally completed. The following month, Lisa's chief clerk, John C. Luttig, casually recorded in his journal an event so important historians are still arguing about whether it really happened at that time and place: the death of "the wife of Charbonneau, a Snake squaw." Luttig added, "She was a good and the best woman in the fort, aged about twenty-five years. She left a fine infant girl." This was almost surely Sakakawea, the Bird Woman, who accompanied the Lewis and Clark expedition; most sources refer to her as "Sacajawea," but the correct Shoshone spelling is probably "Sakakawea." For years many historians believed she lived near Fort Hall, Idaho, until she was very old, but that assumption rested on flimsy evidence (some of it probably false) and has now been quite conclusively disproved. Instead, she lies in an unmarked grave, probably under the waters of Lake Oahe. A monument to her stands on the hill west of the bridge across the Missouri.

By the time Luttig made his brief journal entry, the War of 1812 was in full swing, and British agents were encouraging the Lakota to attack Americans. Hostile Yanktons killed a man at the door of the fort early in 1813 and probably were responsible for burning the fort on March 5, 1813, the last day of Luttig's journal. Lisa abandoned the fort and arrived in St. Louis on June 1. In 1814 he was appointed a subagent for the Upper Missouri and divided his time between the Big Bend post and one near Omaha, working to keep the Indians on the American side. Most other fur traders suspended their Upper Missouri activities during the war.

By 1817 the fur trade was again active, and a thousand men may have been working as traders on the river by 1822. Lisa died in 1820, and other traders began moving into his former territory. His successors, however, were not as well liked by the native inhabitants. About five miles upstream from the bridge is the approximate site of an 1823 attack on Gen. William H. Ashley's second fur-trapping expedition by the Arikara Indians. The journals of James Clyman, one of the trappers, indicate the attack was precipitated when several white men remained in the Indian village overnight, probably for feminine companionship; one of these, Aaron Stephens, was killed. The rest, who had been sleeping on shore, were pinned down by heavy rifle fire from the Indians. Clyman noted in his novel spelling style that since the party had traded ammunition for horses, "You will easely prceive that we had little else to do than to Stand on a bear sand barr and be shot at, at long range Their being seven or Eigh hundred guns in village and we having the day previously furnished them with abundance of Powder and Ball."

The boatmen were afraid to pick up the trappers huddled behind dead and dying horses on the bank, so several members of the expedition, including Clyman, attempted to swim the river. He stuck the barrel of his rifle in his belt with the lock over his head and dived in. But the current was faster than he thought, and he had to untangle the rifle from his clothing and drop it in the river. He was about to give up his buckskin hunting shirt when a man who had caught a drifting skiff helped him into it.

The man, Reed Gibson, was immediately shot, and Clyman rowed both of them to the opposite shore, where he led several Indians away from the wounded man in a running chase of several miles. After he'd outrun the Indians, he returned to Gibson, and the two men were picked up by the keelboat; Gibson died on board that night. Clyman survived to become one of the excellent record keepers of the fur trade, witness his *Journal of a Mountain Man*. More flamboyant fur trappers like Jedediah Smith received more media attention, but none was a more successful trapper, astute observer, or faithful recorder than Clyman.

The Fool Soldier Band

Also near Mobridge is a monument, erected in 1909, commemorating the tale of the Fool Soldier Band, one of the most intriguing stories in Dakota history concerning Indian-white relations. Even today, details given by historians vary wildly. Karolevitz says that two white women and seven children were captured in Minnesota, probably after the 1862 Sioux Uprising; Will G. Robinson, in *Dakota Panorama*, names the women as Mrs. Duly and Mrs. Wright and

Carl Bodmer portrayed the Mandan chief Four Bears wearing a war bonnet and holding a coup stick. Buffalo horns and an unsheathed knife surmount his war bonnet. Plains Indian custom required that every eagle feather be awarded for a brave deed witnessed by one or more warriors, so Four Bears was obviously much respected by his tribe. Ermine tails dangle from the headdress and shoulders of his war shirt.
—State Historical Society of North Dakota

187

says there were only six children. By November of that year, the captives were in the camp of White Lodge, which numbered about 180 Santee, though it is probable that those Santee were not their original captors.

Eleven young Lakota boys—Karolevitz names Martin Charger, Kills Game and Comes Home, Four Bear, Mad Bear, Pretty Bear, Sitting Bear, Swift Bird, One Rib, Strikes Fire, Red Dog, and Charging Dog—decided to rescue the captives by trading food and blankets for them. White historians have often remarked on the selfless nature of their quest. It must be noted, however, that the boys' motives may not have been entirely altruistic: Realizing that it would be unwise to join a war party at that time, they may have used the rescue as a chance to prove their mettle by showing the bravery and concern for weaker members of the tribe that characterized a Lakota warrior.

Whatever their motives, the young Lakota were required to bargain away all they owned for the captives—not only the food and blankets they had planned to trade, but also their guns and horses. They were left only one horse and wagon to carry the frail and wounded captives nearly a hundred miles back to the nearest white settlement at Fort Pierre. The boys walked; Karolevitz adds that, according to the legend, Martin Charger "even gave up his moccasins to one of the barefooted women."

Meanwhile, a Major Pattee, commander of the post at Fort Randall, had been notified of the women's capture and started to the rescue with two companies of the Iowa Infantry and a company of Dakota Cavalry. Their progress was slow in the bad weather, and two days' march from Fort Pierre, according to Doane Robinson in *South Dakota History*, "they met two half-breeds with the women and children, who had in fact been rescued by the Fool Soldier band of Sans Arc boys led by Charger and Swift Bird."

Whatever the details of the rescue, the Lakota were never rewarded in any way by the U.S. government, though Major Pattee's troops took up a collection of several hundred dollars for the white victims. Perhaps because of the lack of gratitude, the young Lakota were known afterward as the Fool Soldier Band for their difficult and risky effort.

But that is not quite the end of the story.

Another chapter was written in late 1991, well over a century later, when a descendant of one of the captives met a descendant of one of the rescuers and gave his thanks. Paul Carpenter, a cardiologist in Sioux Falls, had read the story of the rescue years ago; his research indicated that one of the children freed by the Lakota was six-year-old Lillian Everett, the niece of his great-grandfather. She was one of nine women and children taken captive after a band of Sisseton Lakota attacked a settlement at Lake Shetek in southwestern Minnesota and killed fourteen people. When Carpenter discovered that Harry Charger of Swift Bird was the great-grandson of one of the rescuers, he wrote a letter. Charger, intrigued, replied, "I've always wondered what happened to those descendants of those people who were captured and rescued. Nobody ever said, 'Thank you' or 'Go to hell' or nothing."

When they met, Charger and Carpenter smoked a traditional Lakota pipe and shared soft drinks, cookies, and stories they'd heard about the 1862 incident. "It was as if something that should have been done a long time ago was being done," explained the cardiologist. "Even though I'm not a direct descendant of hers, I feel like I can speak for her and say, 'Thank you.'"

Charger said he was happy about the gratitude. But he explained that the Teton Lakota didn't rescue the whites for appreciation. "They didn't expect anything like that," he said. "They just did a man's job."

SD 50
Fort Thompson—Minnesota
156 Miles

SD 50 begins on the east side of the Missouri River at Fort Thompson, hugs the river bank as it ranges north-south, crossing I-90 east of Chamberlain, and zigzags to Platte. There the highway joins SD 45, and its surface improves at once. From Platte, the combined highways lurch east-southeast to Richland, South Dakota, on the Minnesota border. The Buffalo County/Fort Thompson region is covered in another section (SD 34); this discussion covers the stretch from Platte to the state line.

CHARLES MIX AND
BON HOMME COUNTIES

All of the communities in this rich farming region began collecting settlers during the late 1870s and early 1880s. Even in modern times, alert travelers can see signs of that early settlement history; highways and county roads were built on the boundaries between quarter sections to avoid cutting across fields and destroying crops. Thus, roads tend to bolt straight ahead, then, suddenly, "hang a hard right," as locals say; unwary speeders can be fatally surprised by ninety-degree turns. Slow down!

Because farmers were unable to take time out for long shopping trips, communities are about as far apart as a wagon could travel and return in a day—ten to fifteen miles. Even now, on a clear day, dust rises from a half dozen directions, hanging in geometric curtains over the flat plain as farmers plow their ground. Drivers of nearly all the farm vehicles you meet will wave; watch out for immense, slow-moving tractors, which have the right-of-way. Some farmers do not fence their fields on the sensible theory that corn hardly ever escapes—but periodically they turn cows into the fields after harvest. Watch for cows grazing ditches and farm dogs whiling away long hours waiting for cars to bark at. Local drivers know where these canines are, but a sudden snarling rush could startle an unwary driver into running over one.

At some crossroads, you'll find a "corner"—Stanley Corner, for example (closed now), a gas station with a few groceries and necessities tucked onto the shelves. Another common sight in the fields are churches, sometimes set at the corner of a quarter section on land donated by the farmer. Many of these modestly lovely churches house Mennonites who built the church with their own work-roughened hands and now gather on Sundays from the surrounding farms. Small cemeteries often lie nearby, sheltered by gaunt old spruce trees planted by the first settlers to bury a loved one in this new land.

Numerous communities were settled entirely by colonists who arrived together from a particular country, or even a single city in the old country. These families often took adjoining homesteads, continued to speak their native language, and traded in villages settled by members of the same ethnic group. Norwegians, who started plowing while Easterners were still referring to the "Great American Desert," were probably the first South Dakota settlers who were not trappers or fur traders; Irish and Polish neighbors were less welcome than Indians in those days. In 1859 and 1860 groups of Norwegians settled on fertile bottomland in the area called "the lakes" near the site of modern Gayville. Within a short distance in this region you may still find remnants of Dutch, Czechoslovakian, Norwegian, Bohemian, German, Russian, Irish, Polish, or other European cultures. Many people who grew up in the early 1900s spoke their parents' tongue, along with English and a smattering of Sioux learned from playmates.

Old-timers still talk about the German Russian settlers' method of getting to town. In the old country, travelers had formed wagon caravans as protection against thieves, and they followed the same practice in their new home. The farmer who lived the greatest distance from town would start early on the agreed day, putting hay in the wagon for the children to sit on and for the horse to eat on the trip. His neighbors joined him, one by one, until twenty or thirty wagons in single file were headed for the city. Adults and children swapped seats with people in other wagons to visit with friends on the way. News and gossip were exchanged—and sometimes marriages were arranged—on the way to town.

On arrival, they watered and fed their horses, and families separated to shop. At midday they met at a grocery store provided with tables and chairs, where they spread lunches brought from home— homemade bread and wurst—and continued to visit. When shopping was completed, the wagons reassembled in line and headed back over the plains until each family turned off at its homestead. Though they soon realized the caravan wasn't necessary as protection from bandits, the settlers continued the custom because it was fun.

Platte, Wagner, Avon

Platte, settled in 1882 by a colony of Dutch immigrants, was named for Platte Creek, named in turn for Platte Lake, which the creek drains. The persistent researcher, however, will discover elsewhere that Platte Lake was named for Platte Creek, and so the cycle begins again. Somewhere along the line, the name was probably mispronounced or otherwise distorted from the name of Bernard Pratte of St. Louis, an early trader and partner to Pierre Chouteau, Jr. The town serves a large trade territory of farmers living northwest along the river; in the late 1930s it had a creamery and flour mill. South of town are the breaks of the Missouri River, where the country becomes more hilly and broken.

Wagner, laid out by the Milwaukee Land Company in 1900, was named for Walt Wagner, a pioneer postmaster and storekeeper. Mr. Wagner had a town named after him because he took a group of railroad officials on a successful fishing trip—railroad men must have been getting a little giddy by this time and seemed to be running out of ways to name towns. Wagner became a trading center for the Indians of the Yankton Reservation and acquired a very western flavor, even though it is in farming country east of the river.

Avon, birthplace of Sen. George McGovern, was established in 1879 as a post office at the home of George Phoenix, the first local postmaster. Some say the postmaster named it for his old home town, Avon, New York; others say Mrs. Phoenix named it for Shakespeare, the bard of Avon.

Tyndall and Tabor

Tyndall, founded in 1879, is the seat of Bon Homme County. Settled primarily by Germans and Bohemians, it was named by Dr. O. Richmond for John Tyndall, a British scientist who lectured throughout the United States in 1872. For a time in the late 1890s, the town's flour mill was one of several in the state that were supplied by area farmers and generated electricity as a by-product; others were at Beresford, Bowdle, Springfield, and Vermillion. By about 1910 such mills were unable to compete with larger facilities that were in larger towns and could blend different grades of wheat. By 1961 the Tri-State Milling Company in Rapid City was the only operating commercial flour mill left in the state. Modern notions of efficiency drove out small businesses that filled a local need, employed local people, and yielded a useful by-product. Now the region's farmers sell their wheat through large corporations that can manipulate prices and buy their flour the same way they buy electricity—one reason fewer farmers exist.

Tabor, current population about four hundred, lies at the center of a rural Bohemian community begun when Frank Bem advertised for Czechs who wanted to take up new land. A large group came in 1869 and named their city for the one they had left behind; it is still known as the "mother city of Dakota Czechs." In the 1930s most business in Tabor was conducted in Bohemian; the newspaper was printed in Bohemian, and the city had a Bohemian baseball team and the only all-Bohemian American Legion post in the state. Tabor still holds *sokols*, performances of military exercises, followed—sensibly—by feasts featuring rich food including pork dishes, potato dumplings, sauerkraut, beer, and *kolaches*, sweet biscuits filled with fruit or poppy seeds. Many residents now speak English in public but speak—and cook—Bohemian at home.

Townspeople did ambitious advance planning from the time they arrived in 1872. First citizens voted to buy the homestead of Johanna Kocer for a town site. The 160 acres were divided into fifty-three lots; 40 acres were set aside for the town and 3 acres each for the cemetery, church, and school. Matt Petrik, described as a "music man," came in 1872 and organized a band, making Tabor famous for fifty years. The 1880 census listed 569 mostly Bohemian surnames; many are still listed in the modern telephone book. The first Catholic

Felix Vinatieri, born in Italy in 1834, was Lt. Col. George Custer's bandmaster. Vinatieri was with Custer's troops wintering near Yankton before the Battle of the Little Bighorn; he later returned to Yankton and became a prominent citizen.
—Yankton County Historical Society

church was built in 1872 of chalk rock hauled from the Missouri bluffs; the town's first schoolhouse followed shortly, built in 1873 of logs.

In 1873 Lieutenant Colonel Custer and his Seventh Cavalry troopers camped in the vicinity of Tabor and Yankton for a time. Custer's force included eight hundred officers and enlisted men, as well as some officers' wives. Also with the troops were forty "laundresses," seven hundred horses, and two hundred mules. Most of the wives lived in the town's hotels, but Mrs. Custer and her servants moved into a small cabin without a stove near the regiment. Shortly after Custer's arrival, a blizzard struck. Horses and mules were moved into any shelter the men could find, and Mrs. Custer took ill soldiers into her cabin, wrapping them in carpets because she had no stove. Custer later commended the people of the area for saving the lives of his soldiers and animals.

YANKTON

Sadly, the highway approach to the historic city of Yankton is much like that of any growing town these days: a long strand of fast-food joints, shopping malls, warehouselike buildings selling bargain furniture, gas stations, pizza joints, and rows of houses built in no recognizable architectural style. A traveler might shoot through town on wide bypasses that seem designed to encourage just that—avoiding the town without sampling its long and colorful history. Even a brief drive through the broad, tree-lined streets will reward the eye with rows of prim Victorian houses; the streets were laid out wide enough so teamsters could turn a wagon hitched behind an eight-horse team, not cramped together as is common in modern cities. One of the oldest settlements in South Dakota, Yankton has witnessed much of the history of both the white and Indian inhabitants of the state.

The first permanent white settlers in South Dakota were probably two Frenchmen, Pierre Dorion and Joseph Garreau. Dorion married a Yankton Sioux in 1785; he'd been living with the tribe in the southeastern part of the state for more than twenty years when Lewis and Clark met him. Garreau, who came to the Upper Missouri in 1787, settled among the Arikaras a few years later. When Lewis and Clark came back downriver in 1806, opportunists had already begun trotting along behind: Robert McClellan's trading post stood at the mouth of the James River, which emptied into the Missouri about half a mile south of where it does today.

Strike-the-Ree: Yankton Statesman

Another important early resident was ignored by many historians: the Yankton leader Padaniapapi, Strike-the-Ree, who was born during the visit of Lewis and Clark in 1804 on Green Island in the Missouri River, opposite the city's site. When the baby was only a few hours old, Meriwether Lewis—seeing an opportunity a modern political campaign director would drool over—wrapped an American flag around the child and delivered a speech contrived to persuade the watching Indians to cooperate with the expedition. "This boy will be a great chief among his people," said Lewis, "and will live to be a good American."

Perhaps not coincidentally, Strike-the-Ree was the leader who agreed to the 1858 Yankton Treaty of Cession, in which the tribe gave up its land and agreed to move to a reservation on the east bank of the Missouri (just north of the present state border with Nebraska). Though a small and hostile faction of Yanktons had sec-

Charles Picotte was the son of a fur trader and nephew of Chief Strike-the-Ree. Like many half-breed children of French fur trappers, he was educted in St. Louis. He helped government officials persuade the Yankton Indians to cede land to the United States. His reward, 640 acres of land, was the site of the original town of Yankton.
—South Dakota State Historical Society

ond thoughts about the treaty, Strike-the-Ree spoke with resignation of the inevitability of white settlement. "The white men are coming in like maggots," he said, advising that resistance was useless because whites outnumbered Indians. Brave warriors would die, and women and children would be left alone. "We must accept it," he said, "get the best terms we can get and try to adopt their ways."

In 1862 Inkpaduta tried to persuade Strike-the-Ree's warriors to join him on the warpath in Iowa and Minnesota, but the leader refused and kept the terms of the treaty all his life. His insistence on peace often brought him into sharp conflict with young men in his band who wanted to fight for their hunting grounds. Helen Rezatto, in *The Making of the Two Dakotas*, says the chief and his family were "persecuted, insulted, and their lives were threatened. Old Strike, whom many grateful whites honored by calling 'noblest Roman of them all,' was shot at, his ponies slaughtered and disemboweled, his cabin destroyed."

The tombstone of Strike-the-Ree rises above the grass and other graves in the cemetery of the Yankton sub-agency at Greenwood, South Dakota. —South Dakota State Historical Society

Despite this harsh treatment, Strike-the-Ree remained a leader among the Yanktons and retained a loyal following among those who believed an imperfect peace was better than war. Because Lakota leadership depended not on heredity or financial power but on supporters' free choice, he must have been a man of extraordinary honesty and excellent judgment. He kept the provisions of the 1858 treaty with "a fidelity which amounted to a religious zeal," said Doane Robinson, state historian.

Historians disagree about whether the leader's name was Strike-the-Ree or Struck-by-the-Ree, Robert Karolevitz points out in *Challenge*. In one version, the young Lakota warrior speared an Arikara opponent; in another, he was defeated by the Ree and wore a kerchief over his head for the rest of his life to hide the scars of a partial

George Kingsbury, a pioneer and friend of Strike-the-Ree, became a newspaper editor and historian. He wrote the two-volume History of Dakota Territory.
—South Dakota State Historical Society

scalping. George W. Kingsbury, who moved to Yankton during its early years and knew Old Strike—as whites insisted on calling him—always used the former name.

White Settlement Begins

Like most Indian treaties, the Yankton Treaty of Cession was intended to open up vast new territories to white settlement. By early 1858 settlers anxious to get at the Yankton lands had gathered on the Nebraska side of the Missouri River. Some of the same conditions that made the site ideal for the Indians drew white town site agents: The region offered easy access to wood and water, and the gentle slope to the river facilitated river traffic and commerce. From the beginning, two rival land companies wanted to establish a town on the spot occupied by Strike-the-Ree's villagers. One, the Upper Missouri Land Company, began negotiating with the Yanktons in February 1858. The other party, led by C. J. Holman, came up from Sioux City, Nebraska, to a point directly opposite present-day Yankton. After cautious reconnoitering, Holman's men crossed to the Dakota side on March 20, 1858, and set up camp, the first white settlement on the present site of Yankton. Its existence, however, was short-lived; since they were not licensed traders, the Sioux Citians were considered trespassers and were chased off by the Indians. A log house they built on furtive trips across the river is now considered the first "improvement" in Yankton, though it was burned down by Indians almost immediately.

At the same time, George D. Fiske, who worked for Frost, Todd & Company, pitched a tent nearby; because he was a licensed trader, his residence was legal. In July 1858 he built a two-room log house on the riverbank east of Walnut Street and began trading with the Sioux, thus becoming the first permanent, legal white resident of Yankton. The building he erected still stands on Walnut Street just west of the northern approach to the US 81 bridge over the Missouri. But Fiske did not survive to see Dakota become a territory; he tried to walk home one night in February 1861 in a raging blizzard and was found three days later face down in a snow drift, defeated by the Dakota weather.

In 1859 Chief Smutty Bear assembled hostile tribe members near the future town to resist being moved to a reservation. A confrontation might have resulted, but the new Indian agent, Major A. H. Redfield, diplomatically announced that he was preparing a great feast for the tribe at their agency at Greenwood, sixty-five miles to the west. He then climbed into his boat and headed upstream; as it struggled against the current of the Missouri River, the Yanktons kept abreast of it along the banks and were led peaceably away. Helen Rezatto says that as the "orderly exodus of men, women, children, horses, and dogs" moved up the river, the crowd of eager homesteaders who had been waiting on the Nebraska side of the river started paddling across in anything that would float to lay immediate claim to the vacated land.

The employees of Frost, Todd & Company had put together a raft of logs and held it against the bank until the signal was given, then worked all night marking off town lots and laying foundations for log houses. The Indians had cut all the trees from the village site, so early settlers floated new ones across the river from Nebraska's

North Yankton in 1874 still had mud streets and frame storefronts typical of towns in the early stages of development. —State Historical Society of North Dakota

forests. The first buildings were typical for the early days of the territory, crude shelters with sod roofs and dirt floors around log frameworks.

Like most towns in what had very recently been Indian territory, early Yankton suffered several Indian scares. Rumors frequently spread that the former inhabitants were on the warpath. Many such reports were false, based on fear and perhaps a little bit on guilt. But when word spread in 1862 of the Sioux Uprising in Minnesota, Yanktonians responded briskly. Volunteers built a fort at the intersection of Broadway and Third (today, markers between Broadway and Cedar on SD 50—also called Fourth Street—outline all four corners of the stockade). The 450-square foot structure was built of cedar posts and boards, packed sod and earth. About three hundred settlers moved into or near the stockade for several weeks, and troopers from the Dakota Cavalry gave instruction in the use of weapons.

When that rebellion was quelled, and with the Yanktons safely ensconced on their reservation, settlers were free to begin creating white civilization at Yankton. Settlers flocked into the new town, named after the people they'd driven out. "Yankton" is a corruption of the Sioux tribal name *Ihanktonwan*, meaning "end village," a position that implies the band guarded the rear approach in encampments. The original Yankton town site, about nine hundred acres, reached along the river from what is now Summit Street to Ferdig Avenue and north to the river bluffs. The town was incorporated in 1862.

The steamer Far West, *piloted by Capt. Grant Marsh, hauls firewood in this photograph, but in 1876 it brought the wounded of Reno's company from the Little Bighorn down the Yellowstone to Fort Lincoln on the Missouri in fifty-four hours, a record.* —State Historical Society of North Dakota

By 1867 gold seekers were beginning to pass through Yankton on their way to Idaho and other gold-mining regions. Their trade increased business but spurred the migration of travelers and potential settlers west, away from Yankton. Still, business boomed, and Yankton became one of the territory's most important shipping and supply points. Though some came overland, travelers and businessmen interested in speed often relied on steamboats. Today, with good highways extending like spider webs in all directions, it is easy to forget how useful the river was for fast, efficient transportation—even in days when the boats weren't as well built as they might be today.

The ferocious Missouri River exacted a heavy toll, however; wrecks were frequent. In 1865, for example, the *Tempest* sank at Bon Homme island just west of Yankton, at the same spot where the *Imperial* was crushed by ice in 1867. Thrifty builders often used salvaged pieces of a wreck to build another boat, and townspeople became adept at recycling pieces of boats into other useful objects—for example, the bell from the *Imperial* was recovered for use by the

Congregational Church, the Yankton Academy, and the local high school, finally moving to the Yankton Territorial Museum.

The West's most famous steamship, the *Far West*, was built in 1870 to the specifications of Capt. Grant Marsh. It was light, strong, and fast: Stretching 190 feet long, the boat drew only 4 feet, 6 inches, even when it was fully loaded with four hundred tons—a full cargo. In 1872, under Capt. Sanford B. Coulson, the steamboat chopped almost six days off the speed record for travel from Sioux City, Iowa, to Fort Benton, Montana, making the trip in seventeen days.

During the Indian campaign of 1876, the *Far West* ferried supplies from Fort Lincoln at Bismarck, North Dakota, up the Missouri River. On Sunday, June 25, 1876, Captain Marsh was ordered to continue up the Big Horn River so supplies would be within reach of troops during the Battle of the Little Bighorn; only the *Far West*'s shallow draft could have made the move possible. He was anchored at the mouth of the river when he received word that Custer's entire command had been killed; some men on board the steamer heard rifle fire from the battle. Three days later, Gen. Alfred H. Terry, whose soldiers fought in the battle, chartered the steamboat at $350 a day to carry his wounded men back to Fort Lincoln; Comanche, the horse that became famous as the "only survivor" of the Custer fight, rode along. The *Far West* traveled more than seven hundred miles to Bismarck in fifty-four hours, establishing the all-time speed record for a steamboat on the Missouri, an average of thirteen miles an hour.

This undated photo shows downtown Yankton looking east from the corner of Walnut Street. A storefront sign at left advertises "Chicago Millinery." —Yankton County Historical Society

Yankton: A City of Firsts

The details of Yankton's early years are so varied and interesting they fill pages in histories written of the town and state. In *Yankton Celebrates: The Centennial of South Dakota 1889-1989*, Don Allan notes Yankton's impressive list of "firsts," including the arrival of Bridget Stanage, considered to be the first woman in the territory. Stanage helped her husband, John, set up a ferry on the James River in 1859. Mrs. George Ash, who also arrived in 1859, is listed as the territory's first white female citizen. In addition, Yankton claims to have had South Dakota's first physician, minister, church, carpenter, blacksmith, saloon keeper, butcher, brewer, banker, hardware dealer, harness maker, druggist, drugstore, telegraph, bank, train, fire-fighting unit, paid fire chief, motorized fire truck, high school, school paper, institution of higher learning, jail, white child, social gathering, circus, and night football game. Today, Yankton is often called the "Mother City of the Dakotas."

The first newspaper in Yankton (and in the territory), also the first daily, was the *Dakota Democrat*, now the *Press and Dakotan*. The paper was started here in 1858, an event recorded on a plaque at the west end of Eighth Street. However, a tablet on Fourth Street claims that the *Weekly Dakotian* was the state's first newspaper, established June 6, 1861. If not the first, the *Dakotian* (occasionally spelled *Dakotan*) was certainly among the cleverest of the early papers; on October 6, 1863, it printed a punning plea for a pressing community need: "A first-class shoemaker would make his everlast-

Christ Episcopal Church, the first in Yankton, was built by Rev. Melancthon Hoyt in 1868; it was torn down in 1882. —Yankton County Historical Society

William Jayne, President Abraham Lincoln's personal physician, was thirty-five years old when he was named first governor of Dakota Territory in 1861. He chose Yankton as his capital and shared a small log cabin with the territory's attorney general.
—State Historical Society of North Dakota

ing fortune in Yankton. The soles of our people are in a deplorable condition and demand immediate attention. Who wants to get rich?"

The Reverend Melancthon Hoyt brought religion to Yankton in 1861 when he organized an Episcopal church. The town's first school was built for $1,000 at the southwest corner of Walnut and Fourth in 1866; unimaginatively, it was called the Brown School because of its exterior color. The first teachers were Mrs. H. M. Stewart and James Foster, territorial superintendent of public instruction, who had raised the money from among the women of Yankton.

To all these amenities, Yankton's residents hoped to add one more marker of civilization—the territorial capital. Almost from its inception, Yankton battled for the honor with various other Dakota communities. The struggle began when President Abraham Lincoln appointed his personal physician, Dr. William Jayne of Springfield, Illinois, as the first governor of Dakota Territory. J. B. S. Todd, a cousin to Mrs. Lincoln, resented the choice of Jayne; as a partner in the

In 1868 male voters gathered at the first territorial capitol building in Yankton to cast ballots. Though they could not elect a governor, they named a territorial assembly that met in this building. —South Dakota State Historical Society

Frost, Todd & Company fur-trading operation with Daniel March Frost, Todd owned land in Yankton and was already deeply involved in the town's finances. If he'd become territorial governor with Yankton as his capital, his personal profits might have been staggering. Indeed, almost every organized town wanted the position of capital, and half the men in the territory saw a chance to profit. Almost none of them emerged with an impeccable record for honesty.

When Jayne arrived in Yankton as the territorial governor in the spring of 1861, he ensconced himself in a log cabin office and called for a census. The tally, including mixed-blood citizens but not Indians, totaled 2,376 people. The Yankton district reported 287 people, 9 of whom were half-Indians and the rest non-Indians. After a haphazard election, nine councilmen and thirteen representatives were named to the first territorial legislature. The assembly provides clues to the composition of the new territory's population: When the legislature wanted copies of the governor's first speech printed and distributed throughout the territory, it ordered two thousand copies in English, six hundred in Norwegian, four hundred in German, and two hundred in French. Moreover, Reuben Wallas of Bon Homme, aged fifty, not only was the oldest man in the fledgling legislature but in fact was believed to be the oldest white man in the *entire territory*. Pioneering either didn't draw many folks above middle-age or didn't let people live long enough to reach it.

Delegates spent part of the first session arguing about whether Yankton, Vermillion, or Bon Homme should be the permanent capital when statehood was granted. The debates were as polite and sophisticated as could be expected—i.e., not very. During one argument, Speaker of the House George M. Pinney thought proceedings were getting rowdy and had the governor send twenty men from the Dakota Cavalry to keep peace. The sergeant-at-arms, insulted by the governor's action, tossed Pinney through a window in the town's only saloon. Two legislators—John Boyle of Vermillion and Enos Stutsman of Yankton—debated the issue over dinner at the Ash Hotel, throwing "cups, glasses, condiment bottles and the carcass of the chicken they were eating at each other," according to Robert Karolevitz. Later, the governor got into a hair-pulling fight with another state official.

In spite of all this roughhousing, the session did enact a few laws, prohibiting gambling and bawdy houses and forbidding swine and stallions to run free. Indians also were required to get a pass to leave the reservation. As for the capital, it was awarded to Pierre after a long, costly campaign. In a kind of poetic justice, Yankton was awarded the state insane asylum as a consolation prize.

The territorial asylum was opened April 11, 1879; before that, mentally ill Dakotans had been sent to institutions in Nebraska and Minnesota. Records indicate that most of the early patients were female and that officials may have been more concerned about housing staff than patients. The asylum is at the center of a favorite Yankton story, probably told in dozens of other western communities. It is said that a farmer once mournfully brought his wife to the state insane asylum and told the doctor his wife's mental state was inexplicable. "Doc," he said, "I don't know what there was to make her crazy; she ain't been off the farm for thirty years."

If you laugh at the story, also remember that women in the rough frontier settlements were often left alone in sod shanties with their children for weeks while husbands worked at other jobs. Isolated from one another and from the comfortable lives they had left behind, they sometimes watched their children sicken and die, struggled to stay warm in Dakota blizzards, fought prairie fires, and worked at hard physical labor. Their diaries record their fears, the struggle to keep a sod home clean, to provide enough food, to grow a little garden in the midst of drought; they speak of watching grasshoppers

Moses K. Armstrong, a surveyor who came to Dakota in 1859, described the territory's first election as "wide-open, red-hot and mighty interesting." Armstrong was elected five times to the territorial legislature, held several offices at Yankton, and was twice a delegate to Congress.
—State Historical Society of North Dakota

devour every blade of grass, even the curtains at the windows. Many of these women went slowly mad in such surroundings or suffered nervous breakdowns that might be easily treated today; in those times, they were simply locked away with their terrors.

Jack McCall: Wild Bill's Killer

In 1877, Jack McCall, the man who had killed Wild Bill Hickok in Deadwood on August 2 of the previous year, went on trial in Yankton. Some vigilantes with a coil of rope were ready to hang

McCall immediately after the shooting, but he persuaded them he'd killed Hickok in revenge for the killing of his brother. However, a U.S. marshal arrested him and turned him over to the only authori ties in the territory at the time, in Yankton. He was tried spectacularly for three days in December 1876, found guilty by a jury, and sentenced to hang. Followed by every vehicle in town and hundreds of riders on horseback, he was taken to a gallows located on what is now US 81 at the southeast corner of the state hospital grounds. As the noose was adjusted around his neck, he said, "Draw it tighter, Marshal." Ten minutes later, the unrepentant murderer was dead. He was buried in the Catholic cemetery; when the body was later moved, diggers discovered the noose still around his neck. History doesn't record whether they removed it.

Yankton Today

Yankton now has more than nineteen thousand people; the residential developments around Lewis and Clark Lake add nearly three thousand more residents, according to city officials. The city is the chosen retirement locale for many natives who lived elsewhere during their busiest years. These folks have come home to enjoy life at a more leisurely pace but are informed about issues confronting larger cities; they appreciate the past but are highly interested in Yankton's present and future. Their influence is already apparent. For example, whereas many other cities in the state still consider dumping truckloads of refuse into landfills to be responsible garbage disposal, Yankton has evolved a public-private partnership that involves recycling. A private company, Arens Recycling, runs a plant that recycles much of the city's garbage into usable metals and plastics and makes fuel pellets out of the remaining material. In 1990 Yankton won the Innovations Competition for 1990 for its waste management and recycling program. The competition, sponsored by the National League of Cities, is an annual program that identifies a current issue of concern to local governments and highlights creative solutions.

Yankton history buffs sponsor free mapped architectural walking and auto tours of the town's residential district, listed on the National Register of Historic Places. On the tour are the 1887 meeting place of the Grand Army of the Republic and nearly twenty historic homes, some of them virtually unaltered since they were built in the late 1800s. Architecture is varied, with gingerbread trim, ornate parlors, embossed wallpaper, crystal chandeliers, wide verandas, and formal gardens. Unfortunately, only the Cramer-Kenyon Heritage

Home, a Queen Anne-style building constructed in 1886, is open to the public—it is now a museum—but the tour provides fascinating insights into the town's history.

The Garden Terrace Theatre on the former Yankton College campus became the first open-air theater west of the Mississippi River in 1915, and the campus observatory housed the finest telescope available in 1888. The Carnegie Library at Fourth and Capitol, built in 1902, has been skillfully converted into a restaurant; wrought-iron spiral staircases rise giddily out of the original black and white marble tiles. An octagonal oak design on the ceiling echoes the floor design.

Gayville, Meckling

East of Yankton, Gayville was established as a post office in 1872 and named for Elkanah Gay, first postmaster and first depot agent. Just east of town at the Clay and Yankton county line is the site of Post Vermillion, Robert Dickson's post, established on Audubon's Point in 1822. A marker denotes the site, and a few remains of the post may still be visible. Meckling, founded in 1873, was named for Jones S. Meckling, a railroad contractor. Before that, the site was known as Lincoln Post Office, probably in honor of the assassinated president.

VERMILLION

Vermillion's first documented visit by white men occurred when Lewis and Clark visited Spirit Mound in 1804 to check a rumor that it was inhabited by eighteen-inch devils with human forms. Neither saw devils, but they did find artifacts and concluded the mound might be an Indian burial ground. They were wrong; it's a natural formation. From the top, according to Clark's journal, they enjoyed "a most butifull landscape; numerous herds of buffalo were seen feeding in various directions." Hot and thirsty, the explorers trudged to the Vermillion River, where they found water and "delisiouc froot such as grapes, plumbs, and blue currents." The mound is eight miles north of Vermillion on SD 19.

August Bruyer, his wife Josephine, and their sons John and Julius were settled about four miles east of the later site of Vermillion by 1858. The land east of the Vermillion River was soon surveyed and opened to settlement. In 1859 Bruyer donated ten acres for a Catholic church and cemetery; by the next year the first Catholic church in Dakota stood on the site. Vermillion's first school met in a room over McHenry's store and was taught by Dr. Franklin Caulkins; a rival school in the Presbyterian church was taught by a Miss Hoyt. Bored army troops stuck at the fort during the winter of 1864 built a log schoolhouse.

Clay County, of which Vermillion is the seat, was officially established in 1861, the smallest in the state at 403 square miles. Vermillion originally lay under the bluffs east of the Vermillion River; the 1860 census showed forty families and 215 people there. The busy town soon included a store, sawmill, post office, hotel, churches, private schools, and a newspaper. In January 1875 a fire destroyed all but three of the nearly three dozen buildings, but citizens rebuilt in the same location.

Rev. Joseph Ward founded Yankton College, the first in Dakota Territory, in 1881. He also wrote the state motto: "Under God the people rule." He died nine days after statehood. —Yankton County Historical Society

A whirlpool on an oxbow bend near the original town was a hazard to river travel for years. It was known as the Grand Detour. Steamboats often placed their passengers ashore before negotiating the long, dangerous curve. Water roaring around the narrow bend struck the seventy-foot-high bluffs, creating a whirlpool. Legends abound about deaths, but only one was substantiated.

The whirlpool also endangered the tracks of the Dakota Southern Railway, which reached Vermillion in 1872. They were originally laid on a wide expanse of ground between the river and the bluff. Gradually the river washed closer to the tracks, until part of the bluff had to be cut away to accommodate the roadbed. By June 1878 the railroad had spent more than $3,000 on the piece of track near the whirlpool. On June 15 of that year, the *Vermillion Standard* reported that the river washed away track nearly as fast as it could be laid. By July 6 the roadbed was completely washed away, and the company was considering cutting a new one halfway up the bluff. In a last, desperate effort, willows were woven into a mat a hundred feet wide and three feet thick and sunk around piles driven into the riverbed and weighted with stones. The work was nearly completed by May, but the June rise of the Missouri washed away part of the willow mat. Eight more carloads of stone were dumped in at that point.

The great flood of 1881 brought the whirlpool its most dramatic moments—and its death struggle. Vermillion's population was about seven hundred then. During the last week of March, floodwaters and ice rampaging down the river took out 132 of the town's approximately 200 buildings, ripping them to shreds in the whirlpool and damaging the rest. In the same flood, however, the Missouri River broke through the half-mile neck of land at the base of the great oxbow bend, so the river actually shifted several miles south of its previous course. With water no longer flowing around the curve, the whirlpool ceased to exist. Survivors of the great flood, finally convinced they couldn't beat the river, moved the remnants of the town to the present site on top of the bluffs and continued building.

Water remained in the defunct river bend for years, giving rise to stories that it was bottomless; one old-timer even stated that the water continued to whirl after the river shifted. A map of the area published in 1900 designates the lonely area accessible by Ravine Road as the "Haunted Pool," which suggests that its reputation persisted. A pool nearly fifty yards in diameter was occasionally replenished by the Vermillion River at its spring rise, but by 1964 the pool was dry. It was still possible, however, to see through the underbrush, trees, and shacks that the center of the circular area was considerably lower than the rims.

University of South Dakota

The University of South Dakota was founded near Vermillion in 1862 on seventy-two sections of public land. Today, SD 50 passes between student dormitories and University of South Dakota buildings. USD's enrollment in 1991 was more than seven thousand, an all-time high, which helped jolt the town out of a decade-long housing depression by launching a mini-boom in the construction of houses and apartments. The city's newspaper, *Plain Talk*, lived up to its name, stating: "The University of South Dakota is a recession-proof industry . . . community leaders should take care that pieces of it do not slip away to Sioux Falls, for once a state campus becomes established in that town, growth in Vermillion will likely cease." The town's population in 1990 stood at just over ten thousand.

Besides classes, USD hosts the Shrine to Music Museum (a collection of antique musical instruments from around the world); the W. H. Over State Museum, with hundreds of oral histories of citizens; and the Austin-Whittemore House.

SD 34
Stanley County–Jerauld County
86 Miles

This segment of SD 34, part of which joins US 14, runs east-west between the western edges of Stanley and Jerauld counties, west of Wessington Springs.

The highway rocks and rolls through the broken hills along the Missouri River, diving into creek bottoms and swooping up long, grass-covered hills to the top of the plateau. The region may seem empty to a city-bred visitor, but it is full of history, as well as the beauty and potential that attracted men and women to the Plains. Even on a sunny day, clouds will sometimes drop low over the river like angry white-capped waves on an inland sea. It is harsh country; in the winter of 1934, farmers drove their wagons over the flats along the river collecting buffalo and cow chips (dried manure) for fuel, just as their homesteading ancestors did in the late 1800s.

From some of the bluffs along this highway, it is possible to see the Big Bend, a forty-five-mile loop in the Missouri River south of Pierre that frustrated many travelers who came by steamboat. Occasionally, as happened during painter George Catlin's trip, a boat would venture too far into shallow water and become mired. Passengers sometimes would get off at the beginning of the bend, walk across a four-mile neck of land, and catch the boat when it came around the curve. The hike provided exercise for passengers after the trip of nearly thirteen hundred miles from St. Louis. A writer named Elias J. Marsh recorded in 1859 that his party had to wait all night for the boat to round the bend. Because they brought no camping equipment or food, they huddled on the shore in considerable discomfort.

STANLEY COUNTY

North of the highway on the west side of the river, near Mission Ridge, in one of the most sparsely populated counties in the state, is one of the nation's smallest schools. During the fall of 1990, only three students enrolled at Orton School—tripling enrollment over the previous year. A first-year teacher lived with his dog in a mobile home next to the school. Each of the three students was in a different grade—the second, fifth, and sixth—so the teacher was required to prepare twenty-one lessons every night. The bell atop the freshly painted white schoolhouse is the original, and the teacher rings it three times a day, possibly just to hear it. Mail arrives three times a week; Fort Pierre, an hour away down a bumpy, winding road, is the nearest town.

The school system in Stanley County enrolls 566 students in seven buildings, but none of the four rural schools in the district had more than 8 students in 1990, according to an elementary principal. Nationally, country schools are being phased out in favor of consolidated schools, but almost one-fourth of the elementary schools in South Dakota still have only one or two teachers. Legally, schools can be closed if enrollment drops to fewer than 5 students, but it would be more expensive to pay the families of the displaced students for mileage to and from school each day—or pay for them to live in town—than it is to pay the single teacher to live in the remote spot. After eighth grade, many students must drive long distances to school daily or board in town; some families rent or own a home in town, where a parent lives with children during the school year while the other tends to the ranch.

CROW CREEK INDIAN RESERVATION

Lewis and Clark called this area the "Sioux Pass of the Three Rivers" because the Lakota traditionally crossed the Missouri River near where three creeks—Crow, Wolf, and Campbell—emptied into

As they settled on reservations, some Indians quickly adopted symbols of citizenship, such as the American flag. In 1883, only seven years after the Custer fight at the Little Bighorn, this band paraded in the capital city of Dakota Territory, Bismarck. Signs read "March of Civilization" and "Dakota as a Territory." Historians say the figure carrying the huge American flag is Sitting Bull; certainly he had learned something from whites—on this occasion, he charged $1 for each photograph taken of him. —State Historical Society of North Dakota

it. Much of the land along the Big Bend of the Missouri lies on the Crow Creek Indian Reservation. The reservation is named for Crow Creek, which rises in western Jerauld County and empties into the Missouri west of Selby—not, as many writers claim, for American Crow Creek at Oacoma.

Clark was wrong about the bird, too. Lewis had shot one near the as-yet unnamed stream; Clark got the family right, calling it a "remarkable bird of the Spicies of Corvus," but what Lewis had shot was a magpie. Neither explorer had ever seen one before, but Clark was naturalist enough to detect the species—and the creek had a name. Land speculators made things even more confusing when they began applying the name Smith Creek to it, calling only the northern branch Crow Creek. No wonder exploring and settling were such a confusing business; every traveler considered it a right to go around naming the landscape.

When Indians were moved from near Yankton to this reservation by steamboat in 1859, the Reverend John S. Williamson stayed with them, sharing their hardships, conducting religious services, and teaching them to read and write. The government hadn't provided enough food, and many of the Indians were starving until Williamson

213

persuaded the Indian agent, Col. Clark Thompson, to let them hunt. Williamson accepted charge of them—an astonishing responsibility, as many tribes were still warring against the whites.

Accounts of the hunt vary wildly, with estimates of the number of Indians allowed to leave the reservation to hunt under the Reverend Williamson's good conduct guarantee ranging from one hundred to as many as eight hundred. The entire band, weak from hunger and badly clothed for the cold weather, had fewer than ten guns; many hunted with bows and arrows. When the scouts finally found buffalo, the group followed the herd as it grazed over the prairie for three months. The long journey provided the Indians a chance to eat well and regain their strength, to preserve meat, and to tan hides for future use as clothing, moccasins, and tipis, items that had been destroyed, lost, or worn out in their long trek to the reservation. The group returned with the meat and hides of as many as two thousand buffalo. When the hunt was over, every Indian who had gone out with Reverend Williamson returned with him, and none were punished for the long absence.

The hunt might have convinced Indian agents and others charged with the tribes' welfare to take another look at the system of forcing them to give up nomadic ways and become farmers living in log cabins. These people had left the reservation near death, almost weaponless; they returned well fed and in possession of everything they needed to survive. Surely some astute agent must have recognized the truth: that given the chance and a herd of buffalo, these people could provide for themselves better and more cheaply than the government could provide for them.

The town of Fort Thompson was established as an Indian agency on the reservation in 1863 at the mouth of Crow Creek. The agent there administered both the Crow Creek and Lower Brulé reservations and supervised the distribution of rations, among other duties. Fort Thompson was named for Col. Clark Thompson, superintendent of the northern division of Indian agencies and commander of troops there, another case of conflicting responsibilities. As agent, he was responsible for protecting and feeding the Indians; as a military man, he was trained to fight them. Many agents felt contempt for the weak, hungry, confused wretches they were asked to supervise, never having seen them as an independent people living in their own surroundings. They had no knowledge of the Indians' traditions, the strict discipline of the tribal organization, or the mechanisms by which these undomesticated nomads ensured restraint when it was necessary. Other agents learned the language, spent time talking with the Indians, and began to realize the depth of the Indians' culture; their voices were, unfortunately, usually drowned out in the clamor for making the tribes "behave" on white terms.

Oscar Howe: American Artist

Oscar Howe was born in poverty in Fort Thompson but eventually became known around the world for his unique art. John Milton, who knew Howe and wrote extensively about him, noted that although Howe's art was deeply important and brought him both fame and respect, "it cannot be separated entirely from his personal history as a Sioux Indian in South Dakota working against the odds imposed upon him by physical ailment and ethnic prejudice." Several times, Howe was attacked by both the Lakota society in which he was born and the white society in which he worked, "apparently leaving him in the difficult position of a man without a country. Yet he remained loyal to both cultures."

Howe was born May 13, 1915. One of his great-grandfathers was Chief White Bear, a noted orator and one of many chiefs who signed the 1876 agreement that transferred ownership of the Black Hills to the United States; his paternal grandfather, Unspesni, was the last hereditary chief of the Yankton; and his maternal grandfather, Fearless Bear, was made a chief at general council of his tribe in 1876. Howe may have inherited his interest in art from his maternal grandmother, Shell Face; she drew in the sand with her fingers the symbols of the Sioux tribes that he later used in his paintings.

But when Oscar began to draw, his father tried to discourage him and took away his pencil; after that, he drew lines in the dirt with a stick. He spoke only Sioux when he went to the federal boarding school in Pierre, but the rules required that students speak English, which set him apart. He was isolated further by a skin disease that resulted in open sores and once considered suicide. He was sent back to the reservation, Milton says, "as a hopeless case, both physically and psychologically, having suffered near-blindness (as a result of trachoma) in addition to the skin disease and the shame of having his abnormalities exposed to his fellow students."

Howe eventually returned to school, completed the eighth grade, and won several art contests. Two years later he was diagnosed with tuberculosis and sent to New Mexico, where he enrolled in the art department of the Santa Fe Indian School. When he graduated in 1935 as salutatorian of his class, several of his paintings had already been exhibited in San Francisco and Brooklyn and been included with a traveling exhibit. He painted designs on the domed ceiling of the Mitchell library and produced ten historical murals in Mobridge's new auditorium before serving in World War II. During the war he met his wife, Adelheit (Heide), in Germany.

Back in South Dakota, Howe was asked to design and supervise installation of the large murals made of colored corn on the outside of the famous Corn Palace at Mitchell. Under the G.I. Bill of Rights, he enrolled as a student at Dakota Wesleyan and was named artist-in-residence. Upon his graduation in 1952, Howe went to the University of Oklahoma and earned a master's degree. He returned to South Dakota and became art director in the Pierre public school system and continued winning prizes for his paintings. One of his students was Fritz Scholder, a New Mexico artist who later became famous for his own unique painting style.

Milton says that despite winning many awards in Indian contests, Howe eventually grew bitter because he was considered an "Indian curiosity rather than a painter per se. It angered him that he was not able to show his work in eastern galleries or in nearby city art museums such as the Walker Art Center and the Minneapolis Art Institute."

In 1957 he was appointed artist-in-residence and assistant professor of art at the University of South Dakota in Vermillion. At that time the department had no facilities, so Howe opened a creative arts laboratory. Still, he felt stereotyped as an Indian artist in a white society. After his work was rejected by the Philbrook Competition in 1958, he wrote an angry letter denouncing the whites' view of the Indian as a child who had to be guided. Milton is unsure how much influence the letter had, but the following year the Philbrook revised its rules and Howe took the Grand Purchase Prize. His former student, Fritz Scholder, won honorable mention. At the same time, Navajo artist R. C. Gorman began winning prizes; all three artists had stressed the necessity of being recognized as artists, not in a separate category as Indian artists.

In 1960 Howe was appointed South Dakota's artist laureate by Governor Ralph Herseth and named a fellow in the International Institute of Arts and Letters. These honors were followed by others, including important one-man shows and a 1968 honorary doctorate from South Dakota State University at Brookings. In 1971 he was awarded a similar honor by Dakota Wesleyan when the Oscar Howe Art Center opened in Mitchell, and he went on a lecture tour of nine countries for the U.S. Department of State. He received a third honorary doctorate from Hamline University in St. Paul in 1973, the same year he became the first recipient of the annual South Dakota Governor's Award for Creative Achievement. Howe's health deteriorated and he had to stop painting in the mid-1970s; he retired from the University of South Dakota in 1980 and died October 7, 1983.

Oscar Howe was one of the first Native American artists to gain wide recognition; his geometric works portraying traditional culture have been frequently reproduced and now sell for extremely high prices. Much of his work is displayed at the Oscar Howe Memorial Art Center in Mitchell. He deserves every bit of recognition he has won for his art, but he also deserves to be remembered for stressing the need for white society to accept Indians as full-fledged members of society, not place them in some special category.

The Other Borglum

Another great artist took his inspiration from the Crow Creek Reservation. Though the family name is familiar enough, Solon Borglum is nearly unknown in the state, and none of his works remain here. Solon Hannibal Borglum lived and studied among the Indians at Crow Creek. He was a pioneer in the world of western art, creating works that gained worldwide fame long before his brother Gutzon was employed to cut into a mountain in the Black Hills. But Solon's myriad brilliant works are almost forgotten, whereas Gutzon's single massive carving—Mount Rushmore—has drawn millions of visitors to the state.

Solon Borglum was born in the frontier town of Ogden, Utah, in 1868, and traveled widely with his father, a doctor. While still a teenager, he ran his father's Loup River ranch in western Nebraska, growing up as boss to a tough bunch of cowboys and earning the spurs of a real Westerner. At some time during this period, he visited Crow Creek and was determined to return; he may have sold cattle to the Indians and delivered them with a trail drive from Nebraska. In 1893 Solon sold the ranch and joined Gutzon in California. He studied painting in Los Angeles, then went to Cincinnati to work in clay. At the end of the second year he exhibited seventeen pieces and sold enough work to pay for a trip to Paris, where two sculptures were accepted by the prestigious Paris Salon. Another horse sculpture won honorable mention. Several noted sculptors, including Augustus Saint-Gaudens, assisted him, and he met and married Emma Vignal.

In the summer of 1899 Solon returned to the United States with Emma and set off at once to the Crow Creek Reservation. There they visited a camp of six hundred lodges, and Emma was thrilled with the "horsemen with painted faces and torsos, brilliantly colored clothes, plumes in their hair, little bells and spangles everywhere." Borglum's precision, the faithfulness with which he reproduced detail, might be compared to that of Remington and Russell; however, his work has considerably more polish and power. One of his finest works—"Burial on the Plains," a study showing two mourning Indian women—was exhibited at the Pan-American Exposition in Buffalo, New York. Other works done at or inspired by Crow Creek include "On the Border of White Man's Land" (which won him a silver medal in Paris in 1900), "On the Trail," and "The Sun Dance." Solon won the right to portray themes in the St. Louis World's Fair in 1904, where twelve small pieces earned him another silver medal. A copy of one of his most stunning pieces, "The Mares of Diomedes," featuring a Lakota youth stealing horses, now stands in the Whitney Gallery of Western Art in Cody, Wyoming.

Borglum died in 1922 at the age of fifty-four. Visitors to Mount Rushmore are numbered in the millions, but asking one about Solon Borglum usually brings nothing more than a blank stare, a tragedy in the state that witnessed his artistic birth and provided material for his triumph.

BUFFALO COUNTY

Buffalo County, population about seventeen hundred, never had a railway and currently has no real towns; even Gann Valley, the county seat, remains unincorporated. Mac's Corner and Lee's Corner are gas and supply stops for fishing enthusiasts on the dammed waters of the Missouri. Lee's Corner is one access to the Native American Loop Road, providing a closer look at the modern Indian communities along the Missouri River, accessible also on SD 50 from Chamberlain.

This territory may have been more heavily populated in prehistoric times, when thousands of Indians lived at Elm and Crow creeks, Medicine Crow, and Skunk Island, in villages that predated even the old Arikara settlements along the river. These villagers, ancestors of the modern Arikara, were farmers, planting corn, squash, beans, and sunflowers. Ancient droughts drove them north along the river, closer to a source of water for their crops.

When archaeologists were hastily excavating along the river in advance of the rising waters of Lake Francis Case, they unearthed evidence of a mysterious massacre of the inhabitants of a fortified village above the river. About A.D. 1325, nearly five hundred people were killed, scalped, and mutilated in a single day, and their bodies were buried in a fortification ditch surrounding their earth-lodge village. More bodies were buried in a mass grave covered with clay that must have been carried up from the river below the site.

The village itself was on a V-shaped piece of land more than seventy feet above the river, protected on two sides by steep cliffs. Across the open end of the V was a stout log wall, enclosing about twenty acres. No one knows what group of Indians might have been powerful enough to slaughter the inhabitants of a village so well defended. The mystery is compounded by the covering of the mass grave with clay and the labor required to haul the material from the riverbank. Perhaps survivors returned and carried out the latter deed; analysts think about eight hundred people might have lived in the village. This is the largest known prehistoric massacre site; evidence is still being studied, but much of it was damaged before excavation by natural forces such as wind and water erosion, as well as by looters.

Why, one wonders, is a region that once supported a vigorous hunting and gathering culture now so empty? The easy answer may be that farmers here produce more nourishment with modern methods than nature provided for older civilizations. But differences are intriguing. The older cultures clustered in villages near the river to satisfy their needs; enough leisure time existed for them to create works of art and travel to other regions for trade. Now white descendants of settlers who disrupted those archaic ways live in widely scattered homes and buy much of what they need for daily life. They worry about the crisis in farming, and many are in serious danger of bankruptcy.

The Crow Creek Indian Reservation occupies half the county, and Episcopal churches in Gann Valley use hymnals in both English and Lakota. East of the river, a few more villages exist, including Stephan (pronounced "stef-FAN"), named for the patron saint of Hungary and the site of a Catholic mission.

Drifting Goose (Magabobdu), a chief of the Yanktons, is buried in the Catholic cemetery, though his original home was in the James River valley southeast of Aberdeen. Drifting Goose's band took up settlers' ways even before they were asked to, planting corn and building log cabins, as well as hunting and fishing. But their attempt to peacefully adapt to the white man's ways didn't do them much good. In 1868 white officials promised Drifting Goose that he and his band could occupy their ancestral lands. After the Indians were confined for one winter at the Fort Sisseton Agency, however, they returned to find their log homes occupied by whites and their harvest stolen. Despite the intervention of several army officials, who argued that Drifting Goose's cooperation deserved more consideration, the group was not allowed to return home. Instead, agents moved them north into a barren area of Spink County; the only water was on white-occupied land, and even though the whites were illegal squatters, no official would help the Indians. Peacefully, Drifting Goose tolerated even this outrage. Finally, when he was old and worn out, his band reluctantly moved to the Crow Creek Reservation. The chief often traveled in a horse-drawn wagon back to the Aberdeen area to visit his former lands. In 1904 he was asked to speak at a Fourth of July celebration—the token Indian, one supposes. Calmly, he said that if he were younger, he'd cut out the hearts of white people. He died in 1909.

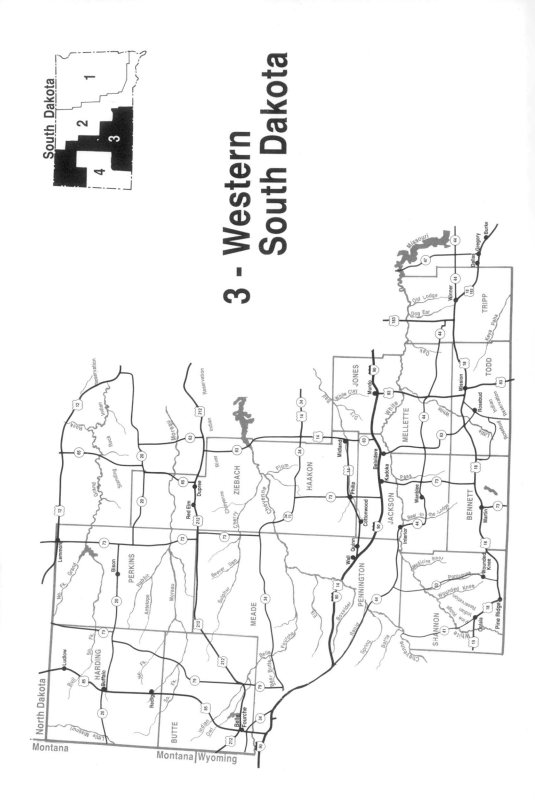

3 - Western South Dakota

South Dakota

PART THREE

Western South Dakota

Signs that you have left the tallgrass country of the East and Midwest and entered the short-grass country of the Great Plains begin to appear soon after you cross the hundredth meridian heading west. But these signs weren't erected by the highway department; they're more subtle, natural. The vegetation is shorter, tougher, browner, and thornier than that to the east. Annual precipitation west of the James River averages less than twenty inches. Towns and cities tend to be more widely spaced, and barbed wire becomes more common than wood for fences. Buildings are often placed on

Cattle graze under the watchful eyes of two cowhands on a cattle ranch in western Dakota's semiarid region. —South Dakota School of Mines and Technology

top of a hill for the view, and often there are no windbreak trees on the north side.

The western half of the state, eroded by water and wind, has always been emptier and quieter than the eastern half. Its silence and its beauties draw most of the millions of tourists who visit South Dakota each year, and new pioneers are moving in from crowded cities in search of clean air, wilderness, and less crime. Farms and ranches are larger here, and ranches predominate. It's important to know the distinction: Ranchers raise cattle rather than crops, and they hate to be mistaken for "dirt farmers." However, farmers and ranchers are lumped together under the term "agriculture" by economists and politicians—one reason for the often confusing voting patterns on the Plains.

On secondary highways, drivers wave, even though they may have a rifle rack in the rear window of their pickup. The men wear cowboy boots and wide-brimmed hats instead of rubber overshoes and caps stamped with the name of their favorite cattle feed. Women commonly drive pickups or other four-wheel-drive vehicles, are often tanned, and wear short-sleeve shirts that reveal well-muscled arms.

You'll see dams across small valleys, called "draws" or "gullies" by local folks, that look as if they've been dry since the beginning of time. In spite of appearances, the little barriers catch rainfall or melting snow—any water that runs off the slopes. Rectangular water holes are usually man-made and cut deep enough into the earth that groundwater seeps into them. Natural streams are few and glacial lakes nonexistent in the West, so residents have to be frugal with water and clever to catch any that falls.

Standing Bear's Plains Legend

Chief Luther Standing Bear told a Lakota legend of the creation of the Great Plains. The first man, he said, awoke in the midst of a vast prairie facing the sun, with only his head visible. The rest of his body was not yet fashioned. No mountains existed, no rivers, no forests; nothing but soft and quaking mud covered the earth. The man pulled himself up until he freed his body from the mud and walked slowly through it. The sun shone, and he kept his face turned toward it. Slowly the sun's rays hardened the earth and strengthened the man until he leaped and bounded, a free and happy creature.

"From this man," said Standing Bear, "sprang the Lakota nation and, so far as we know, our people have been born and have died upon this plain; and no people have shared it with us until the coming of the Europeans. So this land of the great plains is claimed by the Lakota as their very own. We are of the soil and the soil is of us."

White residents of the plains, especially rural dwellers, have also felt they became part of the soil, even though they arrived after the Lakota began thinking of the region as their own. Differing views on what to do with that soil have led to racial and cultural conflicts.

Ranchers Followed Astorians

The first whites known to have seen this area were members of the Pacific Fur Company expedition (the Astorians) being led to the mouth of the Columbia River by Wilson Price Hunt in 1811. Other white or part-white trappers and traders surely preceded them, but the Astorians get credit for keeping records. During the half-century that followed, more trappers and explorers traversed the region. But settlers had not yet established themselves here when Lt. Col. George A. Custer and his troops camped nearby in 1874 en route from Fort Abraham Lincoln to the Black Hills. About twenty-five miles west of Buffalo, at the northern end of the Short Pine Hills, the cavalry passed through a place Custer called Prospect Valley; the blooming wildflowers grew so tall there that the soldiers could make wreaths for their horses' necks without dismounting.

Pioneers made extra money by collecting buffalo bones for sale as fertilizer after the herds were slaughtered. —State Historical Society of North Dakota

225

Building railroad tracks on prairie sod west of the Missouri River was a difficult job. Using hand tools, hired crews suffered from blowing dust and intense heat; they drank whatever water was available, sometimes out of muddy gullies where cattle and buffalo also drank. Food was scarce and often limited to dry staples like beans and hardtack. This crew was photographed building tracks in northern Dakota Territory.
—State Historical Society of North Dakota

Permanent white settlement came to this area in the late 1870s. Drovers bringing cattle up from Texas had already begun using the Plains as summer range for their herds. Then, after most of the bison were killed off, the height and abundance of ungrazed Dakota grass caught the eye of adventurers entering the region to look for gold or other opportunities; some became ranchers and established cattle herds that remained on the northern Plains all year.

Those who raised cattle where Indians still roamed were considered daring; they were willing to fight for the land they used. The boundaries of their ranches were established by informal agreement or simply by having enough armed cowboys to protect their parcels. As long as a rancher had a legal lease or a government contract to supply beef, and if he controlled the local water supply and enough men to support his operation, few questioned his right to use the land. Few ranchers had much actual cash except at sale time; their power and influence came from the amount of land they controlled, the number of cattle they ran, and the number of men they employed. But power also lay in capital. Some large outfits bought land or herds with money provided by investors from eastern U.S. cities as well as from England, Germany, Scotland, and Holland.

The high status ranchers could achieve is illustrated in a story often told about the funeral of James "Scotty" Philip, a prominent cattleman in western South Dakota who died in 1919. After Philip's death, Alex Johnson, the vice president in charge of the Chicago & Northwestern Railroad's operations, called company engineer Chester Dike to ask about the condition of the railroad spur to Philip's ranch.

"There isn't any spur," replied Dike. "We tore it up yesterday. Hauled the steel out."

"Well," said Johnson, "put it back."

Dike naturally protested but was told that a lot of Philip's old friends would expect to ride to his funeral in a special train from Belle Fourche. Working without rest, the crews replaced the track; after the funeral, they tore it out for the last time.

The 1870 federal census indicated a total of 12,467 cattle in Dakota Territory; by 1880 the number had grown to 140,815—and that's assuming the ranchers actually told the truth about how many cows grazed ranges too remote for government inspection. But the era of the cattle baron ended abruptly, and the unpredictable Dakota weather was at least partly responsible. The winter of 1887-88 killed thousands, perhaps millions of cattle in the West; as much as 90 percent of the cattle on the open range died of cold or starvation because few ranchers harvested hay or arranged to feed or shelter livestock in winter.

Losses in South Dakota were not as severe as on the northern ranges in Wyoming and Montana, but they were bad enough. One herd numbered eighteen thousand going into the winter, nineteen hundred afterward. The Hash Knife outfit reportedly saved only nine thousand head out of a herd of eighty thousand, though not all were on the Dakota range. A man who resigned from the Pennington County brand commission figured that most ranchers lost between 85 and 90 percent of their herds and said, with restraint characteristic of the breed: "Many of the cattlemen are disheartened." The ranchers were dealt another blow by the government's decision to open the Great Sioux Reservation to homesteaders in 1889, reducing the amount of land available for grazing. Ranchers had to learn to borrow money to buy land they'd formerly used free—hence, Gus Craven of the Open Buckle outfit described a cow as a four-legged animal with horns and a tail surrounded by mortgages.

Some of these brands used in Dakota are still registered. From left to right, top to bottom: Seven Slash Seven; Circle D; Circle Cross; ZOS; Bar Six Bar; Rake; A Bar S; Twenty-Four Connected; Flower Pot; U Up and U Down; L Slash Y; JV; C Cross; Tumbling Box L; TJ Connected; Reverse FL Connected.

Homesteaders Blown Away

Dakota Territory became one of the last areas of cow country to be opened to settlers by the arrival of the railroads. Edward E. Dale notes that in 1875, just after the Northern Pacific reached Bismarck, fewer than fifty thousand people lived in the two Dakotas. Gold was discovered that year, and the region came to the attention of settlers; eighty-five thousand more residents had come to the region by 1880.

Railroads enabled ranchers to ship beef to eastern markets, first on the hoof, then in refrigerated cars. But the railroads also enabled settlers to move in with fences and plows and claim the land to which the ranchers held no legal title. Cattlemen hired cowboys to file claims on good pieces of land, particularly those that contained water holes, springs, or creeks, so homesteaders could not move in. As homestead claims caught up with them, cattle raisers lost the land they had been using and had to move further west. Some ranchers, assuming farmers would soon be plowing the native grasses up anyway, got in the habit of using land as radically as possible, overstocking and abusing it.

Cattlemen had been warning for years that the western limit of crop production had been reached; however, farmers kept adapting to new conditions with new technologies and making things grow. But when plows tore into the arid soil west of the river in Dakota, the cattlemen's prediction finally came true. Small farmers simply could not survive on the open Plains. As Ian Frazier wrote in *Great Plains*: "To expect a person to make a living on a little square of this vast region where animals and Indians used to travel hundreds of miles looking for food . . . was like expecting a fisherman to survive on just a little square of ocean."

Still, homesteading was supported by federal law and by the widespread public belief that everyone was entitled to own land. By 1915 much of the land immediately west of the Missouri River, and an astonishing amount of the entire western half of the state, had been plowed. Most ranchers didn't shoot homesteaders who tried to farm the grasslands, but they regarded them as stupid or criminal and believed they'd been misguided by a national government located too far away to understand conditions. As government restrictions on the use of public lands became more severe, ranchers increasingly regarded government officialdom as impractical and ignorant; as a group, they still deplore government interference in agriculture.

During the 1930s, most of the topsoil on land that had been plowed by the eager homesteaders blew away; the tough prairie grasses—which ranchers called collectively "buffalo grass" because it sustained the bison herds—had developed long, twisting roots. Once that grass was killed by plowing, the roots no longer remained to hold the earth in place when drought turned the top layers into dust. An old rhyme described conditions in the western part of the state and what some settlers did about it:

> *Fifty miles from water,*
> *A hundred miles to wood,*
> *To hell with this damned country.*
> *I'm going home for good.*

The fertile Plains became the Dust Bowl; in the four or five driest, windiest years of the Depression, the level of the land was actually lowered four or five feet in many areas. Many farmers and ranchers still remember being able to walk over fences five to six feet high on drifts of dust. Ranchers, who grazed the grass instead of plowing it under, generally fared better, as did the land they controlled. Though they couldn't sell the starving cattle, their families could and did survive. A federal relief program provided that cattle too thin to sell or survive be gathered together and shot; their emaciated corpses

Most land west of the Missouri River, considered less desirable for farming, was homesteaded after 1900. Some homesteaders moved into the region as late as the Great Depression of the 1930s, when this photo was taken. The rough-frame shanty appears to be two separate shacks cobbled together. —South Dakota State Historical Society

were bulldozed into mass graves. Many ranchers remember the grim program but won't talk about it.

The ranchers were right in believing the West River country was not suited for farming, but by the time settlers learned that painful lesson many of the ranchers had been driven out, unable to make a living by raising cattle on the acreage left to them. A few had enough cash to buy land that had defeated farming settlers at $2 or $3 an acre and thus expanded their acreage to a practical level.

Ecologists continue to study the process of desertification, trying to discover if recent years of drought are turning the Great Plains back to the desert of blowing sand dunes they apparently once were. What the ranchers and farmers of the 1800s didn't know was that the soil of the Great Plains is fossil soil, "easy to use up with intensive farming but slow to be replaced," wrote John Opie in *The Law of the Land*. He noted that between 250 and 1,000 years were required to build one inch of topsoil and that modern agriculture, using chemicals and single crops, consumed the soil farmers thought was indestructible at an incredible rate. "They were cannibalizing their own resources," he concluded.

Most professional environmentalists and government officials say farmers and ranchers in western South Dakota manage land wisely; the few problems that occur are due to spells of bad luck, such as drought or dust storms. A local newspaper quotes a plant scientist at Chadron, Nebraska, who said western U.S. ranges appear to be "in better shape than 80 years ago." But officials of the U.S. Geological Survey are beginning to suspect that traditional farming methods are responsible for increasing erosion since farming began on the Plains.

Cattle Raising Today

Cattle raising is still important in South Dakota: Three-fourths of the state's agricultural cash comes from livestock. South Dakota usually ranks between seventh and ninth in the nation in production of cattle. The numbers of beef cattle in the state rise and fall with drought and rainfall as well as market highs and lows. Ranching and farming used to be entirely separate, but both ranchers and farmers now diversify; about 80 percent of farms and ranches in the state have cattle operations, including feedlots and dairies. The state ranks between eighth and tenth in the nation in hog production, ninth in grain, and fourth or fifth in sheep.

Sheep and cattle raisers still bicker over some aspects of their respective lifestyles; those who raise sheep charge that ranchers raise coyotes, which feed on sheep. A bumper sticker reads, "Eat lamb; 50,000 coyotes can't be wrong," and one of the state's nicknames is "The Coyote State." Cattle and calves account for 70 percent of livestock receipts, with 10 percent coming from dairy and 15 percent from hogs. Sheep, lambs, poultry, eggs, honey, and other livestock products supply the remaining 5 percent.

Various industries based on farming boost state income, including meat packing, flour and feed mills, dairy products, food processing, implement manufacture, and the handling and shipping of farm products. Farm products brought nearly $2.5 billion into the state in 1980, a low production year. However, profit and loss are not the whole story and probably never were. Farming and ranching are being altered by forces outside the control of South Dakotans. Mechanization and developments in chemistry and genetic engineering have turned ranching into agribusiness.

West River residents in general, and ranchers specifically, see themselves as independent, tough survivors determining their own destiny; some historians say this is no longer true and may never have been true in the state's century of existence. Many ranchers have television sets where their children see the toys a middle-class lifestyle demands; lately, their wives have been taking jobs in town instead of relying on the land to produce the family's needs. As economic hardship has returned, some farms would have been lost without an additional income. The whole family visits a shopping mall in the largest nearby city on weekends instead of going to church, visiting the neighbors, or shopping in local stores.

Some ranchers are experimenting with raising bison, exotic animals, new breeds of lean cattle; all are concerned about their future in a diet-conscious world. But ranchers often feel disoriented when they see television advertisements implying that beef is unhealthy. In a world that eats less beef, regards cowboys and cowgirls as myths, and views guns as dangerous, ranchers cannot help but worry about their future.

For Further Reading:

A Man from South Dakota by George S. Reeves is a fictionalized account of the author's life on the plains near Rapid City. Two accounts from homesteading days are Grace Fairchild's story, retold by Walker Wyman in *Frontier Woman*, and *Bachelor Bess*, a series of homesteader Elizabeth Corey's letters edited by Phillip Gerber. My *Windbreak: A Woman Rancher on the Northern Plains* is a contemporary record of a year on a West River ranch; also my collection of essays, *Going over East*, discusses some of the dilemmas modern ranchers face.

John Neihardt's *Cycle of the West* tells the story of trapper Hugh Glass in rhymed verse, and Frederick Manfred tells it in novel form in *Lord Grizzly*. Glass barely survived a grizzly attack, then crawled two hundred miles for help. Neihardt was a tiny man with a hunched spine, but his prose and poetry were big enough to make him one of the West's most important writers. Manfred is built along western lines, nearly seven feet tall, with hands the size of saddles. To make his novel authentic, he crawled part of the distance and ate as Glass did before he found meat: grubs, beetles, worms.

Black Elk described some of his visions in *The Sacred Pipe*, and Frederick Manfred's novel *Conquering Horse* presents a vivid depiction. The best source of information about Spotted Tail and his times is *Spotted Tail's Folk* by George E. Hyde. *A Pictographic History of the Oglala Sioux*, with drawings by Amos Bad Heart Bull, is an extraordinary document, showing the Indian version of events like the Custer battle at the Little Bighorn. Another rendition of the book, including paintings by Bad Heart Bull and other Indians of the time, is *Wind on the Buffalo Grass.*

Crazy Horse, whose life exemplifies the ideals of Lakota manhood, is best depicted in Mari Sandoz's *Crazy Horse: Strange Man of the Oglalas*; only in the last few years has this book been available at the Little Bighorn Battlefield National Monument.

Two of the most interesting contemporary accounts of the 1973 confrontation at Wounded Knee are *Voices from Wounded Knee*, published by "Akwesasne Notes" (a Mohawk operation) and Bill Zimmerman's *Airlift to Wounded Knee.* The novels of black homesteader Oscar Micheaux include *The Forged Note*, with a Dakota setting; *The Conquest* and *The Homesteader* draw on his homesteading experiences here.

Worthwhile books about Mount Rushmore include Gilbert Fite's *Mount Rushmore*, Howard Schaff's *Six Wars at a Time*, and Rex Alan Smith's *The Carving of Mount Rushmore.* Mary Borglum's *Give the Man Room* is an intriguing account of living with an eccentric artist.

I-90
Jackson County—Lyman County
87 Miles

The western part of I-90 extends east-west between Jackson and Lyman counties. Most communities welcomed the interstate highway system, fervently believing it would make each little town grow larger. Instead, the highway has made it easier for tourists and locals alike to go to the next town. Big billboards reflect communities' desperation for business, and the ages of some of them show that it's already too late. Many of the towns have ceased to be real communities offering diverse services and entertainments that reflect the preferences, nationalities, and interests of the local citizens; now they're simply strips of fast-food joints, gas stations, and supply shops. One town is hard to distinguish from another.

Large ranches and farms have grown from dozens of small homesteading units as populations dwindled and the size of an individual landowner's acreages increased. Some farmers drive their big tractors to the gas station in town because that's cheaper than taking gas delivery at the home place; watch out for slow-moving machinery even on the interstate.

This old chuck wagon calls to mind the era when cowboys from a big ranch like the Open Buckle might camp on the prairie for weeks gathering a herd. Each day, the cook drove the wagon to a convenient water hole and provided hot meals when the cowboys had time. —Rose Mary Goodson

KADOKA

Kadoka's name is a corruption of a Sioux word meaning "opening" or "hole in the wall," the "wall" referring to the Badlands. The area was also known as a "jumping-off place" because of the abrupt drop from grassland to the Badlands just west of town on SD 73. Kadoka, present population about seven hundred, was founded in 1906 when the Chicago, Milwaukee & St. Paul Railroad (usually known simply as the Milwaukee) was extended from Chamberlain to the Black Hills, but ranchers and Indians had been grazing cattle in the area for years before that.

One of Kadoka's most memorable denizens was Cornelius Augustus Craven, better known as "Gus." Craven operated the Open Buckle, one of the best-known ranches in western South Dakota. Born in New Jersey in the 1850s, he was educated at Notre Dame, and his family wanted him to be a priest. Tired of study, he headed west and arrived broke in Abilene, Kansas. According to Bob Lee in *Last Grass Frontier*, he talked himself into a job trailing cattle to Wyoming; for six weeks he carried firewood and water for the cook, took the exhausting job of night guard, and helped with the ox team. He trailed cattle from southern ranches into the Upper Plains for several years.

In the late 1870s Craven bought three heifers and branded them with the cinch buckle on his saddle, creating the Open Buckle brand,

234

which the family believes to be the oldest in continuous use in South Dakota. With a friend named Mike Dunn, he bought other cattle. The men owned no land, so they grazed the herd along on the open range from Cheyenne to Fort Collins, Colorado, and back. Eventually they bought land near Hat Creek, where they could winter a herd. Craven joined Hank Simmons in buying cattle and hay to deliver to Fort Robinson, near Chadron, Nebraska, and obtained a contract to deliver cattle to the Indians at Pine Ridge.

During this time Craven owned a racehorse with Jim Dahlman. One day, according to Joy Keve Hauk in *South Dakota History*, an Indian challenged them to a race. They looked at the Indian's thin, swaybacked horse and bet all the money they had or could borrow, as well as their own horse, on the race. The Indian horse won by such a distance that, as Craven told the story later, "If he'd had a rope on our horse he'd have dragged him to death." The Indian took their money, and Craven was out of the racing business.

By this time Craven was well known among ranchers and cowboys in western South Dakota. He met and married sixteen-year-old Jessie McGaa, whose father had homesteaded where Denver, Colorado, now stands, and the couple ran cattle on the Nebraska-South Dakota border. Later they moved to the mouth of Indian Creek on the east side of the Cheyenne River near the mouth of Rapid Creek. Gus collected fossils in his spare time and shipped them to the Smithsonian Institution. In 1890 he went back to work as a scout for the U.S. Cavalry, leaving his family alone. Mrs. Craven and the children took refuge in Hermosa during the Wounded Knee hostilities; when they returned with Gus, the ranch was in ruins, destroyed by both cavalry and Indian parties. Disgusted, the Cravens moved to the White River a few miles north of Wanblee and established another ranch. The Open Buckle became one of the largest outfits in western South Dakota, with about ten thousand cattle roaming from the White River to Wanblee, from Cottonwood Creek on the east to Bear Creek on the west. The expanse totaled nearly thirty-three thousand acres, much of it owned by his wife through her Indian heritage. Marketable steers were shipped by train to Omaha or Chicago. Gus taught farming in Kyle, where his wife was the first teacher in the Indian school, and was also postmaster for a time; when he received a request for a quarterly report from the postal department, Hauk says, he replied: "Never received a letter nor sent one. C. A. Craven."

About 1914 the family moved to Kadoka, where Gus entered politics while his son ran the ranch. When banks failed in 1921, he was plunged into debt, not an unusual situation for the old-time cowman. But the custom is those days was that "a man was as good as his word"; Gus Craven's word was good enough to borrow $60,000 over the telephone. After he died in 1929, his wife and children paid off his debts.

BELVIDERE

About eighteen miles east of Kadoka, the interstate sweeps by Belvidere as casually as it bypasses most places of interest. Don't ignore this little town, filled with community spirit. Eighty people who still call it home grew tired of the shabby buildings and empty storefronts a few years ago and got a grant from the South Dakota Arts Council and the National Endowment for the Arts. They fixed up the old buildings, hired artist Ida Jansen to paint murals depicting the businesses that once flourished inside each store, and asked descendants or friends of old merchants to tell their stories. During the last weekend in June 1988, residents staged a celebration that included music from a local band begun in 1906, possibly the oldest continuing community musical group in the state. Residents and visitors told stories, enjoyed a community supper, and wore pioneer costumes, some of them authentic garments worn by their ancestors.

East of town at Exit 170 is an intriguing replica of an 1880s prairie town, with original buildings salvaged from the neighborhood. A similar spirit exists at Okaton, twenty miles east of Belvidere. Though many towns fight the "ghost town" label, Okaton wears it proudly; "Ghost Town" has been added to the names of several surviving businesses. The town was founded in 1906 as the Milwaukee railroad laid tracks toward the Black Hills. Okaton means "nails on" or "drives in" in one Sioux dialect and "give birth" in another; either might have a metaphorical meaning as the town's name. During early homesteading days, the local region often produced large wheat crops, but because of scanty rainfall and the sandy character of the soil, many farms have been allowed to return to grass for stock raising.

The Cowboy Governor

South of Belvidere was the thirty-thousand-acre cattle ranch owned by Tom Berry, South Dakota's "Cowboy Governor" from 1933 to 1937 and one of the few politicians who actually worked on the land. Pictures of him riding his pinto cow pony appear in many old histories. South Dakotans have traditionally been strongly Republican, but in 1932 voters were tired of national Republican policies

Reservation Indians. —South Dakota State Historical Society

and financial scandals and responsive to the strength of Franklin D. Roosevelt. Berry, a Democrat, was elected governor, and his party took control of every state office for the first time in history. His election at this crucial time, just as the devastation of the Great Depression got under way, had a far-reaching effect: Federal bailout policies were initiated to help farmers survive, and some have been receiving federal money ever since. From a more distant perspective, the assistance efforts of the New Deal, which Franklin D. Roosevelt originated and Berry enthusiastically supported, appear to have done agriculture more harm than good in the state.

After a year or two of drought, 1932 was a relatively good year for agriculture in the state, but the following two years were much drier, and the migrations to California began. Berry beat his Republican opponent in 1934, as Roosevelt's New Deal policies were proving popular with farmers: Many counties had been declared disaster areas, and federal relief was pouring into the state. After serving two two-year terms, Berry attempted in 1936 to defy tradition and take a third but was defeated by Leslie Jensen of Hot Springs. In 1938 Jensen ran for but lost the Senate seat Peter Norbeck held until his death. Harlan J. Bushfield took over as governor. Berry won the Democratic nomination for the Senate in 1942 but was beaten by Bushfield.

MURDO

Trappers were the first white visitors to this area. James Clyman, heading west to open the fur trade with one of Ashley's brigades in 1823, led his men to water near here while Jedediah Smith retrieved two men he had buried in sand to minimize their dehydration, which saved their lives. Trapper Hugh Glass crawled through this vicinity while nursing wounds he received from a vicious grizzly attack on the Grand River two hundred miles north. Later, the American Fur Company's trail passed nearby on its way from the Little White River to Fort Pierre. The route was traveled by some of the West's most fascinating figures; most of them didn't stay long.

Murdo McKenzie, an early cattleman and manager of the Matador and Drag V ranch companies, may not have intended to stay long, either. In 1904 McKenzie was responsible for shipping so many trainloads of Texas steers to this area to graze on South Dakota grass that a grateful railroad named a town after him; the town's name was originally Murdo McKenzie, though it is known only by his first name today.

The railroad chose this site for a town because it was at the center of what was to become the great White River cattle range. No highways, no railroads, and few settlements existed between Chamberlain and the Black Hills, and Murdo immediately became the largest settlement along that line. A few post offices and tiny stores, some housed in a family dugout, served the cowboys that worked for the big ranches. The land officially still belonged to the Sioux of the Rosebud Reservation or the government when big ranches simply appropriated grazing rights.

McKenzie (or MacKenzie; authorities differ) was born in Scotland and came to the United States in 1885 when he was thirty-five to manage the vast Prairie Land and Cattle Company holdings in Texas and Wyoming for its owners. The Scottish company, formed in 1882, reported nearly a hundred thousand head of cattle on its American ranges when McKenzie was hired as manager. Ed Lemmon, another prominent rancher, later said McKenzie's practice was to market only enough mature beefs each year to declare an 8 percent dividend for the stockholders. This practice helped the Matador become one of the great cattle empires of the world. McKenzie had just finished a term as president of the Texas and Southwestern Cattle Association when he moved the ranch into South Dakota in 1904, running more than twenty thousand cattle on South Dakota ranges and several other herds on land that reached from Mexico to Canada.

McKenzie was one of the cowmen who went to Washington in 1902 to plead with President Theodore Roosevelt to rescind his order to take down the fences on government land in the West. Actually, says Bob Lee in *Last Grass Frontier*, "fencing of public land to keep settlers from homesteading it had been prohibited as early as 1885," but enforcement of the law had been sporadic, and most of the big operators ignored it. The sometimes fraudulent filings through which big ranchers acquired land, along with pressure from the increasing numbers of settlers in the early 1900s, probably dictated Roosevelt's reply: "Gentlemen, the fences will come down!" He promptly arrested a number of cattlemen in what was called the "Roosevelt Roundup," sent several to jail, and vetoed a bill passed by Congress that would have allowed grazing on the public domain.

Later, however, Ed Lemmon wangled a lease of more than eight hundred thousand acres on the Standing Rock Indian Reservation and fenced it. Shortly afterward, Cap Mossman and McKenzie obtained adjoining leases of about a half million acres each on the Cheyenne River Indian Reservation, and the Matador and Mossman's Hansford Land and Cattle Company became part of South Dakota history. Mossman and McKenzie, says Lee, "divided the expense of erecting a four-wire fence between their leases from the Missouri River for a distance of about forty miles westward." The Cheyenne River was the southern boundary of Mossman's lease. In all, about four million acres on the Cheyenne and Standing Rock reservations were stocked by cattlemen.

In 1906 McKenzie was elected president of an organization formed when the National Livestock and the American Stock Growers associations merged in Denver, becoming the American National Livestock Association. McKenzie immediately contributed $300 for a fund to promote legislation favorable to cattlemen and said if anyone disagreed with the plan or the purposes to which the money was devoted, they could get their money back. McKenzie died in Denver in 1939.

Several Matador cowboys stayed in South Dakota when McKenzie put together a herd and took it to Brazil to start another ranch. During World War I the South American enterprise failed, and the Matador men came back to South Dakota to find settlers and fences blocking much of what had been open range. Many left cowboy work as the drought years of the 1930s settled in. The Matador retained its reservation lease until 1914 and then moved its herds to the Fort Belknap Reservation in Montana; Dan Zimmerman's DZ outfit took over the Cheyenne agency lease. An English company bought out the Matador's vast holdings in 1950 for $19 million, bringing the stockholders over thirty times their original investment—a profit that came on top of an average annual dividend of 15 percent paid out during the thirty years of its operations.

McKenzie was one of three Scotsmen who developed major ranches in the Murdo area. The other two were Burton C. "Cap" Mossman of the Diamond A and James "Scotty" Philip, namesake of the town of Philip, of the 73 Ranch. It seems unfair that Mossman didn't get a growing town named after him, but his compensation might have been having the biggest ranch in the state. At one time, the Diamond A covered more than a million acres, including an entire county, and ran more than fifty thousand head of cattle. Before reorganization, what is now northern Stanley and southern Dewey counties was called Armstrong County and lay entirely within the boundaries of Mossman's ranch. One writer described the population of Armstrong County in 1939 as forty-eight Indians, two "other," and a lot of cows.

A typical story about these larger-than-life ranchers says that once a group of western Dakota cowboys gathered around a campfire

Lt. Col. George Armstrong Custer had long curls and wore a campaign hat with his army uniform in this photo, though he'd cut his hair before the Battle of the Little Bighorn. Brevetted a brigadier general in the Civil War, Custer was both hated and loved by his cavalry.
—State Historical Society of North Dakota

at night and fell to studying the full moon overhead, wondering if life existed on its surface.

"Do you suppose there is grass and water and trees on the moon?" queried one.

"I know for a fact there ain't," replied another.

"How do you know that?"

"If there was any grass and water, Cap Mossman would have had it leased for pasture years ago," he answered.

US 212
Wyoming–Dewey County
114 Miles

This east-west portion of US 212 extends from the Wyoming state line near Belle Fourche to the western border of the Cheyenne River Indian Reservation near Faith. Technically, the stretch west of Mud Butte lies slightly inside the boundaries of what has been designated the Black Hills in this volume, but to avoid chopping the highway into segments too small to make sense, I have included the entire western portion here.

BUTTE COUNTY

When George Custer first rode through these rolling plains in 1874, he saw them as a cattle-raising paradise with abundant grazing. As evidence he offered the fact that although the company marched west an average of seventeen miles a day after leaving Fort Lincoln, the party's mules and beef cattle constantly grew fatter, eating nothing but the native grasses. The broad prairie west of the Missouri River came to be considered the best cattle range in the world. Here the buffalo ranged free and grew fat, and before the last buffalo chip dried, cattlemen were moving in to establish ranches, long before the Indians' land was officially opened to white settlement.

Though this is primarily a ranching region, farming has also thrived with the introduction of irrigation. Today about 90 percent of Butte County is grazing land, and 5 percent is used for dryland wheat farming. Lately, wheat raisers have been criticized for plowing up native grasses in an attempt to profit from high wheat prices. Four percent of the county's land is irrigated, and officials estimate that seventy-four thousand tons of alfalfa hay, forty-six thousand tons of silage, more than seven hundred thousand bushels of corn, and more than a hundred thousand bushes of oats are produced annually. The crops supplement feed supplies for local cattle raisers and support feeding industries worth more than a $1 million.

Two-thirds of the county is drained by the Belle Fourche River; the county's water area totals just over ten thousand acres, eight thousand of which are in the Belle Fourche Reservoir behind Orman Dam northeast of town. Though the dam is on Owl Creek, most of the water actually comes from the Belle Fourche River through the Inlet Canal, six and a half miles long with a capacity of sixteen hundred feet per second of water. The reservoir irrigates nearly seventy-five thousand acres in the Belle Fourche Valley.

Orman Dam was begun in 1905 and completed in 1917. At 6,200 feet long, 115 feet high, and 19 feet wide on top, it was the largest earthen dam in the world at that time. The project required hundreds of men, often working with their own teams of workhorses; periodically they left the dam project for a month or so at a time to plant or harvest crops on their family farms. Surrounding land units had been opened for settlement by 1908, and water had been supplied to twelve thousand acres.

The promise of irrigated land drew many homesteaders who hoped to supplement their farm incomes by working on the dam. But a number of complications made the dam less beneficial than it might have been. Nearly half of the land the dam's backers planned to irrigate was gumbo, a fine, silty soil nearly impossible to farm because of its gluey consistency. Errors in construction and maintenance added to the costs, and deflation in the 1920s made it difficult to pay off debts. Water shortages in the 1930s hampered irrigation, and many farmers were inexperienced in irrigating. Only 2 of the original group of 580 homesteaders remained involved in the project by 1946. A new contract was negotiated in 1949, and reclassification removed land unsuitable for irrigation from the project; though it was designed to serve about ninety thousand acres, only about sixty thousand were actually irrigated. Thus, two-thirds of the project had to bear 100 percent of the burden of loan repayment.

All of the towns around the county seat—Fruitdale, Newell (named for dam engineer F. H. Newell), Nisland, and Vail—originated in part because of irrigation from the reservoir, which is now also used heavily for recreation. Because water is abundant, most of the streets are lined with trees, and the green fields of the surrounding irrigated farms stand out against the dun-colored prairie. Nisland was named for Nis Sorensen, who sold the town site to the railroad in 1908. The town soon had a bar but no jail; officials housed lawbreak-

Before the railroads extended their tracks west of the Missouri River, ox teams hauled supplies from towns along the river. A frontier photographer shot this view of oxen resting in the main street of Sturgis. One ox in a team could stand while the other lay down. —South Dakota State Historical Society

ers in an abandoned boxcar. By 1920 the county had built a domed wooden pavilion and forty-acre fairgrounds so it could host the Butte County Fair. President Calvin Coolidge visited the fair in 1927, and it's still a major event in the area.

BELLE FOURCHE

Belle Fourche was founded in 1890 by the Pioneer Townsite Land Company, which included among its investors Seth Bullock, best known as a lawman in Deadwood and friend of Teddy Roosevelt. Everyone agrees the town's name comes from the nearby river, but there the confusion starts. The words means "beautiful fork" in French. Some say French trappers named it because they realized the river is the north fork of the Cheyenne. Others say that the Sioux name for the river meant "beautiful river" and that the French trappers made a slight error in translating it. In any event, the river rises forty miles south of Gillette, Wyoming, circles the north end of the Black Hills, and joins the Cheyenne in Meade County.

As soon as the railroad arrived, Belle Fourche became the main point for the shipping of livestock. Forty-seven hundred train carloads of cattle were shipped from Belle Fourche in 1894, and for a time it was the greatest cattle-shipping point in the world, serving an immense territory. The Chicago, Milwaukee & St. Paul Railroad had not yet completed its lines to the West Coast, and the nearest railroad on the north was the Northern Pacific, running through the center of North Dakota. Belle Fourche also became a sheep and wool marketing point. Ever since John D. Hale put a band of three thousand sheep in the vicinity of Bear Butte in 1878, the region has been in a class with New Zealand, Australia, and Scotland as the best sheep-raising terrain in the world. In 1884, when the Sheep Breeders and Wool Growers Association was formed at Sturgis, about eighty-five thousand sheep grazed the Black Hills area. By 1900 sheep numbered about a half million.

By 1895 twenty-five hundred people lived in town, and it did a brisk trade in goods arriving by train. For a time, the main thoroughfare in the business district was called Saloon Street, in honor of its best business, but when temperance advocate Carrie Nation arrived in 1910, friendly barkeepers, confident in the draw of their refreshments, helped cover her expenses.

Early in the twentieth century, various industries came to town. A Belle Fourche creamery did well enough to build branches throughout the Black Hills, but the biggest manufacturer was the Black Hills Sugar Plant. Sugar beets were grown in the valley after 1912 but processed in Scottsbluff, Nebraska. The Utah-Idaho Sugar Company built a Belle Fourche plant in 1927 at a cost of $1.5 million, and more than 10 percent of the irrigable farmland was immediately planted to sugar beets. The new plant covered eight acres and could convert fifteen hundred tons of beets to thirty-six hundred pounds of sugar every twenty-four hours. About five hundred farmers eventually participated in the industry, growing nearly ten thousand acres of beets. A farmer received one-half the value of the sugar extracted from the beets, minus the cost of manufacturing. Beet pulp from which sugar had been extracted, and beet tops and by-products, were used as feed for livestock; between 1927 and 1938 about fifty thousand cattle and three hundred thousand sheep were fattened for market on sugar leftovers, many of them in feed yards owned by the sugar factory. After World War II, alfalfa began to replace sugar beets, and in 1965 the sugar factory closed, which ended beet production in the state.

Today, the 1911 Belle Fourche courthouse, with its copper green dome, is an aristocratic reminder of the town's position as the seat of Butte County. The rest of the town has a distinctly western look, with false fronts that might come from movie sets. With a population of more than four thousand, the town relies on diverse agricultural businesses for the bulk of its income: More than seventy-five thousand head of cattle, three hundred hogs, and thirteen hundred horses are sold annually at the sale yards in Belle Fourche, along with fifteen hundred purebred bulls, well over a hundred thousand head of sheep, and eleven million pounds of wool. These activities bring more than $35 million into the region.

Petroleum and natural gas reserves are known to exist in Harding and Butte counties north of Belle Fourche, and the region regularly anticipates an increase in drilling activity, welcomed for its infusion of cash. Like many small towns and isolated areas, Belle Fourche promotes itself by noting that South Dakota has no corporate income tax, no personal income or property taxes, no inventory tax, low real property taxes, low worker's compensation rates, and low unemployment insurance rates.

Promoters also work to attract tourists to the free Tri-State Museum's collection of pioneer artifacts and the cabin built in 1876 by John T. Spaulding, a scout. Orman Dam's recreational possibilities—fishing, water skiing, boating, sailing, and swimming—are being emphasized, though recent drought years have cut water supplies. Another local attraction, the Black Hills Round Up, began in 1918 as a three-day celebration to benefit the war effort. The event was so successful it has been held annually ever since, with proceeds used for community and regional enterprises. The usual competitions include bucking contests, bull-dogging, steer-roping, and wild-horse racing, as cowboys and cowgirls re-create the days of the open range. Troops from the Fourth Cavalry from Fort Meade often participated in a parade, as did Indians from the various reservations. Now, nationally ranked cowboys and cowgirls compete for more than $24,000 in prizes.

The Sundance Kid

The Sundance Kid, minus his cohort Butch Cassidy, was once in Belle Fourche as part of the Curry Gang just long enough to botch a holdup attempt of the Butte County Bank. The story might make a more entertaining movie than the 1969 classic that made Sundance famous. The robbers included Harvey Logan (alias Curry), Tom O'Day, Walter Punteney, Tom Jones, and a man called Frank Jones, who was actually Harry Longabaugh—alias the Sundance Kid. Witnesses said the gang couldn't seem to figure out what to do after ordering "Hands up!" A shopkeeper peered in the window and gave the alarm, and the five bad men ran from the bank with only $97 from a cash drawer. Tom O'Day's horse got away from him, so he pretended to be an innocent bystander until he could steal a mule;

unfortunately the animal stubbornly plodded in the opposite direction until the frustrated O'Day got nervous and hid in an outhouse, where he was promptly caught. Belle Fourche's town jail had burned down a few days before, leaving only the steel jail cell standing, so O'Day was locked into the open air cage for a few days. When townspeople threatened lynching, he was locked into the bank vault he'd tried to rob; eventually he was sent to jail in Deadwood.

Meanwhile, an armed city councilman took careful aim and shot the horse out from under the town blacksmith, Joseph Miller, who was in hot pursuit of the robbers. The rest of the gang, except for Curry, were captured near Red Lodge, Montana, and locked in the Deadwood jail with O'Day. But on Halloween night, they overpowered the jailer and his wife and departed in haste, taking along William Moore, a black man accused of murdering another man for mistreating a dog. O'Day and Punteney were caught near Spearfish and returned to Deadwood for trial.

In what one reporter called "a bizarre series of events"—the understatement of the entire story—they were acquitted of the robbery even though O'Day pleaded *guilty* to another charge (assault with a deadly weapon). Another indictment for the jailbreak was set aside by the Lawrence County state's attorney, the report continues, "since they were seemingly innocent men, they had merely walked away from the jail when the opportunity presented itself."

MEADE COUNTY

Meade County is the largest in the state at nearly 4,000 square miles. It is larger than Delaware and Rhode Island together, stretching 140 miles from one corner to the other. More than fifty post offices once dotted the county, but only about fifteen remain. As residents learned to drive distances for mail, they stopped shopping in small, family-owned businesses around former post offices. The southwestern corner of the county is dotted with caves, including Bethlehem, Wonderland, and Stagebarn, which was used as a stage station. Below Stagebarn Cave is Botany Canyon, with wild orchids, mossy rocks, and an almost arctic climate in summer.

Mud Butte, northeast of Belle Fourche, looks like a large mud pie dropped on the prairie from above. A wide region around it is known as "the gumbo" after the mud James Clyman called "particularly adhesive." Geologists know it as Pierre clay, a black soil that becomes incredibly sticky when wet. In the days when merchandise was shipped by wagon, freighters had to remove the brake blocks from their wheels as soon as the gumbo began to roll up; otherwise,

it would lodge between the brake and wheel and eventually halt the wagon. The goo accumulates with each step a human or animal takes when walking through gumbo. Cattlemen can't even move their herds across the stuff when it's wet. When dry, gumbo is creased with wrinkles, like an aged face; as soon as rain comes, the soil flows together into a sea of mud. Homesteaders found it difficult to farm when dry and impossible to handle when wet. No sod exists on gumbo; each spear of grass grows independently. However, the grass is abundant, and ranchers say it is richer even than the buffalo grass by which western Dakotans swear. Cattle or calves raised on gumbo are said to outweigh those raised on buffalo grass.

The Bismarck Trail

East of Mud Butte and a mile west of Cedar Canyon, a highway sign marks the site where some important trailblazers caught sight of the Black Hills in December 1875. Ben Ash, S. C. Dodge, Russ Marsh, Ed Donahue, and "Stimmy" Stimson were exploring Indian country, roughly following Custer's meandering route and planning to straighten the trail to the region from Bismarck, North Dakota. The group ran into a guide named California Joe, who showed them the sights before he led them out of the hills and back to Bismarck.

In February of the next year, the Bismarck *Tribune* reported forty-seven teams leaving with steam sawmill machinery for the Black Hills, with a hundred others planning to leave within a few days. Many of those folks turn up often in western South Dakota's history: Fred Hollenbeck took a herd of cows; Joe Pennell, Thomas Madden, and Bob Roberts went as traders; O. Nicholson took miners' goods; George Gibbs planned to work as a blacksmith; Ed Donahue and W. B. Show formed the Black Hills Lumber Company; a Mr. Hobart took a shingle mill; and Mr. Downing took fresh pork, butter, lard, and sausage. Despite the fact that the Black Hills were still Indian country, these men were going to stay. Caravans could travel ten or fifteen miles a day if the weather was fair; if they ran into gumbo, the trip could be considerably longer. Although fields, fences, and roads have obliterated parts of the Bismarck Trail, deep ruts made a century ago are still visible in some places.

Ben C. Ash, one of the trail's blazers, moved to Yankton with his parents in 1859 and drove a buggy for a U.S. marshal while still a boy. At the age of seventeen, he was already a deputy marshal. In 1872 he worked for railroad contractors and helped build the first house in Bismarck, then part of Dakota Territory. Back in Yankton in 1873, he hired on as a mule skinner with the Seventh Cavalry under Custer, heading with the 22nd Infantry into the Yellowstone country to protect survey parties of the Northern Pacific Railway. After pioneering the Bismarck Trail, Ash intended to start a ranch with S. C. Dodge in Rapid Valley. Dodge went there the next spring but was killed by Indians. Ash settled in Pierre and was twice elected sheriff of Hughes County. For five years he was Indian agent on the Lower Brulé Agency near Chamberlain. Later he operated the Quarter Circle W ranch on the Moreau River.

Maurine and Faith

Maurine was named for Maurine Price, whose family operated a store in pioneer days. Some of the town's best-known natives include Catherine Bach, who played Daisy Duke on TV's *The Dukes of Hazard*; Francis Galbraith, ambassador to Singapore and Indonesia; and Clyde Hull, world welterweight champion in 1929.

Faith might have been named for the quality required to live there. That version of the story is supported by the highway marker at the intersection of US 212 and SD 73, which begins by talking about people's souls and ends on a practical note characteristic of the region: "Our grass is unsurpassed anywhere, producing beef, the backbone of our existence . . . our faith his boundless . . . . In 1910 Faith sprang up on this prairie, so vast in its extent that deceit finds no place to hide and man is known for his true stature—which is well, since the county sheriff is 110 miles away." The livelihood of these ranchers, says the marker, is in "direct ratio with the varying rainfall; our philosophy is 'Next Year Will be Better.'"

Other sources say Faith, nicknamed "The Prairie Oasis," was named for the daughter of Nelson Rockefeller, one of the principal stockholders of the Milwaukee railroad. In August 1940 a woman left town residents a letter containing $100; the letter explained that Faith was named for her, and she had wanted to see it. She did not introduce herself but requested that the money be put to the best use.

Faith was literally on the wrong side of the tracks when it was established in 1910; twenty-five businesses were crammed between the Perkins County line and the railroad line until townspeople took the obvious course and moved the whole thing. By the time the first train arrived in 1911, three hundred residents were waiting for it. After the first depot was destroyed by fire, another was brought in by flatcar. Even after the railroad abandoned Faith in 1978, cattle and sheep sales continued to top ninety thousand head at the Faith Livestock Company.

In the Faith neighborhood, where boots and cowboy hats are everyday wear, the rodeo has always been a way of life: This is the site of the South Dakota Rodeo Association finals. An airport and rodeo grounds jostle each other on the north edge of town. When the old grandstand at the rodeo grounds was ruled unsafe for large crowds, residents responded with typical Plains spirit: They donated labor and materials to build a larger, sheltered seating area, with room for a lunch stand under it and a stage for other events. The same spirit of cooperation is evident in the Faith Memorial Hospital; in 1950 a caravan of 217 ranchers and businessmen drove their pickups and trucks to Rapid City to collect materials to begin the building.

One of the best-known true stories of Dakota's heritage occurred north of Faith, a testimonial to man's courage and falsity. Hugh Glass, a hunter with Maj. Andrew Henry's party ascending the Grand River in August 1823, met a terrible fate. Near the present-day Shadehill Reservoir he was attacked by a grizzly bear that gnawed and mutilated his body, lacerated his scalp, and broke his leg. Ashley expected Glass to die, so he detailed two men to stay behind and wait with the injured man, bury him after he died, then catch up with the brigade. The men waited, but the unconscious Glass wouldn't die. Concerned for their own safety in the territory of hostile Indians, the men finally decided to take Glass's weapons and leave him surely to die. Remarkably, he recovered enough to crawl from the Grand to Fort Kiowa, near Chamberlain, at least two hundred miles. Every cactus that stuck him made him angrier; he drew strength by plotting revenge on the men who left him. The fascinating story is told in books by John Neihardt and Frederick Manfred.

ZIEBACH COUNTY

The Moreau River, which flows east to the north of the highway, was named for a French trader who lived at its mouth and was stabbed to death by his Cheyenne wife. The Sioux called it Owl River, the Arikaras Big Owl River. Moreau was in residence when Lewis and Clark passed by in 1804, because they referred to it as "Murow Creek," though in their later journals they called it "Cerwercerna River." The fur trade route from Fort Tecumseh at Pierre on the Missouri River to Fort Laramie, Wyoming, crossed this area by way of a pass in the Badlands south of Scenic. Gen. W. S. Harney's expedition of 1855 against the Sioux passed through the region as well.

Red Elm and Dupree

Red Elm was founded in 1910 when the Milwaukee railroad built its Faith branch. Perhaps the long struggle to push the rail lines west exhausted the men who named the towns, or maybe they just ran out of Milwaukee officials to name towns after; at any rate, they named this town for the elm trees found in the area.

Dupree, established in 1910 when Frank Barnes set up a wall tent by the tracks, also came with the railroad. It was named for one of the first white settlers in the region, an Indian trader and rancher named Fred Dupris (pronounced as the modern town is spelled). He originated the bison herd Scotty Philip often receives credit for saving.

As lonely as this dry countryside may look to modern visitors, its promise lured settlers from widely scattered places to new homes. Mable Dora Lee Brownwolf, whose story is told in *Daughters of Dakota*, was born in Missouri and came with her family to claim 160 acres of land in 1910; their homestead was north of the Moreau River, two days' wagon travel west of Wakpala. Her father's first act on the homestead was to dig a nine-foot hole for storage; he roofed it with logs and added a door and steps, and the family used it for years.

Mable's father, like most homesteaders, used a green willow stick to "witch" for water. After selecting the spot, he used a posthole auger and spade and dug a well forty-three feet deep, six feet across. At thirty feet he struck a vein of water coming from the Fox Hills sandstone. He bored into the stone with a crowbar until water gushed into the well. A derrick was placed above the well so that Mable could haul dirt and slush out in a bucket and dump it on the surface while her father was digging below. When he was finished, she hauled *him* up in the bucket. An efficient man, he lined the entire well with granite and later installed a pump.

Mable's family moved to a homestead on Ash Creek in 1915, and by that time Dupree contained a cafe, hardware and clothing stores, and other businesses; it retained its board sidewalks for years. During its busiest period, the town was a marketing center for livestock, small grain grown on the nearby prairies, and the flax that seemed to grow best when the prairie was first broken; many homesteaders paid for their land with the first crop of flax sowed.

One day John Brownwolf arrived at Mable's door with a record player in his buggy and said to her father, "I would like to trade my record player for your girl." Mable's father refused, but Mable coaxed him to let her go to the fair with some neighbor girls. Four days later she returned home with John Brownwolf, who refused to take back his record player. "No, I traded for your girl." Late that year, the two were married.

Mary C. Collins, Missionary

Another resident of the Moreau River neighborhood, missionary Mary Collins, grew up in a "conservative religious household in Keokuk, Iowa," according to Helen Rezatto in *South Dakota Heritage*. At the age of thirty she came to Dakota Territory as a missionary. She had never met an Indian and at first said they were "horrid." Collins taught at Thomas Riggs's Oahe Mission, where she became known as a "medicine woman" for curing a baby with infected teeth and a boy with a stomachache caused by consumption of green watermelon. Before long Collins had earned the name Winona, traditionally given to the first-born girl, for her work with the Sioux. She decided to live among Sitting Bull's people near the Grand River. Her cabin was in Running Antelope's village on the Moreau River, and she knew many of the old warrior chiefs during their transition to white ways.

Collins didn't think much of Sitting Bull at the first meeting, calling him "ignorant, filthy, and superstitious." In later years, according

to Stanley Vestal, she grew more understanding and said Sitting Bull was invariably gracious. The two became friends, though they argued over many topics.

She later recalled that when Sitting Bull first visited her, he stopped outside her gate on his white circus horse and called to her. She paid him no attention until he tied the "historic" white horse to the fence and came to the door. "Do you know who I am?" he asked. When she answered in the affirmative, he asked why she refused to come when he called. She explained that a polite man would not call a woman to him; it was his place to go to her. At once, she recalled, Sitting Bull removed his hat, and said, "No, I did not know."

Whenever he called on her after that, he removed his hat and rapped at the door. Miss Collins may have realized later that Sioux politeness, born of tipi life, demanded that a visitor announce himself subtly, by clearing his throat; only in emergencies did a Sioux even become insistent enough to scratch on a lodge cover. That way, if the tipi's residents chose to ignore the visitor, neither would be embarrassed. Sitting Bull must have felt it would be rude to knock on a door and called out as a compromise.

Nevertheless, Collins got along well because she tried to understand Sioux ways before changing them. She also possessed a sense

Sitting Bull and his family posed for this formal portrait. His daughter, Has Many Horses, is on his left, holding his grandson Tom Fly. The woman to his right may be his mother, Her Holy Door, and the two women behind him are his wives; he had nine children. —State Historical Society of North Dakota

of humor, a valuable and rare commodity in religious folk (especially missionaries), and the Sioux loved a good joke on themselves. Collins reports an exchange between the two of them that illustrates the relationship:

> [Sitting Bull] said, "Are you going to live here?" I responded that I was. He then said, "Shall your horses eat our grass and drink our water and shall you live on our land?" I said, "Is the grass yours?" "Yes," he replied. "Is the water yours?" "Yes," he said. It was pouring down a rain and I said, "Is this rain that is falling yours?" He replied, "It is." I said, "Then I have something to say. I have spent money to have my garden plowed. And money for seeds and paid one of you to plant it. Your rain is ruining my garden and if it is yours I want you to keep it off my garden." For a moment they all looked at me as if I were insane. Then a smile broke out on their faces. And they laughed, came forward and shook hands with me and departed.

After that, Collins reported, she was never disturbed by the Indians, even during times of great tension, and many of them became good friends.

In 1890 Collins tried to convince Sitting Bull's people to give up the Ghost Dance, warning that trouble could come of it from white authorities. When Sitting Bull was shot by Sioux police who were trying to arrest him on December 15, 1890, she mourned his death and suggested that a monument be built to him on the reservation. Later she said the Standing Rock Reservation was "where my real labor for the people began." She became critical of the accepted methods for teaching Indians and lectured widely, suggesting that they should attend only a day school, not the crowded boarding schools where they were away from their language, culture, and parents. Still, she believed the Indians would succeed best if they imitated the whites; her motto was "Never do anything for an Indian that he can do for himself or herself." She was finally ordained as a minister in the Congregational church, one of the few females to be so honored. She retired in 1910 and returned to Keokuk, Iowa, where she died in 1920.

Shannon County—Gregory County
201 Miles

US 18 runs east-west through the rolling southern hills between the Shannon County line west of Oglala and the Gregory County line at Dallas. East of Oelrichs, the highway enters both Shannon County and the Pine Ridge Indian Reservation. Just west of Oglala, the highway crosses the main fork of the White River, which can become an impressive stream with hard rain; Indian families often camped along the stream in pre-reservation days to harvest wild berries and stock up on meat. East of Oglala, the highway crosses White Clay Creek several times.

PINE RIDGE INDIAN RESERVATION

Despite its Irish-sounding name, Shannon County, named after the chief justice of the supreme court of Dakota Territory from 1873 to 1882, is primarily occupied by Teton and Oglala Sioux and known to them as the land of Pajuta Wa Cha Cha, "Indian medicine." The Pine Ridge Reservation is the second largest in the United States and contains the largest Indian school in the nation. On the high buttes that dot the landscape, many Lakota dedicate themselves to a vision quest, a ceremony of fasting and endurance that brings a prophecy for the future. Other ceremonies as old as Lakota culture are performed in hidden places in this landscape.

One of the most intriguing elements of Indian culture is the use of plants in making medicines, religious artifacts, decorations, tools, and food. This knowledge is an important and so far unrecognized contribution of Native Americans to the modern world. We are just beginning to appreciate the medications and foods that can be produced from the diverse species of the Plains. Four to five hundred plant species, one-third of those known to exist on the Plains, can be found in South Dakota; if the knowledge of Indian elders is preserved, our civilization may benefit.

For example, Indians often smoked sumac, skunkbush, red osier, or bearberry instead of tobacco. Umbrella plant was used in tanning and bleaching hides. The root of purple coneflower cures toothache; under the name "black Sampson," it is sometimes used as a mind-altering substance by modern Westerners. Yucca was used for soap and to kill vermin. Diapers and quilts were made of cattails, toilet paper came from small ragweed, and a sugar substitute was pro-

The Oglala holy man Black Elk was photographed in 1947 at Pine Ridge Indian Reservation holding his pi The Black Elk Wilderness the Black Hills includes Harney Peak, where he received a prophetic first vision. —South Dakota State Historical Society

duced from the box elder. Pulverized western sagebrush roots might be spread on the face of a sleeping man to prevent his waking up while one stole his horses.

The desolation of the area may have stimulated the imagination of people who named the area's natural features. Unlike the names given to western settlements by railroad officials, many of these names either tell a story or indicate the kind of personal relationship with the land that the Lakota had in former generations (and still have today). Many of the intriguing names don't appear on some maps; along this highway are Bean Soup Basin, Quiver Hill, Big Foot Hill, Sittin-Up School, Bear-in-Lodge Creek, Wanamaker Creek, and Porch Creek. Though the landscape may look tame to a traveler, it has unique features; on Snake Butte, for example, rock hunters find unusual calcite crystals.

Along the highway stand a variety of homes inhabited by the Indian people who live here. These include modern houses that might fit a metropolitan subdivision but that look flimsy against the sturdy hills and a sky often filled with violent thunderstorms in summer and windblown snow in winter. Older homes built by the Indians during the early reservation period are log cabins with sod roofs. Families create outdoor shade by erecting poles to support roofs of fresh-cut pine boughs. Canvas tipis are also raised for summer living or extra visitors.

Sioux Artists

Before contact with the white man, most Plains tribes kept both oral records, faithfully and accurately passed down through the generations, and pictographic records (usually called "winter counts") of the principal events for families and tribal groups year by year. As contact with white men increased, Lakota artists tended to adopt art materials that could be fitted into traditional styles.

Amos Bad Heart Bull was an Oglala Sioux historian and painter born in Wyoming who died on the Pine Ridge Reservation in 1913. He studied art, history, and the Lakota language with his father and uncle; about 1890 he began to record in a ledger the history of his people. He wrote about the Battle of the Little Bighorn, the Ghost Dance movement, and other events in comparatively recent Sioux history. Most of his illustrations of these events were done in traditional style, without the three-dimensional quality most white painters choose but strictly accurate in accoutrements.

The remarkable manuscript was inherited by his sister, Mrs. William Pretty Cloud, and buried with her. Fortunately, Helen H. Blish had photographed and translated the work, and it was published in 1967 as *A Pictographic History of the Oglala Sioux*. The extraordinary document gave for the first time the Indian version of events that had been told only from the white point of view. Another version of the book, including the paintings of Bad Heart Bull along with those of other Indians of the time, is titled *Wind on the Buffalo Grass*.

Andrew Standing Soldier, another Oglala, has become one of the best-known artists of the reservation period. He was born on the reservation in 1917 and died in Omaha, Nebraska, in 1967. Standing Soldier attended a Pine Ridge boarding school and studied mural

The Oglala leader Red Cloud forced the U.S. government to abandon forts on the Bozeman Trail as part of the Treaty of Laramie in 1868. In this photo, he wears eagle feathers symbolizing brave deeds, called "coups," and a breastplate made of bone over a fringed leather shirt. —South Dakota State Historical Society

painting in 1937 at a special summer school at Oglala Community High School in Pine Ridge. His work has been called outstanding by artists who praise his simple, realistic style and authentically portrayed figures. His work depicted the Sioux among whom he grew up, set against the unusual land formations of the reservation in scenes from daily life: Indian cowboys, families riding in wagons pulled by draft horses, grandmothers drying meat.

In 1939 Standing Soldier won fourth prize in a poster design contest for the Federal Pavilion at the San Francisco Golden Gate Exposition; he worked between 1939 and 1941 for the Works Progress Administration as a muralist in the Dakotas, Idaho, and Nebraska, painting in public buildings and schools. He also illustrated several bilingual readers for the Bureau of Indian Affairs. In 1961 he settled in Gordon, Nebraska, where a local auto dealer allowed him to paint in the auto showroom and collected a significant body of his work, as did many people in western South Dakota and Nebraska. He worked mainly in watercolor but also painted in oils and did pen and ink sketches. During 1948-49 he lived at Crazy Horse Monument, where he worked with Korczak Ziolkowski. Some of his work appears at the Wounded Knee Memorial Museum, and several paintings are on display at the Crazy Horse Monument Museum.

Another Oglala artist, Alice New Holy, works with one of the oldest art forms in Lakota culture and has helped recover a traditional skill for future generations. An Oglala, New Holy does quillwork. For generations Indian artists dyed porcupine quills and worked them into intricate patterns for decorations on clothing and useful articles. After quills were laboriously pulled from a dead porcupine, they were boiled to remove dirt and oils and colored with dyes made from plants found in the region. Then each quill was flattened, usually by drawing it between the teeth. Working with quills requires great dexterity, terrific eyesight, and immense patience. When traders brought glass beads to the Plains tribes, many women welcomed the ease of sewing with beads and the varieties of color; thus, the knowledge of quillwork nearly disappeared during the reservation period.

New Holy learned quillwork from her grandmothers, Sadie New Holy and Quiver, who cut out tiny moccasins for her to bead and quill when she was a child. She also was taught by her father, Joseph New Holy. She is passing the tradition to her five daughters and her grandchildren. The family's work is in permanent collections in museums all over the world and has won many awards. Her husband, Amil, uses the long stiff hairs from the porcupine to make the roach headpieces worn by male dancers at *wacipis*, or powwows.

A more recent Lakota craft, making quilts, has led to a business for reservation residents. Lisa Little Chief Bryan watched older women sew colorful geometrically patterned quilts as a child on the Pine Ridge Reservation. Later, as a student of Indian history, she learned more about the origins of the craft and began designing them in her home in Rapid City. Her mother sewed them together in her home in Norris, just outside the reservation. Bryan formed a company to manufacture and sell quilts and called it Star Route Industries. Reservation women make quilts in their homes so they do not have to find help with child care. Bryan's husband, Shane, collects the quilts, sold through a catalog along with pottery, beadwork, clothing, and silver and horsehair jewelry. Her two children help with packaging and travel to craft shows.

When Bryan began her company, such quilts might sell for $40 or $50; now prices range from $200 for a wall hanging to $1,500 for a

U.S. Marine William "Billy" Mills flashed a smile as he won a gold medal in the 1964 Olympics. —South Dakota Department of Tourism

king-size quilt. Designs are all inspired by Indian traditions, and many of the women choose to stitch their own names to the quilts they make.

Other Lakota residents have found unique ways to achieve and bring encouragement to the reservation. William Mills, a Teton Sioux born at Pine Ridge, gained fame for South Dakota and pride for the Lakota in the 1964 Olympic Games when he became the only American athlete ever to win a gold medal in the 10,000-meter run. Mills often returns to the reservation to sponsor and participate in running contests with Pine Ridge youngsters and to encourage them to retain their cultural heritage while learning how to succeed in a world dominated by white men.

Oglala

The town of Oglala is best known for its Indian boarding school, where children from all over the reservation attended classes designed to fit them into white culture. Students reporting to school were systematically "de-Indianized"—they were prohibited from speaking Lakota, dressed in uniforms rather than their native cloth-

This teacher was photographed standing behind his Lakota students on the Pine Ridge Reservation. On opening day, school officials usually cut the students' long braids and required them to give up Indian-style clothing, often in favor of donated castoffs. —South Dakota State Historical Society

ing, given short haircuts, and told to give up their "heathen" ways in favor of Christianity.

Thisba Hutson Morgan, a teacher at the boarding school from 1890 to 1895, wrote in *South Dakota History* of her experiences there, showing sympathy for the Indians that was unusual for her time and place. Reluctant children, she said, were rounded up by agency police, and the first experience for all of them was a bath; kerosene was used to liquidate "the myriad insect inhabitants of the prairie and the tepees which the children unwittingly had brought with them." The children's clothes were sometimes given to their parents but most often burned. When the boys' long hair was cropped, Morgan says, they felt naked, humiliated by an action unusual in traditional society. The moccasins they found comfortable were burned, and their feet were thrust into what Morgan calls "the awful brogans furnished by the United States Government." As they limped about, their feet became blistered, and the bleeding sores often became infected.

Pine Ridge

Government buildings erected here to serve agency Indians include a school, hospital, and administrative structures. Red Cloud, who is buried in a cemetery above the school, encouraged the "Black Robes" to establish a school so Indian children could learn white ways. The Holy Rosary Mission just west of Pine Ridge is operated by Jesuit priests and brothers and Franciscan sisters.

Armed soldiers stand guard while others throw the frozen corpses of Indians killed at Wounded Knee into a mass grave. —South Dakota State Historical Society

One of the town's important features is the Heritage Center, opened in 1982 in a building constructed in 1888. Its collection of Indian art is one of the nation's finest, including contemporary work as well as old beadwork and traditional artifacts. The Red Cloud Indian Art Show, held annually from June through August, exhibits art from Indians in the largest show of its kind, attracting more than eight thousand visitors from all fifty states and as many as fifteen countries each year. Prizes totaling nearly $10,000 were awarded in 1990, and an annual $5,000 scholarship is given to a young artist to pursue higher education. The center's gift shop sells only Sioux arts and crafts. In front of the school is the Holy Rosary Mission Church, its Gothic interior decorated with traditional Sioux designs by artist Felix Walking.

Wounded Knee

North and east of Pine Ridge is Wounded Knee, where, on December 29, 1890, the last bloody encounter between Indians and the U.S. Army occurred. The confrontation is called the "Wounded Knee massacre" by whites and the "Chief Big Foot massacre" by Indians.

The tragedy has been dissected by several historians, who have given not only the self-serving accounts of the military and white promoters but also the words of the Lakota themselves.

The first Wounded Knee tragedy wasn't the end of the story. In February 1973, after increasing problems with whites, their own tribal government, and the Bureau of Indian Affairs (BIA), two hundred Indians led by members of the American Indian Movement (AIM) took over the Wounded Knee Trading Post in what came to be known as "Wounded Knee II." They took eleven elderly hostages, looted the community's trading post, destroyed a museum, and occupied the seven houses and two churches in the village.

Heavily armed federal marshals and FBI agents surrounded the area with armored personnel carriers and exchanged shots with those inside the village, who were soon joined by reservation residents of all ages. Media representatives arrived in force as the siege continued; South Dakota Senators George McGovern and Jim Abourezk negotiated, as did representatives of the BIA and the Justice Department. The standoff dragged on for weeks. Volunteers air-dropped food and medical supplies, and young Indians recalled their heritage by slipping in and out of the fortified village through firefights that grew more intense as the siege moved into its second month; several Wounded Knee defenders were killed.

When the battle ended in early May, the world was a little better informed about conditions on South Dakota Indian reservations. Since that time, world media representatives have been frequent visitors to the region, with mixed results.

A year after South Dakota's centennial celebrations, in which few Indians participated, and one hundred years after the original Wounded Knee massacre, Governor George Mickelson declared 1990 the "Year of Reconciliation" between white and Indian residents of the state, setting off debate and discussion about both past and present. In December 1991 a group of mostly Lakota people rode Big Foot's route to Wounded Knee and performed private and public rituals to observe the occasion and honor those who died.

Wanblee and Martin

North of Pine Ridge is a network of gravel and dirt roads leading to several fascinating communities. Sharps Corner is on the map but not in most historical sources; nor are historical references to Porcupine and Kyle easy to find, though it is known that Kyle was named for turn-of-the-century U.S. Senator James H. Kyle of Aberdeen. Porcupine was named for a nearby butte topped with pine trees that looks like a huddled porcupine; Scenic, a short distance north, was named for its location in the beautiful Badlands.

East of Sharps Corner near Kyle is Oglala Lakota College, which opened in 1970 with a few part-time faculty members. It is one of only two four-year tribal colleges in the nation and has established branches in each reservation district and in Rapid City so adults may attend college without traveling far. By the fall of 1972, more than three hundred students were taking classes. In June 1983 the college received accreditation through the North Central Association of Colleges and Schools. About forty full-time and fifty part-time faculty members instruct about a thousand students per semester.

Wanblee is named for nearby Eagle Nest Butte, called *Wamblee Hokpila* by the Indians. (As often happens with an oral language such as Lakota, its translation into written form differs in spelling from that of Lakota speakers.) To obtain eagle feathers for ceremonies, Indian hunters would often hide in a camouflaged pit baited with a dead animal and grab the eagle's legs when he landed. That was just the beginning of the battle. Besides buffeting the captor with its wings, the eagle would use its talons and beak to try to get away. It was a sign of strength and courage to have captured an eagle; sometimes the victorious Indian would simply remove the feathers he wanted and let the eagle go.

Martin, called the "metropolis of the Pine Ridge Reservation country," is actually located off the reservation about forty-five miles east of Pine Ridge. It boasts a surprisingly large population in such a thinly settled area. Martin was founded in 1912, when Bennett County was organized, and is still the county seat. It was named for Eben Martin of Hot Springs, congressman from South Dakota's western district from 1908 until 1912. Nearby is Lacreek Lake, part of a migratory waterfowl refuge that attracts thousands of sandhill cranes and other birds.

ROSEBUD INDIAN RESERVATION

At Batesland, US 18 enters the Rosebud Indian Reservation. An Indian community has existed here since at least 1878, when Rosebud Agency was established. At a site sacred to the Lakota (and therefore undisclosed to the public) lies a landmark called Holy Butte, Paha Tanka. According to legend, the white buffalo was said to live in a large cave at the butte. Each spring, the white buffalo led his herd of brown buffalo to be hunted by the Indians. Always, the animals nourished and sustained the Indians—until a foolish youth wounded the white buffalo. Immediately, the great leader took his herd back inside the cave, and they were never seen again. The mouth of the cave collapsed, but it is said that in spring, when the wind is right, the sounds of the buffalo herd still rumble on the wind.

Parmalee, east of Martin, was originally called Cut Meat. In 1916 the name was changed to *Wososo*, the Sioux word for "cut meat," but in 1921 the town was renamed for Dave Parmalee, an early settler. Cutmeat Creek, which flows northeast into Mellette County to join the Little White River, recalls an important part of reservation life. In early days, after a successful buffalo hunt, women would slice meat in thin strips and hang it in the sun and air to dry thoroughly. Called jerky, this concentrated meat could be stored for long periods or pounded into bits and mixed with fat and berries for a nourishing and tasty travel food called pemmican.

Later it became illegal for reservation Indians to hunt, partly because the whites didn't trust them with guns. And, since most of the buffalo had been slaughtered, hunting was pointless. An issue house was established at a central point, and on certain days each month such supplies as meat, flour, and sugar would be distributed to the Indians. The Indians didn't consider the salted pork they were given fit to eat and often gave it to their dogs, but the days when they received beef provided both entertainment and sustenance as

Confined to reservations and no longer able to hunt buffalo, Dakota Indian tribes received government beef. This undated photo shows families from Standing Rock Reservation watching as men butcher cattle on beef-issue day. —State Historical Society of North Dakota

*Ben Reifel was the first
Lakota elected to public
office in South Dakota.*
—South Dakota State
Historical Society

families gathered from a large region. The government agents sometimes turned the cattle loose and, in the spirit of a buffalo hunt, let
the Indians shoot the animals themselves; other times, the agents
shot the cattle and helped divide the meat among the Indians, who
butchered their own portions. Cutmeat Creek may have been named
either for the original meat-cutting or because an issue house was
established at the present site of Parmalee.

Ben Reifel, the first Lakota to hold a major political office in South
Dakota, was born in a log cabin at Cut Meat in 1906 to a Brulé mother
and a German-American father. Reifel graduated from South Dakota State College in 1932 and served as an agricultural extension
agent during the drought years of the Depression, then he became
an administrator for the Bureau of Indian Affairs. He helped push
through the Indian Reorganization Act, which authorized each tribe
to buy back some of its lands and established a revolving loan fund
to encourage economic development and underwrite scholarships.
After serving in World War II, he earned his doctorate at Harvard

and worked first on the Fort Berthold Reservation in North Dakota before becoming the first Indian superintendent at Pine Ridge.

Reifel established a strong chain of command, held meetings throughout the reservation, participated in activities, and published a monthly bulletin that included news about accidents and deaths caused by drinking. He declared war on bootleggers who sold alcohol on the reservation and spoke often about the complexities of federal Indian policy, cultural differences between Indians and whites, and the role of the BIA. After being elected to the U.S. House of Representatives in 1960, Reifel worked to pass agricultural legislation beneficial to white South Dakota farmers as well as Indians. He was reelected by large margins four times before retiring in 1970.

Rosebud

The town of Rosebud lies south of US 18. The old corrals where government agents held cattle until the Indians arrived for ration distribution are on the flat land north of the agency, along with a fairgrounds used for rodeos. On the hill above the agency, soldiers dug rifle pits after the Wounded Knee tragedy, expecting attack on the government buildings.

Spotted Tail, whose name in Sioux was Sinte Galeska or Sinte Gleska, was born between 1823 and 1833 in the Brulé tribe. He became a respected leader but was always a man of contradictions; Sinte Gleska College, at Rosebud, is named for him.

When Spotted Tail was fifteen, he joined a raid against the Pawnee that ended in a drunken orgy; he vowed never again to drink and kept the pledge. Later he killed a whiskey peddler on the reservation and demanded that such individuals be kept away from his agency. In 1870 he wrote to the head of the U.S. Board of Indian Commissioners, "We would like a large garrison of soldiers kept at Laramie and also on the Missouri River to keep off bad whites and whiskey from our reserve. To us whiskey is death."

In 1854 Spotted Tail participated in the killing of Lt. J. L. Grattan and his column of soldiers near Fort Laramie. He and the other warriors who joined in the slaughter surrendered at Fort Leavenworth to prevent their entire tribe from being punished. While in prison, Spotted Tail realized the power of the white man, and when he and the others were pardoned, he returned determined to spend his life bringing peace to his people. He signed the 1868 treaty that created the Great Sioux Reservation, promising the Lakota most of western South Dakota and large chunks of North Dakota, Nebraska, Montana, and Wyoming.

After government officials had moved his agency several times, Spotted Tail reportedly said, with irony: "We have been moved five times. I think you had better put the Indians on wheels and then you can run us about wherever you wish." The Brulé were finally moved to Rosebud in 1878. Spotted Tail was given a large frame house but preferred to live in a tent. He was shot to death on his way home from a council meeting by Crow Dog, chief of agency police, nine years before Sitting Bull was murdered.

Two versions of the motives for the killing are still argued. One theory holds that Spotted Tail had seduced Crow Dog's wife. The other says that Crow Dog wanted to lead a Brulé delegation to Washington and was jealous of Spotted Tail's power. As Virginia Driving Hawk Sneve says in *South Dakota Heritage*, "No matter which version of the assassination is true, it was an ignominious end for a great man." Spotted Tail is buried in the Episcopal Cemetery on the hill north of the Rosebud Agency.

Over the years, as whites have begun to study Native American history and beliefs more thoroughly, opinions about Spotted Tail and Sitting Bull have reversed. Spotted Tail and Red Cloud were revered by their contemporaries, but many modern Indians deride them as indecisive cowards who gave up their lands without a fight. At the same time, many whites have begun to admire Sitting Bull, their ancestors' implacable foe, for his determination to save his people's way of life. Both men probably acted out of deeply held beliefs about which course would be best for their people, with a minimum of interest in personal power. Each did the best he could at the time.

Mission

Mission is home of the main campus of Sinte Gleska College, the school named for Spotted Tail. It opened in 1971 and employs about forty full-time faculty instructing about five hundred students. Like Oglala Lakota College, Sinte Gleska is accredited through the North Central Association of Colleges and Schools. The college offers two- and four-year degrees as well as a master's degree in elementary education, the first tribal college in the nation to do so. Many SGC graduates work in administrative or teaching positions in public schools or BIA schools on the reservation. Both staff and graduates are involved in promoting small businesses on the reservation, including a woodworking cooperative that repairs and renovates homes and businesses and an electricians' cooperative that solicits small wiring projects. SGC's administrative offices are in Rosebud, and there is a branch campus in Winner.

Moses Armstrong drew this sketch of the Lakota Sun Dance in fur trade days. Warriors offered flesh "so that the people might live." Some dancers were fastened to the Sun Dance pole by thongs through the skin or muscle on their chests, and danced for four days, fasting before ripping free. After being banned for a time, the Sun Dance has been resumed in several locations; however, it is a sacred ceremony, not a tourist event. —South Dakota School of Mines and Technology

Museums at Mission and St. Francis contain local history and Indian artifacts. St. Francis Mission, begun in 1885, has preserved the photographs of Father Eugene Beuchel, Joe Zimmerman, and other unknown Jesuit priests who served at the mission. The fifteen thousand photographic images include photos taken by Father Beuchel on the Rosebud and Pine Ridge reservations from 1923 to 1954 and by Father Zimmerman between 1915 and 1919. Beuchel, called Wanbli Sapa (Black Eagle), also gathered and classified the area's fauna. His accumulation of thirty thousand word and phrase cards in Lakota culminated in his 1924 *Lakota Bible History*, and his 1939 work *Lakota Grammar* is still used to teach the language. His collection of beadwork, clothing, and other Lakota artifacts is on display.

Mustang Meadows Ranch

On a thirty-two-thousand acre ranch near St. Francis, Dayton O. Hyde has established a sanctuary for wild mustangs, the horses that are a part of many western legends. By 1970 only seventeen thousand of the horses, descended from horses that escaped from

Spanish herds, were left roaming on public land; many of the rest had been rounded up and slaughtered for dog food or simply shot by ranchers because they ate the forage needed for cattle grazed on federal land. In 1971 a massive letter-writing campaign inspired Congress to enact the Wild Free-Roaming Horses and Burros Act, giving the Bureau of Land Management responsibility for protecting the horses. By 1990 forty-two thousand horses were running free on public range and causing new problems of overgrazing. The BLM's Adopt-a-Horse program sold thousands of horses, but the elderly, crippled, or dangerous horses were penned in feedlots at a cost to taxpayers of $13 million a year.

In 1988, Hyde, an Oregon rancher and writer (*Yamsi, Sandy, The Last Free Man*), founded the nonprofit Institute for Range and the American Mustang (IRAM) and began seeking sanctuaries where the horses could roam freely. His first site was more than twelve thousand acres near Hot Springs; tourists pay $15 to see three hundred mares and geldings running free. IRAM also bought twenty-two thousand acres and leased another ten thousand acres from the Sioux. South Dakota and the BLM pay an average of eighty-five cents per day per horse to subsidize the project; Hyde says the project, besides benefiting horses, will demonstrate how grasslands can be profitably managed for grazing animals. Some environmentalists say the horses have become tame and are no longer an example of the wild breed, and ranchers point out that a herd of horses can damage grass as much or more than cattle.

WINNER

Winner took its name from the fight to establish a town along the railroad when the Chicago & Northwestern built west from Dallas, South Dakota, in 1909. Lamro, which has disappeared from most maps, was slated to be on the line, but the railroad survey missed it by two miles; when the tracks arrived in 1911, Winner was already a growing town. The Jackson brothers, who founded Winner, made a fortune in land deals and established the Mulehead Ranch on two hundred thousand acres, about one-fifth of Gregory County. The town grew quickly and was soon one of the busiest trading points along US 18, with forty-eight blocks of paved streets in 1938 and factories that made ice cream, powdered cleaner, and awnings. Farmers who couldn't raise enough cattle to survive raised poultry instead, shipping it to eastern markets by rail. One year in the 1930s, when tough economic conditions made folks scramble for a living in unusual ways, a businessman bought twenty thousand rabbit skins collected in the surrounding countryside in one season. No doubt the harvest helped preserve grass for domestic animals.

One of Winner's more unusual businessmen was Ben B. Butts. Butts came to Winner with his wife in 1919; she worked at a lumberyard, he at a livery barn. Ben Butts was ambitious; he bought honey, overalls, and gloves and stored his goods in a piano box in the corner of the livery barn. He approached livery customers to ask if they'd like to buy a pair of gloves: If the answer was yes, he'd whip a pair out of his pocket; if it was no, he'd show them the honey and overalls. He soon won the nickname "The Outlaw" from other merchants who thought he ought to be embarrassed to run a store from his pants pockets and a piano box.

Butts adopted the name, and when he'd scraped together enough cash to put his store in a building he called it the Outlaw Trading Post. As business grew, he added shaky sheds to the structure and set up branch stores in Wood, Dallas, Carter, and Clearfield. Later, he bought stock, even wooden matches, in carload lots. His business motto was "We Buck 'Em All" for his habit of competing with larger stores. He also offered unusual services—for example, delivering telegrams to outlying ranches with no mail delivery. When Butts retired, he moved to a ranch near Custer and called it Outlaw Ranch. The building he constructed of logs was destroyed by fire; the land is now operated as a youth camp.

TRIPP COUNTY

East of Winner, at the intersection of US 18 and US 183, is a highway marker noting the accomplishments of Lt. G. K. (Gouvernor Kemble) Warren, a topographical engineer who visited the area at the direction of Gen. W. S. Harney in 1855. If he was not the first white man in the area, he was the first to leave a record for modern historians. His job—and he did it remarkably well with only eight men—was to map the huge region from the Missouri River west to the Big Horn Mountains in Wyoming. His 1857 maps of Nebraska and Dakota closely resemble modern maps. The highway marker details his route, which—as he reported with considerable understatement when he arrived at Fort Kearney—was "unfeasible for the passage of a wheeled army."

Tripp County was originally part of the the Rosebud Reservation, which extended all the way to the Missouri River. It was opened for white settlement in 1908, with more than a hundred thousand registrants for four thousand claims. Many of the small towns in this relatively empty region represent the hopes of homesteaders who came to the area in the great land rush of the early 1900s, expecting to establish farms on land taken from the Indians. However, the land simply wasn't suitable for homesteading or farming, and much of it has reverted to grassland used as forage by ranchers, many of whom are white. Modern Indians could certainly have made good use of this area—had it not been taken from them at the beginning of this century—to graze cattle or buffalo.

One of the most unusual homesteaders here was Oscar Micheaux, one of the few blacks from South Dakota to win fame. Arthur Huseboe says in *An Illustrated History of the Arts in South Dakota* that this grandson of a slave earned enough money as a Pullman porter to homestead on the Rosebud Reservation. Micheaux, who believed that a black person could be anything, was "the only black farmer between Gregory and Omaha, an innovator in agriculture, a novelist, and a successful film writer-producer in New York and New Jersey." He wrote of his homesteading experiences on the reservation from 1909 until 1914 in seven novels that stressed the opportunities available to blacks who could free themselves from urban decadence by coming to the free lands of the West. He is the founding father of the black movie industry in United States; when the Black Filmmakers Hall of Fame honors an outstanding artist each winter, the event takes place at the Oscar Micheaux Awards Ceremony. Micheaux died in 1951.

A long train of pioneers in prairie schooners pauses in tall grass. Some travelers brought extra horses to ride; others walked beside the wagons to save the teams' energy. —South Dakota State Historical Society

US 85
North Dakota—Lawrence County
105 Miles

US 85 runs north-south from the North Dakota border to the Black Hills, exiting the state at its western border and heading into Wyoming. (The segment south of the Lawrence County line is discussed in the Black Hills section.) The highway has only two lanes but is straight and mostly level, with little traffic. Don't think of the country through which it passes as barren; imagine that you are an early homesteader, wary of attack by Indians or bandits. Consider how hard it would be for someone to sneak up on you in this terrain. You may encounter some slow farm machinery here, but it's more likely you'll be baffled by whizzing noises. Don't worry: They're only ranchers' pickups passing at approximately the speed of light.

Count bales of hay to learn how dry the year has been, and thus how difficult for local ranchers: Fewer than five hay bales in a minute of driving time indicates a very bad year indeed. The highway ditches are planted in crested wheat grass, which grows in clumps; the blue gray, soft-looking plants are one of several hundred varieties of sage. Trees anywhere in this country indicate either a watercourse, where they can receive just enough water from the seasonal rains and snows to stay alive, or a former homestead. Where the highway climbs a hill, you can clearly trace the progress of the Moreau River and a few tributary creeks in the distance by following lines of green grass and trees. A few stands from the homestead era survive, long rows planted to demonstrate the homesteaders' toughness and intention to stay.

If a large bird skyrockets from a gully, swoops across the road, and dives into the brush, look for the red patch above his tail that identifies a red-tailed hawk. White frosting along the watercourses

273

The Marquis Antoine de Mores found time to pose with his wife Medora, who is mounted sidesaddle. The Marquis named a town in North Dakota for his wife. He also built a church, an elegant chateau, and a packing plant there.
—State Historical Society of North Dakota

is the alkali that kept this from becoming a farming region and still flavors the water. Watch the eastern skyline for the ghostly blue hump of Bear Butte and the faint line of the Black Hills beyond it.

US 85 generally follows the route of the stage line operated by the Marquis de Mores from his North Dakota ranch at Medora to Deadwood, a distance of 215 miles. The stage ran from late 1884 to early 1885, and the Marquis spent a fortune on his business. He bought 150 horses and purchased four stagecoaches from the Gilmer and Salisbury Stage Company, which had run stages from Sydney, Nebraska, and Cheyenne, Wyoming, to the Black Hills. Lumber was hauled from the Black Hills to build fifteen way stations, each with a house, barn, and corrals. Five stations offered eating accommodations, and most were on open water.

A coach that left Medora in the morning arrived in Deadwood the following evening; the cost was ten cents a mile, a total of $21.50 per passenger. Food was probably bought at way stations. In early 1885 a contract was awarded for the shorter Pierre-to-Deadwood route, and the Marquis's transportation business folded.

HARDING COUNTY

Harding County contains some of the most starkly beautiful scenery in the state. This is the country of buttes, sandstone, and limestone eroded into weird and wonderful shapes. Not all the buttes are on the map, but you may see Eagle's Nest, Flat Top, Antelope, Brush Creek, Square Top, Tee Pee, Saddle, Castle Rock, Two Top, Mud, and Owl buttes—the names are self-explanatory. Anarchist Butte, on the eastern edge of the county, was named for the political leanings of a nearby homesteader. Bam's Butte, to the south, recalls pioneer rancher Bam Mendenhall, whose family still owns land in the region; Dunc's Butte was named for Duncan McLaughlin simply because he used to camp beside it on his trading trips to and from the Black Hills (his ranch was east of Reva Gap). Baby Butte is only

This coach carried passengers in 1884-85 for the Medora-Deadwood Stage Line, the Marquis de Mores's short-lived transportation venture. —South Dakota Department of Tourism

a foot or so high, and Lodge Pole Butte is covered with straight pine trees, valued by the Indians for tipi poles.

Lulu Butte was named for the daughter of David Willett, a pioneer rancher, whereas Peggy Butte was named for a mare who had lost a foreleg below the knee and ranged with her herd in the neighborhood. Profile Butte was named by a homesteader; perhaps it looked like someone he knew. Red Butte stands out because it contrasts with the white limestone cliffs behind it and was a landmark for freighters in the early days. Sheep Butte was named for the Rocky Mountain sheep that once lived on it. Slim Butte is a tall shaft of rock and clay, called Stump Butte by the Indians because it looks like a broken tree. Intermittent patches of land belong to the Custer National Forest, whose campsites are often at or near spots where Custer's expedition camped in 1874.

The west-central part of Harding County is known as the "jump-off country," a perfect ranching area affording both grass and shelter among the broken hills. The name comes from a large fault halfway between Buffalo and Camp Crook: The fault creates a wall facing east with a series of eroded badlands formations at its base. It might have been used as a buffalo jump by Indians.

The rocks of this territory include a sixty-million-year-old coal seam, laid down when the region was a swamp. A layer forty million years old attracts fossil hunters and geologists, who find bones of small rodents and mammals; deeper layers have yielded a sixty-five-million-year-old triceratops skull.

One of the most exciting fossil finds in the region was a *Tyrannosaurus rex* skeleton unearthed near Haystack Buttes, east of the highway and northeast of Belle Fourche. Only six *T. rex* skulls have been found with their skeletons in the world; this was the first in South Dakota. The creature, the largest meat-eater known, may have weighed eight tons, been around seventeen feet tall, and reached forty-five feet from tail to its sixty serrated teeth.

The bones were found by a rancher in the area—archaeologists prefer not to identify the site too clearly, for fear it will be visited by vandals. The rancher was fixing fence when his son began digging out what he thought was an old buffalo skull. But the find was much too large, and the rancher consulted Dr. Philip Bjork, director of the Museum of Geology at the South Dakota School of Mines in Rapid City. Between haying and caring for cattle, neighboring ranchers worked all summer with professionals to excavate parts of the dinosaur. Along the way they also recovered the remains of two turtles, two kinds of crocodile teeth, garpike scales, and three teeth from a meat-eating albertosaurus, all around sixty-five million years old.

Eventually, the excavated bones were covered with plaster, loaded onto a flatbed trailer, and hauled to Rapid City. More than 50 percent of the dinosaur has been recovered, and the skull is now on display at the Museum of Geology at the South Dakota School of Mines.

Ludlow

In a recent census, Ludlow's population was listed as ten. The cafe/bar is open and the concrete schoolhouse in use; the frame church is disintegrating, though residents decorate graves in the tiny cemetery beside it. The town was settled in the homestead boom of the early 1900s and named for Ludlow's Cave, one of many in the Cave Hills west of town. Custer visited the cave in 1874 and named it in honor of the expedition's engineer, Maj. William Ludlow. (The party's campsite of July 11, 1874, is about three miles southwest of town.) The cave is three hundred feet deep and about twenty feet high at the entrance. When it was excavated by the director of the University of South Dakota museum in the 1920s, hundreds of artifacts were found, demonstrating that the cave was known to Indians and early travelers in the region. His finds are now displayed in the W. H. Over State Museum in Vermillion.

Buffalo

The small community of Buffalo is the county seat of South Dakota's most sparsely populated county. Harding County has less than 2,000 people spread over 2,682 square miles, giving everyone plenty of room, which most of them may prefer. The county has been dropping in population almost since it was founded: In 1925 the population was 3,508; in 1945 it was 2,546. Residents count three head of cattle and twenty-eight sheep for every person in the county.

One of Buffalo's most famous residents was Tipperary, a bucking horse who became famous for bucking at the Tri-State Roundup in Belle Fourche between 1915 and 1928. Mention of his name can still bring a faraway look to the eyes of old ranchers, who mutter, "*That was a horse*," and recall his long career and peculiar twisting bucking style. Late-night arguments rage over whether the horse was ever properly ridden. World champion rider and movie star Yakima Canutt, Belle Fourche cowboy Harold Ekberg, and possibly one other cowboy stayed on the horse for ten seconds, but some folks insist at least two of them should have been disqualified for losing a stirrup or allowing too much air to develop between the seat of their pants and the saddle. Tipperary died on his home range during a blizzard

Some pioneers found tar-paper shacks quicker to construct and easier to keep clean, but others believed sod houses offered better protection against Dakota winters. A homesteader mounted a grindstone so it could even be turned by a child. —State Historical Society of North Dakota

in 1932; his bones were positively identified by several local men and entombed under a tasteful plaque: "World's Greatest Bucking Horse, Tipperary, 1910-1932." The bones were interred in an eight-square-foot concrete block because townspeople fear unscrupulous folks from some other town might try to steal them.

Another famous four-legged resident of the jump-off country was a buffalo wolf—not a timber wolf—named Old Three Toes. He was named after losing a front toe to a trap. Charlie Wilson met the wolf limping down the trail toward him one morning in 1912, holding up a bloody paw. When Wilson realized it was not a dog, he galloped back to the ranch for a rifle, but the wolf escaped. Later, his tracks were often seen in ranch yards, even under windows, leading to speculation he had once been someone's pet.

If so, his pet days were over when he hit Harding County. Old-timers say that Three Toes, unlike most wolves, killed for the pure fun of it. One of his first mass killings—thirty-four sheep in one night—occurred at the Matt Henri ranch near the Cave Hills north of Buffalo. Three Toes dropped by the Lahti Ranch about twice a

278

year, killing dozens of lambs and ewes in a night. When the rancher bought registered rams to keep the wolf away, Three Toes slaughtered every one of them in a month. The wolf also killed several horses and colts on the Gus Haivala Ranch. Four men chased him for two days, borrowing fresh horses at each ranch they passed, before the wolf escaped into terrain so rough they couldn't follow. He seemed to delight in ducking through fences to slow his pursuers, who had to remove then replace the wire.

The wolf began to grow into a legend in his own time. Stories told of him hiding inside the carcass of a dead horse, scattering sheep to obliterate his trail, and treading on frozen creeks to leave no tracks. He was too smart to poison or trap and too fast to shoot. Bill Foreman tried to run him down with a Model T one day; each time Bill got close, the wolf sidestepped and lay down to rest until he reached the edge of the jump-off and dived out of sight. Wolves mate for life, so Three Toes became a loner when hunters found his den and killed the female and her pups.

By 1922 Three Toes was credited with killing an average of $1,000 worth of livestock a month; one July the total reached $6,000. Ranchers estimate the total value of his kills at between $50,000 and $100,000—that's a lot of beef, mutton, and horse meat. In 1922 the Harding County Stockgrowers Association announced a bounty of $500. A federal trapper spent eight months after Three Toes, using horse relays to chase him two hundred miles in three days. When the exhausted wolf took to the ice of the Grand River, the trapper gave up and went home.

In 1925, after Three Toes killed thirty-six sheep as an appetizer, ranchers called for federal help again. Clyde F. Briggs, a master wolfer from the Ozarks, trapped the old predator on a high rocky hill northwest of Buffalo near the Little Missouri River. Briggs and Gus Haivala took the wolf alive, muzzled him, tied his legs securely, and loaded him into a car. By the time they reached Haivala's ranch, though, Old Three Toes had died. He weighed only seventy-four pounds, not large for a wolf. He was at least twenty-three years old. Briggs got a watch from the appreciative ranchers.

And Still More Buttes

South of Buffalo, look for more buttes on the horizons. Finger Butte was named for the shape of its needles—though from a distance they look more like thumbs. The twin Crow Buttes just south of Redig mark an old battleground of the Sioux and Crow; because the slopes aren't covered with grass, they more resemble the Bad-

A cowboy wearing flashy sheepskin chaps poses with his horse in front of a log cabin in the Black Hills. —South Dakota Department of Tourism

lands heights than other buttes of this area. Haystack Butte is distinguishable from Castle Rock Butte by its flattened top. At Two Top Butte, a scenic overlook provides a broad view of the rolling, heaving countryside and a chance to reflect on being at the geographical center of the nation.

One of Dakota's worst fires occurred in this area in 1886, jumping the Moreau River and burning to the Cheyenne, blackening more than a million acres in five counties. Large cattle companies kept fire drags—twelve-foot-square sheets of asbestos woven with steel rings and wire—at scattered cow camps all over the range. Six cowboys tied ropes to rings in one end, snubbed the other to their saddle horns, and spurred their horses. As the asbestos wore out, cowboys shot and split steers and tied the carcasses on the drags for weight and moisture. When big fires struck a ranching area, entire herds of steers were driven to the fire line for use as fire equipment. Another blaze, the Big Dakota Fire of 1905, cost the Matador a dozen steers.

Redig

Redig was named for two brothers, pioneer cattlemen, and is in the news more often than its size would indicate: It often registers the coldest temperatures in the state and sometimes the hottest. Local ranchers cope with the extreme climate with practicality and humor. They could write a book about local folks who have frozen to death. One favorite story has been attributed to several people, including Abe Jones, who built railroads, freighted, worked wood, ranched, mined, and traded horses all over the northwestern part of the state. One hard winter his brother died. A blizzard made an immediate trip to the undertaker impossible. Abe—with laudable foresight—installed his brother in a chair on the porch, where the corpse froze in a seated position. When the roads cleared, Abe placed the icy remains in the back seat of his car and drove to Sturgis. The car needed work, so he left it at a service station and attended to other errands. Abe neglected to mention his brother's condition to the attendant, however, and when he returned the man was stuttering with fear. Some bum, he thought, had crawled into the car and frozen to death. "That's no bum. That's my brother," said Abe, and headed for the funeral parlor.

A similar tale, related by a source who prefers to remain anonymous, concerns a young courting couple of an earlier day. Caught in the buggy miles from a ranch, they tried for several hours to keep warm. At last the young man left his sweetheart and walked to her father's ranch. But by the time he got there the storm had worsened; the two men dared not try to find the buggy in the dark. By morning, when they struggled out over the drifts, the girl was dead. They took her to the undertaker, who had devised a regular procedure for thawing frozen corpses: He built a huge fire in the stove, propped the dead woman up next to it, and took the men into an adjacent room, where he poured whiskey into them until they could help him straighten the body.

Minnesela

About three miles above the junction of the Redwater River with the Belle Fourche was the first county seat, Minnesela, its name allegedly taken from the Lakota word for "Red Water." A. A. Chouteau, of the fur-trading family of St. Louis, was an early settler and a member of the territorial legislature. By 1882 a flume a mile and a half long and eleven feet wide brought water from the river to a rancher-owned flour mill with a capacity of sixty barrels a day. An irrigation ditch near town made crops flourish, especially wheat. The town had a post office, hotel, general store, hardware store, drugstore, blacksmith shop, schoolhouse, church, several saloons, and a dozen families before Belle Fourche was settled.

When the railroad selected a town site at the forks of the Belle Fourche River and scheduled a day to sell lots at the chosen site,

Minnesela citizens published a map showing their town as the railroad center of the region and listing forty or fifty reasons why Minnesela was destined to be a metropolis. Eager citizens met the train bearing prospective lot buyers and distributed the map, and not a single lot on the Belle Fourche site sold—that day. But when the railroad arrived in Belle Fourche, the buildings of Minnesela were gradually moved there. One man refused to go. He moved into the old hotel and cut it to a third of its former size, converting it into a farmhouse with a lot of spare bedrooms. He made a living farming and remained there until his death in 1936.

SD 20
Wyoming—Dewey County
133 Miles

SD 20 is a good secondary highway but one heavily used by the local populace—watch out for hay-moving equipment, cattle trucks, and occasional herds of cattle that have slipped out an open gate or are being thriftily pastured in the wide highway ditches. This part of the highway runs east-west between the Wyoming state line and the western border of the Cheyenne River Indian Reservation.

HARDING COUNTY

Camp Crook, founded in 1884-85, was named for Gen. George Crook, who campaigned against the Sioux here during the mid-1870s. South of town on a gravel road is Sky Ranch, a juvenile detention and education center established by a Catholic priest whose parish was so large he eventually traveled it by airplane. The priest, Father Don Murray, established the ranch as a refuge for boys in trouble with the law or in their home life. As part of their rehabilitation, he taught them to fly. Murray was killed in an airplane crash with two of his boys, but the ranch, supported by the liquor industry, continues its work.

Reva and Reva Gap were both named for Reva Bonniwell Johns, daughter of John Bonniwell, whose large ranch, the Meat Hook, lay west of the gap in Bonniwell Basin. The gap was the site of the area's

first post office in 1895 and provided a wagon passage through rough terrain. Large, crenellated buttes nearby are called the Castles.

East of Reva Gap and west of the town is the site of an 1876 battle between U.S. soldiers and the Sioux. General Crook's troops were spoiling for revenge after Custer's defeat at the Battle of the Little Bighorn. A large band of Sioux had gone north into Canada with Hunk-papa leaders Gall and Sitting Bull, but Crazy Horse, the Oglala war chief whose strategy figured prominently in Custer's destruction, headed east toward the Dakota plains, burning the grass as he went.

Crook's column was short of provisions, his horses were starving, and movement became nearly impossible in the wet gumbo soil. Finally the troopers hit upon the obvious solution and started eating the horses. From the surrounding hills, the Indians watched and rapidly spread scornful news of the "Horsemeat March."

Finally Crook detached Capt. Anson Mills with 150 men on the best horses to go to Deadwood for supplies. When Mills discovered a Brulé Sioux village en route, however, revenge took precedence over chow. He attacked, surprising the Sioux after an all-night rain. Apparently no scouts were out, and the attack caught the Indians inside tipis tightly closed against the rain. They had no time for the usual exit; warriors slashed tipis open and leapt into the dark to fight. American Horse, a famous chief, took refuge in a ravine with his family and six warriors; by noon four of the men were dead and American Horse fatally wounded. Crook's command joined Mills. Crazy Horse was in the area but unable to battle the larger force. The soldiers captured a large supply of dried meat but—incredibly— destroyed it along with the village. Crook ordered the three dead Americans buried and marched the column over the graves in an attempt to conceal them. The troops did capture some horses, riding some and eating others on their way to Deadwood. There settlers held a welcoming party and fed the men enough to make up for their starvation march; presumably no one was impolite enough to ask who was responsible for destroying enough dried meat to have fed all the settlers in the Black Hills for months. One of the whites killed was scout William White, a friend and follower of Buffalo Bill, to whom Gen. William Sherman had given the nickname "Buffalo Chips"—where you saw one, he said, you saw the other.

The Brulé camp attacked by Mills had been on the eastern slope of the Slim Buttes, which lie along the eastern border of Harding County. The landmarks were named in translation from the Sioux— *Paha-zibzi-pila*—because they are thirty miles long and only one to three miles wide. The buttes are mentioned in the journals of Wilson Price Hunt's 1811 Pacific Fur Company party, and Gen. William Ashley's party also noted them in passing. Among the beauties of the region is a sharp, detached rock at the north end of the buttes, rising to a peak known as the Saddle Horn. Cliffs two hundred feet high face each other across a deep draw. On the west edge of the buttes is Government Knob, named for the survey marker on its summit and the highest point in the county.

The East and West Short Pines are visible west of Slim Buttes, and beyond them rises the long blue line of the Long Pine Hills in Montana. Near Reva Gap, at the crest of the Slim Buttes, is Battleship Rock, along with a perpendicular column two or three hundred feet high known as Flag Rock. Several campsites exist in the area, which is also rich with petrified wood, huge turtle tracks, and the fossils of the three-toed horse, the type of tusked pig, and the saber-toothed tiger.

Calamity Jane's working clothes included a broad-brimmed hat and a jacket that looks like leather—note the fringe over her left hand. She accompanied the Jenney-Newton party to the Black Hills in 1875 and later worked as a scout for General Crook. Her rifle sports a pistol grip.
—Centennial Archives, Deadwood

In this region was the ranch of A. H. Dean, who hired a college graduate named Archer B. Gilfillan to herd his sheep for ten years. The owner got more than he bargained for; in his spare time, Gilfillan wrote *Sheep*, one of the funniest and most accurate renditions of life in the Dakotas. Gilfillan's humorous columns were published in *The Saturday Evening Post* and *Atlantic Monthly*, as well as in local newspapers and several books. Residents claim that within a radius of a few miles are more sheep than anywhere else in the United States, and sheep wagons are still sent out with herds.

The Last Winter Buffalo Hunt

Thomas L. Riggs was known to the Sioux as Eyanpaha Wakan—Sacred Herald—because of his remarkable history as a missionary to the Dakota Sioux. But Riggs wasn't just a delicate, collar-wearing cleric; in *South Dakota History* he wrote of accompanying Clarence Ward, known to the Lakota as Roan Bear, to Slim Buttes in 1880 on the last winter buffalo hunt the Lakota ever held. About a hundred people, both men and women, composed the party, with thirty-three horses and five hundred dogs. Touch-the-Cloud, a friend of Crazy Horse, was along. Someone loaned Riggs an experienced buffalo-hunting horse that "knew all that a horse could know about running buffalo, besides being very fast. Every man in camp knew him, for he was the horse that Can-pta-ye (Wood Pile) had on the Little Big Horn against Custer in '76."

The hunters came upon the buffalo suddenly, and the horses were at a gallop before the riders realized that the snow covered a wide sheet of ice. Nearly twenty horses fell, and Riggs tried to stop his but could not do so. He said the horse was across the spot "before I had time to think," and then the leaders began shooting. When the hunt was over, they packed back to camp the meat from fifty carcasses. "One of these," wrote Riggs, "was killed by Little Bear in the way of his fathers. The arrow was driven entirely through the body, entering the right flank and its steel point sticking out low down on the opposite side." Though driving an arrow entirely through a buffalo on the strength of one arm might seem a superhuman feat today, it was reported by many whites who observed buffalo hunts before the Indians got rifles.

BISON

Bison was clearly named for the longtime dweller of the Plains commonly known as buffalo; technically, the North American *Bison bison* is a not a buffalo, but the common name applied by the early explorers has stuck. One of the first settlers in the vicinity, George Carr, is said to have found a large pile of bison skulls and bones nearby before the town was laid out in 1907. By 1936, as the seat of Perkins County, Bison qualified as a typical prairie town, with false-front wooden buildings arranged along a single main street and a population of no more than a few hundred people.

Bison roamed most of the state before white settlement, but especially liked the freedom of the western grasslands. A few private herds exist, but the traveler's best chance to see the animals is in one of the parks in the Black Hills. Exercise caution, particularly with lone bulls like this one. Buffalo are dangerous because of their speed and ferocity, and an animal that seems peaceful can charge without warning.
—South Dakota
Department of Tourism

SD 73
White Butte—Nebraska
251 Miles

SD 73 is an old but well-kept highway reaching from the northern to the southern border of the state. It joins I-90 for a few miles near Kadoka, then resumes its north-south orientation, winding through the breaks along the White River and crossing the Pine Ridge Indian Reservation. At Tuthill, south of the Pine Ridge Reservation, the highway turns to gravel. Though isolated, this route lies in some of the most beautiful, untouched country in South Dakota. Once you leave the protection of the few towns, particularly once you get south of I-90, you are on your own; you may find no gas stations. Driving this road could provide a real taste of the silence early settlers experienced in coming to this new land.

LEMMON

Lemmon, just south of the North Dakota border, bears the name of G. E. "Ed" Lemmon, one of the best-known early cowboys and ranchers in the state and manager of the L7 Ranch. When the town site was settled during the homestead boom of 1907, he provided the land.

Lemmon was raised southeast of Hastings, Nebraska, on the Liberty Farm Station of the Ben Holliday stage line and later lived in Cheyenne, Wyoming, where his father worked on a Union Pacific construction crew. He began riding the range at fifteen and helped work several Texas trail herds on the northern frontier. Lemmon and other cowboys picked up Texas herds at railheads such as Dodge City, Abilene, and Ogalala and drove them north to grass or Indian agencies. From 1877 until 1908 Lemmon worked for the Sheidley Cattle Company, the Flying V. He returned to the Black Hills in 1880, put a Flying V herd on the Cheyenne River at the mouth of French Creek, and soon bought into the West River cattle business. Eventually he became part-owner of several prominent range companies, ran cattle on more than 865,000 acres of land leased from the Indians on the Standing Rock Reservation, helped lay out a route for rails across northern South Dakota, and assisted in the formation of several stock grower organizations. He became influential in the state's cattle industry and was involved in most of the historical events of the northern range.

An energetic writer, Lemmon wrote an account of his experiences in *Boss Cowman*, which manages to be entertaining in spite of its poor organization and choppy style; if he'd had a decent editor, it might have been a best-seller. He is at his best when telling about the West as he experienced it—how to stop a stampede—and rebutting images of the West distorted by movies.

The small town of Lemmon claims to have the largest petrified wood park and museum in the world. The claim is probably correct; if not the largest such park, it's certainly one of the most unique. In the distant past the town site was covered by a freshwater lake. O. S. Quammen, an early settler and amateur geologist, asked for help from government geologists to study the area and found petrified bones of prehistoric animals, fish, plants, and insects. He began building the park in 1930 to display and study his finds, as well as to provide work for jobless men during the Depression.

One structure, described as "fairylike" by normally clearheaded journalists, has walls and a floor made from 320-foot-tall petrified tree trunks. Visitors can see teeth marks, petrified snakes, and marine creatures on the stone logs, which weigh more than ten

Bernard Murphy, at right, poses in November 1907 in front of a tiny sod house he built for his mother-in-law, Mrs. Sarah E. Gambrel. At left is Murphy's sister-in-law, Miss Laura Gambrel. Between the two is a triangular crate, a type used by homesteaders to protect free-range chickens or hogs from coyotes. —South Dakota Agricultural Heritage Museum

thousand pounds and are eight to ten feet in diameter. The roof boasts five spires of fossilized wood in various shades. The circular museum building is also built of petrified logs, with slabs identified as petrified grass making up the floor. More than a hundred pyramids of petrified wood and other geological oddities dot the park, mingled with stacks of "cannonballs," naturally round stones varying from half an inch to several feet in diameter. A grotto contains petrified bones of large animals. Admission is free, just as the builder insisted during his lifetime.

PHILIP

Philip lies at SD 73's intersection with US 14 at the center of a large farming and ranching area. The town, founded in 1907, was named for its most prominent citizen, James "Scotty" Philip, whose life on the Dakota plains resembles that of many others who came for one reason and stayed for another. Born in 1858 in Morayshire, Scotland, he first came to the Dakotas in 1875 seeking gold. Like many early prospectors, the military escorted him out of the Black

Hills to Fort Robinson, Nebraska, and confiscated his supplies. After several more failed attempts at prospecting, Philip joined Edgar Beecher Bronson's Three Crows ranch in 1878, working part-time as a scout for the army. The following year he married Sarah Larabee, whose mother was an Indian. The marriage gave Philip the right to occupy a quarter section on her reservation, and he gained access to thousands of acres of reservation land simply by letting his cattle graze on it. Bob Lee says in *Last Grass Frontier* that, like other cattlemen who married Indian wives (including John Utterbeck, the LaPlants, and Fred Dupris), Philip "gained grazing privileges as a dowry. But that approach had only limited appeal. There weren't enough Sioux women to go around for all the white stockmen who wanted on the reservation, and, besides, most of them needed grass more than a mate."

Philip built his ranch along the Bad River near the mouth of Grindstone (Butte) Creek east of the present-day town of Philip. Because he was married to a tribal member, he did not have to leave the reservation when the Office of Indian Affairs said reservation lands couldn't be leased or sold to non-Indians, and he had a market for beef at the Indian agencies. By 1893 Philip's stock ran from his home on Bad River north to Fort Pierre and to the Cheyenne River breaks northwest of present-day Hayes. Eventually he and his wife controlled more than ten thousand acres of rangeland. He helped create several organizations of stock raisers, including the South Dakota Stockgrowers Association, and became one of the state's most prominent ranchers, honored in the National Cowboy Hall of Fame. He also served in the state senate from Stanley County in 1898.

Although Philip did much in his lifetime, he received his greatest fame for something he didn't actually do: save the buffalo of the grasslands from extinction. David Miller says in *South Dakota Leaders* that the honor should go to Frederick Dupris. With several of his sons, Dupris and Basil Claymore spent several months in the early 1880s hunting buffalo along the Cheyenne River; they found a small herd, captured five buffalo calves, carried them back to the Dupris ranch in wagons, and kept them in a specially fenced pasture. By 1901, when Philip bought it, the herd had grown to about nine head. Under Philip's management, it grew to nine hundred head, the largest privately owned herd of its time. Philip built a breeding band that contributed to herds all over the world and became known as "the Buffalo King." He knew how to use publicity, and the herd garnered excellent attention for his enterprises, as well as for the state.

An example of Philip's manipulation of publicity, as well as a clear demonstration of the natural power of the buffalo, occurred in 1907 when he staged a fight between a bison bull and a Mexican fighting bull. After much preparation and hoopla, Philip arrived in Juarez, Mexico, with his battling bison, Pierre, who promptly lay down on the warm sand. The arena gate opened, and in trotted the finest, fiercest, meanest fighting bull in Mexico, wicked horns gleaming. He snorted, saw the buffalo, and bellowed. Pierre, perhaps slightly warm in his winter overcoat, slowly stood up. The Mexican bull began to paw, throwing dirt over his shoulders. Pierre stared and pawed a bit. Then the Mexican bull charged. Pierre lowered his massive, shaggy head; the bull ran straight into it and dropped to his knees. He shook his head and stood up, then strolled around Pierre. When he got to the stern end he charged, hooking a wicked horn at Pierre's flank. With incredible speed, the bison whirled, and again the bull slammed into his skull and dropped to his knees. Each time the Mexican bull charged, the bison's massive head knocked him flat. The Mexican crowd booed and howled until a second bull was brought in. The same scene was repeated, several times. The Mexicans consulted and brought in another bull, and finally a fourth. Pierre never seemed to get excited or annoyed; he just lowered his head at the correct moment and knocked every one of the bulls down. Finally, when all four bulls were let into the ring at once, Pierre began to get grouchy; he finally charged, and the bulls tried to scramble up the walls of the arena.

A few days later the Mexicans scheduled a contest between a professional bullfighter and a younger bison, Pierre, Jr. The bullfighter performed admirably, making lovely passes at the buffalo's nose with his cape, until the buffalo began to paw. But before the question of whether a matador could kill a bison was settled, the fight was stopped.

The city that bears Philip's name was founded with the extension of the railroad to the Black Hills in 1907. In 1914 its citizens campaigned against four other towns—Nowlin, Powell, Midland, and Lucerne—to become the seat of the newly created Haakon County. Philip won easily: Since then, Lucerne and Powell have completely disappeared, and Nowlin barely exists.

Philip itself might have dwindled after the homesteading period, but it has been revitalized by Scotchman Industries. The company is one of the largest manufacturers of the ironworker, a device that uses hydraulic pressure to cut, shape, and punch holes in steel. Today the city's population stands at about twelve hundred.

The original caption on this 1889 photo reads: "The Indian Girls' Home, Cheyenne River Reservation. A group of Indian Girls and Indian police at Big Foot's village on the reservation." The girls' clothing is a mixture of Indian and white styles, including cloth dresses and bone hair pipe necklaces. Most of the men wear broad-brimmed hats. —South Dakota State Historical Society

SD 34

Cheyenne River Indian Reservation—
Stanley County

57 Miles

SD 34 runs east-west between the western border of the Cheyenne River Indian Reservation through ranching country to the western border of Stanley County. It's a good highway but, like many of these secondary roads, mostly traveled by locals. Watch for wildlife native to the grasslands, and be wary of slow-moving farm machinery and loaded cattle trucks.

HAAKON AND STANLEY COUNTIES

Grace Fairchild's experiences as a homesteader, recorded in *Frontier Woman*, typify those of many in the West, though she may have been more independent than some women. She lived on a claim ninety miles west of Pierre and thirty miles south of a now-defunct town called Pedro halfway down the stage road between the Missouri River and Rapid City. When she first traveled to the homestead with her husband, the wagon trip took eight days. She later recalled that a road ranch and post office, where stage drivers changed horses, stood along the trail about every thirty miles—her house *was* one. She and her husband made extra money by boarding extra horses for the stage. When it reached their place, Grace and her husband fed the drivers and passengers and bedded them down for the night. At times she cooked for twenty-three people and found each a place to sleep, if only on the floor, in a two-room log cabin. Rather than complaining about such difficult conditions and such hard work, Grace looked on the bright side, remarking that the drivers and passengers provided her with contact with the outside world as well as extra cash. She charged twenty-five cents for meals and the same for a bed, "whether it was on the floor or on a cot."

When the Chicago & Northwestern Railroad reached Philip in 1907, Fairchild felt that her isolation was nearly at an end; no longer would she have to face a long wagon trip to Pedro to buy necessities. Such trips were rare, because they took so much time; after she moved to her homestead, it was three and a half years before she went back to Fort Pierre with her husband. "The rails," she remarked "now connected me with everything I knew before I went West—my sisters, my parents, and store goods—and some of the lonesomeness began to go away."

But her hardships weren't over. The blizzard of 1905 struck in May just after her husband, Shy, went into debt to buy Texas longhorns. These cattle were tough, but they had never lived through a South Dakota snowstorm. Water holes were full from a rain which preceded the storm, and for two nights and a day the snow piled up, turning the water to freezing slush. "The cattle began to drift on the second day," wrote Mrs. Fairchild, "and one by one they froze to death or drowned in the waterholes." The Fairchilds found some of their cattle forty miles southeast of their home; herds owned by larger ranchers on the Cheyenne River drifted to the Fairchild claim, dying by the hundreds. Of the 168 head they owned, the family lost 91. Many other ranchers had purchased the Texas cattle, mortgaging the livestock for security. Now, with the cattle dead, many ranchers simply turned whatever was left of their holdings over to the bank and filed for bankruptcy.

Mrs. Fairchild chose to stick it out. It took her fourteen years to pay off the debt, with interest at 10 or 12 percent. "Everything we made from livestock was turned over to the bank," she recalled. During those difficult years she raised a garden and chickens to keep

Many homesteaders built a sod structure this size as their original home, then turned it over to the chickens after building a better house for themselves. —South Dakota Agricultural Heritage Museum

her family fed, sewed their clothes, and even made shoes. She did complain mildly: "Between Shy's lack of sense and the snowstorm of 1905, we nearly lost our goddamn claim."

Mrs Fairchild eventually threw her husband out of the house and ran the homestead herself with her nine children, but when her husband became ill, she nursed him until his death. She also recorded many of the region's sayings, folk wisdom, and predictions. For example, a difficult winter is supposed to ensue if woolly caterpillars have narrow instead of broad brown bands, if corn husks are hard to pull apart in the fall, and if skunks come early to make their lodging under the barn.

This area also attracted homesteader Elizabeth Corey, whose Iowa relatives kept her lively letters detailing her adventures in Dakota between 1909 and 1919. Her brother edited some of them for the South Dakota Historical Society; in 1990 the University of Iowa Press published them as a book titled *Bachelor Bess*.

Corey was twenty-one when she left Iowa in 1909 to stake out a claim in Dakota, intending to support herself by teaching school. As soon as she left home, she began writing letters filled with cheerful determination to her family in Iowa; the letters continued as she settled near Lindsay, a small Stanley County town north of Hayes. Homesteading offered Bess, and many other single women, a chance at independence from a family that might limit her freedom, a chance to be self-supporting, to find adventure, to make a profit.

Her letters provide a detailed account of homesteading, which appears to have been less isolating than modern readers expect. Corey speaks of a busy community life, though being neighborly could be inconvenient. In one note, she remarked that she'd cooked a piece of pork with beans three times when a "Dutch neighbor borrowed it to cook with beans when he had company. Then the old dunce left it on the plate. When the dog washed the plate he ate it. I wanted Irish stew tonight and had to get out a fresh piece." Food was always an interesting topic in homesteaders' letters home, and Corey later entertained her family with an account of how she started bread in a chilly homestead shack where a pail of water standing by the stove might freeze overnight. Once she'd started the yeast, she put it in a tight can, wrapped it well, and took it to bed with her. She told her family her cellar was well stocked with winter provisions, including four pie pumpkins, a grain sack full of vegetables, a pail of beets, four citrons, and a dime's worth of onions.

Corey's adventures included a struggle with sticky Plains gumbo, which could almost kill a team of horses struggling through it. Once when she was obliged to walk home through it, her feet were "like tubs" when she reached her shack. Rattlesnakes kept her hopping: Her claim was so infested with the venomous snakes that she might kill half a dozen in a single walk, and she tells hair-raising tales of children bitten by them. Bess was better prepared than many homesteaders; she was a big woman, and her country experiences had made her self-reliant, strong, and courageous. She could already ride a horse and was experienced in nursing the sick, burying the dead, handling animals, and most of the tasks solitary folks had to learn.

Corey eventually moved to Midland, a town created by and for the railroad, and remained in the state as a teacher most of her life. She died in 1954 in Pierre.

One of the clever inventions of settlers in this neighborhood was the barbed-wire telephone line. In 1908 Preacher Davis, who lived near Hayes, rigged a buzzer on a barbed-wire fence so his wife, alone on the claim, could signal the nearest neighbor. Later he proposed to connect telephones to the barbed-wire line so his wife could talk to the neighbors. Twelve neighbors agreed to try it, paying $13 each for the experiment, and Preacher Davis furnished the phones and installed them. Soon other neighbors joined, and the line eventually stretched for a hundred miles. Each group of eight settlers was responsible for repairing and maintaining twelve miles of the makeshift line. There were no hired telephone operators, of course, or repairmen, but if the bell didn't ring, neighbors went looking for the trouble, which might be a tumbleweed caught in the fence or a cow scratching her back on the telephone system.

The Narcelle Ranch

Paul Narcelle was a fur trader who saw an opportunity to become a rancher and worked with the Indians of his chosen region to develop his business and his family. Narcelle, a trader for the American Fur Company, discovered a good site for a ranch on the south side of the Missouri River near the Great Bend, where Fort Defiance once stood. When Pierre Chouteau sold Fort Pierre to the U.S. Army in 1855, Narcelle began ranching with a herd of four hundred cows and maintained a trading post at Fort Sully. He married Pelagie Sarpe (or Scarpy), the daughter of a trader, and developed his ranch in partnership with his sons, Narcisse and Edward. Records show that in 1887, the year of the Big Roundup on the free range, the Narcelle family had more than 15,000 cattle, 2,500 saddle horses, and 23 wagons, employing 325 men.

In 1879 Narcisse married Cecelia Benoiste, one of the first schoolteachers in the Cherry Creek area, and established his headquarters on the south side of the Cheyenne River; the original log building is part of the present home of Hans T. Hanson. He had three children while serving as Boss Farmer at Cherry Creek Station; with a second wife, Katherine Blackbird, he had three more. In 1883 Narcisse moved to the Circle Dot Ranch north of the river and west of a bridge over Narcelle Creek, about halfway between the present towns of Philip and Faith. By the early 1900s he had moved again, to Cherry Creek, about twenty miles south of Faith near the community of Red Scaffold. He introduced irrigation to increase the yield of hay fields and built his ranch for protection and self-sufficiency.

Like many ranchers of the era, Narcelle lost much of his rangeland when the Cheyenne Reservation was opened for homesteading and another portion was leased for two cents an acre by the Bureau of Indian Affairs to larger ranches, the Matador and the Diamond A. Narcelle was eventually forced into bankruptcy. He died in 1909 when he and his team of horses were drowned in a flooding creek on the way back from a shopping trip to Philip.

US 14 is a good two-lane blacktop, often used by South Dakotans as a shortcut to Pierre. Watch out for occasional slow-moving farm machinery and highballing eighteen-wheelers on these rolling hills and curves. In fall, the teardrop-shaped ornaments on the fence-post tops are hawks waiting for road kills or for rodents frightened foolish by passing cars. Lucky and observant drivers may see a golden eagle, another scavenger.

QUINN AND PEDRO

Quinn was named for Michael Quinn, a pioneer bullwhacker who freighted between Fort Pierre and the Black Hills and later ranched nearby; a group of Jewish farmers also settled here. Ruts of the old Deadwood Trail and the remnants of an old telephone line may still be visible ten miles north of town. The country is considerably emptier in modern times than it was a hundred years ago; in 1936 Quinn's population was 144, but it is doubtful half that many live there today.

A century ago one of this region's busiest trading centers was Pedro, north of Quinn on the banks of the Cheyenne River. This trading post was begun by Elmer Hawks and his wife Jennie in the early 1890s. The store supplied most of the needs for early settlers in the remote region, selling everything from sewing needles to threshing machines. Indians later joined white settlers in building homes of native cottonwood and cedar in the area, and Pedro soon had a livery stable, Odd Fellows hall, hotel, barber shop, blacksmith, post office, log schoolhouse, and a community icehouse. The store burned in 1917, and since then the town has settled into prairie sod.

Even earlier, there were several fur outposts northwest of Pedro at the forks of the Cheyenne, an area now accessible only by dirt roads. Francis (or François) Chardon arrived in Fort Pierre on April 9, 1830, from the forks with over four thousand buffalo robes and a quantity of other furs and merchandise; he'd lost a canoe with four hundred robes descending the river. Chadron, Nebraska, is named for him, despite the error in spelling. Earlier posts probably occupied the site by 1827.

Even in pioneering times, water was scarce here; the Stokes Ditch was built by the Chamberlain Company for irrigation. Settlers joined forces to dam the Belle Fourche River with large bundles of willows and small trees tied to boulders with wire cables. The headgate was built of heavy cedar logs. Workers dug a canal twenty feet deep, and the homemade irrigation project worked beautifully during the summer of 1894. Early the next year, when the Belle Fourche River flooded, the high water changed the course of the river, buried the willow dam with silt and debris, and left the log headgate isolated on the south side of the river. Settlers recalled later that flooding Bull, Pine, and Teepee creeks demolished everything in their way.

COTTONWOOD AND MIDLAND

Founded in 1906, Cottonwood was named for a nearby creek; but the state had fifteen other streams also named Cottonwood, because those trees commonly appear along water sources, so some confusion may have ensued. The town no longer appears on some maps, and its school is gone, but two stores continue to operate by a retired Air Force couple who are militant about defending the settlement from charges that it is dead. When a local newspaper reported that only one streetlight burned at night, they counted and hotly noted "about twenty." An antique store and bar (with an accompanying purple two-hole outhouse) draws enough customers to be called the "Cottonwood Mall" by local teenagers. The town's original jail, a wooden structure with rusted window bars, stands in front of the antique store, and the town gets positively boisterous when the train goes through. Still, its residents insist, with the spirit that kept the pioneers going, that it is a community, a good place to raise their children.

Midland sits midway between the White and Cheyenne rivers and between the Missouri and the South Fork. The town's first post office was opened in 1890, shortly after the Great Sioux Reservation was opened to settlement. The name was significant because the tiny town was the center of a cattle empire, free of pesky settlers. Before the cattlemen came, only the Lakota roamed the plains in this region. Early cattlemen—Scotty Philip, Dan Powell, and Mike Dunn—married Indian wives and were well established by the time the region was officially opened to settlers. During roundups, cowboys from all the ranches gathered cattle and pushed them to Big Prairie Dog Creek, about ten miles north of town. There representatives of each ranch cut out cattle with the ranch brand, sorted some off for sale, and headed home.

Midland remained a cow town until the railroad reached it in 1907. By 1910 settlers with plows, fences, and plans for farming began moving in, and the town's population reached 210. During the high point of homesteading, a shack stood on nearly every quarter section, but harsh winters and dry summers drove many of them away; only those interested in large cattle and wheat-raising efforts remained.

Today Midland has the wide streets of the original town—wide enough to park wagons—and the Pretty Nice Bar across from Tom's Welding, half a block down from the hotel, which still advertises hot mineral baths. The hotel is unpainted, but you can still check in and get a private bath and steam better than modern spas have to offer. During the uranium boom of the mid-1960s, before the dangers of excess radiation were well known, the owner lined a room with radioactive "hot rock" from the Edgemont mining operations, intending to have customers sit inside and bask in "healing" rays. Concerned citizens forced removal of the room.

North of Midland and west of Hayes was the Plum Creek Station, which served stagecoach passengers on the Pierre-to-Deadwood trail.

This Whirl Washer was once the highest technology for farm women who washed the family's clothes every week. The moveable arm helped agitate the clothes, and heavy blankets could be more easily wrung out with the wringer mounted on the end. The prudent housewife kept her old tub and washboard for especially dirty clothes. —Rose Mary Goodson

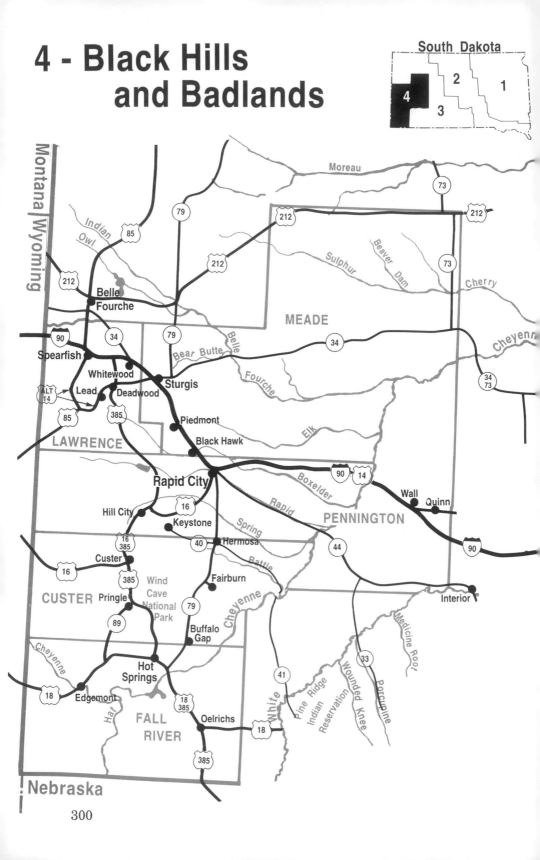

4 - Black Hills and Badlands

South Dakota

PART FOUR

Black Hills and Badlands

The Black Hills contain many valuable minerals and precious stones. In the late nineteenth century this attracted just about everyone who passed by. Few places on the North American continent contain rocks older than those found in the Black Hills, which began to rise about 1.6 billion years ago. Scientists estimate a granite outcropping north of Nemo at 2.5 billion years old. Even though the Black Hills contain some ancient rocks, however, they are not especially old mountains; most of what we see today emerged within the past 50 million years. Actually an eastern extension of the Rocky Mountains, the Black Hills appear isolated by the vast plains that surround them. The highest point in the Hills, Harney Peak, is more than seven thousand feet high above sea level; most of the surrounding terrain lies at three thousand and forty-five hundred feet above sea level.

The Land

The Hogback Ridge, composed of hard sandstone, forms the outer rim of the Black Hills, encircling the uplifted center. Streams have eroded a few openings in this nearly continuous outer circle. Immediately inside the ridge is a valley of red soil several miles wide. This band, which also runs almost completely around the Hills, was called the "racetrack" by the Lakota. According to the myth, in ancient times animals and people lived in harmony until they began eating one another. The Great Spirit decided a race would determine who would eat and who would be eaten. Only animals were allowed to race, not humans. Ironically, a magpie represented two-legged humanity and won the race.

The Limestone Plateau, in the northwestern hills, includes Spearfish Canyon and other spectacular cliffs rising above creek valleys; the mass is as full of caverns as a block of Swiss cheese. The central area of the Hills includes the Harney Range, containing some of the oldest exposed formations anywhere in the world—the Precambrian igneous and sedimentary rocks and granite. Many of the major Black Hills peaks—Harney, Terry, and Custer—are granite, as are the Needles formations, where climbers from all over the world exercise their skills on slender spires.

Neither visitors nor promoters have been entirely happy with the name "Black Hills." Mountains seven thousand feet tall, they argued, should be given a more dignified name. The name derives from an Oglala band, which called the ranges "Paha Sapa" about 1776 because the slopes appeared so dark from a distance. *Sapa* is Lakota for "black," and *paha* refers to any height, whether mountain or hill. Whites tried the name "Black Mountains" briefly in the 1800s, as well as "Purple Mountains" and "Magic Mountains." Somehow, the less spectacular name stuck.

Prehistoric tribes left few artifacts. Radiocarbon dating of potsherds, hearthstones, and bison bones in the Badlands indicates Indians lived there as early as A.D. 900, hunting and gathering over a wide region. Other clues, including petroglyphs and pictographs, indicate probable prehistoric occupation, but the dates are difficult to pinpoint. Most authorities believe the Kiowa and Arapaho probably lived in and around the Black Hills before the Cheyenne, but they left little trace of occupation.

Petroglyphs like this one, called "Coronado's Map" and found in Red Canyon, were probably carved by prehistoric Indians. —Joseph Gullian photo

Arrival of Whites

Knowing exactly when the first white settlers appeared is also challenging. Agnes Wright Spring tells us in *The Cheyenne and Black Hills Stage and Express Routes* that the prospectors who arrived during the gold rush of 1876 found evidence that other nonnatives had preceded them by many years. They found pieces of rusted picks and shovels; a pine tree that had grown enough to engulf an abandoned wagon chain; a long chain and sluice boxes buried eight feet below the ground surface; stumps bearing aged ax marks; an ash wheelbarrow so old it had decayed nearly to dust; a prospector's pit with an oak growing in its center; and timbered mine shafts and tunnels supported by aged and rotting wood. Spring suggests some Spaniards may have struck north from Coronado's 1541 expedition through the southern territories. Clearly, *someone* mined the Hills long before the gold rush of the 1800s, but no one knows who it was.

Gen. W. S. Harney led a military and exploratory expedition into the Black Hills in 1855, making note of feasible travel routes and mapping rivers. Lt. G. K. Warren, a topographical engineer who accompanied Harney, searched the Hills during the next two years for a good site for a military post, in spite of Harney's treaty with the Sioux forbidding white travel through Indian country except along the Platte and White rivers.

Dr. Ferdinand V. Hayden was one of the best early explorers of the Black Hills and Badlands; his explorations laid the foundations of modern geologic understanding of most of the West beyond the Mississippi River. A man named John Evans had briefly mapped the Badlands in 1849 and collected some fossils; Hayden was sent back in 1853 to investigate more completely; he was twenty-three. With an assistant, Hayden first followed the White River; later he made several trips alone and unarmed, learning to carry his needs on his back. The Sioux approached him on several occasions and were amazed at his ability to run and pick up fossils at the same time. They named him "He-who-picks-up-rocks-running" and, as was their habit with the demented, left him alone after that.

In the spring of 1855 Hayden found Pliocene mammal bones on the summit of Eagle's Nest Butte. In 1866-67 the U.S. Congress established what was to become known as the U.S. Geological and Geographical Survey of the Territories, usually called the "Hayden Survey." For the next eleven years Hayden drew maps, measured streams, identified and collected fossils, and drew more maps throughout the Rocky Mountains from New Mexico to Montana and all over the Plains. He was the first scientist to survey the cliff

dwellings of Mesa Verde and examine the wonders of Yellowstone,
which became a national park largely because of him.

In spite of all this traffic, the Black Hills remained one of the last
unmapped areas in the United States when Lt. Col. George Custer's
1874 thousand-man military expedition confirmed, near Custer, the
rumors that had been heard for years: The Black Hills contained
gold. Wagon ruts from Custer's heavily supplied party are still visible near several Hills highways, and the graves of men who died
during the trip are marked with monuments and shown on maps.

Custer's discovery of gold "at the roots of the grass" spurred a
rush of prospectors, creating a need for merchants, prostitutes,
freighters, churches, schools—all the underpinnings of civilization.
Though fur traders, homesteaders, farmers, and other varieties of
pioneer were already steadily settling the Plains, gold lust brought
an explosion of development in the western part of the territory.
Some folks got rich and had streets named after them; others remained poor and made up jokes about the weather. The Homestake
mine, discovered the same year Custer visited the Hills, is still the
largest gold producer in North America.

The next year, the government-sponsored Jenney-Newton expedition penetrated the Hills to estimate the gold potential so its value
could be taken into account when negotiating with the Lakota to
give up the Hills. Army Lt. Col. Richard I. Dodge came along to write

Dr. Valentine T. McGillycuddy, shown with his first wife, Fanny Hoyt, was a South Dakota pioneer. The Lakota called him Wasichu Wakan, Holy White Man. He was the first white man to climb Harney Peak, and his ashes were scattered there in 1939.
—Clara Lobdell collection

an official report, but he had difficulty making a straightforward positive remark. He reported in *The Black Hills*, "Nature seems to have been at pains to set barriers around and about" the Hills; he griped about the "nauseous water" and said the "barren plains, cut with innumerable ravines and gorges," were succeeded as the party got closer by steep, almost impassable ridges and canyons without any water at all. Even a moderately good country, he said, would seem like paradise after the purgatory of a trip to the Hills. Finally, however, Dodge admitted after several months of living there, he could "pronounce the Black Hills, in many respects, the finest country I have ever seen."

The Jenney-Newton expedition estimated the Hills held enough gold to make many fortunes—and cost a few more. Dodge predicted that after the gold fever died down, the miners would become valuable citizens in a region that would be an important part of the United

305

States. Since the Dakota territorial capital in Yankton lay so far away, miners in the Hills tried to form a separate territory to be called El Dorado or Lincoln.

The Dakota Gold Rush

The rush to Deadwood, the nation's last gold-mining district, changed the character of the entire territory. The Lakota were driven away from the mines and herded away from the grass. Profit dictated land-use policy: Flat land was for the rancher's cows and the homesteader's plow, and pointed land was opened to the miner's pick. Some residents say profit is still the deciding factor in decisions made about the Black Hills, but conflict arises when modern mining, an employer of residents for a century, threatens to damage the profitable tourism industry and pollute water and soil.

One of the best accounts of the realities of mining, published as *An Illinois Gold Hunter in the Black Hills*, was the diary of Jerry Bryan, a young miner from Illinois who came to the Black Hills with

This photo of Dr. Valentine T. McGillycuddy may have been taken when he was a surveyor with the Jenney-Newton party exploring the Black Hills in 1875. The object that looks like a tiny haystack is probably an overnight shelter made of tree limbs. McGillycuddy met Sitting Bull and George Custer, danced with Calamity Jane, and got advice about traveling in Indian country from Wild Bill Hickok and Buffalo Bill Cody. Later he attended the dying Crazy Horse.
—South Dakota State Historical Society

two companions to hunt for gold in 1876. Bryan had traveled overland at least as far as Wyoming in 1859, but his friends were completely inexperienced in frontier living; in that, they were probably typical of gold seekers who came to the Hills. They arrived by train in Cheyenne in a terrific storm and found the town full of people and excitement. The only boarding house they could get to offered standing room; by furnishing their own blankets, the three had the privilege of sleeping in the dining room.

The trio bargained for passage to Custer and finally made a deal with a teamster who agreed to take them and 150 pounds of gear apiece for $18. When the expedition started, they discovered the freighter was carrying only their gear; the men had to walk. The first day they hiked eighteen miles in a blizzard. The weather continued to be cold and snowy; wrote Bryan, "I think here is where wind is manufactured." Fifteen days later the travelers arrived in Custer after "pushing or pulling the Wagon half the way." Bryan called Custer "a Ruff crowd" and concluded, "dont like the looks of the country. and I dont like the looks of the men dont believe there is a claim on the creek that will pay Wages." Later, after prospecting in several places and, as Bryan says, "spending 10 Days eating up all our Grub Wearing out all our clothes and very materialy lessning our faith in the Hills," the group headed for Deadwood.

By the time they arrived, Bryan was somewhat cynical about the chances for success in the gold rush, saying, "Now comes the Tug of War No chance to get work. The country all claimed. Grub very high and our Money geting low." Desperate, he and a partner were hired to dig a claim for another man; in fourteen hours of hard work, they took out gold worth $5.28 and had to pay the claim owner half the sum. More businesses sold whiskey than food, Bryan observed; "Evrything fluctuates here except Whiskey and Labor Whiskey is at the top notch and labor at the lowest."

A few days later, when Bryan found a good claim, he changed his tune. In May he bought another man's claim for $505; many prospectors made more money by selling their claims to newcomers than they did panning gold, especially if they already knew the spot was worthless. Bryan didn't pay cash for the claim but was hoping to dig enough gold to pay for it and supply his needs. On June 15, after four days' work, the three partners' gold was worth $211; they panned $134 more a few days later.

By July Bryan had become disgusted with Deadwood, where he saw nothing but gambling and drinking. He left in August and returned to Illinois after an absence of five months and five days. His earlier frontier experiences probably made him more cautious than many miners, and he spent more time working his claim than drinking and seeing the sights of the boomtown, pastimes with which many miners were preoccupied. Some accounts say hundreds of young men died in their flimsy tents of hunger and exposure. Living in a tent or in a busy town with dusty streets wasn't conducive to cleanliness and good health. One bullwhacker said, "It is an absolute fact that I was lousy with but an intermission of about twenty-four hours, for about six years, so was everyone else. I once went into Cheyenne with a roll of $700 in bank notes, and it was full of lice and nits."

Another factor helped keep the average life expectancy fairly low: As the population grew and prospered, bad men naturally multiplied. The Sam Bass gang of Texas dropped in to pull off a holdup or two, and Persimmon Bill was rumored to be killing and robbing miners on the way home with loot. The gold coaches were robbed so many times *The Black Hills Pioneer* got a bit cynical, reporting in 1877:

HAT CREEK—Coach from Deadwood was stopped again last night near Cheyenne River. Both treasure boxes were taken. The passengers were not molested. The Road Agent sent word by the driver to the manager of the stage line to send them a pair of gold scales. They say dividing the dust with a tablespoon is not always satisfactory. They also would prefer to have the box carried loose in the coach. If that can't be done, they want a hammer and hatchet sent up.

The Dakota gold rush may seem romantic and exciting to modern readers, but the people who actually lived it had almost the opposite perspective. In fact, a popular song of the era was titled "The Dreary Black Hills":

> *Kind friends, won't you listen to my pitiful tale,*
> *I'm an object of pity and looking quite stale,*
> *I gave up my job selling Aire's Patent Pills*
> *To prospect for gold in the Dreary Black Hills.*

The chorus went like this:

> *Don't travel away, stay at home if you can,*
> *Stay away from that city, they call it Cheyenne,*
> *Where the blue waters roll and Comanche Bill*
> *Will lift up your hair in the Dreary Black Hills.*

Other verses spoke of folks who returned from the Black Hills with no clothes on their backs and no bills in their pockets, and of the rain, hail, and snow that froze miners "plumb to the gills." Prospectors were warned that they would only fill the pockets of railroad speculators "by taking a trip to the Dreary Black Hills."

(The song is included on *Songs of the Seventh Cavalry*, a cassette recorded for the benefit of the Fort Abraham Lincoln Foundation.)

Black Hills Tourism

Just after World War II the Black Hills were proposed as the permanent headquarters of the United Nations. South Dakota's governor joined those of Wyoming and Nebraska in formally inviting the UN to locate here, and the plan received serious consideration along with invitations from cities like Geneva, Brussels, and Philadelphia.

Naturally, sophisticated Easterners didn't grasp the Hills' charm; *Time* magazine sneered at the idea, saying of a meeting in London, "The star performer was Paul Bellamy, a bull-necked businessman who represents no city, but the bleak Black Hills of South Dakota where men are men and steaks are three inches thick."

Local promoters argued that the Hills location was ideal because it was the most interior spot on the continent, most remote from the oceans; in every direction, the Hills are eleven hundred miles from a saltwater sea and thus the safest possible spot from hostilities. The plan even included a "world highway" that would have connected South Africa with Argentina. In the Black Hills, they predicted, the organization would be unique, whereas in New York it would be just another group.

Although the UN initiative failed, the region today draws visitors from all over the world. Tourism is now South Dakota's most profitable business. Visitors can hike, bicycle, or drive. The Black Hills save their best secrets for the slow explorer, the prowler who goes quietly and leaves few traces—the hiker, fisherman, mountain biker, walker, or stroller. The most interesting "roads" can't be covered here—little gravel and dirt lanes that disappear seductively into the trees as you cruise along a paved highway. Even if space had been available in this book, I'd have left them out; if everyone travels them, some government official will insist upon having them paved, and their charm and loveliness will be gone.

But if you're a person who treats the wilderness with respect, drive some of those secret roads. Better yet, take a mountain bike or walk along old railroad rights-of-way. If you go quietly, without a motor, you'll get a more intimate look at wildlife, trees and flowers, lonely meadows where pioneers built their lonely cabins. But watch the weather; rain or snow can turn a lovely road into a dangerous spot. Never go into the Black Hills without extra jackets; the temperature can drop suddenly at any time.

Jewel Cave and Wind Cave—both among the ten longest in the world—contain rare rock formations. The Black Hills contain almost seventy other calcite caves as well. —South Dakota Department of Tourism

One route through the heart of the Hills is the Centennial Trail, which opened in 1989 and runs 111 miles from Wind Cave National Park to Bear Butte State Park. A total of eleven hundred signs guide users, and there are twenty-four trailheads with parking lots. The trail covers varied territory, from the lush prairies of Wind Cave to the granite outcroppings near Mount Rushmore to the evergreens of the Black Hills National Forest and the highland prairies of Custer State Park. It is open to hikers, horseback riders, and mountain bikers; motorized vehicles are prohibited everywhere except for a 30-mile stretch in the northern Hills. Ask locally before setting out; mountain bikers who have traveled the entire trail report that some stretches are extremely rough. The U.S. Forest Service offices distribute maps of other hiking trails in the Black Hills National Forest; they range from one accessible to wheelchairs at Sheridan Lake to the 14-mile path along the historic Rockerville Flume to Sheridan Lake.

Another good way to hike is to follow old railroad beds, which are abundant; Black Hills National Forest maps and books by local authors show many railroad rights-of-way. Railroads have been entwined with Black Hills history since the early mining days. Beginning in 1879, tiny locomotives ran on narrow gauge rails three feet apart, hauling supplies in and ore out of the mining communities. The Fremont, Elkhorn & Missouri Valley ran its first train into Deadwood on December 29, 1890, the day of the tragedy at Wounded Knee.

Dozens of ghost towns litter the Hills, and old mining camps lurk in every gulch wide enough for a cabin. The spirit of the era is reflected in local place-names, though some are a tad misleading. For example, Bloody Gulch east of Rochford commemorates not a gunfight but the properties of the water. An Englishman tasted the heavily mineralized water and experienced its strong laxative effect. Upon returning to camp, he moaned weakly, "Oh, I drank the water in the bloody gulch." A surveyor who lost his way was responsible for another name that stands out on a map. He met a prospector carrying a heavy pack and asked the name of the gulch the two were in. "Go to hell," the miner snapped—and the surveyor duly recorded the name. Four miles north of Deerfield stands the aptly named Nipple Butte. Big Nasty Creek in northern Harding County was named for its terrible smell; the stream's original name is unprintable. The considerably more obscene name of an area southwest of Red Shirt in western Shannon County remains; it is a sneering reference to white men who cohabited with Indian women and to the women themselves.

The Badlands

The Badlands are a vast rock garden of sandstone, clay, black shale, and volcanic ash carved by wind and water into a sculpture hall and a standing record of the region's prehistory. Today's tourist often stands silent, camera dangling uselessly, when seeing the spectacle for the first time. Lt. Col. Richard Dodge, one of the first white visitors to the region, was stunned by what he saw. "No one," he said, "can imagine or realize, from any picture or description, the wonderful and weird beauty of a view in the Bad Lands." Dodge, whose prose was slightly less than scintillating, really floundered when he tried to describe the sharp, narrow ridges known as "hogbacks," but he clearly was impressed by the great bowls and excited by the "thousands of isolated castles, towers, domes, obelisks, pyramids, carved by water and frescoed in various colored earths," as well as the bone fields, "the burying-ground of races extinct before the advent of man." As early as 1830, travelers reported seeing huge bones exposed in the earth. Alexander Culbertson sent a wagon load

The Badlands, sixty miles east of the Black Hills, frightened most early travelers and still remain dangerous to careless explorers. The Lakota knew travel routes and water holes, allowing them to hunt and camp comfortably in this terrain. —South Dakota State Historical Society

of fossils out in 1843, and paleontologists have been gleefully digging up new fossils ever since.

The earliest sediments in Badlands National Park formed in shallow, muddy seas during the Cretaceous more than sixty-five million years ago. During this period, great rivers wandered over wide floodplains, leaving huge loads of dark sediment that became the Pierre Shale. This layer, often visible today, has yielded fossils of mosasaurs and sea turtles up to twelve feet long. At the end of the period, upheaval resulted in the folding of the earth's surface, lifting the Rocky Mountains and causing a bulging dome that became the Black Hills. Small streams and millions of years of sun, rain, and vegetative growth sculpted the landscape and caused chemical changes, resulting in the bright yellow soil visible in some areas of the Badlands.

Near the beginning of the Oligocene period, about thirty-five million years ago, rivers heading north and east from the Black Hills flooded, filling valleys with hundreds of feet of sand and gravel. This material formed the gray green Chadron formation's rounded hills, filled with fossil titanotheres (slightly smaller than today's elephant and resembling a rhinoceros). Resident horses were about the size of a collie; the species eventually reached nearly its present size before becoming extinct on this continent. Saber-toothed tigers and camels the size of modern sheep also roamed the region, as did the giant pig, about the size of a modern cow. Fossils of three kinds of rhinoceros have been found in the Badlands, along with protoceras, which had as many as five pairs of horns on its face at different angles.

The Brulé formation, in which the Badlands' fantastic shapes are carved by wind and rain, is banded in yellow and red and contains fossilized remains of the oreodont, a piglike animal with tusks. Though they have no living descendants, closely related animal groups resulted in camels and llamas. Above this formation are layers of whitish volcanic ash.

Ferdinand Hayden claimed that when he explored the Badlands in 1866, the thermometer read 112 degrees in the shade and no potable water existed within fifteen miles. He concluded that only geologists would ever be permanently attracted to the place. For once, Hayden was wrong; though the Badlands were slow to attract settlers, a few found homesteads around or on top of the flat-topped buttes that dot the landscape. This environment is more hostile than that of the Black Hills, but it is more hospitable than its name suggests, with secret springs and hidden green valleys—a fact lost on the state's first poet laureate, Badger Clark, who wrote in his first collection of poems, *Sun and Saddle Leather*:

No fresh green things in the Bad Lands bide
It is all stark red and gray,
And strewn with bones that had lived and died
Ere the first man saw the day.
When the sharp crests dream in the sunset gleam
And the bat through the canyon veers,
You will sometimes catch, if you listen long,
The tones of the Bad Lands' mystic song,
A song of a million years.

A poem about southwestern South Dakota written by a less renowned wordsmith, Custer pioneer Frank G. Mills, seems curiously applicable today, when many Lakota are asking for a return of their former lands:

We live in South Dakota, just inside its western line,
The country's mostly sagebrush, low hills and scrubby pine.
We took it from the Indians and we swiped it from the Sioux
Then we put them on a reservation to see what they could do.
The Indian must have chuckled as he rounded up his stuff
For he knew white men would starve if they farmed it long enough.

The weather's been the driest the world has ever seen
And those little runty pines are all we have that's green.
The 'hoppers got the pastures and the crickets got the grain
And half the old men on the place have never seen it rain.
The wind removed the top soil and the sub-soil turned to rock,
So there's nothing high nor low we can find to feed the stock.
The cows get thin and thinner while we're waiting on the weather
'Til they die from irritation caused by sides that rub together.
Uncle Sam, he dug a well, but that's been dry for years
'Cause the only sub-soil moisture was the poor old settler's tears.
Then the settlers quit their crying and stopped no more to think
They just couldn't spare the water from what was left to drink.
After years and years of farming, and fighting drought and pest
We have come to the conclusion that the Indian's way was best
So come back, old Crazy Horse, bring all your Indian band
Come back, and set your teepee on this great South Dakota land.

For Further Reading

Gold-mining days in the Hills have received the bulk of writers' attention. The best fictional treatment is the novel *Deadwood* by Pete Dexter. His account of Calamity Jane, Wild Bill Hickok, Charley Utter, and Jack Langrishe sings with authenticity. Historical works include *Old Deadwood Days*, written by Estelline Bennett, who lived downtown during the town's wildest days. Watson Parker's *Gold in the Black Hills* is a reliable, scholarly history that avoids common myths, and *Pioneer Years in the Black Hills* by Richard B. Hughes, who came to Deadwood during 1876, is a journalist's account. George W. Stoke, who was in Deadwood from 1876 to 1879, working for a newspaper, told his firsthand account to Howard R. Driggs for *Deadwood Gold*. Doug Engbretson gives a good summary of outlaws in the region in *Empty Saddles, Forgotten Names*.

Donald Jackson's *Custer's Gold* is a good account of the 1874 campaign, including the photographs taken by expedition photographer William H. Illingworth. *Prelude to Glory* by Herbert Krause and Gary Olson reproduces newspaper accounts. Another intriguing book is *Crazy Horse and Custer* by Stephen E. Ambrose, detailing parallels in the lives of the two American warriors who battled at the Little Bighorn.

For pure entertainment, based on solid fact, Helen Rezatto's *Tales of the Black Hills* provides all you really need to know about Hills history; her *Mount Moriah: Kill a Man—Start a Cemetery* does the same for Deadwood, providing considerable enjoyment. *Seth Bullock: Frontier Marshal* was written by Kenneth C. Kellar, Bullock's grandson.

For hikers and folks who prefer the back roads, I recommend *Black Hills Ghost Towns* by Watson Parker and Hugh K. Lambert, or Mildred Fielder's *Hiking Trails in the Black Hills*. If the stage routes are your primary interest, look for Agnes Wright Spring's *The Cheyenne and Black Hills Stage and Express Routes*. Laura Bower Van Nuys's book, *The Family Band*, reveals a great deal about small town and home life in settlement days. Dr. Vallentine McGillycuddy's story, and considerable information about the region and time, is told by his wife, Julia B., in *McGillycuddy, Agent*.

Edward P. Hogan, state geographer, has published *South Dakota*, an illustrated geography that is constructed like a coloring book but packed with information. *This Curious Country: Badlands National Park* by Mary Durant and Michael Harwood offers great photos, along with plenty of intriguing information. *Black Hills Badlands: The Web of the West*, with photos by Craig Blacklock, is a stunning display of some of the best scenes in both areas.

While driving, read Badger Clark's rollicking poetry in books like *Sun and Saddle Leather*, *Grass Grown Trails*, and *Sky Lines and Wood Smoke*.

I-90 crosses the southern third of South Dakota from east to west, skirting the Black Hills within sight of the major peaks. Between Sturgis and Rapid City, western I-90 lies in "the racetrack," a broad valley that surrounds the Hills almost completely. East of Rapid City, it passes through the valley of the Cheyenne River and the edge of the Badlands onto the broad, rolling grasslands of the northern Plains.

SPEARFISH

Spearfish, founded in 1876, was named for the nearby creek, which received its name either because Indians speared fish in it or because the pioneers thought they did. Whereas mining supported most of the region's early towns, Spearfish developed alternate industries and became the center of a rich agricultural and gardening region. Wheat and oats were grown in dry areas and milled locally; irrigated bottomland grew fruit, berries, and vegetables in large plots and garden markets. Two irrigation ditches were built (they still flow under downtown streets). Sugar beets grown here were first shipped to Nebraska, then to the sugar factory in Belle Fourche. The Squire Dingey Pickle Company of Chicago contracted with local and Belle Fourche gardeners for cucumbers, which were shipped in brine-filled railroad tanks to Chicago for canning. A million head of cattle grazed in the neighborhood; sheep, hogs, and dairy cattle provided food for townspeople and meat, milk, and butter to sell in mining towns.

Settlement at Spearfish came in 1876 with the arrival of the Centennial Party—fourteen men who traveled from Iowa to explore the gold fields. Only six of them settled in Spearfish, but town site speculators followed, believing that fertile land could be worth more than gold. The settlers knew they were in dangerous territory and built their town as a fort; four cabins became corners to a stockade at the present intersection of Hudson with Fifth and Sixth streets. The first school, sawmill, and hotel all opened in 1877, and J. C. Ryan of St. Joseph, Missouri, built a twenty-by-forty-foot store. By 1883 he had constructed a two-story Masonic Hall with a fireproof cellar.

M. C. Connors brought a herd of cattle from Texas in the spring of 1877 and turned them out to graze along the Redwater River. By 1879 the valleys of the Redwater, False Bottom, and Spearfish creeks

Mrs. John Murray washed clothes the hard way— with a washboard and tub—outside her home in Spearfish about 1910.
—South Dakota Agricultural Heritage Museum

were filling with settlers. Reiley & Son brought brood mares and stallions to their ranch in Spearfish Valley in 1878, and J. P. Gammon raised horses on his False Bottom Ranch. On the Belle Fourche River, Sol Starr and Seth Bullock—who was later famous as Deadwood's sheriff and Teddy Roosevelt's friend—raised standardbred horses. The livestock operations were all in country that still belonged to the Sioux, who later attacked outlying farms.

The town maintained its frontier look throughout the 1880s, with log cabins and false-front buildings on the main streets. The first bank appeared in 1883, and by 1884 Spearfish had five lumber mills. In 1889 a sawmill was built on Spearfish Creek; lumber is still an important industry here. Churches, a law office, a flour mill, furniture stores, and a newspaper (the *Queen City Mail*) were established as families grew, along with a stucco mill, brick factories, and machine shops. As an agricultural center, the town grew gradually— much to the dismay of the city fathers—but the slow growth seemed to provide the stability that was lacking in the boom-and-bust

317

An eight-mule freight team moves through a narrow canyon near Deadwood bound for Homestake's mine and mills in 1889. —Centennial Archives, Deadwood

towns of the gold rush. By 1890 Spearfish had a population of nearly seven hundred.

Not until the 1890s was the town connected to Deadwood by a railroad; by that time, businessmen had already realized they could not compete with larger towns in the region. Searching for ways to make money, they began to tap the economic potential of tourism. To encourage sport fishing, they stocked trout in northern Black Hills streams in 1889; in 1899 the fish hatchery began raising fish to stock other streams and man-made lakes in the Black Hills.

Spearfish has experienced phenomenal growth over the last hundred years. Today its economy relies heavily on tourism and lumbering. Most of the orchards are gone; the soil that nourished market gardens has been covered by sprawling housing developments. Spearfish is filled with people who like its small-town atmosphere and cultural and educational advantages. Many new residents are young families and retirees. The city recently annexed property in three directions as new retail and light industrial businesses moved in. A shopping area stands where the orchards flourished west of town, and a mall has been built out east. A manufacturer of waterproof bentonite products sells plastic liners for waste disposal sites, and another plant makes screens for crushers in gold, gravel, and coal mining operations. Tourism is bigger than ever; the town hosts an annual convention of Corvette owners, and during 1989 nearly fifteen hundred contestants arrived for the World Horseshoe Tournament.

Spearfish is home to Black Hills State University, which began in 1883 as Spearfish Normal School with $2,000 in operating funds from the legislature in 1881. Van Buren Baker was hired as the first principal, and during the second term he employed a female teacher to conduct classes so he could campaign for county superintendent of schools. When he was defeated, he closed the school and left the country; he'd spent the money. The next year, the legislature cautiously appropriated $5,000 for two years' operating costs and enrolled sixty-five students; the first building was finished in 1894. The school provided two-year teaching programs by 1907 and four-year degrees by 1922. In 1941 it became Black Hills Teachers College. In 1961 extension classes at Ellsworth Air Force Base were added. Management courses created for the business and travel industries have expanded enrollment. By the last decade of the twentieth century, 92 percent of the school's graduates were born and raised in South Dakota.

Cultural events are brought to the Matthews Opera House, built in 1906 for touring shows, minstrels, vaudeville, and Shakespearean plays. After serving as a motion picture theater, shooting gallery, dance hall, and pigeon roost, it was renovated and reopened with actors in a melodrama by a resident writer. Another local attraction is the Black Hills Passion Play, permanently established in Spearfish in 1938, with Joseph Meier portraying Christ. The company of players spends the winter in Florida, where the play depicting the last seven days in the life of Christ is also performed. The play has become central to the Spearfish economy, drawing tourists from all over the world. Tourists also come to the High Plains Heritage Museum, overlooking I-90 on the south side of town. The museum displays artifacts from developments in mining, lumbering, ranching, and the native Lakota culture.

Safe and Sane Flying

The Spearfish airport is named after Clyde Ice, the "Father of South Dakota Aviation." Ice, who celebrated his hundredth birthday in 1989, taught himself to fly in 1919 on a barnstorming tour with another pilot. A few days after he took his first flight and earned his pilot's license, Ice began carrying passengers for $5 each. He traded two used cars to get his first plane, which a North Dakota farmer had won selling newspaper subscriptions.

After barnstorming a few years, Ice and two other men formed Rapid Airlines and later operated a line from Minneapolis to Spearfish. Ice was the ticket agent, baggage handler, flight attendant, and pilot. He was also chief of public relations, coining the phrase "Safe and Sane Flying," which he painted on each airplane he flew. During World War II, Ice trained more than two thousand pilots, many of them later Air Force officers. He was one of the first to dust crops from the air and developed the technique of pouring herbicide through a tube connected to the plane's fuselage. He pioneered winter flying, making wooden skis with metal runners for snow landings. He used the skis to fly mercy missions to isolated areas of the Great Plains.

Ice flew for sixty-two years without injuring himself or passengers; once, when a plane's engine stopped while he was flying up a canyon, he landed among rocks and damaged only the propeller and landing gear. He elected not to renew his pilot's license in 1981, when he was ninety-three years old.

Near Spearfish

West of Spearfish stands the brooding shape of Crow Peak, a big-shouldered mountain nearly six thousand feet high, named either because the Sioux killed some Crow warriors there or because someone was hard of hearing—one authority says it was named "Joe's Peak" after California Joe (this is a doubtful theory, however).

Another nearby landmark, the Thoen Stone, was discovered in 1887 by a man named Louis Thoen. This block of sandstone with words scratched on it was found near Lookout Peak; the site is east of I-90 behind the Holiday Inn south of Spearfish and marked with a concrete "X" visible from the highway. The stone was concealed in

Homesteaders in western Dakota, 1882. —South Dakota State Historical Society

a crevice ten feet underground near two large oak trees that may have been markers. The message on one side said:

CAME TO THESE HILLS IN 1833, SEVEN OF US, DE LA COMPTE, EZRA KIND, G.W. WOOD, T. BROWN, R. KENT, WM. KING, INDIAN CROW. ALL DEAD BUT ME, EZRA KIND. KILLED BY IND BEYOND THE HIGH HILL GOT OUR GOLD JUNE 1834

The other side read:

GOT ALL THE GOLD WE COULD CARRY. OUR PONYS ALL GOT BY INDIANS. HAVE LOST MY GUN AND NOTHING TO EAT AND INDIANS HUNTING ME.

The stone has intrigued researchers for years. Frank Thompson of Spearfish spent much of his life trying to prove it was genuine. He discovered that men bearing the listed names left eastern settlements at about the right time, headed west, and were never heard from again. Skeptics, however, pointed out that Thoen was an experienced mason, capable of creating a stone hoax.

If these men really found gold here, they may have been the first gold miners in the West, fourteen years before the California gold rush. However, it's hard to believe a starving man being hunted by Indians would take the time to laboriously scratch a message into a stone by hand. No trace of the seven miners, their ponies, or their gold was ever found. Indians did tell about killing white men they found panning gold and using the gold to buy goods from the Hudson's Bay Company. The Thoen Stone is now in the Adams Museum in Deadwood.

WHITEWOOD

Agents with the Pioneer Townsite Land Company of the Fremont, Elkhorn & Missouri Valley Railroad bought the site of Whitewood from a settler and opened a post office in 1877, before mail service reached Lead, Spearfish, or Central City. Once railroads reached Deadwood and Belle Fourche, which became the nation's largest livestock shopping center, as many as twelve trains a day passed through Whitewood. The town was platted in 1888 and got its name from groves of birch and aspen trees.

The fertile valley was much like that of Spearfish in early days; settlers grew grain and fruit. A flour mill opened in 1889, when 60 percent of the Black Hills wheat crop was grown within a radius of fifteen miles. Fred Borsch, a German immigrant who lived between Whitewood and Sturgis, won a gold medal at the 1893 World's Fair for the quality of his grain. Dairy farming north and west of town

Pupils and teachers at a schoolhouse in western Dakota.
—South Dakota School of Mines and Technology

encouraged the building of the Danish American Creamery in 1907, which lasted until 1954. By the early 1900s, about five hundred people lived in the town, which included three hotels and a doctor's office. The sawmill and railroad were the main employers, and quarries supplied sandstone and limestone for area buildings. Enos Lane built a hotel of local sandstone, featuring a special parlor for women. Rodeos and Labor Day celebrations attracted visitors, and in the 1920s the town had a theater (with movies Wednesday and Saturday evenings) and a newspaper.

One of the last bank holdups in the northern Black Hills was a $25,000 heist at the Whitewood Banking Company in 1932. The bandits were caught, but the bank closed a few years later. The town lost more establishments over the years: Whitewood's stockyard was moved to Sturgis when a larger one was built in Belle Fourche, and passenger rail service was cut back steadily, finally ending in 1958. Though the economic base has narrowed and the population declined, agriculture still helps support the town; Livestock Energy Systems produces a feed supplement, and businesses dependent on logging are still active. Now the town is becoming a residential community for people who work in nearby towns. The same is true of Tilford, a few miles down the interstate—founded in 1888, it was named for Col. J. G. Tilford of the Seventh Cavalry.

For a hundred years, Whitewood Creek was one of the most notoriously polluted creeks in the nation, carrying deadly concentrations of cyanide from Homestake Mine and raw sewage from Deadwood. Residents tolerated the pollution because they needed jobs. As Sven G. Froiland remarks in *Natural History of the Black Hills and Badlands*, "the track record of the mining interests in the Hills, in regard to concern for the environment, has been less than exemplary." When the dumping finally stopped in 1985, the South Dakota Game, Fish & Parks Department built structures in the stream to encourage trout habitat, and the fish population flourished; some grow more than sixteen inches long.

STURGIS

Lt. G. K. Warren recognized the strategic importance of the Black Hills when he conducted his topographical survey in 1857. In 1866 the Dakota territorial legislature asked Congress to establish a military post at the southern end of the region. By the time the federal government seriously considered establishing a post, the military's primary job had become keeping whites out of the land promised to the Sioux by the 1868 Fort Laramie treaty. After the Charles Metz family was slaughtered in Red Canyon in April 1876, Lt. Gen. Phil Sheridan, commander of the Department of the Missouri, suggested the army build a post near the Black Hills as a way of keeping the Sioux under control. As a result, the short-lived Camp Collier was established near the Cheyenne River at the mouth of Red Canyon in the southern Black Hills; it was abandoned after a year.

As fighting continued between Indians and the whites illegally invading the Hills, other commanders recommended a permanent post, and in 1878 Congress appropriated $50,000 for construction. Lt. Col. Michael Sheridan (Phil's brother) was ordered to choose a site and actually bought twelve lots in the heart of Rapid City for $500 after deciding that a post near Bear Butte would not be suitable. A rivalry developed between Deadwood and Rapid City over the post, and Phil Sheridan was sent out in mid-1878 to settle the matter. He established Camp Sturgis, named for Lt. J. G. Sturgis, killed on the Little Bighorn with Custer's Seventh Cavalry. The town of Sturgis was later named for his father, Maj. Samuel D. Sturgis, commander of the post.

The cavalry abandoned the original post site in the fall of 1878 and moved to present-day Fort Meade. The site covered an area six miles by two miles where log buildings, a stockade, and a wooden reservoir had been built; many original fort buildings, including one

housing a museum, still stand. The fort was well located at the mouth of a natural gap in the hogback ridge around the Black Hills and on the main Indian trail to good hunting areas. Also, the Bismarck, Fort Pierre, and Sidney trails used by freighters and homesteaders converged nearby. While moving to the new site, soldiers found the remains of the two Magnus brothers and one of their wives, all killed by Indians while trying to catch up with a wagon train on the Bismarck Trail. Ironically, they were *leaving* the goldfields, homesick and disappointed. A marker two miles north of Bear Butte on SD 79 identifies the massacre site, where ruts of the wagon trail are still visible.

There are numerous intriguing stories about the fort where the Seventh Cavalry re-formed after the Battle of the Little Bighorn. A horse named Comanche, the only survivor of the companies that died with Custer during the fight, was nursed back to health and retired here. Four years after the battle, Maj. Marcus A. Reno was court-martialed here for spying through windows at Colonel Sturgis's daughter. Col. Caleb H. Carlson claimed that he became the first army officer to order the playing of "The Star Spangled Banner" at formal ceremonies in 1892, forty-one years before the song became the national anthem. One monument on the post recognizes two of the hardest drinkers in the Eighth Cavalry's D Troop. The black "buffalo soldiers" stationed at Fort Meade won twenty-three Congressional Medals of Honor during their history.

Fort Meade had no troops between 1914 and 1917, and then it had only National Guardsmen being trained before going overseas to fight in World War I. From 1933 to 1935 the post served as state headquarters for the Civilian Conservation Corps camp, with officers of the Fourth Cavalry assigned to command them. Guard detachments from the fort helped with the army's balloon flight experiments at the Stratosphere Bowl near Rapid City.

When the Japanese bombed Pearl Harbor in 1941, most of the fort's troops were undergoing winter training; they quickly posted guards to protect the post's reservoir and water pumps from sabotage. By April 1942 all but a few of the Fourth Cavalry's members had turned in their horses and been assigned to tanks. That fall, the last troop of cavalry was transferred to Camp Hale, Colorado. Glider troops from the Eighty-eighth Infantry trained at the fort for a year in 1943, but active-duty troops left Fort Meade for the last time in 1944, the same year the first group of Women's Air Corps volunteers arrived. That fall, six hundred German prisoners of war were imprisoned, some helping convert barracks into hospital wards, others working in the beet fields near Belle Fourche. The fort is now a Veterans Administration psychiatric treatment hospital.

The best-known modern attraction in Sturgis is the annual Black Hills Motorcycle Classic, a week-long series of events attended by more than fifty thousand bikers and spectators each August. Officials say three hundred thousand people came to the fiftieth anniversary of the event in 1990, doubling the population of western South Dakota for a week.

The Black Hills Steam and Gas Threshing Bee is also held annually in August, drawing examples of the farming machinery that eventually displaced horses, as well as early autos, quilting demonstrations, and examples of all kinds of early-day crafts and products. Each May Sturgis is host to a balloon rally with colorful gas bags from all over the nation; balloon chasers have a wonderful time roaring along obscure roads hoping their craft doesn't land on a granite peak.

"Poker Alice," a loving wife and mother who went into a different line of work after her husband, Warren Tubbs, died. —South Dakota Department of Tourism

Another potential tourist attraction in Sturgis is the old home of "Poker Alice" Tubbs, a loving wife and mother, a compassionate nurse, a professional gambler, a brothel madam, a good shot, and a certified killer. Existing photographs show Tubbs with a sour look and a cigar stuck in her mouth, but she was beautiful when young and learned her gambling skills as a cheery widow in the 1880s. She came to the Hills in the 1890s and married Sturgis resident Warren Tubbs, a housepainter who gambled at night. Not every night, apparently; they had seven children. When Mr. Tubbs died of tuberculosis, Alice started a sporting house and bootlegging establishment in Sturgis, catering to soldiers. During a drunken brawl, someone started shooting, and when it was over Alice had killed one patron and wounded several others. She was tried for murder but acquitted on a plea of self-defense. She died in Sturgis at seventy-seven and is buried in St. Aloysius Cemetery.

Bear Butte

Just north of Sturgis stands Bear Butte, nearly forty-five hundred feet high. Its prominence on the horizon attracted a steady stream of early visitors: It was probably the first real landmark explorers had seen after days on the open prairie. Verendrye, Warren, Hayden, and Custer all mention the peak. However, Col. Richard I. Dodge, who accompanied the 1875 Jenney expedition, argued vehemently with the title in *The Black Hills*:

> our surveyors changed the name to what the original namer evidently intended. The elevation is a cone of solid granite rock, entirely devoid of all vegetation. "Butte" means an elevation too high to be called a hill, too low to be called a mountain. This peak rises to the height of five thousand two hundred feet above tide-water, and, standing on the plain several miles from the nearest mountains, appears yet higher. It is not a "butte." "Bare Peak" expresses exactly what it is.

In spite of Dodge's assertions, the name he preferred didn't stick; he was wrong about the height, too. Dodge also asserted that the rest of the prairie region was a desert and that the alkali water was unfit for use. Residents have gotten used to the water, though many

Bear Butte, a gold rush landmark sacred to the Lakota and Cheyenne, stands on the plains east of Sturgis. —*South Dakota Department of Tourism*

Custer's photographer, William H. Illingworth, took this picture of Bear Butte in 1874. Some members of the Custer expedition climbed the sacred shrine, which offended the Sioux, and led them to predict death for the whites. Illingworth survived the Battle of the Little Bighorn but eventually committed suicide. —South Dakota State Historical Society

support a scheme to pipe water from Oahe Reservoir to the West River country for domestic use.

Dodge thought the Hills' greatest potential was as farming country and rhapsodized that it would be filled with "cozy farms and comfortable residences." Not all of Dodge's forecasts were inaccurate: He acknowledged that farming this area might be difficult and said the region's splendid grass, pure water, and good shelter made it valuable for stock grazing. He also predicted the rise of tourism, saying, "the tourist will find an ample reward in climbing the rugged heights, or exploring the dark defiles of this wonderful land"; however, he didn't visualize neon signs and billboards in front of the beauty he enjoyed.

Plains Indians gathered at nearby Bear Butte Creek for important meetings. In 1857 the Lakota met to discuss how to resist the white advance, particularly into the Black Hills. One of the young warriors, Crazy Horse, probably conducted a vision quest here, a three- or four-day fast in search of a life-guiding vision. Though the Indian tribes could not keep whites off Bear Butte, they have regained the right to hold ceremonies there. The Cheyenne, who call the Butte *Nowawaste*, and the Lakota, to whom it is *Mato Paha*, often hold religious gatherings on or near the mountain, and some trails are closed to visitors because they lead to ceremonial sites. Strings of cloth tied with bundles of tobacco hang from trees, visible symbols of prayer. Indians frequently camp in the area, often conducting ceremonies or prayers; visitors should conduct themselves as they would in any church.

In 1945 and again in 1951, descendants of old Cheyenne leaders came to Bear Butte to pray for the ends of World War II and the Korean War, respectively. Many Sioux believed that two years before the Battle of the Little Bighorn, Custer had doomed himself and his men to death by ascending the butte during the 1874 Black Hills expedition; they also believed the suicide of William H. Illingworth, the expedition's official photographer, was part of the spirits' revenge.

PIEDMONT

Three of the four major pioneer routes to the gold camps of Deadwood led through Piedmont Valley: the Bismarck Trail from the northeast, the Fort Pierre Trail from the east, and the Sidney (Nebraska) Trail from the south. The Spring Valley Way Station, estab-

Firewood has always been plentiful in the Black Hills; some modern residents take advantage of this fact to get practical use from items that would be antiques elsewhere. Wood cookstoves, like the one in this drawing—used daily in Piedmont Valley—provide for heat as well as cooking. —Rose Mary Goodson

lished in 1876, hosted many travelers, as did the Piedmont Hotel, built in 1895. The Covered Wagon Resort, opened in the 1940s, was the state's first privately owned campground.

Capt. C. V. Gardner, one of the Spring Valley station's early owners, was among the first to send Black Hills goods to eastern markets. By the 1890s excursion trains to the northern Hills towns left from Spearfish, where the Homestake Mining Company's narrow-gauge Black Hills & Fort Pierre line linked with the Fremont, Elkhorn & Missouri Valley. South Dakota's first oil wells were sunk in Piedmont, but the quality was poor and they were eventually capped. Logs and lime were sent to Hills mines, and gypsum for building materials and calcium carbonate for animal feed were also mined nearby. Bethlehem and Stagebarn, and Crystal Cave, lure visitors to the area. The first fossil bones of a barosaurus, "heavy lizard," were found near Piedmont in 1889. The town's history has been best collected by John Honerkamp in *At the Foot of the Mountain.*

Along I-90 several miles north of Piedmont, boulders the size of small cars are scattered in fields. They were washed out of the deep canyons of the Black Hills to the west, probably in a mud flow. No one knows when the flood that moved them took place, but it must have been a monster, even greater than the floods of 1883, 1907, and 1972. Old-timers theorized such a flood might have exterminated the buffalo in the Black Hills in 1852; Lakota legends tell of a great flood in the 1850s, after a terrible winter during which snow piled thirty feet deep. Early pioneers wrote of finding stumps cut off nine feet above the ground and elk skulls lodged twenty-five feet high in a pine, evidence that might point to deep snow and a resulting flood.

As you drive past the rocks, consider the size and power of the flood that washed these massive rocks a mile out onto the flat prairie—then check the clouds. The 1972 Rapid City flood obliterated Canyon Lake Dam and killed 238 people, yet it still wasn't forceful enough to move rocks that large.

BLACK HAWK

Pierced in all directions by highways and rapidly being overwhelmed by Rapid City, Black Hawk has been busy since regular travel first began to the Black Hills. It was a prime camping spot for exploring expeditions. Its settlers were mostly Swedish immigrants who farmed and cut timber for the gold camps. The communal Black Hawk Threshing Company used a gas-powered Case engine to thresh grain from ninety farms from Box Elder Creek to Piedmont and sometimes as far east as Wall. The Dakota Plaster Mill processed

Pioneers cut hay on the site of Rapid City, which was first called Hay Camp. —Minnelusa Historical Museum

gypsum mined further up the valley. Bingo Bangs's Black Hawk Supper Club was a hot nightclub in the 1940s and hosted the Ink Spots and Nat King Cole before they became famous. After the 1972 Rapid City flood, Black Hawk experienced a housing boom when folks became uneasy about living beside creeks.

RAPID CITY

Lakota campfire ashes were still warm in the Paha Sapa on February 25, 1876, when the eleven founders of Rapid City camped on what the Sioux called "water swift creek." Their town has called itself "the gateway to the Black Hills" ever since. Around the campfire that night, John R. Brennan, Martin Persinger, Thomas Ferguson, W. P. Martin, Albert Brown, William Marston, J. W. Allen, James Carney, William Nuttal, Major Hutchinson, and surveyor Samuel Scott dreamed of the city they would build. Brennan carved his name on a sandstone cliff above the campsite, identified today by a marker. The men held a raffle, each drawing five times, to divide the center lots among themselves. The following day, the founders laid out a square mile for the town site. But Rapid City has since spilled well beyond that boundary. The original square mile can still be detected where some downtown streets bend abruptly, even though surveyors have corrected the plat to make streets run true north.

The settlement was called "Hay Town" or "The Hay Camp" because it supplied hay, among other needs, for the mining towns in the region. The fledgling town nearly went defunct in August 1876: Four men were killed in a fight with Indians just west of town, and when a wagon train left for Pierre the next day, most of the population went with it; barely a month after hearing the news about Custer on the Little Bighorn, their frayed nerves had not yet healed. Remaining residents built a two-story blockhouse, thirty feet square, at Fifth and Rapid streets. For a month, townspeople posted guards; some said they battled Indians almost every day as their food and ammunition stores dwindled. But the Indians rarely conducted a siege, and when the settlers finally ventured out, they found the warriors had gone.

A sawmill was in operation by 1876 and a gristmill by 1882. The Fremont, Elkhorn, & Missouri Valley Railroad reached town in 1886, to the delight of merchants, who no longer had to rely on ox teams to haul groceries. The line required more than a hundred trestles in the fifty miles it ran along Rapid Creek and was advertised as the "crookedest railroad in the world"—a statement with a double meaning that the railroad officials probably didn't appreciate. Profit was the name of the game during the gold rush days (cynics would say it still is). An enterprising man could buy a steer in Texas for $10, drive it to the Black Hills, butcher it, and sell it to gold miners for $125.

Rapid City: Rough and Raw

One of the most memorable of Rapid City's early events, though townspeople tried hard to forget it, was the 1877 vigilante hanging of three supposed horse thieves. The men, caught near Deadwood with horses stolen from the stage company, were jailed in Rapid City. During the night the jail was attacked, and the men were hanged on a high hill overlooking town by "unknown parties." Several days later, someone dug a grave and put a pine board over it, sporting some of the region's earliest, and worst, poetry:

HORSE THIEVES BEWARE:

Here lies the body of Allen, Curry and Hall.
Like other horse thieves they had their rise, decline and fall;
On yon pine tree they hung till dead,
And here they found a lonely bed.
Then be a little cautious how you gobble horses up,
For every horse you pick up here, adds sorrow to your cup;

*We're bound to stop this business, or hang you to a man,
For we've hemp and hands enough in town to swing the
whole damn clan.*

Most authorities now believe the youngest man hanged, only nineteen years old, was innocent; the other two prisoners said he had been hitchhiking and they offered him a ride. He died screaming curses and protestations. The prospect that they had hanged an innocent man, or perhaps the poetry inscribed on the headboard, rendered the citizens unwilling to discuss the hanging. The dead tree embedded in cement on Hangman's Hill is not the actual hanging tree—just a reminder to hitchhikers.

Happier memories of Rapid City's early days involve Alice Gossage, the first woman to work on a newspaper in South Dakota. She married Joseph Gossage in 1882, and from then on was active in the publication of the *Rapid City Journal*. In 1890, because of her

Alice Gossage married the publisher of the Rapid City Journal *and after his death took over publication. When she wasn't writing news, she provided clothing and food for the needy.*
—Carl Leedy, South Dakota School of Mines and Technology

Dora DuFran was one of the best-known madams in Deadwood, Lead, and Belle Fourche before moving her business to Rapid City. When she died in 1934, the local paper eulogized her humanitarian work.
—Dr. Leland Michael

husband's ill health, she assumed full responsibility for the paper. She handled circulation, wrote a daily column of local news, collected accounts, signed the payroll, and read proof on every edition and all the outside jobs printed. She also helped the needy, sang in the church choir, reported society events, worked as a volunteer nurse, helped direct the YWCA, and was an active member of the Women's Christian Temperance Union. Her sister, Laura Bower Van Nuys, later wrote *The Family Band*, bringing fame to the family name.

Another memorable Rapid City woman, Dora DuFran, ran brothels throughout the Black Hills. Her establishment on Coney Island in Rapid Creek thrived during the 1920s and 1930s. Many prominent city businessmen were marooned there when the bridge went out during a flood. When the sun rose and the water level began to drop, the men rolled up their pants legs and began wading back across the creek. On the opposite bank their wives waited—with rolling pins and umbrellas. Dora later wrote *The Low Down on Calamity Jane* under the name D. Dee. She is buried in Mount Moriah Cemetery in Deadwood with her husband and pet parrot.

Rapid City's most renowned cop was "Hooky Jack" Leary, a former hard-rock miner who blew off both hands while thawing dynamite on a stove. After he was fitted with hooks on both hands, he became the town's night policeman and held the job the rest of his life. His hiring might seem odd—Hooky Jack couldn't even fire a gun—but Rapid Citians took pride in assisting the crippled officer. If a stranger got rowdy and the night policeman couldn't control him, townspeople stepped in. When a group of prankish high school boys celebrating a football victory hung Hooky Jack by his hooks from a tree limb, the town reacted with fury. A delegation of cowboys from Ed Stenger's ranch near Hermosa dropped into town the next night, picked up the leaders of the plot, and spanked their naked bottoms in front of a raucous crowd at the Harney Hotel. No one ever embarrassed Hooky Jack again.

During the first half of the twentieth century, Rapid City's economy was busy and diverse. The state cement plant opened in Rapid City in 1925 and with the Warren-Lamb Lumber Company was one of the city's biggest employers. Leading industries included lumber milling, a flour mill, burial vaults, cigars—more than six thousand a day—and tin production. The Duhamel Brothers and Ackerman Hardware and Saddlery made about five hundred saddles and six hundred harness sets a year. A rancher's cooperative established a pork and lamb processing plant; as the Black Hills Packing Company, it is still in operation, though downtown businesses are beginning to complain about its odors. Modern commerce includes a particle board plant, several jewelry factories, and a credit card operation. An important economic boost is provided by Ellsworth Air Force Base, established in 1941 in a cornfield ten miles east of Rapid City; a museum near the main gate displays a variety of aircraft and is open to the public.

Tourism is now crucial to the local economy. President Calvin Coolidge's visit to the Black Hills in 1927 is often cited as the beginning of the region's tourist industry; reporters followed him everywhere, but his vacation adventures paled in comparison to the announcement by his local office in the Rapid City High School that he would not run for president in 1928. By the mid-1950s, tourism had become a prime objective of Rapid City planners. Today the community is particularly proud of its regional airport. The Rushmore Plaza Civic Center and a large hotel, a complex intended to draw conventions to the city, were built near Rapid Creek after the 1972 flood. The completion of Rushmore Mall, the Black Hills Regional Eye Institute, the City/School Administration Center, and the Wesleyan Health Care Center during the 1980s symbolize the town's economic progress to businessmen; however, older buildings downtown have slowly emptied of businesses. With a 1990s popula-

Dr. Valentine McGillycuddy was called to treat the wounds of Crazy Horse when he was shot at Fort Robinson, near Chadron, Nebraska. He also served as president of the South Dakota School of Mines and mayor of Rapid City.
—South Dakota State Historical Society

tion of about fifty-five thousand residents, Rapid City is South Dakota's second largest town.

The most devastating disaster in Rapid City's history was the flood of 1972. At least fifteen inches of rain fell and caused flash floods that killed 238 people and injured more than ten times that number. Five bodies were never found. Property damage totaled $165 million. The flood brought media attention to the former hay camp. When the mayor was interviewed for seventeen minutes on a major network talk show, he spent half his time describing the flood's horrors and the other half urging tourists to visit the state. As mayor of a tourist town, he couldn't resist free advertising, even though the subject of the interview was disaster.

The flood had positive effects besides media attention. It unified people in Rapid City and surrounding towns as volunteers rushed to save lives, clean up the mess, and rebuild. The flood also inspired a massive program to relocate poor Indian families who had camped along the creek for years; those who survived were helped to find housing on higher ground. City planners had known for years that the floodplain posed dangers to those who lived near it, but the prevailing attitude was that property owners had the right to do what they wanted. Building along the floodplain is now better regulated and urban renewal programs more firmly established. A series of bicycle and walking trails have been built through the entire town alongside the creek, both as a memorial to the dead and as a green zone for city dwellers. A complex including baseball and softball fields, outdoor tennis and racquetball courts, horseshoe pits, picnic shelters, and flower gardens were added to the enlarged Sioux Park. Storybook Island, a children's park destroyed in the flood, was moved and rebuilt.

The South Dakota School of Mines and Technology was established in Rapid City in 1885. Cash and residents are attracted by researchers' projects, which include studies of nuclear and solar energy, weather modification, building materials, robotics, mechanical aides for the disabled, and lunar soils. Eighteen percent of Tech's graduates stay in South Dakota, despite the fact that their starting salaries in-state will be several thousand dollars less than they could make elsewhere. Other educational institutions in the city include the business-oriented National College and Western Dakota Vo-Tech.

The Sioux Indian Museum, with a vast assemblage of Indian artifacts, is located downtown in Halley Park, as is the Minnelusa Pioneer Museum's pioneer gear exhibits. The collections have outgrown their space, and several others, including one amassed by Pete Duhamel, are not on display, so city officials have pledged to build a new museum.

PENNINGTON COUNTY

New Underwood, founded in 1906, was named for Johnny Underwood, who sold the right-of-way across his land for the right to christen the new town. Ranching has been the area's backbone for more than a hundred years. Texas-born George Moore settled nearby after all but fifty of the five thousand Texas longhorns he was herding died in Wyoming in the 1886 blizzard. He established a ranch at a spot eventually known as Elm Springs; his 160-acre tract, chosen two years before South Dakota statehood, now supports its fifth generation of ranchers.

Wasta was named by former state historian Doane Robinson from the Lakota word *waste* or *wastah*, meaning "good." At Wasta, I-90 dives into the vast and beautiful canyon of the Cheyenne, headed toward its confluence with the Belle Fourche, Elk Creek, and other

Doane Robinson, South Dakota's first state historian, suggested Gutzon Borglum carve something on a Black Hills mountain, and continued his faith in the Mount Rushmore project.
—South Dakota State Historical Society

notable Black Hills streams rolling east to swell the Missouri River. The broad plain is rich with cottonwoods, twisted and bleached white by the wind and floodwaters. A few homestead ruins lie along the banks. North of Wasta lie the remnants of old Camp Cheyenne, manned by five companies, two Hotchkiss guns, and a detachment of Indian scouts before the Messiah War and used as a base of operations for the army in the Wounded Knee massacre.

The Cheyenne River was named for the Cheyenne Indians, but each explorer had a unique interpretation of the spelling. Old Spanish maps show it as the Chyanne; Jean Truteau, in 1794, called it the Chaquiennes; Evans, in 1796, referred to it as the Shayenne; Perrin du Lac as the Chaquyene. Lewis and Clark, apparently misled, called it the Chien, which translates as "dog" in French. The second largest tributary of the Upper Missouri, after the mighty Yellowstone, the Cheyenne rises west of the Black Hills in Wyoming, curves around the southern end of the Hills, and angles northeast to its junction with the Missouri above Pierre. The southern length drains an area as large as Massachusetts, Rhode Island, and Connecticut combined, yet it still doesn't have enough water to float a canoe most of the year.

However, if the trickle of water is disappointing, passersby should note the width of the channel and the debris caught high in the old cottonwood trees along it. The Cheyenne was once a far more powerful river—early stockmen recall swimming their horses across it. Reservoirs, thousands of stock dams, and irrigation now limit its flow.

WALL

Founded in 1907, the town was named for the high "wall" of the Badlands, beautiful but dangerous, as Corb Morse discovered. One of the early cattlemen of the region, Morse had a ranch near Wall and a couple more on the White River. He was a leader in importing blooded stock, and his Wall herd, his proudest possession, included ten thousand head of registered white-faced Herefords. A photograph of the herd hung on the wall of the International Hotel in Rapid City, where cattlemen gathered to socialize. Morse spent a lot of time in the hotel, talking to other ranchers and giving orders to his cowhands.

One cold November night Corb rode horseback to the hotel from his place east of town; he put the horse in the livery barn across from the hotel and got lost crossing the street in the blizzard. "It's a hell of a night for a cow to be out without a fur overcoat," he remarked over a hot toddy. Morse planned to ride a snowplow to Buffalo Gap about midnight to look over some cattle the next day. Just as he came out of the dining room, ready for his snowplow ride, a half-frozen cowboy stumbled in the doors of the hotel, clutching his snow-crusted hat.

"They're all gone, Corb," he gasped. "All of them!" Every one of the ten thousand beautiful Herefords had fallen over the cliff at Big Foot Pass in the blizzard, while the cowboys struggled to turn the herd. About $500,000 worth of blue-blooded cattle was now a pile of chilling beef. Suddenly Corb Morse was no longer a big cattleman, just a man nearly broke. His expression didn't change. "Well," he said, "Easy come, easy go."

That, say the men who saw him, was the spirit of the West, and especially the spirit of the rancher: A brave man must not show his feelings in public.

Wall Drug

Wall has less than a thousand residents, but it is known worldwide for Wall Drug, the "ice water store." You may see signs advertising this establishment anywhere: During the Second World War, soldiers put them up on Pacific islands; they're on subway trains in London, beside a canal in Amsterdam, and even in the outback of Australia, usually with fanciful estimates of the distance.

Pharmacist Ted Hustead opened the store in 1931 with his wife, Dorothy. By 1936, in the midst of the Great Depression, with farm prices low and widespread drought choking their business, they feared they had made a terrible mistake. Three-quarters of all land in the area had been repossessed by the county because the taxes weren't paid, and most ranchers worked for New Deal agencies such as the Works Progress Administration for wages. Ted gave up his car to keep the business going, and his family took up residence in part of the store. Farmers and ranchers could barely afford essentials like medicine; they certainly couldn't buy ice cream. And the Husteads couldn't afford to advertise.

Then Dorothy got an idea that made the enterprise famous. They started offering free drinks of ice water to hot, thirsty travelers. She began composing jingles, and Ted started painting signs and putting them up along local roadways. The next summer, they had to hire eight local women to keep up with business. Ted installed a cistern and hauled water. To motorists crossing the dusty Plains, the crude log building became a haven; the simple gesture attracted customers by the millions.

Today the store is a fascinating maze of shining pine hallways leading to rooms full of souvenirs, clothes, knickknacks, rocks, and antiques. Old-timers drink coffee—still a nickel a cup—and eat homemade pie under displays of Indian crafts and local brands. A bar top is embedded with silver dollars. Animated cowboy singers and an orchestra entertain at the drop of a quarter. Life-sized carvings of western characters stand everywhere, along with stuffed "jackalope," the mythical hybrid of a jack rabbit and an antelope. The Wall Drug bookstore is one of the state's best, specializing in titles on regional history, wildlife, and plants. The store's collection of western art is world famous, and visitors can view historical photos in the backyard. The Hustead family still runs the place, and it hasn't turned its back on the tradition that brought it success: You can still get free ice water.

Vanishing Trails

In 1960, Leonel Jensen, a Wall rancher, and Will Robinson, secretary of the South Dakota State Historical Society, began a series of motorized trips to historical areas in the neighborhood of Wall.

Hundreds of people—some former residents or descendants, some tourists—have battered car tires on these informal and entertaining trips. Sometimes only the memories of old-timers had preserved the sites before the trips began; now many are accessible and marked with signs.

Jensen and Robinson's first trip was to Harney Springs, where Lt. G. K. Warren wrote one of the first descriptions of the Badlands in 1855. Warren's daughter Emily met Buffalo Robe, son of a Sioux Chief who had spoken to the lieutenant on the same spot 105 years before. The second expedition went to Peno Springs and Smith Crossing, north of Wall, stations on the old Fort Pierre-to-Deadwood freight route. Other excursions went to the Indian stronghold on Cuny Table, where Indians took refuge before the Wounded Knee massacre. In 1964 the history buffs followed Big Foot's trail through Big Foot Pass, Potato Creek, Kyle, and Porcupine Butte to the site of the massacre. In 1965 the group went to Conata, a town that thrived in the 1900s in spite of the townspeople's refusal to sell hard liquor, and Sheep Mountain Table, where a ranch perched 3,200 feet above sea level, atop the huge butte. Harvested hay was pushed down a natural chute in the butte's eroded side to buyers in the valley below.

BADLANDS NATIONAL PARK

South Dakota leaders lobbied many years for the creation of Badlands National Park. Congress first responded in 1929, when it established Badlands National Monument and Calvin Coolidge signed the legislation into law. Ten years later Franklin D. Roosevelt proclaimed the monument a national park, but Congress did not concede the new status until 1978, two years after land from a former military gunnery range was added, more than doubling the park's size to a total of 243,302 acres.

The Pinnacles entrance to the Badlands is eight miles south of Wall on SD 240. From there, paved or improved roads lead northwest to the Sage Creek primitive campground and a scenic rimrock road. From this route you can head south to Scenic and take the turnoff for Sheep Mountain Table, one of the most startling sections of the Badlands.

Another entrance to the Badlands lies twenty miles southeast of Wall near Cactus Flat. A half mile north of this entrance is Prairie Homestead, the intact early-day dwelling of Edgar I. Brown. At the age of fifty-five, he built the dirt-roofed structure for his wife, Alice, and son, Charles. A homesteader in the Badlands could secure title

The Prairie Homestead in the Badlands is so well preserved that it can be visited by modern travelers. —Rose Mary Goodson

to a 160-acre claim by living on it for eighteen months, plowing and planting at least five acres, and paying fifty cents an acre, or a total of $80.

Cedar Pass, headquarters of the Badlands National Park, is eight miles south of the Cactus Flat entrance. Cedar Pass Lodge is operated by the Oglala Sioux Tribe and offers rooms, informative programs by National Park rangers, a dining room, a fudge shop, and Indian arts and crafts as well as traditional souvenirs. Three short hiking trails are available near Cedar Pass: Door Trail, less than a mile long; Cliff Shelf Nature Trail, a half-mile paved loop; and Fossil Exhibit Trail, five miles west of the visitor center.

The Badlands Loop between Wall and Kadoka on SD 240 gives a good look at the scenery and access to several old and intriguing communities on the Pine Ridge Indian Reservation south of the interstate. Temperatures in the Badlands can still boil the mercury in your thermometer, so rangers suggest that you take plenty of water with you on hikes and inform the visitor center if you plan to leave marked trails. However, exploring the Badlands in more detail is worth the effort. Geologically, they are like a textbook illustrating the earth's creation, and their living wildlife is fascinating. Wear boots—the wildlife includes rattlesnakes.

Wyoming–Shannon County
99 Miles

US 18 arches generally east-west from the Wyoming state line through Edgemont, Hot Springs, and Oelrichs to Oglala, where it enters the territory covered in the section on western South Dakota.

FALL RIVER COUNTY

Edgemont, named for its position at the edge of the mountains, began its growth about 1891 when the railroad arrived. By that time E. W. Whitcomb had been ranching in the area for thirteen years.

These petroglyphs and pictographs were copied from several sites near Edgemont. If you locate them there, please do not touch or disturb them; they are fragile, and the sandstone on which they were placed thousands of years ago is crumbling.

Local builders—inspired by sandstone deposits in the southern end of the Black Hills—created a city called Cascade south of Hot Springs along a route some believed the railroad would take. The tracks reached Hot Springs instead and most of the buildings were torn down, including this sanitarium. —Helen Magee Collection

After his marriage to an Indian, he established the Bar T Ranch on Hat Creek about fifteen miles south of Edgemont and built his herd to about fifteen thousand head before selling out to the Anglo-American Cattle Company. Later he was involved in the Johnson County range war in Wyoming, joining other big ranchers against settlers. In his old age, he was found dead near the Upper Belle Fourche River; the cause of death was officially listed as "struck by lightning," but there were no witnesses. An old western joke tells of a man who called his rifle "Lightning," which may account for the verdict. Range wars were no joke in this country, and violence wasn't confined to the movies.

The name of Hat Creek, which joins the Cheyenne River east of Edgemont, is perhaps a punning white translation of the Indian name: Warbonnet Creek. The country southwest of Edgemont, before the highway climbs into the Black Hills, is more deeply eroded than the Plains, with sharper embankments and lighter, more gravelly soils. To the casual observer it can look barren, but, like the Badlands to the northeast, it keeps secret water holes for the native antelope, deer, coyotes, and smaller mammals.

Seven miles south of Edgemont is Igloo, officially dead for decades now but the site of much recent controversy. The story begins with the federal government searching for an ammunition storage and shipping site during World War II, before Igloo existed. The site had to be isolated from population centers in case of explosion, dry enough to retard deterioration of the ordnance, and near rail lines. The region south of Edgemont at first appeared unsuitable because it had no electricity. Congressman Francis Case of Custer, first elected to the U.S. House of Representatives in 1936 and later elected to the U.S. Senate, sought workers from the nearby Pine Ridge and Rosebud reservations and encouraged local power companies and rural electric officials to provide power.

Late in 1941 Congress chose Provo as the site of the Black Hills Ordnance Depot; at that time, the town had twenty residents, six houses, one store, and no electricity or running water. It became a boomtown as workers arrived; within seven months the population mushroomed to a thousand, and workers had to sleep in cars and tents. During 1942, as construction of government buildings, workshops, and the utilities plant continued, permanent employees asked permission to build accommodations for other services, such as homes, schools, and a hospital. The first ammunition arrived in 1942, and the following year a government housing project helped five hundred families move onto the depot grounds. Workers built a new high school and named the sports team the Rattlers, after the resident snakes, which were probably getting grouchy about all the human activity. Private businesses permitted to operate on the depot included a store, a gas station, a restaurant, a bowling alley, and a barber shop. The local population soon exceeded four thousand, and residents decided the community needed a name. A fourteen-year-old boy suggested "Igloo" because of the shape of the ammunition storage buildings.

After the war, workers drifted away; by 1950 only about seven hundred people remained. But U.S. involvement in Korea revived the depot, and by 1956 Igloo's population shot back to about twenty-five hundred. But the town lived on Defense Department appropriations, and cutbacks on government spending in 1964 doomed Igloo. Residents have since tried to revitalize the area with such ideas as building a state penitentiary, establishing a military training site, or installing Bureau of Indian Affairs offices. A Texas cattleman started a feedlot, but it closed in 1974. A railroad car repair facility closed in 1978. A proposal to use the site as a national low-level nuclear waste dump was overwhelmingly defeated in 1985 by a statewide referendum. A waste company convinced the state that

The Soldiers' Home built at the west end of Minnekahta Aven in 1889 was the firs major sandstone building in Hot Spr
—South Dakota State Historical Society

gold could be extracted from sewage ash and promised to pay $9 million to dump nearly three hundred thousand tons of the material from St. Paul, Minnesota. The ash was dumped, but the company defaulted, and the state was stuck with the bill for burying the ash that hadn't blown away during the controversy. In 1989 South Dakota approved a permit for an out-of-state company to bury bales of municipal garbage for Igloo in what became the "Lonetree Balefill," named for the single tree growing in the region. Environmental groups defeated the plan in 1993.

HOT SPRINGS

Indians frequently camped at Minne-kahta, or "warm waters." Tradition insists that even war parties were obliged to behave peacefully there, because it was used by so many tribes. One of the first whites to visit the warm springs was Col. W. J. Thornby. As a reporter for the *Deadwood Pioneer-Times* in 1879, he took a horseback ride with professor Walter Jenney, the geologist who led an expedition to the Black Hills in 1875. They followed the warm river to its source, where Thornby chopped the top out of a cedar sapling and wrote his name on the trunk in lead pencil with the notation, "This is my spring."

Not long afterward, Thornby dropped by to find two tough-looking men, Joe Larive and John Davidson, building a log cabin. Badger Clark, later poet laureate of South Dakota, says in *When Hot Springs Was a Pup* that when the two announced they were going to "jump his claim," Thornby gave it to them; it was probably a wise choice under the circumstances. Some say Dr. Valentine McGillycuddy, with the Jenney expedition as a mapmaker and surgeon, had already stumbled upon the bubbling thermal bathtub in 1875. The claim is probably true—he was in the area.

When white settlers began arriving in 1879, they gave names to individual springs. Cascade Springs lies two miles north of the Cheyenne River and is still a favorite swimming hole; Catholican Springs supplied a large Catholic sanitarium; Lakota Springs was named in honor of the original owners; Mineral Springs is descriptive of the water. Mammoth Spring was named because it is the largest in the Black Hills, flowing at ten thousand gallons an hour; now that mammoth fossils have been discovered here, the name seems even more appropriate.

A man named Joe Brimdschmidt once traded these springs to Joe Petty for a horse worth $35, but as soon as the new settlers discovered that towns in the sophisticated East were advertising themselves as "health spas," Hot Springs caught on to the possibilities. City fathers published brochures claiming miraculous cures. A 1901 edition promises that the waters will cure rheumatism, kidney disease, urinary problems, stomach intestinal disorders, skin diseases, asthma, tuberculosis, paralysis, nervous prostration, liver complaint, gout, syphilis, chronic diarrhea, habitual constipation, and, in case they'd left anything out, "other kindred disorders." Patients both drank and bathed in the water, and bathhouses and business flourished. After 1891 customers disembarked at the Union Depot, "the smallest Union Depot station in the world," serving both the Elkhorn

"The smallest Union Depot station in the world" was built in Hot Springs in 1891. —South Dakota State Historical Society

Fred Evans owned the largest freighting business in South Dakota. He used bulls to pull his wagons; ox teams are always steers. Carl Leedy, a pioneer in Rapid City, said this photo shows Evans last bull train about 1887. —Minnelusa Historical Museum

and Burlington railroads. The depot closed in 1938 and now houses the Chamber of Commerce.

Hot Springs originally sprawled over "seven hills and valleys," according to an engineer's report that reads like a promotion piece and may lean too heavily on myth. A natural amphitheater in the southern Black Hills is enclosed on the south by the Sawtooth or Seven Sisters Range, with Battle Mountain on the east and lower pine-covered hills on the west and north. Hot Brook and Cold Brook unite to make Fall River, which flows through town and joins the Cheyenne River several miles south.

The canyon is five hundred feet deep in places, its walls vivid with gray and pink Minnekahta limestone, purple shale, and red and yellow Minnelusa sandstone. All these colors and more are visible in the distinctive Victorian buildings downtown; look for the face surrounded with leaves on the Petty Building. The town has been called "a gallery of architectural art," and self-guided walking tours are popular. The Miss South Dakota Pageant is held here yearly in June, along with an arts and crafts festival.

Fred Evans, one of the Black Hills' most colorful immigrants, saw the possibilities of Hot Springs early. He'd already had a successful career as a freighter, beginning about 1875. The Evans Transportation Company was the largest in the West, hauling twelve million

The Minnekahta Block, built in 1891 by Fred Evans, was one of the largest and most ornate sandstone buildings in Hot Springs. —South Dakota State Historical Society

pounds of freight, mostly between Fort Pierre and the Black Hills, during the dozen years it existed. Fellow bullwhackers claimed Evans could "swear an ox's horn off in two minutes." Once, when Evans used every word in his vocabulary trying to get a team to pull a wagon out of a mud hole, a preacher chastised him for his profanities. Evans patiently explained that the team didn't understand anything else and that, by the way, his work was a lot harder than the minister's job of getting souls to heaven. In fact, Evans declared, he'd give the preacher $1,000 if he could drive one yoke of oxen for one day without cussing. The offer was declined.

Evans was one of the first to observe the medicinal properties of the springs and to recognize their money-making possibilities. He built the Minnekahta Hotel and, after it burned, the Evans Hotel and Evans Plunge, both still standing despite later fires. He was generous, donating land for every church in town—perhaps a little insurance after his confrontation with the preacher—and he also provided land for the Soldiers' Home. After a typhoid epidemic caused by impure water, he paid for a new water system and later a city band and baseball team.

WIND CAVE NATIONAL PARK

Wind Cave was discovered in 1882. Badger Clark says, "like the Springs themselves, the Cave is likely to have been discovered several times." Of course, the Sioux knew of it, and several legends concern the noises it makes. Doc Pierce, an early pioneer and supreme storyteller, said Cornelius Donahue had discovered it in 1877 and used it as a hideout when he was better known as Lame Johnny. Donahue was later hanged for stealing horses, but that's another story—and another highway (SD 79).

Perhaps because of Lame Johnny's poor reputation, two other men are given credit for the official discovery of the cave. Jess and Tom Bingham were attracted to the cave by its habit of breathing in and out. Understandably unnerved by the sound of giant gasping breaths in an isolated canyon, the two young men galloped back to town to spread the news, and a new tourist institution was born. Before long, regular social expeditions were made to the cave; courting couples were suspected of getting lost on purpose. With nearly sixty miles of mapped passages and explorers adding a few more each year, the cave is turning out to be one of the largest in the world. Spelunkers suspect it is connected with Jewel Cave. Both caves are stunning in their beauty, with many types of intricately built crystals from the water flowing through the cave's limestone formations. Tours include easy ones that nearly anyone can take and more strenuous tours to the cave's natural entrance, as well as a strenuous candlelight climb. Some spelunking tours require a hard hat for off-trail crawling.

In 1903 Theodore Roosevelt, with a little help from Congress, created Wind Cave National Park, more than ten thousand acres roamed by buffalo, antelope, elk, and other wild native species.

The Morris Grand Theater, with its impressive stone arch, was built in Hot Springs in 1911 and advertised as the "Grandest Little Theater in the Whole Northwest." —South Dakota State Historical Society

Prehistoric Bones

In 1974 some of the very earliest history of the region was discovered: the remains of dozens of mammoths and other prehistoric creatures who died in the Pleistocene era, about twenty-six thousand years ago. During construction of a housing development on the south edge of Hot Springs, workers found a large bone and called in experts from Nebraska's Chadron State College, who discovered a concentration of mammoth bones. Eventually, a nonprofit corporation was formed to fund excavation and allow visitors to watch its progress. Most of the bones found so far are from *Mammuthus columbi*, commonly known as the Columbian mammoth, a warm-climate counterpart of the wooly mammoth that lived in Arctic regions. The creatures stood fourteen feet high at the shoulder and weighed ten tons.

Today Earthwatch volunteers dig each summer. Bones of a giant short-faced bear, peccary, prehistoric camels, coyotes, and a carnivorous bird have also been found. Dr. Larry Agenbroad, who has supervised excavation, says in *Mammoth Site of Hot Springs, South Dakota*, that the creatures may have tried to drink at a sinkhole with steep sides and became trapped, unable to climb out again. The well-marked visitor center, just off US 18 on the west side of town, invites tourists to stop and watch the excavation in progress.

OELRICHS

By 1882 about a hundred thousand Texas cattle a year were being trailed to the Black Hills; one Rapid City banker paid $60,000 for incoming stock. In that year, Harry Oelrichs, a New Yorker, came to the region as representative of an English syndicate and bought several ranches, including the TOT, the TAN, and the Bar T. He incorporated all of his acquisitions as the Anglo-American Cattle Company. When a town was founded in 1885, it was naturally named for him. For a time, Oelrichs and Hot Springs held the usual debate over which would be the county seat, with accusations of illegality on both sides.

In 1888 Oelrichs established a packing house with a spur to the railroad tracks so his Anglo-American Cattle Company could more easily supply retail meat markets with beef and pork. Bob Lee says in *Last Grass Frontier* that a feud developed between butchers in Oelrichs and those in other Black Hills towns who accused the "foreign" corporation of trying to monopolize business. A Rapid City butcher said the English company didn't feed its stock corn and called it "a big, rich English company" that lined the pockets of its rich

Horses hitched to buggies in 1901 stand outside the Hot Springs establishment now known as Evans Plunge.
—South Dakota State Historical Society

members with money, leaving none for the development of the Black Hills. Oelrichs accused small Wyoming stockmen and farmers of wantonly shooting his stock. The feud simmered down after Oelrichs fell ill and left the West.

US 14/14A
Spearfish—Sturgis
67 Miles

US 14 is part of I-90, the direct route from Spearfish to Sturgis. US 14A (Alternate 14) makes a wide loop through Spearfish Canyon to Cheyenne Crossing, then back through Lead and Deadwood and down Boulder Canyon to Sturgis.

SPEARFISH CANYON

The drive through Spearfish Canyon is beautiful at any time, spectacular when autumn frosts turn the leaves a rainbow of colors. The upper portion of the canyon is comparatively shallow, wide, and sunlit, but as the rock walls rise, the sun strikes the road only briefly during the day. Visible in the walls is the Deadwood formation, composed of sandstone shading from gray to red, greenish shale, and limestone.

In 1887, when the Black Hills interested white folks primarily as a source of gold, two men took a water right on Little Spearfish Creek and built a ditch and flume nine miles long to take water for placer mining to Iron Creek. Later, the Buckeye Placer Mining Company took over the flume, but it was a costly and ultimately unsuccessful gold-mining method. Traces of the flume and the iron cables from which it was suspended can be seen high on the walls of Spearfish Canyon in several places; energetic and skilled hikers can reach it, but careless ones have been killed or injured climbing in the canyon.

By 1910 citizens of Spearfish were beginning to realize that the beauty of the canyon and the area around it might be a financial asset. The city's businessmen formed a commercial club and began working to attract visitors to enjoy Spearfish Canyon's beauty, reasoning that in the long run the canyon would be more valuable if it

U.S. Marshal Seth Bullock brought law to the lively gold camp of Deadwood. He never killed anyone. —South Dakota State Historical Society

were preserved than if it were mined. About a hundred volunteers built the first road up the canyon, and Spearfish began to advertise the area almost as if the town owned it. Hunters also found beauty and game in the canyon, including Theodore Roosevelt and his sons, who often hunted with Seth Bullock, one of Deadwood's best-known peace officers.

When Bullock was appointed a deputy U.S. marshal, he invested in mining and ranching. In *South Dakota Leaders*, Dr. David B. Miller quotes Charles C. Haas, who ranched near Whitewood, as saying that Bullock not only obtained the land by illegally "squatting" on it but also did so by proxy. The land had not been surveyed, nor was it available to anyone but homesteaders willing to take it 160 acres at a time. Beginning in 1878, Bullock, like many big cattlemen of the time, paid ranch hands to file for homesteads on the land he wanted. He furnished the money to construct buildings and stock the land and paid his employees to remain there until they made final proof on the homestead; then they turned it over to the rancher. Bullock, said Haas, spent only a small part of his time at his ranch.

Still, he experimented with selective cattle and horse breeding on his S-B Outfit and introduced alfalfa—"perhaps the first ever grown on the Northern Great Plains"—brought from Utah, where farmers called it "Lucerne."

When the United States went to war with Spain in 1898, Bullock was fifty years old. He managed to get his physical deficiencies waived and raised a company that went to Georgia, but the war was over before they could leave for Cuba. Bullock didn't let this stop him from assuming the title of "Captain," which he used the rest of his life.

Later he became supervisor of the Black Hills Timberland Reserve, which he saw transformed into the Black Hills National Forest. Before he would take the post, he asked for four concessions: to report only to the Washington office; to hire local people who knew the Black Hills; to be allowed administrative staff sufficient to process applications and permits at the local level; and to have local authority to authorize small timber sales. He didn't get the latter compromise, but the other requests were granted.

During his tenure, he helped make Devil's Tower in Wyoming the first landmark to be designated a national monument and later helped secure the same status for Jewel Cave. He probably was involved in establishing Custer State Park in 1912, according to Miller. When political pressure grew to open forest reserve meadowlands to homesteading, Bullock quit as forest supervisor and returned to law enforcement. He was appointed U.S. marshal in Sioux Falls in 1906.

Bullock's friendship with Theodore Roosevelt brought him considerable influence. The two had met sometime between 1884 and 1893. Roosevelt said they met on the trail from his ranch at Medora when Bullock, in his capacity as U.S. marshal, confronted Roosevelt's party because he suspected they were a "tin-horn gambling outfit." As vice president, Roosevelt helped Bullock become forest supervisor. When Roosevelt was inaugurated to his second term as president in 1905, Bullock took fifty cowboys from the Dakotas, Wyoming, Montana, and Nebraska, complete with loaded pistols, to the parade. President Roosevelt often corresponded with Bullock on politics, and the families of the two men became close. The president's children, cousins, and friends came annually to Deadwood to hunt and fish with Bullock, who helped Roosevelt's Bull Moose candidacy in the presidential election of 1912.

When the United States entered World War I in 1917, Roosevelt asked Bullock to form a division of twelve hundred cowboys, railroaders, and miners from the Black Hills and surrounding regions, a unit similar to Roosevelt's own Rough Riders. However, President Woodrow Wilson declined to accept the volunteers, so Bullock worked for the Red Cross instead and tried to persuade Governor Peter Norbeck to locate the state cement plant at Deadwood instead of Rapid City. After Roosevelt died in 1919, Bullock worked to create a monument for him on Sheep Mountain in the Black Hills, renamed "Mount Theodore Roosevelt." Bullock died on September 23, 1919, before he could get parts of Spearfish Canyon dedicated as the Theodore Roosevelt Bird and Wildlife Sanctuary. He is buried above Mount Moriah Cemetery, on a plot he donated to Deadwood, with a view of Mount Theodore Roosevelt.

Bridal Veil and Spearfish Falls

When Lt. Col. Richard Dodge first saw Spearfish Creek and the canyon it had cut in 1876, he described it vividly in *The Black Hills* as "rising with a bound from the earth" and rolling "purer, colder, clearer, softer, deeper, and much more rapid" than other streams in the Hills, "rushing between its banks with the force of a cataract." Many Black Hills creeks he observed disappeared underground; this one cut a canyon of "not less than two thousand feet in depth."

As soon as the first miner diverted water for a flume, the character of the creek was changed. The Homestake Mining Company is primarily responsible for transforming the torrent of early days into today's tame trickle. Homestake's water rights date from early riparian and vested rights, and the company diverts much of the flow

From a special excursion train, passengers could look sixty feet down Spearfish Falls. Brave ones are standing on the old trestle, which shook from the water's force. —Centennial Archives, Deadwood

for domestic use in Lead and Deadwood, for electricity generation, or for mining. These uses amounted to six thousand gallons per minute in 1990. Homestake officials say less than half of the total diversion was caused by mining; the city of Spearfish uses between seven hundred and twelve hundred gallons per minute. Several irrigation ditches below Spearfish also use water from the creek. South Dakota law allows total appropriation of a stream and does not provide protection for stream flow or for fishing rights, so Spearfish Creek might eventually dry up, though area residents are working to protect the stream for its beauty, fishing, and historical and cultural importance.

Bridal Veil Falls is slowly diminishing as Hills stream flows are decreased by drought, overuse, and an abundance of trees. Spearfish Falls was once the biggest in the Hills and a highlight for those who rode special excursion trains through Spearfish Canyon. Halted on a trestle that shook from the water's force, train passengers looked sixty feet down the cataract. The excursion train's tracks curved 375 times in about thirty linear miles from Deadwood to Spearfish. The round-trip cost $2.40, and the crew was happy to let fishing enthusiasts, berry pickers, or picnic parties off anywhere along the creek in the morning, and pick them up in the evening.

Spearfish Falls is now dry most of the time, because in 1917 Homestake Mining Company diverted all the waters of Little Spearfish Creek into a hydroelectric pipeline. In the incredibly dry summer of 1988, the company released enough water to make the falls flow for a few days; local residents and tourists drove miles to witness the rare sight.

OLD MINING TOWNS

Though the canyon of today hums with tourist traffic, it is likely that fewer people actually live in it now than at any time in its history. During the early days of gold mining, the WYOD, Tuesday, King, Dividend, Shugar, Star, Old Ironsides, and OK mines were located near Maurice. None of them made much mining history, though the Old Ironsides did ship ore to Denver. Part of a flight of eight hundred wooden steps leading to the Homestake hydroelectric plant may still be visible, though they are far too rickety to be climbed. The persistent hiker may find traces of other once-populous mining camps everywhere; the ghosts of Moskee, Preston, Mineral Hill, Nugget City, Victoria, Flatiron, Astoria, and Carbonate—where silver was mined—are all in or near the canyon.

More gold-mining settlements were located up among the ridges west of Spearfish Canyon. At Tinton, the richest mining area became known as "Nigger Hill" and retains that name in spite of the efforts of embarrassed citizens to change it. The diggings there were worked successfully by a group of black miners who avoided the saloons and gambling joints and actually got the gold out of the Hills, unlike most miners. The creeks draining from the hill—Iron, Potato, Beaver, and Bear—were thoroughly prospected at various times, and the gold mentioned by the Thoen Stone (if the story is true) probably originated on one of those drainages.

Savoy may have been named for a French region bordering Switzerland by a homesick Frenchman who saw a resemblance to his native soil in the rough limestone cliffs hung with vines, trees, and flowers. The Lepke-McLaughlin Sawmill, owned by the Tie and Timber Company, was built here in 1892. The small building used for the company office became the first room of the Latchstring Inn; visitors as recently as 1989 could see the marks of a handsaw in the six-inch timbers in the floor. The inn, a popular place for tourists to dine and stay overnight, was a living museum; its massive stone fireplace warmed generations of hikers, gold seekers, and others who enjoyed dozing in front of it or having a drink in the tiny bar nearby. The dining room was perched on the cliff edge so it seemed to hang in space, and one could dreamily sip coffee for hours watching birds cruise the air currents up and down the two-thousand-foot canyon walls. The scarred logs of the interior walls had seen as much history as the region offers, and hundreds of people had lurched down the narrow halls, known as "Hard Boiled Alley," on uneven floors to cozy rooms and an unparalleled view of the canyon walls at sunrise and sunset. Displays in the "museum room" included a spinning wheel dated at 1840, an iron-bound, handmade chest for gold, a lady's sidesaddle, gold weighing scales, Civil War-era guns, pottery candle molds, and a wool carder dated 1826. Scattered on the grounds among sunny openings were ancient trees that provided deep shade on the hottest day for venerable log cabins rented by hunters and fishermen.

The Latchstring was living, vibrating history, a building that even by its silence told much of the history of the Hills. Even taking it apart carefully and excavating its site might have given us clues to the daily life of the canyon's first courageous residents. The Homestake Mining Company bulldozed the building over citizens' protests in 1990, saying modern technology could not save it. Now a visitor center made of shiny yellow logs preserves a few artifacts saved from the rubble.

Roughlock Falls

On a narrow gravel road beyond the former site of the Latchstring is one reason people came to it: Roughlock Falls. The named refers to the only method of braking a wagon on these steep downhill grades—chaining the wagon wheels together, called a "roughlock." Even if the teamsters prayed instead of using their normal profanity, the brake didn't often work; old-timers tell stories of spectacular wagon wrecks.

Visitors can walk along a trail overlooking Roughlock Falls, then continue on to look up at the falls from the middle of the creek, as this photographer did. Watch for the elusive water ouzel.
—South Dakota Department of Tourism

358

A short path with footbridges over three branches of the creek leads to the falls; though the drop is only about thirty feet, the spot is one of the most beautiful in the Hills. The paths are fragrant with chamomile, which grows despite the heavy foot traffic, and dippers, or water ouzels, nest in the walls and hunt bugs in the spray. If you see a small bird that bobs up and down on a rock and then seems to tumble into the water, don't plunge in to save it; that's a dipper. If you watch closely, you'll see him strolling nonchalantly along the stream bottom, gulping aquatic life before he finally comes up for air.

One of the strangest characters of the neighborhood was Potato Creek Johnny Perrett, who has been adopted—or stolen—by Deadwood to add to its gallery of eccentrics. John Perrett was born in Wales in 1867 and drifted through the northwest into the Black Hills, where he built a cabin on Potato Creek. Fame found him late in life when he supposedly panned the largest nugget ever found in the Hills, later sold to W. E. Adams of Deadwood for $250; the stone, alas, is now lost. Stories persist that he constructed his find by melting several nuggets together. Johnny became Deadwood's pet,

Potato Creek Johnny may have panned the largest gold nugget ever found in the Black Hills.
—South Dakota Department of Tourism

played his fiddle on its street, posed for photographs, let his hair grow, and played at being a genial prospector for tourists. One old-timer recalled stopping to visit Johnny and his wife, Maude; it was lunchtime, and she served nothing but a huge bowl of lettuce, which they ate with sugar. People remember Johnny as likeable; store-keeper Nels Brakke of Spearfish often filled his order for flour, beans, bacon, and other staples, then tore up the bill, which Johnny couldn't pay anyway.

Another colorful early prospector was Jim Timan, a bartender in Deadwood. According to H. A. Smith in *Latchstring Inn*, Timan married and set up housekeeping with his new bride. The couple planned a honeymoon trip, and Jim set out for the saloon to pick up his guitar and say a round of goodbyes. One goodbye led to another, and before long Jim was filled with good will and whiskey. He noticed a train going by, and in a freight car saw a load of furniture that looked exactly like what he'd bought for his bride. He marveled at the

The Borglum Memorial Highway, SD 244, offers alert motorists this profile view of George Washington. A tiny gravel apron allows room to pull off the highway, if you're quick. Don't try to climb up for a closer look; rangers frown on the practice, fearing vandalism as well as injury to climbers.
—South Dakota Department of Tourism

coincidence but knew she was waiting patiently at home for him. Finally, he staggered in that direction. Unfortunately, his bride and the furniture had gone back to her mother—on the train.

US 16 (or US 16/16A)
Custer–Rapid City
36 Miles (or 54 Miles)
SD 244, Mount Rushmore, 14 Miles
SD 87 (Needles Highway), 14 Miles

US 16 in South Dakota runs only between the Wyoming border and Rapid City (beyond which it becomes I-90). The highway divides at Custer, with the main route briefly joining US 385 and heading north until it again turns east beyond Hill City, then it skirts the northern boundary of Mt. Rushmore National Memorial and continues on into Rapid City as Rushmore Road; US 16A (alternate route) heads east out of Custer, enters Custer State Park, then turns north and rejoins US 16 thirty-six miles later just north of Keystone. SD 244 connects US 16 and US 16A and leads only to Mount Rushmore National Memorial. SD 87 also connects US 16 and US 16A via the Needles Highway, which is closed in winter but provides a beautiful drive through the northwestern portion of Custer State Park.

ROCKERVILLE

One of the richest gold deposits in history was found near Rockerville, twelve miles southwest of Rapid City—as usual, by accident. William Keeler drove a string of burros from Sheridan, a town now under Sheridan Lake, to Rapid City. Bedding down near in a dry gulch, he found the ground too rocky for comfort. While he squirmed and tried to get comfortable, he looked at rocks under him and found that gold—not for the first or the last time in human history—was causing his discomfort.

Rockerville was originally called Captain Jack's Dry Diggins after Captain Jack Crawford, "the poet scout" who worked for Custer and spouted lengthy rhymed verses both before and after he learned to write. The gold deposits in the gulch, six miles long, were nearly as rich as Deadwood's, but water was so scarce placer mining didn't work well. Rockerville miners had to do most of their work in spring, when melting snow filled nearby streams. They used a system of

Hydraulic mining in Rockerville in 1889. The method causes terrific damage to hillsides. —Minnelusa Historical Museum

placing ore and water in a cradlelike device, rocking it back and forth until the gold settled, then pouring off the water and fine dirt. Eventually, the settlement was called Rockerville, after this mining method, though the post office referred to it as Rockville.

The town boomed in the gold rush period from 1876 to 1878; the hillsides, valley, and prairie plateau in the vicinity were honeycombed with holes dug by individual miners. Johnny Hunt, a pioneer, called the spot "the prettiest little mining camp in the Black Hills." During the first two years of the camp's existence, more than $400,000 worth of gold was mined. For a dozen wild years Rockerville made national headlines.

Even at its best, Rockerville was pretty informal. Many of the residents perched wherever space existed; they didn't dare leave a claim, so most camped beside the hole they were digging. A nearby highway marker says Main Street followed the creek line and crossed it "whenever it felt like it." In 1880 a fabulous and unlikely scheme to bring water from Spring Creek by way of a flume seventeen miles long actually succeeded. Strong streams of water were forced through nozzles to break down large chunks of ore before it was sluiced down the flume. The diversion dam for the flume was half a mile north of Spring Creek from Sheridan Lake. The Black Hills Placer Mining

Like the Needles and most high-altitude rock in the Black Hills, the summit of Harney Peak is limestone, rough, and overgrown with lichens. Here the Sioux holy man Black Elk had his first vision as a boy of nine. "Then I was standing on the highest mountain of them all, and round about beneath me was the whole hoop of the world," *he said.* —Rapid City Chamber of Commerce

Company raised $300,000 for the amazing engineering achievement under the direction of Ambrose Bierce—whose career in the gold-fields was good practice for the ups and downs of his later life as a writer. The flume operated for several years, but weather and water pressure made it leak; a boy was hired for a time to walk the seventeen miles every day, stuffing rags in the holes. Other hydraulic gold-mining operations in the Hills also failed for lack of water. Today, hikers can find many traces of this and other flumes and ditches.

A mile and a half east of Rockerville is the Stratosphere Bowl, where the space age took a great step forward in 1934. In flights sponsored by the National Geographic Society and the U.S. Army Air Corps, two helium balloons were launched here to study high-altitude conditions. The first ripped at a height of sixty thousand feet and was forced to descend at Holdredge, Nebraska. The second, launched November 11, 1935, climbed thirteen miles—an altitude record that stood for twenty-one years—and supplied data on high-altitude photography, cosmic rays, and atmospheric conditions.

Upper picture shows an outside view of the Holy Terror Mine in old Keystone about 1900. Below, miners pose at the entrance to the dangerous mine workings, where miners were sometimes killed by fires and gas explosions. Underground flooding forced the mine to close in 1903. —Edwald Hayes photo

KEYSTONE

Founded in 1891, the town was named for the Keystone mine, which in turn was named for the Masonic emblem worn by the prospector who located the mine. The new section of town throbs with tourist trade much of the year and has charm, antiques, and fudge. The older, original section of town still serves local citizens more than tourists and features some intriguing buildings, including what could serve as a museum exhibit of the old-time western general store. Legend says the establishment was begun about 1885 by a traveling salesman who used a ventriloquist show to peddle his wares throughout the Hills; later it was operated by four generations of the Halley family. The Halleys stocked oxbows until well into the twentieth century, and customers could pump kerosene into their own containers from a barrel in the basement.

The last Halley grew frustrated with modern regulations on handling food and held a three-day auction in 1980. The store was placed on the National Register of Historic Places in 1981. New managers modernized the store between 1981 and 1983, and the authentic kerosene barrel was replaced by that scented, colored stuff in little glass bottles, which no more resembles real kerosene than Keystone might be mistaken for Phoenix.

James Halley V brought the store back into the family but sold it in 1989 to Bob Nelson, a Keystone resident who had been a teacher, a logger, a salesman, and an auctioneer. The grandchildren of people who have told nostalgic stories about the place for years often visit to look at the memories and find that many of the old fixtures are still in place, including the ornate iron handles on the front door, the teller's cage from the old Keystone bank, the original maple shelving, and the green bins with porcelain knobs holding nuts, bolts, screws, and plumbing fittings. Displays of bank statements, letters, and photos decorate the walls. Coffee is served at a table next to the old wood-burning stove; local residents hide their own mugs everywhere to have them handy when they need them.

Keystone became one of the centers of the mine-dotted district, and the air seems to echo the fantastic names of some of the mines, reflecting the hopes and fears. The Holy Terror mine looms above the streets; stories say a prospector's wife asked her husband to name his mine for her, so he did—perhaps not quite in the way she intended.

Not far away are the sites of other mines named with a fine regard for the realities of life: Accidental, Big Hit, Broken Nose, Chief of the Hills, Giant, Golden Star, Hard Nut, at least two Hardscrabbles, Hoodlebug, June Berry, several Last Chances, Kicking Horse, Old Love, Rainy Day, several Rattlers, Sunrise, Sunset, Sunshine, Sunbeam, Swamp Angel, Swamp Eagle, Yankee Boy, Weasel, Window Light, and Black Nell—named for the proprietress of Black Nell's Golden Palace in Deadwood. The women who operated businesses like hers probably profited more from the mining industry than most of the prospectors.

MOUNT RUSHMORE NATIONAL MEMORIAL

SD 244 leaves Alternate US 16 at Keystone and leads directly to Mount Rushmore National Memorial, then along a scenic route through the woods to US 16.

A highway marker at the intersection of US 16A (alternate) and SD 87 southwest of Keystone vividly describes the international background of Gutzon Borglum, the artist who carved Mount Rushmore into a memorial honoring four significant U.S. presidents.

"His birthplace was Idaho," the marker reads. "California first taught him art. Then France, who first gave him fame. England welcomed him. America called him home." The artist had already won deserved fame for his sculptures in bronze and marble as well as his paintings before he came to South Dakota in 1924 at the invitation of Doane Robinson, who had been the state's historian for twenty-two years, to look for a mountain suitable for a carving.

When Robinson asked Borglum, then fifty-six years old, to come to South Dakota, many local residents were not enthusiastic about the idea, preferring their mountains as nature left them. Robinson originally visualized the mountain carving as a way to capitalize on the state's history: He suggested carvings of an Indian leader, a trapper or trader, a farmer, a noted woman, and a statesman. In

Mount Rushmore, "The Shrine to Democracy," is the most widely recognized symbol of South Dakota; it's even on state license plates. —South Dakota Department of Tourism

modern times, a variety of people have suggested adding carvings to the mountain to recognize groups other than white males; few appreciate Robinson's foresight.

Borglum explained during a 1931 radio appearance how he selected the men to carve into the mountain. Jefferson, he said, had drafted the Declaration of Independence; Washington was "a great presiding officer he guided in council, was great in battle, and made possible and successful the struggle that followed"; Lincoln had kept the union together; and Roosevelt had "completed the dream of Columbus, opened the way to India, joined the waters of the great East and West seas. Roosevelt did more; alone he stayed the encroachment of organized privilege against the principles of government."

The ferociously patriotic Borglum was inspired by his vision of the carving's meaning to Americans, particularly Westerners—each of the four chosen presidents was also connected with the westward movement. He was a bit cynical, perhaps, about the American habit

Gutzon Borglum sometimes rode a crude cage up a cable to take a close look at the carving of Mount Rushmore.
—South Dakota State Historical Society

of destroying one monument to build another and said he wanted his memory of the nation's greatness "placed so high it won't pay to pull it down for lesser purposes." He originally intended to carve the entire figures of the four presidents but didn't have enough stone. The original plan also included a Hall of Records, a tunnel beneath the mountain to contain documents of historical and cultural interest that might survive a disaster capable of destroying the carving and wiping out history. Discussion of the unfinished tunnel was revived during the state's centennial celebrations.

Sitting in Borglum's chair, you could gaze into Thomas Jefferson's eyes; stone projections make the eyes more lifelike from a distance. White lines in this photo show where cracks have been repaired by Park Service workers. —South Dakota Department of Tourism

In 1927 Borglum began carving the head of Washington, and President Calvin Coolidge dedicated the project; Borglum unveiled the final part of the sculpture, Theodore Roosevelt's head, in 1939, the same year the Panama Canal was finished. The intervening years were busy. Senator Peter Norbeck, who had encouraged Doane Robinson to pursue the project, helped obtain congressional funding several times; the federal government eventually contributed most of the total project cost of $990,000. Norbeck also forced Borglum to behave himself; the temperamental sculptor was famous for tantrums. Borglum died in 1941; his son Lincoln refined Roosevelt's face and finished the lapel on Washington's coat. Fifty years later, the Mount Rushmore Society began soliciting funds to complete an amphitheater, more parking, and elevators.

369

The mountain on which the Mount Rushmore carving appears was originally known as "Slaughter House Mountain" for a nearby butchering operation. When a New York mining promoter sent his attorney, Charles Rushmore, into the Keystone area to check on mine titles in 1885, David Swanzey was hired as a guide. The two men rode the area on horseback and stopped to rest near the base of the impressive granite mountain. Rushmore asked the name, and Swanzey was embarrassed to tell him what it was really called, so he volunteered, "T'ain't got a name, but we'll call it Mount Rushmore." When Rushmore returned to Keystone, he boasted about having a mountain named for him, and the name stuck. The U.S. Board of Geographic Names officially recognized it in the 1920s.

Gutzon Borglu strapped hims into a sling- chair device to inspect his artistic creatio and supervise blasting on Mount Rushmore.
—South Dakota Department of Tourism

BLACK HILLS NATIONAL FOREST

The Needles Highway takes visitors through some of the most beautiful parts of the Black Hills National Forest and Custer State Park. Keep the map handy, though; it's easy to lose your bearings.

Sylvan Lake Lodge is one of several beautiful old wood and stone buildings that welcome visitors in the area; others include Legion Lake Lodge and the Game Lodge on 16A and Blue Bell Lodge on SD 87. Sylvan Lake exists because two hunters, Dr. H. B. Jennings of Hot Springs and Joseph Spencer of Chicago, climbed Harney Peak and thought it would look nice with a lake on top of it. Spencer bought land in Sunday Gulch, built a 75-foot dam between two granite boulders, and created a mountain lake that is one of the real beauty spots in the Hills. The lake sits at 6,250 feet of elevation atop the ridge between Hill City and Custer on US 85A. A small hotel was built of native pine, cedar, and stone, with separate log cabins scattered in the trees.

Gutzon Borglum (left) placed the American flag on top of Mount Rushmore for the first dedication in 1925.
—South Dakota State Historical Society

SD 87 spirals down several hairpin curves through pine, birch, quaking aspen, and stone buttresses to the Game Lodge. The story of Calvin Coolidge's visit—the first to South Dakota by a reigning president—is a series of hilarious encounters between official Washington and native South Dakota. The only losers were the fat trout secretly penned in the creek by game officials who wanted to be sure the president caught all the fish he wanted. Photographs of the little man holding huge trout probably did more for Black Hills tourism than anything else in history; the number of tourist camps doubled between 1927 and 1929. It is probably only rumor that the private golf course constructed for the president was engineered so that all the greens sloped down toward the cup.

Coolidge was the last president to take three-month vacations, and he was encouraged to come to South Dakota partly because Senator Peter Norbeck wanted him to see the farmers' problems firsthand. A coalition of Hills residents scrambled to be sure the president could keep track of his duties while in the Hills; telephone lines were installed, highways graveled, and office space for his staff arranged in record time. Residents weren't just being generous and

Harney Peak, at 7,242 feet, is the tallest point between the Rocky Mountains and the Swiss Alps. This photo from the air shows its lookout tower.
—Rushmore Photo

patriotic; they knew that a president's visit was the best advertising for the fledgling tourism industry. Besides making the Game Lodge famous, Coolidge visited the Days of '76 celebration in Deadwood, the Tri-State Roundup in Belle Fourche, the Butte County Fair in Nisland, and other events.

The Needles Highway is named for tall, slender spires of granite southeast of Sylvan Lake. These shafts of rock are the weathered remnants of the core of the Black Hills. In warm weather, travelers see bright spots of color clinging to the tops and sides of rocks: climbers practicing their skills. A traffic jam is standard at the Needle's Eye, as earthbound folks photograph climbers working to the top. For years, local residents often drove the highway on the chance of seeing a recreational vehicle stuck in one of the narrow tunnels blasted from solid granite. Recent highway "improvement" has enlarged some of the tunnels, making things handier for trailer campers but altering the views of Mount Rushmore and other scenic spots.

JEWEL CAVE NATIONAL MONUMENT

Jewel Cave, thirteen miles west of Custer, was originally developed as a mine by Frank and Albert Michaud. It might have ended up looking like the Homestake Mining Company's Open Cut in Lead, but wiser heads prevailed, and it was turned into a national monument. Jewel Cave contains spectacular crystals, first mined, then protected for their beauty. Spelunkers Herb and Jan Conn have probably spent more time underground than above it. They've mapped more than fifty miles of new passageways since September 1959, work that still influences modern cavers conducting surveys and scientific studies. Jewel Cave, at more than one hundred miles, now ranks as the fourth longest cave in the world. Some passages are not now and probably never will be open to the public. The Miseries, a ninety-minute half-mile series of passages, so narrow it sometimes removes the cavers' jeans, is the only known entrance to regions of the cave still uncharted. If Jewel is connected to Wind Cave, twenty-two miles south of Custer—as some spelunkers believe—the resulting single cave would probably be the longest in the world. Air volume studies lead some researchers to estimate that only 5 percent of the caves has been explored. Both caves contain unusual and delicate underground formations in sparkling shades of color.

SD 79
Hermosa—Nebraska
68 Miles

SD 79 runs north-south in South Dakota between North Dakota and Nebraska. Few towns exist along the northern portion of this route, north of I-90, so in this book they have been lumped into the section on US 85. This segment deals only with that stretch of SD 79 between Hermosa and Nebraska.

This is an old highway. It is straight but lethal and is often called "the deadliest highway in the state" by highway patrol officers. State officials blame alcohol and excessive speed as major factors, but local residents say freight trucks changing routes between I-90 in South Dakota and I-80 in Nebraska or I-25 in Wyoming are another cause. Although SD 79 has frequent passing lanes, slow-moving traffic accesses the highway from numerous side roads. Be careful when driving this route.

HERMOSA

Hermosa began with settlers camped on Squaw Creek about 1882. A small community grew up around the original Battle River Stage Station, located beside SD 79 about a mile south of town. Locals knew it as Strater Post Office, for the family that ran the mail service. When the Chicago & Northwestern Railroad reached this place in 1886, it was called Battle River, but Nebraska had a town named Battle Creek and the railroad wanted something more distinctive. In Spanish, Hermosa means "beautiful"; maybe Chicago & Northwestern officials had more imagination than other railroad officials. The railroad carried ore from several area tin mines with names like the Golden Summit and the Etta. Hermosa writer Rick Mills offers considerable local history in his book *Making the Grade*, a study of Black Hills railroads; Mills hopes Hermosa will someday become the site of a major railroad museum.

By 1887 the town had two banks; one constructed of local sandstone still stands, though it is now empty. As in many western towns, citizens stayed busy erecting new businesses and rebuilding them after they burned. Within one two-year period fire had destroyed two hotels, a restaurant, two general stores, two saloons, a livery barn, and a hardware store. The premium booklet for the Second Annual Custer County Fair, held at Hermosa in September 1888, said the town had "good schools, religious societies, a church build-

The bank building in Hermosa, built in 1910 of native sandstone, still occupies the same corner at Second and Main streets. —Rose Mary Goodson

ing in process of erection, secret societies, business men's association, an excellent flouring mill, and nearly all branches of business." The booklet also explained that the area owed its fine climate to the "Japan current," which "strikes the Pacific coast near British Columbia," makes its way across the Rockies, obligingly follows the Missouri River, and pours its warm bounty directly on eastern Custer County.

The booklet included an advertisement for the Bower Family Band, which would one day be the subject of a book (*The Family Band*) and a television show. In another ad, *The Hermosa Pilot* called itself the "Official Paper and Leading Organ of Custer County" and heralded its newsy location on "the only possible route to the wonderful tin mines"; a subscription was $2.50 a year. Oddly enough, two pages away in the fair booklet, *The Custer Chronicle* called itself the "Leading Paper and Official Organ of Custer County." The Battle River House, billed as "The Only House in the West where every one must pay," sternly advertised: "NO DEAD BEATS ALLOWED." Rates were $2 per day, cash—"And Don't You Forget It."

The Baron de Mandat-Grancey may have stayed at the Battle River House in 1887 during a trip to the Hills to establish a horse ranch; he didn't get much sleep, as he reports in *Buffalo Gap*, because some local cowboys were "comparing the different whiskies of the town." Toward midnight, he was awakened "by an unbelievable uproar, singing, swearing; furious galloping of a troop of horses, finally a violent fusillade followed by a great noise of breaking windows." The next morning, he saw from his hotel room three horses, still saddled and bridled, grazing on the street and occasionally sniffing their riders, "stretched dead drunk on the ground."

In several places on either side of the highway, it is possible to see traces of roads followed by the Cheyenne and Black Hills passenger stagecoaches in the early 1870s; residents still occasionally find ox shoes. All these locations are on private land and cannot be explored without landowners' permission, but when grass is short during a dry spell, which is fairly common, you may spot wagon ruts from the highway.

FAIRBURN

Fairburn is named for its beautiful creek, or "fair burn." The town's earliest resident was not a Scot, as the name suggests, but a black man who grazed horses on the fine stands of hay along the creek banks. Several families settled in Fair Valley in 1883; one resident dispensed both mail and dental care from a tent office. The town wasn't platted until 1886, when, on the Fourth of July, the railroad arrived. Because the first man buried in the cemetery had been a shooting victim, the story arose that the citizens had to shoot a man to start a cemetery. Much later, after its reputation for rowdy doings had subsided, the town became famous among rock hounds because the surrounding hills are filled with Fairburn agates, the state gem— lovely, multicolored, striped confections polished for jewelry.

Between Fairburn and Buffalo Gap, a bridge crosses Lame Johnny Creek, site of the vigilante hanging of a supposed stage robber, horse rustler, and cattle thief. The bad man's name was really Cornelius Donahue, an orphan from Philadelphia who went to Girard College and became crippled when his horse fell on him in the cobblestone streets. After graduating with high marks in conduct and moral science, he drifted to Texas, where some sources say he learned to repossess stolen horses for the Texas Rangers from the Indians. Since taking horses from any Indians, let alone the Comanches and the Tonkawas, was risky at best, this story deserves some suspicion.

Donahue, or "Lame Johnny," appeared in the Black Hills about the same time as Texas outlaw Sam Bass, which may or may not have been coincidence. He went into legitimate work, possibly serving as a deputy sheriff of Custer County, then as bookkeeper for the Homestake in Lead. While there, so the story goes, an old acquaintance recognized him and spread the story that Johnny had been a thief in Texas, and he soon left the job. Homestake's records for this period were lost when its headquarters was burned following the San Francisco earthquake of 1906. Rumors persisted that Johnny was robbing stages and stealing horses and cattle, especially those bearing the brand of the Indian Department, as the Bureau of Indian Affairs was then called; the practice was fairly widespread among white residents at the time.

Donahue was eventually captured and sent under armed guard to Rapid City for trial. Along the creek that now bears his name, the guards reported hearing an order to halt and the sound of a gun being cocked. They obeyed, but by the time they realized the men who issued the order had gone, Lame Johnny was already hanging from an elm. Boone May, the Deadwood lawman whose captives had a nasty habit of dying before they could be tried, was apparently among those who yanked the rope, though rumor insists some of the vigilantes were local stockmen tired of Johnny's thieving ways. The story has many loose ends and discrepancies, but one wonders if May—who often was conveniently elsewhere when the stage was robbed—had something to hide that Johnny knew and would have told to save his neck if he'd reached jail. Some of the complexities of the story are told by Jesse Brown and A. M. Willard in *The Black Hills Trails*, a fascinating anecdotal history.

Somewhere nearby lived the Sage Hen, girlfriend of a freighter named Dave Madison, who traveled the route from Sidney to Rapid City. To keep his girl out of trouble, he left her in a cabin on Lame Johnny Creek and picked her up on the return trip.

Once two men visited her shack and ordered her to fix dinner for them. She figured they were bandits and resented their rudeness but agreed to boil up some stew with garden greens. On her way to get the greens, she picked up a pistol. While adding the greens to the stew, she also added a generous dose of castor oil. After one taste, the robbers protested, but she drew the pistol and forced them to eat every nauseating drop. She disarmed them, took a dollar apiece for the dinner, threw their guns in the creek, and suggested they leave quietly.

Later, Madison asked her why she didn't just kill them and get the reward. "Killing was too good for them," she answered demurely. Madison probably tasted his meals with great care for a long time.

BUFFALO GAP

Named for the nearby opening in the Black Hills where buffalo entered and left the high country, Buffalo Gap was an 1874 stage

From near SD 79, the Buffalo Gap in the southern Black Hills appears much as it must have to Jedediah Smith and his men in 1823. They are hailed as the first whites to enter the region. —South Dakota State Historical Society

station. The town was located by the Fremont, Elkhorn & Missouri Valley railroad and soon became notorious for having twenty-three saloons, two large "sporting houses," and "a whole row of small ones." To be fair, it also had four blacksmiths, seventeen hotels and restaurants, two drugstores, four Chinese laundries, three livery barns, a hardware store, ready-to-wear and furniture stores, and a population of around two thousand. Among the attractions of the town was the sandstone quarried for buildings that still stand in Omaha (Nebraska) and Hot Springs, as well as Buffalo Gap. Nearby Calico Canyon is the location of a natural arch of purple, peach, and yellow sandstone that furnished materials for the sturdier buildings.

The Baron de Mandat-Grancey, whose 1887 stay at the Battle River House had been so poor, also lodged in Buffalo Gap, where he persuaded the hotel owner to let his personal chef prepare a meal. The cook found eggs, onions, lard, an old pot, and a frying pan, and within twenty minutes "the first onion soup which had ever been conceived and executed in Dakota simmered gently on the fire, sending throughout the building delicious aromas." The cook followed this creation by preparing an omelet. Everyone wanted to taste the new foreign dish, and Colonel Thompson, editor-in-chief of the *Buffalo Gap News,* declared that he would write an editorial about the two exotic French dishes.

The Baron also remarked that on at least one occasion, Buffalo Gap's citizens had acted against a house of prostitution by collecting the town's fire pumps, directing them at the chimney, and pumping enthusiastically until water poured out the front door of the house—along with the bedraggled inhabitants, who moved to a town where their charms received more appreciation.

Archie Riordan was hired as marshal to "tame" Buffalo Gap in the best western tradition. His first successful encounter was with Charley Fugit, a well-known and boastful gunfighter who wasn't fast enough. Then the frightening rumor spread: Fugit was a nephew of the gunman Doc Middleton. When Middleton showed up to identify the body, however, he said mildly, "Whoever shot my nephew did the right thing and has nothing to fear from me."

Another early Buffalo Gap denizen, Augustus A. "Gus" Haaser, first came to Rapid City in 1878 from Sidney, Nebraska, on the stage, walking most of the way because the trail was deep in gumbo. In 1880 he and a partner named Bill Blair trailed 3,500 cattle and 250 horses from Oregon to the Cheyenne River near Wasta for the Haft and Conrad outfit. In 1883-84 Gus was at the old Walker Stage

Most businesses built wooden porches and boardwalks next to buildings, but pedestrians fought for street room with wagon trains and buggies. This 1890 photo shows the temporary offices of the First National Bank in Hot Springs. The wagon at right has upright stakes to hold loose loads, like lumber. —Earl Chace photo

Station at Hermosa to cut local cattle out of passing trail herds, a tough job since most trail crews resented the time lost—and the implication. More than 180,000 head of cattle passed through Hermosa in two years.

In 1888 Haaser became foreman of the Gunstock Ranch, a horse outfit twelve miles east of Buffalo Gap. During the Indian scare of 1890, he was a scout for Captain Wells of the Seventh Cavalry and saw the Wounded Knee massacre from six hundred yards away while carrying dispatches. Later he started a ranch of his own on Lame Johnny Creek. Haaser was one of the last of the old-time cowboys; he took part in the first big roundup in Dakota Territory in 1881 and the last one in 1902. But homesteaders moved into this area as they did all over the West, and today smaller places predominate.

Another early rancher, Frank Stewart, helped organize the Western South Dakota Stock Growers [now Stockgrowers] Association in 1892 and served as its secretary until in 1927. Born in 1860 in Pennsylvania, he moved to the Black Hills in 1886 to cure his asthma, as did many Easterners. The cure must have worked, because he settled on the Cheyenne River near Buffalo Gap and raised cattle and horses. Records kept in his careful hand reflect the growth of the cattle industry in western South Dakota. By 1903 the stockgrowers association was taking in more than $20,000 a year, and Stewart reported that more than two hundred thousand head of cattle valued at $9 million had been shipped out of state the previous year.

In 1906 Stewart demonstrated forethought by deploring the disappearance of ranches in the state and predicted that the three highways cutting west from the Missouri River would further reduce their numbers; still, in 1907 the association reached a peak of 667 members. Appointed by President Theodore Roosevelt to advise the Public Lands Commission on grazing legislation, Stewart suggested that overgrazing could be stopped if local groups were allowed to supervise cattle on public lands; he also wanted a tariff on cattle produced in other countries, which reduced markets available to American producers.

An important innovation was the publication of books listing members' brands to help both stock detectives and ordinary ranchers prevent the theft of stock. Under an 1897 state law, anyone could adopt a brand by filing it with the secretary of state and paying a fee of $1.50. Any cattle brought in from out of state wearing a brand already registered here had to be rebranded. The penalty for violations was a $1,000 fine and up to one year in the county jail, or both. Stewart went to Pierre to help pass the law. In spite of these efforts, however, rustling increased, and the stockgrowers' organization constantly hired more range riders and stock detectives to patrol the state's broad western range.

When Stewart died in 1927, his daughter Queena was unanimously elected to succeed him as secretary, an unusual move for the largely male group. Women were expected to be members of the women's auxiliary, known as the Cow Belles until the name was changed a few years ago. By 1937, though rustling was still a problem, it was apparently becoming more difficult for rustlers to be convicted; Bob Lee reports in *Last Grass Frontier* that Miss Stewart wrote at the bottom of her December financial report that year, "Another dumb jury released _____, the king of rustlers. Can't seem to get him." When Queena Stewart resigned as secretary, she and her father between them had held the post for fifty years, serving under seven presidents.

SD 44
Rapid City—Interior
133 Miles

SD 44 is a good secondary route to the center of the Pine Ridge Indian Reservation and the Badlands. Some stretches, however, contain craterlike potholes, and the road often narrows without warning, especially at bridges. Drive alertly.

Take time to look at the spectacular sweeps of grass-clad hills, the sharp-edged ridges of the Badlands, cottonwood trees along streams, and isolated, simple homes of reservation residents. The land the Indians received from the government is certainly not farmland, but it has a wild grandeur and beauty; with care, it is excellent grazing land for herds of cattle, horses, and buffalo. Gravel roads often lead to high points with magnificent views of the Badlands and the Black Hills; some high bluffs are prayer sites or family burial grounds, so be respectful of these shrines. But the view is open for all, and you may find you are not alone in appreciating it.

PENNINGTON COUNTY

Among the few settlements in this region is Caputa, laid out in 1907 by the Chicago, Milwaukee & St. Paul Railroad; even with such encouragement, settlement didn't begin until the next year.

Farmingdale was originally a post office located on a ranch half a mile from the present site. The first postmaster, Americus Thompson, named his office for the great number of farmers who settled in the region. Scenic, founded in 1907, was aptly named.

Sarpy's fur post stood between Farmingdale and Scenic, about twenty-five miles above Wasta near the junction of Rapid and Spring creeks. The site is visible on the north side of Rapid Creek where SD 44 crosses it. Established by John Jacob Astor's American Fur Company, the post was run by Thomas L. Sarpy at least as early as the winter of 1829-30. Though the water of the Cheyenne never looks very deep at the highway crossings, it was deep enough to float pelts to Fort Pierre in huge skin canoes. In March and April 1830 nearly six thousand buffalo robes reached Fort Pierre in this manner from Sarpy's post.

Indian and white trappers brought their furs to the post, where they were examined, valued, and traded for supplies needed during the coming trapping season. The crowded huts that served as fur posts contained everything a trapper might need: traps, candles, blankets, lead for making bullets, and fifty-pound kegs of black powder used in muzzle-loading guns. Most trappers didn't want to carry fifty pounds of powder, so there was always an open keg from which lesser amounts could be weighed out to each customer. On January 30, 1832, an assistant passing robes over a counter knocked a candle into an open powder keg. The resulting explosion killed Sarpy and destroyed the post, but the assistant lived; the post was rebuilt and operated for several years after the mishap.

Sheep Mountain Table

Sheep Mountain Table, about six miles southeast of Scenic, took its name from nearby Sheep Mountain, which leads to considerable confusion. Some authorities say the mountain was named because Rocky Mountain sheep were found there; others say its shape, from some angles, looks like a sheep. School of Mines Canyon separates the two, named because students dig for fossils at a summer camp established by the Rapid City technical college.

A tenacious settler named Mary Hynes made a living for herself and her family atop this desolate mountain. When she arrived in Scenic in 1907, most of the choice homesteading spots had been taken. She heard men talking about Sheep Mountain in the local saloon, but they told her no one would be fool enough to file a claim up there. Hynes promptly hired Bill Osborne's team and buckboard to take her to the mountain. Osborne used his pocket knife to cut

Modern Lakota Sun Dancers fast and pray for days during the ceremony. Calling upon Wakan Tanka, they blow eagle-bone whistles and wear headdresses of sacred sage decorated with feathers. —South Dakota State Historical Society

steps into the walls and boosted his customer up. She saw the great view, noticed waist-deep grass, and staked her claim for a $5 fee.

Hynes bought four horses and twenty milk cows, loaded her five children in the wagon, and headed for Sheep Mountain, sleeping outside most of the way. Their first home was a tar-paper shack at the foot of the hill; two of her sons used a pick and shovel to dig a road accessible for a team and wagon. The family built a sod house, barn, and sheds. With a team, they hauled food and supplies up the mountain in a stone boat. A spring several hundred feet from the mountain's base supplied the only water, and a gas motor and bucket system brought it to the house. For cash, the family sold milk and cut wild hay from the tabletop, selling it for $8 a ton. An earlier entrepreneur shoved hay down a "hay chute," a natural trough in the side of the mountain. A legend is told about a cowboy named Frank Hart who rode a load of hay down the mountain. Halfway down he lost the hay, and the rough slide peeled off his pants, then started paring off layers of hide. He only did it once.

In 1915 a Model T climbed Sheep Mountain—in reverse, so the motor could get enough gas on the steep grade. Ten years later a sign at the foot of the hill advised, "Put your car in low, step on the gas and don't look back."

BADLANDS NATIONAL PARK

Among the well-known people who knew and admired Mary Hynes for doing the impossible was Senator Peter Norbeck, who encouraged her work to create a Badlands National Monument in 1929. Mary did not live to see the monument become reality; she was thrown from a buggy and stubbornly hung on while it careened wildly down the mountain. She never recovered from her injuries and died three years later.

Interior

Interior, named for its position inside the Badlands, was founded on the White River in 1891 and originally named "Black." Cowhands objected to the name, and the town site was moved when the Chicago, Milwaukee & St. Paul arrived in 1907. The town sponsored an all-woman rodeo in the early 1900s. Mildred Douglas was one notable performer, donning a fringed skirt for most events; when she rode steers and bucking horses, she wore long, dark bloomers under the skirt.

Rocky spires, buttes, and gorges in the Badlands ensconce petrified remains of prehistoric camels, three-toed horses, and saber-toothed tigers.
—South Dakota Department of Tourism

The Deadwood Treasure Wagon, owned by Wells-Fargo Express, carried four guards besides the driver as it hauled $250,000 in gold bullion from the Homestake mine. Officials claimed the coach's strongbox was impregnable for at least twenty-four hours; bandits proved otherwise. The wagon rushed along the Cheyenne-to-Deadwood Trail. —South Dakota State Historical Society

One of Interior's modern attractions is the Woodenknife Restaurant, run by Ansel Wooden Knife, Jr., a native of the Rosebud Reservation. Wooden Knife turned his mother-in-law's fry bread and Indian tacos into a valuable commodity. An Indian taco is made of crisp, fresh, light circles of fry bread topped with taco salad and sour cream or onion. The fry bread served with honey is a superb dessert. Wooden Knife and his family also produce Woodenknife Indian Fry Bread Mix so folks can make their own fry bread at home. Wooden Knife's recipe differs from other fry bread formulas because it includes a hard-to-find ingredient: *tinpsala*, also called Indian turnip (or common breadroot scurf pea if you're a botanist).

US 85 and 385
Deadwood—Oelrichs
125 Miles

Together, US 85 and US 385 run the length of South Dakota from the North Dakota border to the Nebraska line. South of Spearfish, US 85 is a narrow, winding two-lane highway with steep hills. At

Deadwood US 385 diverges from US 85 and heads south, traveling the spine of the Black Hills. The road passes through many gold-mining districts and the town of Hot Springs to the plains at the southern end of the Hills and into Nebraska.

Next to US 85 as it climbs into the Hills stand the beautiful sandstone buildings of the Frawley Ranch. In 1974 the ranch was placed on the National Register of Historic Places because, as a brochure reads, it "encompasses visually and historically the procession of western rural life from the American Indian through homesteaders to the large ranch. The site is also a testimony to the success of one family where many others had failed."

Still owned by the Frawley family, the ranch comprises seventeen homesteads in nearly five thousand acres, divided into the Upper, Middle, Lower, and East ranches. Upper Ranch was once the site of the Centennial Park Hotel, which burned in 1883. In 1888 the owners built a second hotel and restaurant beside US 85 on Middle Ranch. Courtyards in front of the barns were used to bed down cattle. One of the earliest buildings on the property, still in excellent condition, is a one-story log house believed to have been built in the 1870s on the Lower Ranch.

DEADWOOD

When the gold rush began, Deadwood Gulch was littered with downed timber from lightning-caused fires; thus were both gulch and town named. Later, citizens who thought the name wasn't cheerful or dignified attempted to call the town Miles City, after a general who won fame in the Indian wars. Indians, who consider the Black Hills a sacred source of spiritual rebirth as well as a never-failing hunting ground, find it ironically symbolic that white history in the region began with greed. Gold mining and processing remain important businesses, along with lumbering and tourism.

Greed also remains important: Since 1989 the primary business in town has been gambling. In 1988 Deadwood citizens began campaigning for legalized gambling as a way to boost the tourist trade. The idea's promoters gained support by promising that some of the funds brought in by gambling would be set aside for historic preservation. The legislature set an 8 percent gaming tax, restricted the number of games per business, and put the betting limit at $5. On November 1, 1989, the casinos opened, and the town was transformed overnight. During the first month, gamblers bet more than $13 million, producing an adjusted gross return of more than $1 million to jubilant businessmen. The gaming tax raised $100,000 in that

Many authorities believe this photo, taken June 15, 1876, is the first ever taken of the gold rush town of Deadwood. At left, tents stand beside solid log buildings with shingled roofs. At right, crude canvas shelters are supported by rough-cut poles in front of the framework of a new building. —Centennial Archives, Deadwood

first month, to be split between the state, Deadwood's historic preservation venture, Lawrence County, and the new South Dakota Gaming Commission. By the time the city received its first payment of $500,000 in gambling revenues from the state—only three months later—nearly every other business on Main Street had closed; the buildings had been turned into gambling emporiums filled with slot machines and poker and blackjack tables.

Goldberg Grocery, one of the town's oldest and most beloved businesses, serves an example of how the transformation occurred. Initially, the owners announced they'd stay in the grocery business, merely tucking a few slot machines into the aisles. The news came as a relief to Deadwood's senior citizens, many of whom could walk to Goldberg's but were unable to drive to grocery stores located on the fringes of town. However, shoppers looking for the daily provender were shoved aside by crowds playing the slots; eventually the proprietors gave up and turned the entire building over to the new business.

Car dealerships, hardware stores, and apartments housing the elderly gradually emptied, and the space was rented or sold to casino operators. Residents found it nearly impossible to buy gas, food, and other daily needs in town. As traffic congestion increased, parking was banned downtown and shuttle buses hauled visitors. City

Goldberg's grocery in Deadwood resembled a museum of the American dream before legalized gambling replaced groceries with slot machines.
—Rose Mary Goodson

fathers, astonished by the rapid change in their town, began trying to balance development and history with the needs of local citizens. Leaders in other towns and Indian tribal councils watched the experiment carefully and began debating the merits of gambling as a cure for poverty. Black Hills residents learned about gambling addictions, but smiling winners are still pictured in the newspapers, and their luck makes headlines.

Early Deadwood

Luck has been making headlines in Deadwood ever since gold was discovered in the nearby hills. During the town's first gold rush in 1876, each separate mining camp had its own name. Ingleside, Chinatown, Cleveland, Fountain City, Elizabethtown, and Montana City were among the early camps, but eventually these settlements were all incorporated into Deadwood. Within six months ten thousand miners had swarmed into Deadwood, Whitewood, and the neighboring gulches, all hoping to strike it rich and get out of there as soon as possible. Dozens of men lived in flimsy shacks or tents up and down the gulches.

An artist's drawing shows Jack McCall shooting Wild Bill Hickok in the back of the head. Hickok's hand—black aces and eights—has been called the "Dead Man's Hand" ever since. —Centennial Archives, Deadwood

Between April and November 1876, the Cheyenne and Black Hills Stage Company carried an average of eight passengers per coach between Fort Laramie and Deadwood. In dry weather the coaches could make it in forty-seven to fifty-two hours; in bad weather, with muddy roads, the trip took sixty or more hours, even when passengers walked. That first summer of gold mining in Deadwood was eventful. In July the news reached Deadwood that Lieutenant Colonel Custer's command had been killed, and the town feared massacre by hostile Indians. Still, gold kept them digging; within a few weeks, more than $500,000 worth had been sent back to Cheyenne.

Most of the miners' necessities were brought to town by freighters and teams of oxen; shipping charges from Cheyenne to Custer City ranged from three and a half cents to six cents per pound. The food carried by freighters was simple but nourishing: sides of fat bacon, Arbuckle's coffee (at twelve and a half cents a pound), beans, prunes, dried apples, sugar, blackstrap molasses, and hard tack bread in six-by-six-inch squares a half inch thick. In January 1879 the *Black Hills Daily Times* reported live chickens selling in Yankton at

$2.50 a dozen, but by the time the poultry reached Deadwood its price had increased five or six times. Butter sold for fifty cents a pound, eggs were sixty cents a dozen, onions brought ten cents a pound, cabbage five, and potatoes cost $3.50 a hundred pounds. The receipts of one Lee Street retailer, said the newspaper, averaged $175 a day, mostly in cash—a huge income for the time. One *Daily Times* writer said he'd rather have an apple orchard than a gold mine. "Apples are worth from ten to twenty cents apiece just now," he pointed out.

There were almost as many ways to make a fortune in Deadwood as there were citizens. Mule skinner Phatty Thompson paid children twenty-five cents for each cat they caught in Cheyenne; then he packed the felines onto a wagon and headed north with the howling load. When he got to Deadwood, dance hall girls and "fallen women" rushed to greet him, eager for pets and mouse catchers. He sold the cats by the pound—$30 for a fat one—and made almost a thousand dollars. Some authorities suggest the name "cat house" for a house of prostitution came from this incident; who can prove otherwise?

Actor Jack Langrishe found yet another way to make a buck in Deadwood. Arriving in June 1876 with his wife, Jeanette, and twelve members of their troupe, Langrishe built a crude stage surrounded by a high fence on the main street of town, lighted it with kerosene lamps, hung a canvas roof, and opened for business. Rain poured down during the first show, "Lillian's Lost Love," and "The Banker's Daughter," but the house was packed and nobody minded. Later the actor leased the notorious Bella Union, also used for Episcopal church services. His theater performances, unlike some of Deadwood's other entertainments, were "legitimate," a code word meaning "clean enough for the whole family."

Langrishe stayed in Deadwood three years and eventually built a fancy theater with boxes for the society swells; the building still exists as the Gem Theater. Some of the society ladies used stylish opera glasses; the theater was so small they weren't necessary, but the fad caused great merriment among Deadwood's rougher element. One old prospector broke up the show—and made Langrishe forget his lines—by jamming two beer bottles through holes in a board and peering through his own "glasses." Langrishe eventually went back to Colorado to open the Tabor Opera House in Leadville and a theater in Denver.

By January 1879 a local newspaper called Deadwood "the metropolis of the Black Hills." The burg had a population of six thousand inhabitants, five hundred businesses, churches, schools, and "numerous secret organizations," a sure mark of civilization.

Law and Disorder

According to one historian, ninety-seven murders occurred in the first three years of Deadwood's history. Trials were informal, and the killer was usually set free. One of the town's most famous murders took place on August 2, 1876, when James Butler "Wild Bill" Hickok, who'd only been in Deadwood six weeks and hadn't killed anyone, was shot in the back by Jack McCall. Hickok's reputation as the fastest gun in the Wild West had been earned elsewhere; by the time he reached Deadwood he was married and might have been considering settling down. The poker hand he was holding when he was shot—black aces and eights—has been known as the Dead Man's Hand ever since.

McCall was tried and acquitted, but when he boasted of getting away with the crime he was retried, convicted, and hanged in Yankton. Hickok was buried in Mount Moriah Cemetery, where

James Butler "Wild Bill" Hickok wore two pearl-handled revolvers and an unsheathed knife—thrust dangerously through his belt—when he posed for this undated photo.
—South Dakota State Historical Society

Preacher Henry W. Smith, first minister in the Black Hills during the gold rush, was killed in 1876 on his way to deliver a sermon. The statue was destroyed by vandals. —South Dakota State Historical Society

souvenir hunters have been chipping away his tombstone regularly ever since; it's been replaced so many times local historians have lost count.

Another murder victim, Methodist clergyman Henry Weston Smith, preached in scattered gold camps only briefly before he was killed between Deadwood and Crook City. Signs indicated Indians were the murderers, but some say white men killed Smith and tried to blame the Indians. Many folks who committed crimes in those days seem to have dressed up as Indians to do so, as law enforcement officers almost never chased anyone they thought was Indian. When there was an "Indian scare," the next Indians who happened by, be they hostile or friendly, were usually shot by whites, increasing the tension. Many white settlers, of course, were in favor of driving the Indians completely from the Black Hills or eradicating them as a race.

Because Deadwood was located in Indian territory and the residents were there illegally, law enforcement was an individual business. Men such as Boone May started their careers on the wrong side of the law and only later became bounty hunters, guards, or lawmen. May's captives always seemed to make an escape attempt—

with their hands tied behind them—and usually wound up dead, slung over the back of a horse. Residents were sufficiently suspicious to try May for murder at least once, but he was acquitted. Ambrose Bierce once hired him to guard a gold shipment, listing him on the payroll as "Boone May, murderer." In the only narrative Bierce wrote about the Black Hills, he told how he and Boone were riding from Deadwood on a rainy night when a bandit attempted a holdup. May's speedy work with a Winchester left the fellow full of holes.

Bounty hunters couldn't be squeamish. A man named Frank Towle ambushed the stage, was shot by Boone, and was buried by someone. Then May discovered a reward was offered. He dug up Towle's corpse, cut off the head, put it in a sack, and carried it two hundred miles to Cheyenne. He didn't get the reward; it had been lifted by the time he rolled the skull onto the desk of a startled official in Cheyenne. May carried the trophy around for days, vainly trying to earn some revenue from it. Eventually May drifted down to South America, and only rumors ever drifted back.

Seth Bullock was an early lawman with a better reputation. He arrived in Deadwood with a wagon load of hardware and household goods the day before Wild Bill Hickok's death. Bullock had been seated in the Montana territorial senate at twenty-two and introduced a resolution asking Congress to set aside Yellowstone as a national park. In 1873 Bullock became sheriff of Montana's Lewis and Clark County and arranged the first legal hanging in the state.

In Deadwood he joined Sol Starr in the hardware and auctioneering business; they also sold liquor. In the 1879 Deadwood fire Bullock lost merchandise worth $18,000—but he had $13,000 worth of insurance. He built a larger store in Deadwood, opened branches in Lead, Sturgis, and Spearfish, and directed the Deadwood Flour Milling Company. Bullock entered politics again, becoming one of the five original members of the Board of Health and Street Commissioners, the first governing body in town. In 1877 Lawrence County was officially organized, and temporary county officials were appointed by Territorial Governor John Pennington. Bullock was named sheriff. Unlike Boone May, Bullock never shot his suspects. Instead, he often used his wits. On one occasion, about thirty miners, armed and supplied with food and water, holed up in the Keets Mine and demanded back wages. Bullock bought some sulphur and set it on fire to smoke them out, avoiding bloodshed.

Bullock and most of the other temporary officials were defeated by Democrats in the next election, and he never ran for office again. Back in private life, Bullock acquired ranch land illegally, like most

Seth Bullock, center, is flanked by two unidentified men.
—Centennial Archives, Deadwood

homesteaders, and financed a method of smelting gold ore designed to keep processing in Deadwood. His investment wasn't very successful, but other smelting methods produced a boom in Deadwood. The arrival of the railroad fueled the momentum. Dr. David B. Miller says in *South Dakota Leaders*, "By 1895 Deadwood's population grew to more than 4,000. In large degree, Seth Bullock was responsible." Bullock put $40,000 into the Bullock Hotel, a three-story white and pink sandstone building with sixty steam-heated rooms. It remained Deadwood's main hotel until the Franklin opened in 1903.

The Deadwood Press

Newspaper reporters and editors were often as lively as Deadwood's citizens; if they weren't strange when they came to town, they were probably converted by the weird incidents. The *Deadwood Times* announced in 1877 that the editor was "prospecting through

the murky channels of literature solely for the colors" and that he would not accept for subscriptions "sauer kraut, coon skin, frozen onions, second-hand blankets, watered bug juice, empty fruit cans."

A writer for *The Black Hills Pioneer* took exception to statements made by an eastern paper that Hills dentists pulled teeth with six-shooters and filled them with gold dug in the cellar. "How ignorant our eastern friends must be," said the Deadwood writer; in fact, he said, after loading their revolvers with a good charge of powder, local dentists "insert golden bullets and shoot them into the cavities of their patrons' teeth." Much more sophisticated. The *Black Hills Daily Times* of August 23, 1879, reported a wild incident wherein a "tenderfoot," upon hearing a shot fired by a hunter,

> let a cry of terror out of him that echoed from the top of White Rocks, and then ran down the street like a scared wolf. In front of Chas. Stacy's house he fell prostrate upon his face in the dust of the road, and thinking the man was at the end of his run, Mr. Stacy approached him, and as he attempted to roll him over, the fellow sprang to his feet and letting another squawk . . . lit out down the street with the speed of parole. The last seen of him he had quit cutting up the dust and was laying straight in the air, going like a meteor toward the foothills and the great plains beyond. He will probably never come

Prairie schooners drawn by mule teams stand in Deadwood's main street.
—Centennial Archives, Deadwood

within a thousand miles of the Hills again, but will devote the balance of his life to rehearsing to all who lend to him their ears, of how he was riddled with five-pound bullets by a gang of a dozen giant road agents sixteen feet high.

Not all of Deadwood's journalists were given to fantasy. Freeman Knowles, the founder of three newspapers—the *Independent*, the *Equality*, and *The Lantern*—was an outspoken Populist, an advocate of unions, and finally a Socialist. A Civil War veteran and lawyer, he came to the Hills in 1888, according to Helen Rezatto's *Mount Moriah: Kill a Man—Start a Cemetery*. Knowles was nominated for Congress and served one term as a representative-at-large for the

Black Hills region. He fought for higher wages and better working conditions for poor miners and laborers, battling powerful mine owners and other bosses.

Knowles's most famous editorial was probably one in which, with great restraint, he discussed a respectable woman who had died following a botched abortion. He wrote on May 30, 1908: "Love had its way and God blessed the union with the most stupendous fruit of the universe, a human child, and society steps in and cries 'shame' and causes the mother to kill both herself and the baby." According to an article by Paulette Tobin in the *Rapid City Journal*, the editorial led to Knowles's conviction in federal court of sending lewd, obscene, and lascivious matter through the mail.

When the Homestake Mining Company attempted to prevent its workers from unionizing in 1909, Knowles supported the union men;

Fannie Hill, a madam, ran one of Deadwood's successful businesses in the early days of the gold rush.
—Centennial Archives, Deadwood

Dr. Flora Stanford stands in front of her house in Deadwood. A modest sign advertises her medical qualifications in a region where women seldom followed such professions. The woman standing on the porch is unidentified.
—Centennial Archives, Deadwood

a minority among the twenty-five hundred workers, they had been accused of using pressure tactics to get other miners to join. In an attempt to point out the inherent brutality of their work, the union miners sought a seven-day week, saying they were tired of putting in ten hours a day, eight days a week. They insisted that all miners join the union. The miners threatened a strike, and the Homestake owners retaliated by closing down the mine. Hostility divided the town into fighting factions. Detectives were hired to protect Homestake property, and replacement workers were recruited from as far away as Tennessee and Missouri. Within two months, hunger and desperation brought the local miners back to work—without the union.

Homestake's general counsel Chambers Kellar was so mad he horse-whipped Knowles at the county commissioners' office in front of county officials who made no move to thwart the attact. Knowles died six months later of pneumonia; many miners attended his funeral.

Deadwood's Women

On January 11, 1879, the *Black Hills Daily Journal* attributed to a local man a well-used western saying: "The Black Hills region is a d——d good place for women and dogs, but h-ll on men and horses." Few married women lived in the gulch during its first months, but there were women present, and even a few ladies. Dr. Flora Hayward Stanford, the first woman doctor in the Black Hills, arrived in 1888. Her famous patients included Calamity Jane and Buffalo Bill Cody. Other patients sometimes slipped into her office to have bullet wounds dressed, then zipped out the back door before the sheriff arrived. The first woman to be admitted to the South Dakota bar, Blanche Colman, was born here in 1884. She attended neither college nor law school but studied law in her spare time and was admitted to practice in 1911 at the age of twenty-seven. She worked most of her life for Chambers Kellar, chief counsel for Homestake Mining Company in Lead.

Female dealers were popular in the gambling houses, where they earned their pay in gold dust by dealing a variety of games, including rondo, *vingt et un*, *rouge et noir*, casino, California Jack, euchre, roulette, keno, and the strap trick. Although some of these games remain popular, modern gambling emporiums might do well to revive others that have fallen from fashion; the change might liven up the business. In Deadwood, gambling began to lose its luster—and profits—three years after it was legalized.

Spectators watch as Charlie Brown was hanged in Deadwood on December 17, 1897, for the murder of Mrs. Stone. —Centennial Archives, Deadwood

LEAD

The name of Lead (pronounced "leed") was taken from the miners' term for a rich vein of gold-bearing quartz. Discovery of such a vein launched the Homestake mine, backbone of the community throughout its existence. Some say the name also reflected early settlers' desire that their town become the "leading" city of the Black Hills. Lead did not achieve that distinction, though it was probably the region's noisiest city: By the early 1890s Homestake Mining Company had more than nine hundred stamps pounding day and night to crush gold-bearing ore. The people, their houses, and everything else must have shaken constantly.

The town began in 1876 under the name Washington. Later it joined another settlement called Golden and the two became Lead City. When Lead incorporated in 1890, it dropped "city" from its name. It is nicknamed "the Mile High City"; its actual altitude, 5,320 feet, exceeds the qualification by 40 feet.

Because Lead developed in a narrow canyon surrounded by a major mining operation, it is a city planner's nightmare. No one but the local residents will drive up some of its steep, zigzagging streets, even in the summer. And during the winter, harrowing tales abound as cars skid uncontrollably down icy lanes. Houses cling to the upper slopes with an ingenuity it might be best not to question; they quake and crack when miners set off explosions underground, and longtime residents always know exactly when miners are blasting.

The Homestake

The Homestake was located by two Canadian-born brothers; typical of western mining operations, they found gold by accident. Shortly after the Civil War, Fred and Mose Manuel joined a wagon train bound for Montana from Minnesota. Once there, they joined Henry Harney and Alex Engh and headed for the Black Hills. Fred's horse broke a leg and had to be shot, so he had to walk. Each evening, he bathed his aching feet in a cold creek, if he could find one. One night he noticed some shiny flecks in the water, which he readily recognized as gold. He located his first claim right there, in Gold Run Gulch; nearby he staked another claim he called the "Old Abe," and his mining days had begun. The Homestake vein was found in 1876, and the Manuel brothers hauled ore to Whitewood Creek near the old town of Pennington; there they built the region's first *arrastra*, a stone mill to pulverize the ore. That fall, despite the rich find, Mose left his brother and went to Alaska, and Harney and Engh sold their share to H. B. Young for $300, perhaps illustrating the

This well-constructed cabin, built by James Cozett near Deadwood, may have been intended for a permanent home rather than just shelter for a brief prospecting fling. Logs and a glass window have been skillfully fitted and heavy planks form a sidewalk in front of the cabin. —Centennial Archives, Deadwood

principle that some folks find adventure satisfying enough without wealth. Meanwhile, Fred Manuel was busy developing the mine, scaring off claim jumpers, and getting ready for a cold winter. The brothers may have retrieved $5,000 in gold that summer.

By June 1877 a representative of George Hearst had purchased the options of Mose Manuel, Engh, and Young. Fred Manuel stubbornly hung on, but Hearst allegedly used promises and threats to convince him to sell out for $70,000. Fred Manuel returned to Minnesota, married, and spent his life in Montana mining and dealing in real estate. He eventually retired to California.

George Hearst—a U.S. senator, mining engineer, sportsman, and speculator—developed three of the best-known mines in the West: the Ophir in Nevada, the Anaconda in Montana, and the Homestake. By August 1878 Hearst had transported a monster eighty-stamp mill by railroad and ox team to Lead. He and other business leaders were frustrated by frequent shutdowns when freight didn't arrive and miners ran out of materials. In April 1879 Hearst started building a company store and, two years later, his own railroad. Hearst Mercantile eventually covered nearly an acre and carried not only mining equipment but also dry goods, groceries, clothing, toys, furniture, even buggies—enough stock to sell wholesale to smaller stores.

As his mine became the richest in the Americas, Hearst bought more property, timber, mineral and water rights, and railroad lines. When Hearst's only offspring, William Randolph, refused to manage the Homestake and the store, his daddy gave him the *San Francisco Examiner*. The younger Hearst devoted his energies to the paper and later bought the New York *Journal*, with which he became notorious in the 1890s for crude tactics and "yellow journalism." After George Hearst died in 1891, his widow, Phoebe Apperson Hearst, spent more than $21 million on social causes throughout the nation. From her, Lead got a library building and two thousand books for Christmas in 1894; she later founded a free kindergarten, built an opera house, and encouraged improved labor policies in the mine. By 1895 the Hearsts had invested more than $3 million in the

Phoebe Apperson Hearst had deep pockets for social causes.
—South Dakota State Historical Society

Homestake, but the mine was yielding over $4 million in gold annually. Thirteen hundred miners and five hundred railroad and timber workers were listed on the payroll.

Hearst's store had been built on a street that began sinking from the mining excavations underneath. Workers shored up the street but had to build a new store, which was one of the largest in South Dakota. Miners could charge purchases against their paychecks, so the business thrived. Though the system was handy for those short of cash, some miners had to work most of their lives to pay off the debt incurred by a few impulsive purchases. Hearst's brick store was one of the few structures to survive the fire of March 8, 1900, which burned most of the wooden buildings in a four-block area of the commercial district, to the accompaniment of exploding powder from mining supply stores.

Unlike the rest of South Dakota, Lead survived the years of Depression and the Dust Bowl in style, and its profits contributed to the economy of the entire Black Hills area. Gold prices rose throughout the 1930s; miners got about $6 a day while the average wage elsewhere was just a dollar. Farmers who had lost their land to the bank swarmed to Lead, hoping for jobs. Homestake's stock shot from $60 a share to more than $500 a share. Lead could afford to build a million dollar high school in 1940.

The Homestake paid no state taxes until after a bitter legislative fight. Emil Loriks first introduced a bill in 1933 requiring an ore severance tax, arguing that mining interests had removed over $3 billion from South Dakota without paying for the privilege. In 1935 the legislature passed a 4 percent tax on gold, silver, tin, and all other minerals, and in it 1937 increased the tariff to 6 percent. One year, Homestake's taxes of $750,000 provided one-third of the state's operating budget, according to Elizabeth E. Williams in *South Dakota Leaders*. In 1957, as profits declined and the state made more money from other sources, the legislature cooperatively lowered the ore tax to 2.5 percent.

When World War II began, the federal government classified gold production as nonessential and ordered gold miners moved to cop-

This 1876 photo shows Deadwood's main street jammed with wagons floundering in the mud. —South Dakota State Historical Society

The Wing Tsue Wong family prospered in Deadwood during the gold rush. With one child buried in Deadwood's Mount Moriah Cemetery, Wing Tsue paid for the funerals of other Chinese. Many Chinese returned to their homeland after the mining days; in some cases, they took the bodies of their dead along.
—South Dakota State Historical Society

per and iron ore mining operations, citing strategic importance to the war effort. In late 1941, just as Lead was about to be drained of miners, fire struck the Homestake store, gutting it. The Homestake Recreation Building, with Phoebe Hearst's library and opera house, were saved. The store was not rebuilt; by the mid-1980s, says Steven Kinsela, "the situation was similar to the time when George Hearst first rode into the Black Hills—a miner could not find a pair of mine boots or a box of nails in Lead."

Homestake's vein of gold reaches the surface at the Open Cut, a man-made canyon hundreds of feet deep and two thousand feet across. The chasm was created over the years as miners removed forty-eight million tons of rock in search of gold. By the end of 1949 approximately nineteen million ounces had been mined, says Herbert S. Schell in *History of South Dakota*. North Mill Street originally lay in the center of the cut but was devoured by the mine; US 85, the present highway, will also be rerouted.

The size of the Homestake is hard to comprehend. Some of the more than five hundred miles of mine shafts extend 8,000 feet down. In some areas of town, buildings have collapsed as timbers used to shore up tunnels underneath sagged; modern mining methods include dumping waste ore back into mined-out tunnels to support surface ground. In 1989 the company began exploration of a new three-mile tunnel at the 6,800-foot level of the mine, an expensive search for new deposits. A ton of rock yields a piece of gold no larger than a marble, but modern milling recovers 97 percent of the gold.

The Homestake is still the largest supplier of gold on the North American continent and one of the largest in the world. The gold is sold directly to the U.S. government, and industries buy from the federal supply. The mine is open for guided tours, though visitors are not allowed to go into deep shafts. A tour at the Black Hills Mining Museum simulates underground conditions for visitors.

LAWRENCE COUNTY

The gulches in every direction from Deadwood and Lead are littered with the ruins of several dozen towns that might have become prosperous cities in the northern Black Hills. Mining camps were established everywhere a little "color" was found, and only the complicated process we call civilization made some towns grow and others disappear. Trojan, Balmoral, Preston, Carbonate Camp, Flatiron, Two Bit, Maitland, Galena, Roubaix, Tinton, Gayville, Chinatown, Cleveland, Fountain City, and others were once crowded with tents and crude shacks, bustling with plans and gold; their streets became rivers of waste, whiskey, and a measure of blood. The dreams of men and women blossomed and died everywhere, and a few fragments of those dreams can be found if you look.

Terraville was between Lead and Central City in Bobtail Gulch. The town was probably named for the Golden Terra Mine, founded in 1876 by J. B. Pearson of Yankton, the same man who first discovered gold in Deadwood Gulch. The mine was sold to the Homestake Mining Company in 1877 for $90,000. The Deadwood, Terra, and Caledonia stamp mills kept the place vibrating day and night, and numerous businesses other than mining kept citizens employed.

The first saloon in Central City, halfway between Lead and Deadwood, was called the "Shoofly," a name probably taken from what patrons did while eating. A suburb, Elizabethtown, was named for Elizabeth Card, one of the first white women in the area. In 1883 a huge flood damaged the various mining hamlets that made up Central City; Anchor City and Golden Gate were heavily damaged, and placer mines in the entire gulch washed away or were buried under flood debris, as were settlements clustered at the foot of Poorman Gulch.

The *Black Hills Daily Times* of January 15, 1878, reported a shocking case of women's liberation, in this manly gold-mining town:

> Just as we were going to press there is considerable excitement in the lower end of Chinatown over the jumping of a mother lode owned and recorded by Jeff Cleveland. At noon Mrs. Elizabeth Lovell proceded [sic] to the mine and ordered the men to desist and leave the mine at the same time drawing a six-shooter to enforce her demands. The men left when she started to cut down the windlass and threw the car down the hill. She was arrested by Sheriff Peterson.

Terry, a former mining town four miles southwest of Lead, was home to a thousand people in 1893, when it was a station on the Burlington Northern; by the early 1890s it competed with Spearfish for the status of third largest town in Lawrence County. It was named for nearby Terry Peak, which in turn was named for Gen. Alfred Howe Terry, a well-known Indian fighter who, as commander of the Department of Dakota in 1874, controlled army forces in the Dako-

When Calamity Jane dressed in female finery, she looked like the average woman of her day. Called an angel when she nursed sick miners in Deadwood Gulch, she was more often described as a drunk, a sharpshooter, and a bullwhacker. —South Dakota State Historical Society

tas, Montana, and Wyoming. Terry's chief employer was the Golden Reward Mining Company; the company now mines with the heap-leach method and has expanded its operations to include the ski slopes of Terry Peak.

Calamity Jane, worn out by her wild life at the age of fifty-one, died in a Terry hotel room in 1903. Her last request was to be buried next to Wild Bill Hickok. Old-timers, who say the love was a fantasy of Jane's, think Bill has been spinning in his grave ever since.

Seven miles south of Lead, where the highway crosses Elm Creek, was the town of Brownsville. In 1883 the Hood & Scott lumber mill stood a half mile east on the creek. When the Baron de Mandat-Grancey visited in 1883, he noted one of the side effects of mining. Within a radius of ten miles, miners had cut down every tree for railway lines, homes, and mine shaft supports. Writing in *Buffalo Gap*, de Mandat-Grancey added that the mountains "will be avenged in their own way. With the first rains the water will run down in torrents, carrying away the soil into the valleys, and the houses into the Cheyenne. That is what took place a few weeks ago at Dead-wood." The comment might have been made by a modern environmentalist.

In 1883 a boardinghouse filled with lumber workers burned down, killing eleven men. The story illustrates events that must have been common at the time. Neighbors didn't know the men's names or histories and lacked modern identification methods or any way of notifying relatives in other states. Moreover, no one could afford burial costs or charges for individual tombstones. Therefore, the men were buried in a common grave in Mount Moriah Cemetery in Deadwood. Later, relatives of two of the men came to Deadwood searching for the missing men; they eventually learned the truth and put up headstones for them.

Most of the small mining camps were eventually served by one of several railroad lines, which made for difficult building. When the editor of the *Black Hills Daily Times* first saw a map showing the route of the Black Hills and Fort Pierre line, he wrote, "It looks like an angle worm in excruciating torture. At one point in Whitewood gulch the bend is so sharp as to enable the brakeman on the rear car to receive a chew of tobacco from the engineer of the locomotive." The grade from Brownsville to Woodville was so steep that the engine had to make several trips, bringing one or two loaded cars up at a time until the entire train was at the top. In 1888 the *Times* reported that two flatcars loaded with wood jumped the track and turned completely over. Ben Bell, a conductor, went over with one car and "found himself sitting on a big rock some distance below the

When George Custer set out to explore the Black Hills in 1874, he took along his black cook "Aunt Sally" Campbell, who became the first non-Indian woman to enter Lakota territory. She returned later to homestead and died in 1887. Her grave in Vinegar Hill Cemetery in Galena, near Deadwood, bears the words, "She Ventured with the Vanguard of Civilization." —South Dakota School of Mines and Technology

wreck, with his backbone driven up at least a foot." Well, maybe not a *whole* foot—he made a complete recovery.

US 385

US 385 heads southeast from Deadwood and nearby Pluma. The highway is narrow but mostly straight as it traverses beautiful tree-covered plateaus through the Black Hills National Forest and the heart of the gold rush country. Side roads of gravel and dirt lead to ghost towns and more great scenery.

Claim jumpers were a perennial problem in this region. They did this by replacing a miner's claim stakes with their own while the true claimant was gone to buy supplies. Stories abound of lone miners guarding their claims day and night until they toppled over into sleep, only to find their claim jumped by a superior force when they woke up. To discourage such practices, two prospectors near Rochford posted a sign quoted by Irma Klock in *Yesterday's Gold Camps and Mines in the Northern Black Hills*:

> We, the undersigned, knowing our racket, take up this tree. We claim 1,500 feet upwards and a radius of 300 feet from branches to spread and the first son-of-a-bitch who disturbs our stakes is liable to be cannibalized immediately thereafter.
>
> Signed, C.B. Strong and A.B. Striker from Montany

One of the most famous gold coach robberies occurred at Pluma, though the robbers didn't get the gold. On March 25, 1877, road agents trying to stop the stage killed driver Johnny Slaughter and wounded a guard. Slaughter was reputed to be the best six-horse driver on the line, fearless and dependable, and he immediately became a legend in stagecoach circles.

Silver City, southeast of Lead at the head of Pactola Reservoir, was settled in 1876 as the wild and woolly center of Black Hills silver mining and confidently expected to live up to its billing as a city. The beautiful site now serves as a resort area for Pactola and is reached by speedboats. The reservoir also flooded the route of the old Black Hills & Western Railroad.

West of Silver City on a gravel road is Mystic, once the site of an experimental mill set up to extract gold by a chlorination process. The Frink sawmill now occupies the site, though the Frinks had to endure lengthy battles with local authorities to secure the right to remain. The town was originally called Sitting Bull but changed its name when the railroad came through in the late 1880s; Sitting Bull wasn't popular in those days. The same gravel road winds through the beautiful heart of what was once mining country, leading eventually—be patient! enjoy the scenery!—to Rochford, named in honor of one of its founders.

In 1874 Lt. Col. George Custer shot a grizzly bear on Rochford Creek and posed for an often-reproduced picture. By 1878 Rochford had five hundred people, two hundred houses, a solid block of stores with wooden, covered sidewalks, a couple of doctors, and a good school, all supported by gold mining. The Evangeline and the Minnesota mines both built large processing plants. A flume provided water and power for the Stand-By Mill, a favorite of Hills artists, finally demolished because it was too attractive—and too dangerous—for visitors. You can pick up fishing tips by hanging around the Rochford store and listening to the locals. You might even get tips by asking, if you're lucky. But don't rush; the natives resent it.

Gold Rush Ghost Towns

If you enjoy hiking, you might try looking for a lost nugget or exploring the remains of dozens of ghost towns in the vicinity. One of the most apt names for a ghost town is Oblivion, a former stop on the Burlington Northern four miles east of Hill City. Look for Tigerville on the headwaters of Newton Fork, among gulches that once rattled with the sounds of placer mining as men followed veins of gold-laced quartz. Among the richest mines were the King Solomon,

Hikers often find remnants of ghost towns like this one in the Black Hills. Some have been ransacked by vandals searching for hidden treasure, which probably never existed; others have simply tumbled down from the effects of weather and time. —South Dakota Department of Tourism

the Bengal Tiger (with its unique tiger-striped ore), and the Lucky Tiger, for which the town may have been named. The names of the ghost towns in Pennington County echo the fascinating history of the Black Hills: Addie Camp, Allen's Camp, Alta, Canyon City, Castleton, China Gulch, Horneblende, Hustleton, Nugget Gulch, Teddy Bear, Warbonnet. Always approach mines with caution; deep, dangerous, uncovered shafts may lurk in the grass.

In 1875 Sheridan became the third town established in the Black Hills. Originally called Golden City, it was renamed for Lt. Gen. Phil Sheridan. A man named Williams washed $2 worth of gold from a sandbar along the creek and rode over to Custer the next morning to tell his five partners about it. When the men returned they found the entire area covered with claim stakes from others who thought Williams had left for richer diggings; the place was named Stand-Off Bar on the spot. Incredibly, the usurpers gave Williams's claim back to him when he complained.

That fall General Crook ordered all miners out of the Black Hills because they were trespassing on Indian land. They left, but most of them returned before snow fell. After a group of Montana men took $3,000 worth of gold from the creek side, they renamed it the Montana Bar. Since the town was on Indian land, miners usually built log cabins with portholes large enough to stick a rifle barrel through and shoot without removing any chinking. The town was nicknamed "Valley of a Thousand Smokes" from the number of liquor-brewing stills there; smoke from the boiler fires hung thick among the treetops.

Several rich quartz deposits, the "Blue Lead" mines, were found south of Spring Creek near Sheridan, where the Rockerville flume began. But the town that was once Pennington County's seat has been under the waters of man-made Sheridan Lake since 1942.

HILL CITY

Hill City was laid out as a gold camp in February 1876 by Thomas Harvey, John Miller, and Hugh McCullough; three months later the miners had already moved on, looking for richer strikes in the northern Black Hills. Only a man and a dog remained. A tin boom in the 1880s restored life to Hill City. The few hundred people who live here now live on revenue from lumber and tourism. West, toward Deerfield, is a replica of a gold-processing operation.

The Black Hills Central Railroad, better known locally as "The 1880 Train," travels twenty miles round-trip daily on an old mining spur between Hill City and Keystone. The 1926 steam engine pulls four cars of passengers, who are advised to bring raincoats or blan-

"The 1880 Train" travels the tracks of an old mining spur, a scenic ride with authentic pioneering joys including smoke and ashes from the engine's boiler. —Rapid City Chamber of Commerce

kets to shield themselves from the smoke and soot bellowing from the diesel-fired steam boiler. The train stops at Oblivion, where passengers can tour movie sets left behind after the filming of *Orphan Train*. Travelers get a good view of Harney Peak and see the remains of mines such as the Addie, the Good Luck, and the Bob Ingersol, which yielded more than fifty different minerals.

In recent years, tourists have been entertained by the "Hill City Shootout and Wild West Show." The skit performed by local volunteers features Carrie Nation chasing Poker Alice and Calamity Jane out of the saloon; later, Texas outlaw transplant Sam Bass and his gang rob the local bank and are shot down by sheriff Seth Bullock and bounty hunter Boone May. None of these events actually happened in Hill City, though the play is based on fragments of truth. Demonstrations on gun safety follow the performance.

Another modern business in Hill City is the Black Hills Institute of Geology, housed in the city auditorium built by the Works Progress Administration in the 1930s. The business, known to locals as the "bone shop," houses a homegrown company that supplies mineral and fossil specimens for schools, universities, and collectors worldwide, including the Smithsonian Institution. The institute was started by two brothers, Pete and Neal Larson, who began collecting fossils on their father's ranch near Mission, South Dakota. With partner Bob Farrar, they developed new techniques for field preparation and preservation of specimens, cleaning and repairing the fossils for sale. They have sold several complete fossilized skeletons and keep one on display at the institute's museum, which is now one of the town's leading tourist attractions. In a legal wrangle over fossils allegedly collected on Indian land, federal officers seized a *Tyrannosaurus rex* skeleton.

Harney Peak rises just south of Hill City. At 7,242 feet, it is the highest point in the United States east of the Rocky Mountains. During his topographical survey of the area in 1857, Lt. G. K. Warren named the peak in honor of Gen. William S. Harney, who had conducted a number of military operations in the area and twenty-one years later became commander of the Black Hills military district. The Sioux called Harney "Squaw Killer."

CUSTER

History doesn't record how many people camped in this beautiful valley before George Armstrong Custer rode into it in 1874. The area might have been busy; Indian hunting parties used the same campsite in summer. But the Indians didn't bring along newspaper

The Custer expedition posed for this formal photograph in 1874, before heading into the Black Hills. In direct violation of the Laramie Treaty of 1868, Custer went looking for gold and a good place to build a military fort. —South Dakota State Historical Society

reporters or send dispatches reporting on the gold, though they certainly knew it was there. Custer, by contrast, had nearly a hundred Indian scouts, guides, interpreters, engineers, practical miners, and a photographer in addition to the reporters he brought to make sure he got publicity. As a result, Custer received credit for discovering gold in the Black Hills—and got a town named after him to boot.

The real non-Indian discoverer of Black Hills gold, however, was Horatio N. Ross, a miner who found the precious metal in French Creek on July 27, 1874, at the center of what Custer promptly dubbed "Golden Valley." At that instant, a determination was made about the future of the Black Hills that its citizens are still debating. Until then, the Black Hills had been nothing more than a lovely region filled with natural beauty and wildlife; suddenly, it became a place containing mineral wealth—a very different entity. Two factions have been arguing ever since; today we call them environmentalists and developers. The Sioux claim to the Black Hills is also a part of the modern debate, but Lieutenant Colonel Custer thoroughly ignored that.

The first miners' organization in the Black Hills was formed by the campfire soon after Ross found gold, while Custer was writing dispatches to send with a messenger to Fort Laramie. Custer had to know the news would start a stampede of gold seekers into the area, changing the status of the Black Hills from a Sioux refuge into a white man's mining district. John R. Curtis, correspondent for the Chicago *Inter Ocean,* wrote the headlines that drew the nation's interest to Custer:

The Glittering Treasure Found at Last

A Belt of Gold Territory Thirty Miles Wide

The Precious Dust Found in the Grass Under the Horses' Feet

Excitement Among the Troops

By December a party of miners had entered the Black Hills. With it was Anna Donna Tallent, a teacher and officially the first white woman to enter the Black Hills. Born in 1827, Tallent was raised on a farm near York, New York; she married David Tallent in 1854. Twenty years later she, her husband, and their son Robert joined the gold-seeking party of twenty-six organizing in Sioux City, Iowa, while Custer was still exploring. Though Charles Collins, editor of the *Sioux City Times* and one of the party's leaders, announced he would not enter the Hills until he had consent from federal officials, the group struck out for the Hills secretly in early December; one person died en route. On December 23 the party camped on French Creek, searching for the spots where Custer's men found gold. A re-creation of the stockade in which they lived has been built outside Custer.

Members of the illegal Russell-Collins expedition to the Black Hills in 1874 were J. J. Williams, Thomas H. Russell, Eaf Witcher, Lyman Lamb, R. E. Tallent, and Anna D. Tallent, who was the first white woman known to enter the area. —Centennial Archives, Deadwood

Collins left early the next spring to take news of the gold strike to the outside world, apparently hoping to stimulate enough interest so the military could not keep gold seekers out. On their way back, the party was intercepted by the army; its supplies were destroyed, and the men were made to march on foot back to Fort Randall. Meanwhile, the group left behind had a good time selecting ranch sites, playing cards, hunting game, or prospecting for gold. They laid out the first town in the Black Hills, Harney City, near their stockade, but no buildings were ever erected there.

Six men tired of the routine and returned to Fort Laramie, and the military arrived to remove the remaining prospectors in April 1875. Annie Tallent was allowed to ride a government mule back to Fort Laramie. She and her husband remained in Cheyenne while other members of the party returned to Sioux City; during July, David Tallent and several others tried to slip back into the Hills. They were overtaken by soldiers and brought back to Cheyenne but slipped away again and were again arrested and evicted. On the way back to Cheyenne after their third attempt, the men escaped yet again and returned to the Hills in October.

Within ninety days after the ejection of the first group, prospectors had laid out the town of Stonewall, named for Stonewall Jackson, before being removed by General Crook. Almost immediately, more settlers gathered at the site and defiantly changed the name to Custer. This pattern—the army escorting one party out while others sneaked in—went on for about a year. One man was ushered out four times; another said, "I figure the Army will get tired of it before I do." By that time, dozens of gold seekers were moving in and out of the Hills, and the military was either unable or unwilling to keep them out. Privately, President Ulysses Grant advised the military men to give up, and the last great gold rush was on.

The Tallents returned to Custer in April 1876, then moved on to Deadwood with the rest of the crowd; by that time, the best claims had been taken. Annie and Robert remained in a cabin with a leaky roof while David wandered about. He was apparently involved in several shady schemes and accused of committing various crimes, including perjury. In Deadwood, Annie survived floods and fires before moving to Rochford, then to Rapid City, where David practiced law and sold insurance.

Annie Tallent taught reading, writing, arithmetic, geography, grammar, and other subjects in Rochford, Tigerville, and Hill City and was twice elected superintendent of schools; she also served as president of the Rapid City Board of Education. In 1889 she was made an honorary member of the Society of Black Hills Pioneers,

composed of *men* who had arrived in the Hills before the end of 1876; her son Robert joined in 1892. In 1888, while she was visiting family in Illinois, David disappeared and was never seen again.

In June 1897 Tallent moved to Sturgis, where she wrote her eyewitness history of early years in the Hills. She died in 1901 and was buried with her brothers and sisters in Elgin, Illinois, which has undoubtedly saved her grave site from becoming a tourist attraction. Annie Tallent insisted that at least eleven thousand people came to the Hills between November 1875 and March 1876, and she estimated that fourteen hundred buildings went up in Custer during that time. Fred Whitley, in *South Dakota History*, more modestly estimates four hundred structures had been raised in the valley. One of them, a badly constructed dugout, collapsed on Charley Holt, causing the town's first death and catching the settlers unprepared:

In 1874, William H. Illingworth, the Custer expedition's photographer, hauled a heavy camera and tripod up cliffs for this famous photo, sometimes called "the string of pearls." At center, Custer's wagons move down the valley north of the present city of Custer.
—South Dakota State Historical Society

With no preacher, no Bible, no cemetery, and no embalmer, Whitley reports, they dispensed with the formalities and hastily buried poor Charley Holt.

In addition to the shacks, brush wickiups, wagons, and tents that folks lived in, Custer had saloons, gambling houses, dance halls, a few general stores, three sawmills, and a brewery. In May 1876 the first newspaper appeared, the *Black Hills Weekly Pioneer*. That spring, after a hard winter, supplies were short, and the price of flour went from $10 to $18 for a hundred pounds. Saloons flourished, although one of Custer's twenty-nine saloon owners lost a freight train of a hundred mules, a team of horses, and $10,000 worth of "Early Times" whiskey in a robbery.

Soon, however, richer strikes were made in Deadwood, and much of the population moved. In 1877 some stage trails were rerouted to the plains east of the Black Hills, approximately where SD 79 now runs. Custer lost more trade and became only a place to stop on the way to Deadwood. The remaining citizens tidied the place up by burning abandoned buildings as firewood. The sudden change may have

418

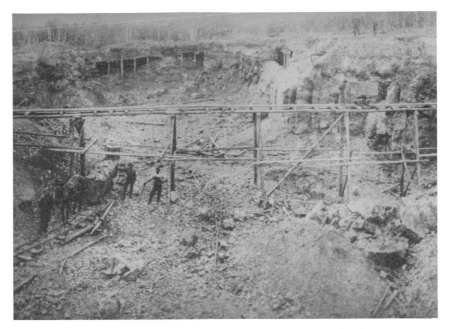

The Open Cut at Jack Gray's Wasp No. 2 mine, a money-maker for years. Gray used an inexpensive cyanide process to treat low-grade ores, an unusual process in the early days but one that has returned to the Black Hills in modern times. —Centennial Archives, Deadwood

saved Custer from some of Deadwood's excesses, such as preserving its broad streets and some of its original beauty and tranquility.

New quartz veins were found near the town in 1879, and within a few years several mines were yielding gold. A second, smaller boom resulted when the quartz began yielding $3,000 worth of gold per ton. Other resources—copper, silver, nickel, tin, graphite, lead, fuller's earth, volcanic ash, coal, and iron—were developed in ensuing years. The silver and tin discoveries led to brief excitement, with wild predictions about the worth of the mines and Custer's future; as always, though, the finds were less valuable than first thought.

By the 1890s the town had become the center of the Black Hills lumber industry, which still provides much of the region's sustenance a hundred years later. The lumber industry was at first dependent on mining, but by 1895 twenty local mills employed more than 250 men, according to the *Custer Weekly Chronicle*. The nearby Holy Terror and Keystone mines each used thirty-six hundred cords of fuel wood a year and more than a million linear feet of lumber to prop up mine shafts, according to an 1898 report. Forty thousand Black Hills residents burned another hundred thousand cords of

At left, white paint outlines part of the projected carving of Crazy Horse, a leader of the warriors who defeated Custer at the Little Bighorn in 1876. —South Dakota Department of Tourism

wood a year to heat homes and cook food. Railroad building between 1885 and 1900 required another 1.5 billion board feet. Some experts speculated that the timber would not outlast the ore being mined.

But the completed railroads brought coal for fuel; in 1893 a series of forest fires—following beetle infestations, low prices, and erosion from clear-cutting—pointed out the need to conserve timber for the future. In 1897 outgoing President Grover Cleveland announced the creation of the Black Hills Forest Reserve, with Custer as its center. Citizens protested that the lumber industry was destroyed and hundreds of families would starve. (Similar complaints were heard in 1991 when Sierra Club members asked for several million acres of additional wilderness area in the Hills.)

Demand for lumber in 1900 was greater in the Black Hills reserve than in any other, and this was the first reserve in the nation with a plan that included lumbering. The area had already experienced more mining, logging, grazing, and settlement than most areas that later became national forests. South Dakota officials asked President William McKinley to remove the Black Hills from the forest reserve program. McKinley refused but agreed to allow some mining, logging, grazing, and other activities; thus, the idea of "multiple-use management" was formulated, according to Dick Willis in the *Rapid City Journal.*

When the uproar died down, forest *management*, rather than forest cutting, was Custer's most important industry, and many lumber mills had moved to the northern Hills. H. G. Hanamaker was the first forest supervisor, setting up headquarters in 1898. The next year, 219 men applied for two jobs as forest rangers. The conservation business still provides a steady income for many residents. The Black Hills National Forest remains one of the top revenue-producing timberlands in the Rocky Mountain region; in 1988 it was the only one in which buyers paid more for timber than the U.S. Forest Service spent on management.

Custer's Characters

Not all the interesting folks moved to Deadwood when the gold rush did; Custer could muster a few of its own. "Fly Speck" Billy Fowler may have been nicknamed for his freckles, or because he was generally filthy. He was already wanted by the law when he

In 1920 members of the Society of Black Hills Pioneers, survivors of settlement times, climbed onto a wagon for this photo. Women had proven their ability to live on the frontier with men, but the society's policy excluded them until 1920. —Centennial Archives, Deadwood

joined Abe Barnes's freight wagons as they neared Custer in 1881. On a saloon tour after he hit town, Billy borrowed Abe's gun. Later, Billy staggered into George Palmer's saloon, pretty well inebriated, and began bullying customers, waving Barnes's large Colt 45 around. Barnes was playing cards; Fly Speck grabbed him by the collar and ordered him to drink, pulling the trigger as he spoke. History always records the last words of people who have been shot, even though they are pretty predictable: Abe shouted, "Oh, I am shot." He ran a few steps, fell, and was dead in fifteen minutes. Fly Speck Billy ran for the door, disentangling himself from several angry citizens on the way, but Sheriff John T. Code nabbed him. The sheriff took his prisoner to a stout cabin, intending to move Fowler to safety later, when angry folks had quieted down and he'd gathered reinforcements. But before Code returned with his deputies, a lynch mob had hanged Fly Speck.

Some say Billy was properly buried in the cemetery; others claim that while the mob was dragging him that way, he accidentally fell into a prospect hole and no one bothered to pull him out. Fred Whitley says in *South Dakota History* that vigilantes put a rope around Billy's neck when they left the cabin and that by the time they got to the woods, "there was no need for a tree. But, as one pioneer observed, it was a time honored custom to elevate a man to where the wolves would not get him if he were to be left out overnight."

Apparently the citizens weren't fond of executions. The first legal hanging in Custer occurred in 1892 when John B. Lehman swung for the murder of constable John H. Burns near Fairburn; that was also the last legal hanging in the county.

The well-traveled Baron de Mandat-Grancey came to Custer, where he saw a curious American custom for the first time. Joining other residents of his hotel on the front porch, he was startled to see one man reach for his knife. The Baron grabbed for his revolver, but the man smiled, sliced a chunk off the bench the men were sitting on, and commenced "cutting it up into chips." Whittling, said the Baron, is a "special malady of the American brain," especially in the West where most men "manifest these symptoms":

> Its diagnosis consists in an irresistible desire to take in the left hand a piece of wood, and to reduce it to morsels of the size of a match by a gentle and regular movement of the right hand armed with a pocket knife, a razor, or a bowie-knife.

Indulging in the custom, he added, usually replaces conversation. He remarked several times on how taciturn Westerners were—compared, one supposes, to the chatty French. But the Baron sincerely wanted to understand the custom, so he asked for a whittling lesson from an old cowboy toting two guns. The man ripped a chunk of wood from a hotel bench and loaned the Baron his bowie knife; other men sitting on the bench encouraged him with kind glances, and the Baron began chipping away. "I am sorry to say," he concluded, "I found no gratification whatever in the experiment." A few days later, when the Baron returned from his nearby ranch, the bench was completely gone; the hotel owner planned to replace it the next day and said it rarely lasted more than three or four days.

The Frenchman was also perplexed by a building method he was told about in Custer. When he checked into his hotel in the evening, it was a one-story wooden frame building. By the time he got up in the morning, it was surrounded by brick walls, already up to window level. The owner explained, "As soon as the building is finished, I shall slide it out behind the wooden house on to the ground yonder, which I have bought likewise." He told the Baron that dragging the inside layer—the wood-frame hotel—out of the brick hotel wouldn't even require moving the furniture, and he'd have two hotels. It's hard to believe the hotel owner was serious, but the Baron believed him.

After his first visit to the United States, the Baron wrote the popular *In the Rocky Mountains*. As a result, two other Frenchmen, Auzias de Turenne and A. Marion, came to the Black Hills in 1885 to establish the Arab and Percheron Stallion Importing and Breeding Company, more often called the Fleur de Lys for its brand. The two arrived in Custer with two Arab stallions, El Keber and El Mahdi, and two Percherons, Vidocq and Vigoreaux. Most of the population of Custer turned out to greet them, and came back a few days later to watch Turenne give an exhibition of El Mahdi's jumping skills.

Afterward, some of the local cowboys blindfolded and saddled a bucking horse for Turenne and challenged him to ride western-style. In *Western Dakota Horse Stories*, Martha Linde, Custer author, tells what followed: "Turenne knew this was going to be bad, but since the cowboys were all yelling for him to get on, he jumped into the saddle just as Spurlock pulled off the blindfold. The pinto bellowed, arched his back and jumped high three times, then zigzagged to the right, then to the left, throwing Turenne ten feet to one side. As Turenne crashed down with an astonished look, the cowboys roared with delight." Turenne later learned to ride cowboy-style but stayed off broncs; to the end of his life he was prouder of being a real cowboy than of any other accomplishment.

The Fleur de Lys was established seventeen miles northwest of Buffalo Gap, and its three hundred or more mares ranged unfenced between there and Custer. The ranch became an attraction for French nobility, many of whom toured the Wild West to satisfy their desire for adventure. When the Fremont, Elkhorn & Missouri Valley Railroad reached Custer, a stock farm was established at Fremont, Nebraska, where the best three-year-olds were readied for Chicago markets, and the ranch established a breeding farm in Montreal. In 1890, when unfenced range was being taken over by homesteaders and squatters, Turenne sold out and went to the Klondike for the gold rush, then settled in Seattle.

Another fascinating Custer citizen was Badger Clark, named South Dakota's first poet laureate in 1937. He spent thirty years living in a three-room log cabin he called the "Badger Hole," now open to the public in Custer State Park. Clark's most famous poem is "A Cowboy's Prayer"; unfortunately, the widely quoted poem is

Badger Clark, poet laureate of South Dakota, lived serenely in a cabin he built and called the "Badger Hole" near Custer.
—Helen Rezatto

usually attributed to another prolific author, Anonymous, who probably lived somewhere in the Hills.

Clark was born at Albia, Iowa, in 1883, the son of a Methodist minister who homesteaded near Plankinton, Dakota Territory. He attended Dakota Wesleyan University, spent two years in Cuba, then came to the Black Hills to work as a newspaper reporter. Diagnosed with tuberculosis in 1906 and advised to move to a sunny climate, he worked on a ranch in Arizona for four years, where he wrote his first verses. He was surprised to receive a check in payment and immediately decided to become a writer. He penned a poetic inscription, later quoted in the introduction to *Sun and Saddle Leather*, that was a pun on "Ridin'," one of his own poems:

> *Just a-writin', a-writin',*
> *Nothin I like half so well*
> *As a-slingin' ink and English—*
> *If the stuff will only sell*
> *When I'm writin'.*

Back in the Hills, he lived with his parents in Hot Springs for fifteen years, then built the Badger Hole near Legion Lake. The image of the ideal Westerner, Clark was tall and lean, and he enhanced the look with wide-brimmed hats, jodhpurs, boots, a western flannel shirt, and a neatly trimmed goatee. After his death in 1957, his cabin was bought by the state and is now open to the public just as he left it. Clark's verses have always been popular because of their comfortable rhythms, like the jog trot of a cattle horse, and Plains philosophy. "Make me as big and open as the plains," he wrote in "A Cowboy's Prayer,"

> *As honest as the hawse between my knees,*
> *Clean as the wind that blows behind the rains*
> *Free as the hawk that circles down the breeze!*

Like many of his poems, it's perfect to read and memorize while cantering over the plains, whether on a horse or in a car.

The Black Hills were blessed with outstanding artists as well as poets. Korczak Ziolkowski spent years blasting granite on Thunderhead Mountain, five miles north of Custer, working on a gigantic sculpture of Crazy Horse, one of the best, and least known, of the Sioux leaders. The memorial was not finished when Ziolkowski died in 1982, so his tomb at the mountain has a handle *inside*—in case he wants to return to work. His wife, Ruth, and several of his ten children continue the sculpture.

Ziolkowski was a successful sculptor when he came to the Black Hills in 1947 at the request of Henry Standing Bear, a Sioux leader.

Korczak Ziolkowski, at right, wore a leather shirt for this photo with his wife, Ruth, and unidentified costumed Indians at Crazy Horse Monument.
—South Dakota State Historical Society

Ziolkowski's portrait of the Polish pianist and statesman Paderewski won an award at the 1939 New York World's Fair, and the monumental marble of Noah Webster he gave to West Hartford, Connecticut, astounded critics. He might have settled into an easy, bountiful career in the world's sophisticated capitals, but Standing Bear asked him to carve a portrait of Crazy Horse to show white society that "the red man had great heroes too." With $174 and a hard-working wife, Korczak started the project, refusing federal aid. When completed, the sculpture-in-the-round will be taller than the Washington Monument, and all four faces of Mount Rushmore would fit into the carved head of the Indian chief.

But Ziolkowski did more than carve a mountain; he also built a fascinating home and studio and managed a farm, dairy, sawmill, and other enterprises. The complex he started now includes a restaurant, a museum with many exhibits donated by Lakota people, and a gift shop featuring Indian-made crafts and a rich selection of books about the region. Ziolkowski's long-range plan called for an Indian university, medical center, and airstrip as well.

PRINGLE

First named Point of Rocks for the prominent natural formation just to the east, Pringle originated when early settlers gathered around a boardinghouse Anna Wolfe ran for passengers on the Cheyenne-to-Deadwood stage. In 1886, with the establishment of a post office, the name was changed to simply Rocks, but when the railroad reached town in 1890, citizens prudently changed the name to flatter W. H. Pringle, the rancher who owned the water rights.

Evidence of an early industry, the Black Hills Lime Company, still exists near town. In the late 1880s lime was produced by digging a vertical hole six to eight feet across and fifteen to twenty feet deep in a hillside rich with limestone. A firebox was tunneled into the base and fired continuously for several days so heat would rise

Korczak Ziolkowski worked on Crazy Horse Monument at his own expense and with hand tools for years before benefactors began contributing to the carving's expense; he received a used bulldozer as a gift. —South Dakota Department of Tourism

This model of the proposed carving of Crazy Horse stands on a porch at the studio below the mountain. A model of scaffolding on the figure's outstretched arm and the horse's nose shows the scale of the work; the mountain to be carved is at right. —South Dakota Department of Tourism

through the lime rock. After the rock cooled, lime was removed through the firebox. Local farmers and ranchers furnished wood for the fires in exchange for stock in the company. Wages were twenty cents per hour for a ten-hour day. Later, a 250-foot-high shaft kiln was built with a firebox on each side at the base. Lime rock was put in at the top and drawn off at the bottom for shipment on the Burlington railroad to lumber yards for construction throughout the territory. Other businesses based on the natural wealth of the area included a sand operation and an enterprise making quartz flint products for the abrasives industry.

EPILOGUE

Many of the vignettes in this history shine a light on South Dakotans' finest virtues; others illuminate things the citizens might rather forget. As a modern woman who cares about the environment, human rights, and women's rights, I wish some things had never happened in the state where my ancestors chose to settle. The trouble is, none of us lives forever in paradise. Many of our ancestors were racists, sexists, imperialists. It's not fair to judge them by today's standards; they lived in a different time and understood things in ways difficult for us to imagine. All we can do is tell what happened and hope we'll all do better next time.

Many white female pioneers, for example, were terrified out of their wits by tall tales and stories they'd heard about Indians before they came west. They labored under the Victorian fear of the "fate worse than death" and were generally forbidden to follow any profession but motherhood. Motherhood, like most professions, is more satisfying if one has a choice. Burdened by too many children, taught to hide their intelligence, denied opportunities to expand their education, women were often more limited than they had to be. Some learned, as one of my female ranch neighbors says demurely, that "anyone with testicles is always right."

This view made some women incapable of enjoying much of what Dakota had to offer. It made them, as well as the men in their lives, especially unable to appreciate the Indians who lived here first. The Indians, by contrast, usually lived in matriarchal societies; the women could toss their husbands out of the lodge for misbehaving, and they knew how to adapt to the natural world instead of trying to put a starched apron on it. Indian women moved around the landscape comfortably, using its plants for medicine, its animals for food.

But every time the wind blew, or a turkey flew overhead, or an Indian passed by, white women became terrified and scurried for shelter. The Indian women often saw the humor of the situation, but they were unable to share it with their white sisters or make it the beginnings of a mutual exchange. The misunderstandings, resentments, fears, and hatred left over from those days are far too prevalent in our society today.

Though now considered passé by many American historians, part of Frederick Jackson Turner's frontier thesis seems to have validity. The West has demanded certain traits, both good and bad, of its long-term residents. People who could stand isolation, who could act independently, who were physically and mentally tough, saw the West as a paradise. They remained, and their descendants are here still. Those who feared and hated wildness and loneliness, who wanted the land tamed and tractable, either tried to change the western landscape or left it for more domesticated lands.

But the beneficial traits that some of us believe were created in Westerners by the land are also the source of some problems. Take Westerners' fabled independence, for example. Sometimes it makes ranchers refuse to act together, even when it is in their own best interests. For years, ranchers have talked of finding a way to demonstrate to the eating public that supermarket beef prices do not reflect the ranchers' profits. They've argued over the morality of selling their lean, mean range cattle to huge corporations that put them in feedlots, stuff them with corn, and sell them to a public that increasingly wants leaner, more organically raised meat. They've screamed that the corporations that own the grain, the supermarkets, and all the processes in between are getting the profits, and that they're the ones allowing feedlot waste products to drain into rivers and groundwater.

But ranchers haven't found a way to explain themselves to most of the public or to unite and change the situation. They're too isolated and independent to organize and stick together. "Nobody's gonna tell me what to do with my land," they say stoutly, while beef prices fall and neighbors sell out to big corporations. Then they take the check they got from the government for not planting a field with wheat, put it in the bank, and buy a new pickup of an American brand with components made in foreign-owned factories.

Conversely, conservative Republican ranchers often support a woman's right to abortion because they see it as an independence issue; no one should own another's body. Ranchers have always been supported—psychologically, and sometimes financially—by women who keep house, raise kids, and work in the fields or in town. If many ranch women didn't have "town jobs," the land would be lost when drought wipes out a crop planted with borrowed money. Yet women's rights issues are a sensitive matter, and to say a woman is "liberated" is not usually a compliment in ranch country.

To outsiders, women who drive their own pickups, brand their own cattle with their own mark, maintain their own checking accounts, shoot guns, ride horses, and rope calves seem pretty emancipated. But you can start a ferocious argument with most of them by saying the Equal Rights Amendment ought to be ratified.

Westerners are tough. Even today, we're usually out shoveling snow when the weather report advises everyone to stay inside. Our historic ability to endure makes us unsympathetic to union workers who demand higher wages until the company goes broke. We can't do that; when times are tough, the whole family tightens its belt, because the family is the company. Ranchers always depend on what the market price is for their cattle; their only other choice is to take them home, where there may not be enough hay to feed them.

Ranchers don't have much understanding of the idea that criminals or Indians deserve sympathy for their childhoods or other difficulties; a rancher's background includes men who strapped the kids for talking back and children who worked in the fields all day at eight years of age. A rancher's answer to mental illness, physical illness, and criminal behavior is to work harder. This toughness has gotten ranchers through some tough times; it has created hardworking folks. But lately, statistics show that this attitude sometimes masks real problems. Rural crime and mental instability are increasing; the use of drugs, including alcohol, is soaring.

A bright spot in all this is that Dakotans, like most Westerners, have always been eager for education. Everyone reads. And ranchers are learning about environmental concerns through their own efforts—partly because they refuse to listen to environmentalists. Many rural people are far in advance of state legislators in their thinking. Since World War I, the attention of prairie folk has been forcibly directed to world affairs. We're more aware of the wider world than it is of us. Visitors are often surprised that most of us can talk knowledgeably about art, music, books, and many topics besides the price of cows and grain.

Because we know a lot about the outside world, we have choices our ancestors didn't have. Many of today's ranchers have been to cities; we went to school, tried being stockbrokers, or teachers, or anthropology professors. We're here not because we can't get a better job, but because we want to be.

And some of us are here because we don't want this world to become like the ones on either side of the plains. As usual, most of us remain silent, so our elected leaders and the business people who make development decisions don't always know how we feel.

Take mining, for example. It's part of our heritage, our history, our state's income. But that doesn't mean we'll tolerate just any abuse. Mining companies that flocked to the Black Hills because South Dakota has few environmental restrictions or taxes have discovered in recent years that citizens may draw the line somewhere, that perhaps heap-leach mining, with its potential to put cyanide in the groundwater, will be too much even for George Armstrong Custer's descendants to stomach.

Still, it's impossible not to notice that there's less diversity in South Dakota than in many regions; we have fewer gays, feminists, blacks, and religions other than Catholic and Protestant than most parts of America. We're so used to seeing white Anglo-Saxon faces that we're nervous about folks we can't identify at a glance as like us.

One way or another, we'll get over this. Given our history, we'll probably change slowly. But individuals who don't fit our mold will likely, one by one, teach us that they deserve respect because they have other traits we recognize—like independence and toughness. If they stay, in spite of harsh weather and sometimes harsh treatment, it will be because they choose to be here, because they love this land.

BIBLIOGRAPHY

PERIODICALS:

Alexander, Ruth Ann. "South Dakota Women Stake Claim: A Feminist Memoir: 1964-1989." *South Dakota History* 19, 4 (Winter 1989).

Anderson, Harry H. "Fur Traders as Fathers: The Origins of the Mixed-Blooded Community among the Rosebud Sioux." *South Dakota History* 3, 3 (Summer 1973).

Anderson, Irving W. "Sacajawea, Sacagawea, Sakakawea?" *South Dakota History* 8, 4 (Fall 1978).

Anderson, William T. "'It Is Better Farther On': Laura Ingalls Wilder Followed Her Western Vision to the Little Houses on the Prairie." *American West* (May/June 1984).

———. "Wall Drug—South Dakota's Tourist Emporium." *American West* (March/April 1985).

Brown, Mabel Stoll. "Mabel Stoll Brown: The Prairie Child." *South Dakota Historical Collections* 39 (1978).

Burba, Evadna Cochrane. "With Horse and Buggy, Yesteryear's Rural Assessor Made Annual Springtime Rounds." *South Dakota High Liner* (August 1988).

Burmester, Ruth Seymour, ed. "Jeffries Letters." *South Dakota History* 6, 3 (Summer 1976).

Chenoweth, Richard R. "The Black Hills—United Nations Capital." *South Dakota History* 5, 2 (Spring 1975).

Clow, Raymond L. "The Sioux Nation and Indian Territory: The Attempted Removal of 1876." *South Dakota History* 6, 4 (Fall 1976).

Conard, Jane. "Charles Collins: The Sioux City Promotion of the Black Hills." *South Dakota History* 2, 2 (Spring 1972).

Czech, Kenneth P. "High Plains Rebellion Rekindled." *Wild West* 3, 1 (June 1990).

DeMallie, Raymond J., Jr. "Joseph N. Nicollet's Account of the Sioux and Assiniboin in 1839." *South Dakota History* 5, 4 (Fall 1975).

Edwards, Paul M. "Great Britain in Dakota Territory." *South Dakota History* 3, 2 (Spring 1973).

Frajola, Ruth Cook, ed. "They Went West." *South Dakota History* 6, 3 (Summer 1976).

Gasque, Thomas. "The Bulletin." Institute of American Indian Studies, University of South Dakota (Summer/Fall 1991).

Giago, Tim. Column. *Lakota Times* (December 4, 1991).

Gish, Robert F. "Hamlin Garland's Dakota: History and Story." *South Dakota History* 9, 3 (Summer 1979).

Goertz, Reuben. "The Battle of the Cows." Paper presented at the 13th Dakota History Conference, 1982.

Haivala, Paul A. "Old Three Toes: Killer Wolf of Harding County." Paper presented at the 13th Dakota History Conference, 1982.

Hamburg, James F. "Railroads and the Settlement of South Dakota during the Great Dakota Boom, 1878-1887." *South Dakota History* 5, 2 (Spring 1975).

Hammer, Kenneth M. "Come to God's Country: Promotional Efforts in Dakota Territory, 1861-1889." *South Dakota History* 10, 4 (Fall 1980).

Hasselstrom, Linda M. "Vermillion's 'Haunted Pool' Now Dry Relic of River's Freewheeling Past." *Sioux City Sunday Journal* (January 5, 1964).

Hauk, Joy Keve. "The Story of Gus and Jessie McGaa Craven." *South Dakota Historical Collections* 27 (1954).

Hensler, Donna L. "1981 Discovery of the Steamboat Era in Yankton." Paper presented at the 14th Dakota History Conference, 1983.

Herseth, Lorna, ed. "A Pioneer's Letter." *South Dakota History* 6, 3 (Summer 1976).

Hill, Pamela Smith. "Haystack Butte Surrenders Terrible Lizard." *American West* (March/April 1983).

Holtzmann, Roger. "A River Tamed." *South Dakota Magazine* 7, 5 (January/February 1992).

———. "An Incident at Crow Creek." *South Dakota Magazine* 7, 5 (January/February 1992).

Johnson, Norma. "Stavig Brothers Department Store." *South Dakota Heritage* 14, 2 (Centennial Series 2 [Summer 1988]).

Joslyn, Kathryn. "Music to Protest By: An Examination of the Songs from South Dakota's Populist Period." Paper presented at the 14th Dakota History Conference, 1983.

Judy, S. S., and Will Robinson. "Sanborn County History." *South Dakota Historical Collections* 26 (1952).

Kinsela, Steven R. "Company Store: The Hearst Mercantile, 1879-1942." *South Dakota History* 20, 2 (Summer 1990).

Kovats, Nancy Niethammer. "*Black Hills Pioneer*: First Newspaper of Deadwood, Dakota Territory, 1876-1877." *South Dakota History* 8, 3 (Summer 1978).

Kovinick, Phil. "South Dakota's 'Other' Borglum." *South Dakota History* 1, 3 (Summer 1971).

Lawson, Michael L. "The Oahe Dam and the Standing Rock Sioux." *South Dakota History* 6, 2 (Spring 1976).

Lewis, Dale. "Fort Sully Is Out of Water." *South Dakota Heritage* 16, 2 (Summer 1990).

McDermott, Louis M. "The Primary Role of the Military on the Dakota Frontier." *South Dakota History* 2, 2 (Winter 1971).

McLaird, James D. "From Bib Overalls to Cowboy Boots: East River/West River Differences in South Dakota." *South Dakota History* 19, 4 (Winter 1989).

———. "The Welsh, the Vikings, and the Lost Tribes of Israel on the Northern Plains: The Legend of the White Mandan." *South Dakota History* 18, 4 (Winter 1988).

McLaird, James D., and Lesta D. Turchen. "Exploring the Black Hills, 1875-1885: Reports of the Government Expeditions—The Explorations of Captain William Franklin Raynolds, 1859-1860." *South Dakota History* 4, 1 (Winter 1973).

Marten, James. "A View from the West: The Territories and Federal Policy." *South Dakota History* 18, 4 (Winter 1988).

Miller, John. "History Carved on a Mountain." *South Dakota Heritage* 15, 3 (Centennial Series 7 [Fall 1989]).

Miller, John E. "The Way They Saw Us: Dakota Territory in the Illustrated News." *South Dakota History* 18, 4 (Winter 1988).

Mittelstaedt, Robert A., ed. "The General Store Era: Memories of Arthur and Harold Mittelstaedt." *South Dakota History* 9, 1 (Winter 1978).

Morgan, Thisba Hutson. "Reminiscences of My Days in the Land of the Ogalala Sioux." *South Dakota Historical Collections* 29 (1958).

"Narcisse Narcelle." *Timber Lake Topic* (September 27, 1990).

Nasland, Francys M. "Historical Markers Keep a Vigil of Faith." *South Dakota Heritage* 15, 3 (Centennial Series 7 [Fall 1989]).

Nichols, David A. "Civilization over Savage: Frederick Jackson Turner and the Indian." *South Dakota History* 2, 4 (Fall 1972).

Parker, Donald D. "Early Explorations and Fur Trading in South Dakota." *South Dakota Historical Collections* 25 (1950).

Parker, Watson. "Booming the Black Hills." *South Dakota History* 11, 1 (Winter 1980).

———. "Some Black Hills Ghost Towns and Their Origins." *South Dakota History* 2, 2 (Spring 1972).

———. "A Westward Heritage." *South Dakota History* 6, 3 (Summer 1976).

Paulson, Howard W. "Federal Indian Policy and the Dakota Indians: 1800-1840." *South Dakota History* 3, 3 (Summer 1973).

Philip, George. "James (Scotty) Philip." *South Dakota Historical Collections* 20 (1940).

———. "South Dakota Buffaloes versus Mexican Bulls." *South Dakota Historical Collections* 20 (1940).

Plain Talk (Vermillion, South Dakota).

Rapid City Journal.

Rhodes, Richard. "A Plundered Province Revisited: The Colonial Status—Past and Present—of the Great American West." *American Heritage* 29, 5 (August/September 1978).

Riggs, Thomas L. "Sunset to Sunset: A Lifetime with My Brothers, the Sioux." *South Dakota Historical Collections* 29 (1958).

Ring, Ray. "Tumbleweeds Triumphant: How the Russians Conquered the West." *High Country News* (July 3, 1989).

Robinson, Will G. "Digest of the Reports of the Commissioner of Indian Affairs as Pertain to Dakota Indians—1869-1872." *South Dakota Historical Collections* 28 (1956).

Russell, William H. "Promoters and Promotion Literature of Dakota Territory." *South Dakota Historical Collections* 26 (1952).

Samp, Ardyce. "History of the Flandreau Santee Sioux Tribe." In *Twentieth Annual Dakota History Conference*. N.p.: Karl E. Mundt Historical and Educational Foundation, 1989.

Schaffer, Connie DeVelder. "Money versus Morality: The Divorce Industry of Sioux Falls." *South Dakota History* 20, 3 (Fall 1990).

Schusky, Ernest L. "The Lower Brule Sioux Reservation: A Century of Misunderstanding." *South Dakota History* 7, 4 (Fall 1977).

Stephens, Melanie L. "Halfway House for Horses." *Time* (January 1, 1990).

Stucker, Gilbert F. "Hayden in the Badlands." *The American West* 4, 1 (February 1967).

Thomas, Norman. "The Hutterian Brethren." *South Dakota Historical Collections* 25 (1950).

WarCloud, Paul. "A Description of Unity through the Great Spirit." *South Dakota History* 2, 4 (Fall 1972).

Wehrkamp, Tim. "Manuscript Sources in Sioux Indian History." *South Dakota History* 8, 2 (Spring 1978).

Youngkin, S. Douglas. "'Hostile and Friendly': The 'Pygmalion Effect' at Cheyenne River Agency, 1873-1877." *South Dakota History* 7, 4 (Fall 1977).

BOOKS

Roadside History of South Dakota is necessarily brief; many of the following sources contain fuller details on important events. Some books may be difficult to find due to age or scarcity, but most are readily available.

Adams, Alexander B. *Sunlight and Storm: The Great American Plains*. New York: G. P. Putnam's Sons, 1977.

Agenbroad, Larry. *Mammoth Site of Hot Springs, South Dakota*. Hot Springs: Mammoth Site, Inc., 1977.

Allan, Don. *Yankton Celebrates: The Centennial of South Dakota 1889-1989*. Yankton: Boller Printing Company, 1989.

Allen, Clifford, et al. *History of the Flandreau Santee Sioux Tribe*. Flandreau: Flandreau Santee Sioux Tribe, 1971.

Allen, John Logan. *Passage through the Garden: Lewis and Clark and the Image of the American Northwest*. Urbana: University of Illinois Press, 1975.

Allred, B. W., and the Publications Committee of the Potomac Corral of the Westerners, Washington, D.C. *Great Western Indian Fights*. Lincoln: University of Nebraska Press, 1960.

Ambrose, Stephen E. *Crazy Horse and Custer: The Parallel Lives of Two American Warriors*. Garden City: Doubleday & Company, 1975.

Anderson, Robert, et al., eds. *Voices from Wounded Knee, 1973: In the Words of the Participants*. Mohawk Nation via Rooseveltown, New York: Akwesasne Notes, 1976.

Andrist, Ralph K. *The Long Death: The Last Days of the Plains Indians*. New York: Collier Books, 1964.

Armitage, Susan, and Elizabeth Jameson, eds. *The Women's West*. Norman: University of Oklahoma Press, 1987.

Bad Heart Bull, Amos, and Helen Blish. *A Pictographic History of the Oglala Sioux*. Lincoln: University of Nebraska Press, 1967.

Barns, Cass D. *The Sod House*. Lincoln: University of Nebraska Press, 1930; reprinted 1970.

Baumhoff, Richard G. *The Dammed Missouri Valley, One Sixth of Our Nation*. New York: Alfred Knopf, 1951.

Bennett, Estelline. *Old Deadwood Days*. New York: J. H. Sears, 1928.

Billard, Jules B. *The World of the American Indian*. Washington, D.C.: National Geographic Society, 1974.

Blackthunder, Elihah, et al. *History of the Sisseton-Wahpeton Sioux Tribe*. Sisseton: Sisseton-Wahpeton Sioux Tribe, 1971.

Blasingame, Ike. *Dakota Cowboy: My Life in the Old Days*. New York: Putnam, 1958.

Blevins, Winfred. *Give Your Heart to the Hawks: A Tribute to the Mountain Men*. New York: Ballantine Books, 1973.

Boone, C. F. *The Rapid City Flood: June 9, 1972*. Lubbock, Tex.: C. F. Boone, 1972.

Borglum, Lincoln. *My Father's Mountain*. Rapid City: Fenske Printing, 1965.

Bray, Edmund C., and Martha Coleman Bray, eds. *Joseph N. Nicollet on the Plains and Prairies*. St. Paul: Minnesota Historical Society Press, 1976.

Bray, Martha Coleman. *Joseph Nicollet and His Map*. Philadelphia: American Philosophical Society, 1980.

Briggs, Harold E. *Frontiers of the Northwest: A History of the Upper Missouri Valley*. New York: D. Appleton-Century Company, Inc., 1940.

Brown, Jesse, and A. M. Willard. *The Black Hills Trails: A History of the Struggles of the Pioneers in the Winning of the Black Hills*. Rapid City: Rapid City Journal, 1924.

Brown, Joseph Epes. *The Sacred Pipe*. Norman: University of Oklahoma Press, 1953.

Bryan, Jerry. *An Illinois Gold Hunter in the Black Hills*. Springfield: Illinois State Historical Society, 1960.

Burnette, Robert, and John Koster. *The Road to Wounded Knee*. New York: Bantam Books, 1974.

Casey, Robert J. *The Black Hills and Their Incredible Characters*. Indianapolis and New York: Bobbs-Merrill, 1949.

Cash, Joseph H. *The Sioux People (Rosebud)*. Phoenix: Indian Tribal Series, 1971.

———. *To Be an Indian: An Oral History*. New York: Holt, Rinehart & Winston, 1971.

Cassells, E. Steve. *Prehistoric Hunters of the Black Hills*. Boulder: Johnson Books, 1986.

Catlin, George. *Letters and Notes on the Manners, Customs, and Conditions of North American Indians*. 2 Vols. New York: Dover Publications, Inc., 1973.

Cheney, Roberta Carkeek. *The Big Missouri Winter Count*. Happy Camp, Calif.: Naturegraph Publishers, Inc., 1979.

Clem, Alan L. *Prairie State Politics: Popular Democracy in South Dakota*. Washington, D.C.: Public Affairs Press, 1967.

Clowser, Don C. *Dakota Indian Treaties*. Deadwood, 1974.

———. *Deadwood: The Historic City*. Deadwood: Fenwyn Press, 1969.

Conn, Herb, and Jan Conn. *The Jewel Cave Adventure*. Teaneck, N.J.: Zephyrus Press, Inc., 1977.

Conway, James. *The Kingdom in the Country*. Boston: Houghton Mifflin, 1987.

Cushman, Dan. *The Great North Trail*. New York: McGraw-Hill, 1966.

Dale, Edward Everett. *Cow Country*. Norman: University of Oklahoma Press, 1942.

———. *The Range Cattle Industry: Ranching on the Great Plains from 1865 to 1925*. Norman: University of Oklahoma Press, 1960.

————. Introduction to *Cattle-Raising on the Plains of North America*, by Baron Walter von Richthofen. Norman: University of Oklahoma Press, 1961.

Deloria, Ella Cara. *Dakota Texts*. Vermillion: Dakota Press, 1978.

————. *Speaking of Indians*. New York: Friendship Press, 1944; rpt. Vermillion: Dakota Press, 1979.

Deloria, Vine, Jr. *Behind the Trail of Broken Treaties: An Indian Declaration of Independence*. Austin: University of Texas Press, 1990.

DeMallie, Raymond J., ed. *The Sixth Grandfather: Black Elk's Teachings Given to John G. Neihardt*. Lincoln: University of Nebraska Press, 1984.

Densmore, Frances. "How Indians Use Wild Plants for Food, Medicine and Crafts." *Forty-fourth Annual Report of the Bureau of American Ethnology to the Secretary of the Smithsonian Institution, 1926-1927*. Washington, D.C.: U.S. Government Printing Office, 1928; rpt. New York: Dover Publications, 1974.

DeVoto, Bernard. *The Sod-House Frontier, 1854-1890: A Social History of the Northern Plains from the Creation of Kansas and Nebraska to the Admission of the Dakotas*. New York: D. Appleton-Century Company, 1937; rpt. Lincoln: Johnson Publishing Company, 1954.

————, ed. *The Journals of Lewis and Clark*. Boston: Houghton Mifflin, 1953.

Dodge, Richard Irving. *The Black Hills*. Minneapolis: Ross & Haines, Inc., 1965.

Duncan, Dayton. *Out West: American Journey along the Lewis and Clark Trail*. New York: Viking Penguin, Inc., 1988.

Durant, Mary, and Michael Harwood. *This Curious Country: Badlands National Park*. Rapid City: Fenske Printing, Inc., 1988.

Engbretson, Doug. *Empty Saddles, Forgotten Names: Outlaws of the Black Hills and Wyoming*. Aberdeen: North Plains Press, 1982.

Erdoes, Richard. *The Sun Dance People*. New York: Random House, 1972.

Fairchild, Grace. *Frontier Woman: The Life of a Woman Homesteader on the Dakota Frontier*. Retold from notes by Walker D. Wyman. River Falls: University of Wisconsin-River Falls Press, 1972.

Fanebust, Wayne. *Where the Sioux River Bends: A Newspaper Chronicle*. Sioux Falls: Minnehaha County Historical Society, 1985.

Fatout, Paul. *Ambrose Bierce and the Black Hills*. Norman: University of Oklahoma Press, 1956.

Federal Writers' Project, South Dakota. *Legends of the Mighty Sioux*. Chicago: Albert Whitman Company, 1941; rpt. Interior, S.Dak.: Badlands Historical Association, 1987.

Federal Writers' Project Staff. *South Dakota: A Guide to the State*. Pierre: State Publishing Company, 1938.

Fielder, Mildred. *Hiking Trails in the Black Hills*. Aberdeen: North Plains Press, 1973.

Fire, John. *Lame Deer: Seeker of Visions*. New York: Simon & Schuster, 1972.

Fite, Gilbert. *Mount Rushmore*. Norman: University of Oklahoma Press, 1952.

Froiland, Sven G. *Natural History of the Black Hills and Badlands*. Sioux Falls: Center for Western Studies, 1978.

Gerber, Phillip L., ed. *Bachelor Bess: The Homesteading Letters of Elizabeth Corey, 1909-1919*. Iowa City: University of Iowa Press, 1990.

Gerloff, Scott. *Hot Springs Architectural Guide*. Hot Springs: Historic Preservation Commission, 1979.

Giago, Tim. *Notes from Indian Country*. Vol. 1. Pierre: State Publishing Company, 1984.

Gilmore, Melvin R. *Prairie Smoke*. Columbia University Press, 1929; rpt. St. Paul: Minnesota Historical Society Press, 1987.

———. *Uses of Plants by the Indians of the Missouri River Region*. Lincoln: University of Nebraska Press, 1977.

Goodson, Rose Mary. *The Rushmore Story*. Stickney: Argus Printers, 1979.

Gorum, Phillis, trans. *Buffalo Gap: A French Ranch in Dakota, 1887*, by Edmond de Mandat-Grancey. Hermosa: Lame Johnny Press, 1981.

Graber, Kay, ed. *Sister to the Sioux: The Memoirs of Elaine Goodale Eastman, 1885-1891*. Lincoln: University of Nebraska Press, 1978.

Grant, Paul WarCloud. *Sioux Dictionary*. Pierre: State Publishing Company, 1971.

Greever, William S. *The Bonanza West: The Story of the Western Mining Rushes 1848-1900*. Norman: University of Oklahoma Press, 1963.

Gressley, Gene M. *Bankers and Cattlemen*. Lincoln: University of Nebraska Press, 1966.

Grinnell, George Bird. *The Cheyenne Indians*. New Haven: Yale University Press, 1923; rpt. Lincoln: University of Nebraska Press, 1972.

Hafen, LeRoy R., ed. *Mountain Men and Fur Traders of the Far West*. Lincoln: University of Nebraska Press, 1965.

Hall, Bert L. *Roundup Years: Old Muddy to Black Hills*. Pierre: State Publishing Company, 1956.

Handley, Herbert. *Old Hands and Old Brands*. N.p.: Frances Fitch, 1981.

Hart, Herbert M. *Tour Guide to Old Forts of Montana, Wyoming, North and South Dakota*. Boulder: Pruett Publishing Company, 1980.

Hasselstrom, Linda M., ed. *Journal of a Mountain Man: James Clyman*. Missoula: Mountain Press Publishing Company, 1984.

Hassrick, Royal B. *The Sioux*. Norman: University of Oklahoma Press, 1964.

Hitchman, Sue. *North of Pierre: 1740-1984*. Vermillion: Dakota Press, 1985.

Hogan, Edward Patrick. *South Dakota: An Illustrated Geography*. Huron: East Eagle Company, 1991.

Hoig, Stan. *The Humor of the American Cowboy*. Lincoln: University of Nebraska Press, 1958.

Holden, David J. *Dakota Visions: A County Approach*. Sioux Falls: Center for Western Studies, 1982.

Holder, Preston. *The Hoe and the Horse on the Plains*. Lincoln: University of Nebraska Press, 1970.

Hollon, W. Eugene. *The Great American Desert*. New York: Oxford University Press, 1966.

Hoover, Herbert T. *Planning for the South Dakota Centennial: A Bibliography*. Brookings: South Dakota Committee on the Humanities, 1984.

Hoover, Herbert T., and Larry Zimmerman, eds. *South Dakota Leaders*. Vermillion: University of South Dakota Press, 1989.

Hoy, Jim, and Tom Isern. *Plains Folk: A Commonplace of the Great Plains*. Norman: University of Oklahoma Press, 1987.

Hudson, Lois Phillips. *The Bones of Plenty*. rpt. St. Paul: Minnesota Historical Society Press, 1984.

Huseboe, Arthur R. *An Illustrated History of the Arts in South Dakota*. Sioux Falls: Center for Western Studies, 1989.

Hyde, George E. *Indians of the High Plains*. Norman: University of Oklahoma Press, 1959.

———. *Red Cloud's Folk: A History of the Oglala Sioux Indians*. Norman: University of Oklahoma Press, 1937, 1967.

———. *A Sioux Chronicle*. Norman: University of Oklahoma Press, 1956.

———. *Spotted Tail's Folk: A History of the Brule Sioux*. Norman: University of Oklahoma Press, 1961.

Jennewein, J. Leonard. *Calamity Jane of the Western Trails*. Rapid City: Dakota West Books, 1991.

Jennewein, J. Leonard, and Jane Boorman, eds. *Dakota Panorama*. Mitchell: Dakota Territory Centennial Commission, 1961; rpt. Freeman: Pine Hill Press, 1988.

Jordan, Teresa. *Cowgirls: Women of the American West—An Oral History*. Garden City: Doubleday & Company, 1984.

Karolevitz, Robert F. *Challenge: The South Dakota Story*. Sioux Falls: Brevet Press, 1975.

———. *The Prairie Is My Garden: The Story of Harvey Dunn, Artist*. Aberdeen: North Plains Press, 1969.

Kellar, Kenneth C. *Seth Bullock: Frontier Marshal*. Aberdeen: North Plains Press, 1972.

Keyser, James D., and Linea Sundstrom. *Rock Art of Western South Dakota: The North Cave Hills and the Southern Black Hills*. Sioux Falls: South Dakota Archaeological Society, 1984.

King, Charles. *Campaigning with Crook and Stories of Army Life*. Sioux Falls: Center for Western Studies, 1978.

Klock, Irma H. *Yesterday's Gold Camps and Mines in the Northern Black Hills*. Lead: Seaton Publishing Company, 1975.

Kohl, Edith Eudora. *Land of the Burnt Thigh*. St. Paul: Minnesota Historical Society Press, 1986.

Kovats, Nancy Neithammer. *Annie Tallent: The Mystery of the First White Woman in the Black Hills*. Hermosa: Lame Johnny Press, 1983.

Lamar, Howard R. *Dakota Territory 1861-1889*. New Haven: Yale University Press, 1956.

———, ed. *Cow-Boys and Colonels: Narrative of a Journey across the Prairie and over the Black Hills of Dakota*, by Edmond de Mandat-Grancey. Philadelphia: J. B. Lippincott Company, 1963.

Lazarus, Edward. *Black Hills White Justice: The Sioux Nation versus the U.S., 1775 to the Present*. N.p.: HarperCollins Publishers, 1991.

Lee, Bob. *Gold, Gals, Guns, Guts: Roarin' Deadwood, Unique Lead, Picturesque Spearfish*. Deadwood-Lead: South Dakota Centennial Commission, 1976.

Lee, Bob, and Dick Williams. *Last Grass Frontier: The South Dakota Stock Grower Heritage*. Rapid City: Black Hills Publishers, 1964.

Lemmon, Ed, with Nellie Snyder Yost. *Boss Cowman: The Recollections of Ed Lemmon, 1857-1946*. Lincoln: University of Nebraska Press, 1969.

Lewis, Faye Cashett. *Nothing to Make a Shadow*. Ames: Iowa State University Press, 1971.

Limerick, Patricia Nelson. *The Legacy of Conquest: The Unbroken Past of the American West*. New York: W. W. Norton & Company, 1987.

Linde, Martha. *Western Dakota Horse Stories*. Rapid City: Grelind Printing Center, 1989.

Link, Mike, and Craig Blacklock. *Black Hills Badlands: The Web of the West*. Bloomington, Minn.: Voyageur Press, 1980.

McClintock, John S. *Pioneer Days in the Black Hills*. N.p.: J. S. McClintock, 1939.

McNeely, Marian Hurd. *The Jumping-Off Place*. New York: Longmans, Green, 1929.

Mails, Thomas E. *Dog Soldiers, Bear Men and Buffalo Women: A Study of the Societies and Cults of the Plains Indians*. New York: Galahad Books, 1973.

————. *Sundancing at Rosebud and Pine Ridge*. Sioux Falls: Center for Western Studies, 1978.

Mills, Rick. *Making the Grade: A Century of Black Hills Railroading*. Rapid City: Grelind Photographics, 1985.

————. *Railroading in the Land of Infinite Variety*. Hermosa: Battle Creek Publishing Company, 1990.

Milton, John. *South Dakota: A History*. New York: W. W. Norton, 1977.

Morgan, Dale L. *Jedediah Smith and the Opening of the West*. Lincoln: University of Nebraska Press, 1953.

Morganti, Helen F. *The Badger Clark Story*. Rapid City: Espe Printing Company, 1960.

Nasatir, A. P., ed. *Before Lewis and Clark: Documents Illustrating the History of the Missouri, 1785-1804*. 2 Vols. Lincoln: University of Nebraska Press, 1990.

Neihardt, John G. *Black Elk Speaks: Being the Life Story of a Holy Man of the Oglala Sioux*. Lincoln: University of Nebraska Press, 1961.

Nelson, Bruce. *Land of the Dacotahs*. Minneapolis: University of Minnesota Press, 1946.

Nelson, Paula M. *After the West Was Won: Homesteaders and Town-Builders in Western South Dakota, 1900-1917*. Iowa City: University of Iowa Press, 1986.

Nurge, Ethel, ed. *The Modern Sioux: Social Systems and Reservation Culture*. Lincoln: University of Nebraska Press, 1970.

Oglesby, Richard E. *Manuel Lisa and the Opening of the Missouri River Fur Trade*. Norman: University of Oklahoma Press, 1963.

Olson, Gary D., and Erik L. Olson. *Sioux Falls, South Dakota: A Pictorial History*. Norfolk, Va.: The Donning Company, 1985.

Opie, John. *The Law of the Land: Two Hundred Years of American Farmland Policy*. Lincoln: University of Nebraska Press, 1987.

Parker, Donald D. *Pioneering in the Upper Big Sioux Valley: Medary, Sioux Falls, Dell Rapids, Flandreau, Brookings, Watertown*. Santa Fe: N.p., 1967.

Parker, Watson. *Deadwood: The Golden Years*. Lincoln: University of Nebraska Press, 1981.

————. *Gold in the Black Hills*. Norman: University of Oklahoma Press, 1966.

Parker, Watson, and Hugh K. Lambert. *Black Hills Ghost Towns*. Chicago: Swallow Press, 1974.

Pierce, Ellis Taylor. *Odd Characters and Incidents in the Black Hills during the Seventies*. Typescript. Pierre: Historical Resource Center, n.d.

Poole, D. C. *Among the Sioux of Dakota: Eighteen Months Experience as an Indian Agent, 1869-70.* St. Paul: Minnesota Historical Society Press, 1988.

Powell, John Wesley. *Report on the Lands of the Arid Region of the United States.* Boston: Harvard Common Press, 1983.

Powers, William K. *Oglala Religion.* Lincoln: University of Nebraska Press, 1977.

Price, S. Goodale. *Ghosts of Golconda: Black Hills Historical Guide Book.* Deadwood: Western Publishers, Inc., 1952.

Progulske, Donald R. *Yellow Ore, Yellow Hair, Yellow Pine.* Brookings: Agricultural Experiment Station, South Dakota State University, 1974.

Reed, Dorinda Riessen. *The Woman Suffrage Movement in South Dakota.* South Dakota Commission on the Status of Women, 1975.

Reeves, George S. *A Man from South Dakota.* New York: Dutton, 1950.

Reyer, Carolyn, ed. *Cante Ohitika Win (Brave-Hearted Women).* Vermillion: University of South Dakota Press, 1991.

Rezatto, Helen Graham. *The Making of the Two Dakotas—A Centennial History.* Lincoln, Neb.: Media Publishing (2444 O Street, 68510), 1989.

———. *Mount Moriah: Kill a Man—Start a Cemetery.* Aberdeen: North Plains Press, 1980; rpt. Rapid City: Fenwyn Press, 1989.

———. *Tales of the Black Hills.* Aberdeen: North Plains Press, 1983.

Riggs, Stephen Return. *Mary and I.* Boston: Congregational Sunday School & Publishing Society, 1887.

Roach, Joyce Gibson. *The Cowgirls.* University of North Texas Press, 1990.

Robinson, Doane. *History of South Dakota.* 2 Vols. Logansport, Ind.: B. F. Bowen & Company, 1904.

Rolvaag, O. E. *Giants in the Earth.* New York: Harper, 1927.

Ross, A. C. *Mitakuye Oyasin: We Are All Related.* Fort Yates, N. Dak.: Bear, 1989.

Russell, Carl P. *Firearms, Traps and Tools of the Mountain Men.* Albuquerque: University of New Mexico Press, 1967.

Schaff, Howard. *Six Wars at a Time.* Sioux Falls: Center for Western Studies, 1985.

Schatz, August H. *Longhorns Bring Culture.* Boston: Christopher, 1961.

Schell, Herbert S. *History of South Dakota.* Lincoln: University of Nebraska Press, 1968.

Schlissel, Lillian. *Women's Diaries of the Westward Journey.* New York: Schocken Books, 1982.

Schuttler, Linfred. *Agriculture and Transportation.* Spearfish: Centennial History Series, 1988.

Smith, H. A. *Latchstring Inn and the Conquest of Nature in Spearfish Canyon.* N.p., n.d.

Smith, Rex Alan. *The Carving of Mount Rushmore.* New York: Abbeville Press, 1985.

———. *Moon of Popping Trees.* New York: Reader's Digest Press, 1975.

Sneve, Virginia Driving Hawk. *The Dakota's Heritage: A Compilation of Indian Place Names in South Dakota.* Sioux Falls: Brevet Press, 1973.

———, ed. *South Dakota Geographic Names.* Sioux Falls: Brevet Press, 1973.

Spring, Agnes Wright. *The Cheyenne and Black Hills Stage and Express Routes.* rpt. Lincoln: University of Nebraska Press, 1967.

Standing Bear, Luther. *My People the Sioux*. New York: Houghton Mifflin, 1928; rpt. Lincoln: University of Nebraska Press, 1975.

Strain, David F., ed. *Black Hills Hay Camp: Images and Perspectives of Early Rapid City*. Rapid City: Dakota West & Fenske Printing, Inc., 1989.

Stuart, Joseph. *The Art of South Dakota*. Brookings: South Dakota State University, 1974.

Sundstrom, Jessie Y., ed. *Custer County History to 1976*. Custer: Custer County Historical Society, 1977.

Tallent, Anna. *The Black Hills: Last Hunting Ground of the Dakotahs*. St. Louis: Nixon-Jones Printing Company, 1899; rpt. Sioux Falls: Brevet Press, 1974.

Thomson, Frank. *The Thoen Stone*. Detroit: Harlo Press, 1966.

Thornton, Russell. *American Indian Holocaust and Survival: A Population History Since 1492*. Norman: University of Oklahoma Press, 1987.

Tillett, Leslie, ed. *Wind on the Buffalo Grass: The Indians' Own Account of the Battle at the Little Big Horn River, and the Death of Their Life on the Plains*. New York: Thomas Y. Crowell Company, 1976.

Utley, Robert. *The Last Days of the Sioux Nation*. New Haven: Yale University Press, 1963.

Van Nuys, Laura. *The Family Band*. Lincoln: University of Nebraska Press, 1961.

Vestal, Stanley. *The Missouri*. New York: Farrar & Rinehart, Inc., 1945.

———. *Short-Grass Country*. New York: Duell, Sloan & Pearce, 1941.

———. *Sitting Bull: Champion of the Sioux*. Norman: University of Oklahoma Press, 1957.

Wagner, Sally Roesch, ed. *Daughters of Dakota: A Sampler*. Vol. 1. Carmichael, Calif.: Sky Carrier Press, 1989.

———. *Daughters of Dakota: Stories from the Attic*. Vol. 2. Yankton: Daughters of Dakota, 1990.

———. *Daughters of Dakota: Stories of Friendship between Settlers and the Dakota Indians*. Vol. 3. Yankton: Daughters of Dakota, 1990.

Wishart, David J. *The Fur Trade of the American West, 1807-1840*. Lincoln: University of Nebraska Press, 1979.

Wyman, Walker D. *Nothing but Prairie and Sky*, from notes by Bruce Siberts. Norman: University of Oklahoma Press, 1954.

Young, Don. *Local Government in Spearfish, Dakota Territory, 1876-1889*. Spearfish: Centennial History Series, 1988.

Zimmerman, Bill. *Airlift to Wounded Knee*. Chicago: Swallow Press, 1976.

INDEX

448

Blair, Norval, black
settler, along Missouri
River, 154-55
Blizzards, of 1888,
"schoolchildren's
storm," 22; of 1880,
effects, 20-22; photo,
77; flood of 1881,
Vermillion whirlpool,
210; destroys railroad
tracks, 137; skeptical
pioneer lost in blizzard,
103-4; Texas herd dies,
337; frozen brother,
fiancée, 280-81
BLM (Bureau of Land
Management),
subsidizes horses, 270
Bloody Gulch, 311
Bluebird, Lydia, Lakota
collection, 139
Blue Cloud, travels with
Father De Smet, 86;
abbey, 86
Blunt, grouchy historical
marker, 151; Medicine
Knoll, 153
Bodmer, Carl, artist,
travels, 160-61;
Missouri River, 124;
Mandan village, 125;
Fort Pierre, 131;
Mandan lodge, 154;
Four Bears, 187
Bohemian settlers, in
southeast, 190; at
Tyndall, Tabor, 192-93
Bolling, Charles and
family, drowned in
river crossing, 141
Bon Homme, Hutterian
colonists settle, 73, 92;
oldest man in
territory, 204-5
Bon Homme County,
189-93
Bon Homme Island, 200
Bonesteel, name, lottery,
146; Battle of, 147
Bonilla, 102
Bonniwell, John, rancher,
282
Bordeaux, W. J.,
interpreter, 179
Borglum, Gutzon,
sculptor, carving Mt.
Rushmore, 365-71;

choice of men to carve,
367; records, 368;
photo, flag-raising,
371; death, 369; wife,
Mary, 233
Borglum, Lincoln,
Gutzon's son, finishes
Rushmore, 369
Borglum Memorial
Highway, 361; photo,
360
Borglum, Solon Hannibal,
artist, Gutzon's
brother, 217-18
Boucher, Father Pierre,
first priest; 52;
grasshopper
pilgrimage, 53-54
Bowdle, railroad
boomtown, 76; flour
mill, 192
Bower Family Band, 375
Boyle, John, feisty
legislator, 205
Bradley, 63
Brandon, burial mounds,
16
Brave, 167
Bridal Veil Falls,
Spearfish Canyon,
355-56
Briggs, Clyde F., wolfer,
traps Three Toes, 279
Brimdschmidt, Joe,
trades springs for
horse, 347
Bristol, 81
Britton, 27
Bronson, Edgar Beecher,
rancher, 290
Brookings, Wilmot W.,
legs amputated, 30;
builds road, 32
Brookings, 30-36
Brotherhood of
Locomotive Firemen,
93
Brown County, name, 103
Brown, Charlie, hanging,
photo, 399
Brown, Edgar I.,
Badlands
homesteader, 341-42
Brown, Samuel J., winter
ride, 28-29
Browns Valley,
homesteaders, 26

Brownwolf, John and
Mable Dora Lee,
settlers, 250-51
Bruguier, Theophile,
ferry license, 54;
trader with Chouteau,
158-59
Brule Creek, first general
election, 50
Brulé (Sicangu) Lakota,
spelling, 52; leaders,
136-37; origin of
name, 137; settle at
Rosebud, 267-68;
Crook's soldiers
attack, 284
Brule City, near
Chamberlain, 137
Bruyer, August,
Josephine, John and
Julius, settle at
Vermillion, 208
Bryan, Jerry, gold miner,
306-8
Bryan, Lisa Little Chief,
modern quilter, 259
Bryan, William Jennings,
presidential
candidate, 46; at Corn
Palace, 58
Buffalo. See Bison
Buffalo (town), 277
Buffalo County, 218-20
Buffalo Gap, bison route,
377-78; stage stop,
378
Bullock, Seth, town sites,
243; horse raising,
317; marshal,
investor, politician,
353-55; establishes
national monument,
354; attends
inauguration, 355;
hardware business,
promoter, auctioneer,
393-94; photos, 353,
394
Burbank, John A.,
governor, railroad
director, 119
Burial mounds, eastern
Dakota, 16; Mound
City, 150
Burke, 146
Burleigh, Walter, corrupt,
Indian agent, photo,

458

Vermillion, history, 208-11; trading post, 37; flour mill, 192; railroad, 210

Vermillion River, fur post, 78, 208; whirlpool, 210, map, 237

Vermont City, 77

Verzani, Frank, first proved homestead claim, 52

Vilas, 116

Vinatieri, Felix, Custer's bandmaster, photo, 193

Vivian, 166-67

Volga, on Black and Yellow Trail, 88; history, 100-101

Wagner, named for postmaster, 191

Wahpeton Lakota, hunting area, 82

Wakpala, history, 179; site, 250

Walker, named for rancher, 179

Wall, 339

Wall Drug, 339-40

Wallace, 63

Wallas, Reuben, oldest man in Dakota, 204-5

Walworth County, 151

Wanblee, 264

War of 1812, 183-86

Ward, Clarence (Roan Bear), buffalo hunt, 285

Ward, Joseph, writes state motto, photo, 209

Warren, Gouvernor Kemble, topographical engineer, at Cedar Island, 139, 155; expedition, 271-72; Harney Springs, 341

Washing, early day, Whirl Washer, drawing, 299; washboard, photo, 317

Wasta, 337-38

Watauga, 179

Watertown, history, 29-30; county-seat fight, 68; rainmaker, 104

Waubay, 26-27

Waubay Lake, grebe refuge, 16; fur post, 83

Webster, 82-84

Welk, Lawrence, first job, 114-15

Welsh colony, near Ipswich, 79-80

Wessington (Elmer), 91

Wessington Springs (Aqua), 211

Wessington Hills, part of *coteau*, 91, 110

Western Town Lot Company, in Brookings, 30-31; organized, 43; founds Frankfort, 63; lays out Redfield, 67; owned by C&NW, 92; objects to name, 100

Westport, 101

West River, definitions, 2-4

Wheaton, 26-27

Whetstone Creek, 87

Whitcomb, E. W., rancher, 343-34

White River (town), 167

White River, reservation boundary, 137; "costive" water, 167; map, 237

White Buffalo Cow, Brulé Lakota, signs treaty, 136-37

White Lake (Siding Thirty-six), 56

White, William, "Buffalo Chips," scout killed, 284

Whitewood, 321-22

Wild Free-Roaming Horses and Burros Act, 270

Wilder, Laura Ingalls, author, homesteader, 96-99; homestead photo, 98; books, photo, 99

Wildlife, in East River and West River, 3, 273-74, 344; in refuges, 16; near Pickstown, 145

Willett, David, rancher, daughter Lulu, 276

Williamson, Rev. John S., hunts with Yanktons,

213-14

Wilson, Charlie, meets wolf, 278

Wind Cave, discovery, 350; National Park, 349-50; possible connections to Jewel Cave, 373

Winfred, 117

Wing Tsue Wong family, photo, 405

Winner, 270-71

Winship, 101

Wintermute, Peter P., fatal political fight, 119-20

Wixon, Eli B., trader, 50-52

Wizard of Oz, set in Dakota, 80; called Populist parable, 81

Wolf Creek, 212

Wolfe, Anna, boardinghouse, 427

Women's suffrage, in Dakota, 93-94; in West, 8

Wonderland Cave, 246

Wood, 271

Wooden Knife, Ansel, Jr., cook, 385

Woonsocket, 57; named by Milwaukee Road, 114

Wounded Knee, 1890 massacre, 262-63; photo, 262; Eastman resigns, 40; Memorial Museum, 258-59

Wounded Knee II, 263; Janklow prosecutes, 40

WPA (Works Progress Administration), builds lakes, 15; restores Fort Sisseton, 29; sponsors murals, 258

Yankton, history, 194-208; fur post, 37; Hutterian colony, 92; battle over capital location, 119-20; photos, 199, 201, 202, 204

Yankton County, 194-208

Yankton Lakota, burns